This book brings together the themes of diet, consumption, the body and human relationships with the natural world, in a highly original study of Shelley. A campaigning vegetarian and proto-ecological thinker, Shelley may seem to us curiously modern, but Morton offers an illuminatingly broad context for his views in eighteenth-century social and political thought concerning nature, culture and society. The book is at once grounded in the revolutionary history of the period 1790–1820, and informed by current theoretical issues, and anthropological and sociological approaches to literature. Morton provides challenging new readings of much-debated poems, plays and novels by both Percy and Mary Shelley, as well as the first sustained interpretation of Shelley's prose on diet. With its stimulating literary–historical reassessment of questions about nature and culture, this study will provoke fresh discussion about Shelley, Romanticism and modernity.

CAMBRIDGE STUDIES IN ROMANTICISM 10

SHELLEY AND THE
REVOLUTION IN TASTE

CAMBRIDGE STUDIES IN ROMANTICISM

This series aims to foster the best new work in one of the most challenging fields within English literary studies. From the early 1780s to the early 1830s a formidable array of talented men and women took to literary composition, not just in poetry, which some of them famously transformed, but in many modes of writing. The expansion of publishing created new opportunities for writers, and the political stakes of what they wrote were raised again and again by what Wordsworth called those 'great national events' that were 'almost daily taking place': the French Revolution, the Napoleonic and American wars, urbanization, industrialization, religious revival, an expanded empire abroad and the reform movement at home. This was an enormous ambition, even when it pretended otherwise. The relations between science, philosophy, religion and literature were reworked in texts such as *Frankenstein* and *Biographia Literaria*; gender relations in *A Vindication of the Rights of Woman and Don Juan*; journalism by Cobbett and Hazlitt; poetic form, content and style by the Lake School and the Cockney School. Outside Shakespeare studies, probably no body of writing has produced such a wealth of response or done so much to shape the responses of modern criticism. This indeed is the period that saw the emergence of those notions of 'literature' and of literary history, especially national literary history, on which modern scholarship in English has been founded.

The categories produced by Romanticism have also been challenged by recent historicist arguments. The task of the series is to engage both with a challenging corpus of Romantic writings and with the changing field of criticism they have helped to shape. As with other literary series published by Cambridge, this one will represent the work of both younger and more established scholars, on either side of the Atlantic and elsewhere.

For a complete list of titles published see p. 299.

SHELLEY AND THE
REVOLUTION IN TASTE

The Body and the Natural World

TIMOTHY MORTON

Department of English, New York University

CAMBRIDGE
UNIVERSITY PRESS

Published by the Press Syndicate of the University of Cambridge
The Pitt Building, Trumpington Street, Cambridge CB2 1RP
40 West 20th Street, New York, NY 10011-4211, USA
10 Stamford Road, Oakleigh, Melbourne 3166, Australia

First published 1994

Transferred to digital printing 1998

Printed in Great Britain by Biddles Short Run Books

A catalogue record for this book is available from the British Library

Library of Congress cataloguing in publication data
Morton, Timothy, 1968–
Shelley and the Revolution in Taste: the body and the natural world/Timothy Morton.
p.   cm. – (Cambridge studies in Romanticism)
Includes bibliographical references (p.) and index.
ISBN 0 521 47135 4 (hardback)
1. Shelley, Percy Bysshe, 1792–1822 – Political and social views.
2. Body, Human, in literature.   3. Man-animal relationships – Public
opinion – History – 18th century.   4. Nature conservation – Public
opinion – History – 18th century.   5. Vegetarianism – Public opinion –
History – 18th century.   6. Diet – Public opinion – History – 18th
century.   7. Man-animal relationships in literature.
8. Vegetarianism in literature.   9. Nature in literature.   10. Diet
in literature.   11. Romanticism.   I. Series.

PB5442.B58M67 1994   94–13360
821'.7 – dc20   CIP

ISBN 0 521 47135 4 hardback

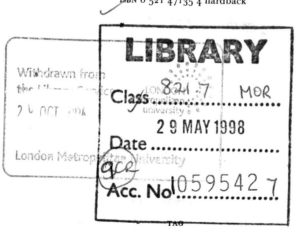

A sense of the body's place in the natural world can provide ...
a social ecology and an alternative rationality that articulate a
cultural and moral challenge to the exploitation and domination
of 'the nature within us and without us'.

Paul Gilroy, 'Urban Social Movements, "Race" and
Community' in P. Williams and L. Chrisman, eds.,
Colonial Discourse and Post-Colonial Theory: a Reader, 407.

The image of the tiger reveals the truth of eating.

Bataille, *The Accursed Share*, 38

Break that deer; ... rear that goose; lift that swan; sauce that
chicken; unbrace that mallard; unlace that cony; dismember
that heron; display that crane; disfigure that peacock; unjoint
that bittern ...

Rabisha, *The Whole Body of Cookery Dissected*, 241

Contents

Figures

Acknowledgements

This book is a further exploration of the doctoral thesis which I wrote at Oxford University between 1989 and 1992, entitled *Re-Imagining the Body: Shelley and the Languages of Diet*. I benefited from the suggestions of my supervisors, Paul Hamilton, Nigel Smith and Timothy Webb, and of my examiners, Marilyn Butler and Lucy Newlyn. Bruce Barker Benfield helped me to read the Shelley manuscripts at the Bodleian Library, Oxford. I would not have been able to complete it without the generous assistance of the British Academy, Magdalen College, Oxford, the Trustees of the Procter Fellowship and Princeton University. In America I received positive guidance from Stuart Curran and Paul Magnuson. The transition of the thesis to a book was skilfully facilitated by Josie Dixon of Cambridge University Press. The illustrations are reproduced by permission of the Bodleian Library, University of Oxford, the British Library and the British Museum.

I wish to thank, in alphabetical order, the many friends and acquaintances who helped in the production of this book: Carol Adams, Alan Baker, Jonathan Bate, Maurice Bryan, CIT Staff (Princeton), Terry Eagleton, Kelvin Everest, Marilyn Gaull, Barbara Gelpi, Stephen Gill, Nick Groom, Yael Halevi, Bill Howarth, Carolyn Howitt, Tim Hunter, Mark Jenner, Barbara Kirshenblatt-Gimblett, Andrew Laird, Grant Lamond, Cathy Lines, Anthony Low, Chris Morgan-Jones, Simon Morrison, Gene Murray, David Norbrook, Nicolas Rasmussen, Donald Reiman, Frank Romany, Andrew Ross, Brian Ruppert, Richard Sennett and the Committee on Theory and Culture at New York University, the Shelley scholars at the 1992 bicentenary conferences in New York and Wales, Sarah Squire, The Staff of the Bodleian and British Libraries and the Staff of the Firestone Library, Princeton University, Georges Teyssot, Rod

Tweedy, Tony Vivanco, Jennifer Wicke, Marcus Wood, Jonathan Wordsworth and Jason Wright.

This book is dedicated to my parents, Garth and Jasmine, and to Dominique Calapai, without whom it would never have been written.

New York University, November, 1993

Abbreviations

[ ]	denotes my insertion within a quotation
⟨ ⟩	deletion within a quotation
A6r	page A6 recto
A6v	page A6 verso
DNB	*Dictionary of National Biography*
J	the 'Julian' edition of Shelley's works (see bibliography)
L	Shelley's letters (see bibliography)
V	Shelley, Percy Bysshe, *A Vindication of Natural Diet* (London: printed for J. Callow, 1813); the *Julian* version
'VSys'	Shelley, Percy Bysshe, 'Essay on the Vegetable System of Diet' (1814–1815)

A note on the text
Notes are given for published works (author, short title and page number). Full titles and other publication data are listed in the bibliography. Short-titles are employed in the text. Bracketed numbers in the main body of the text refer to poetry quotation line numbers. After a displayed poetry quotation, the number of the first line is recorded. Data referring to the publication of Shelley's poems in his lifetime is given in the notes.

Introduction: prescriptions

Shelley and the Revolution in Taste discusses the significance of diet for Percy Bysshe Shelley and his circle, in the period of the French, American and Industrial Revolutions. Drawing on the aversive rhetoric of vegetarianism, Shelley refashioned taste, in revolt against what he conceived to be the hierarchical powers which controlled consumption, production and culture. The revolt in taste delineated new relationships between bodies and their environments.

In literary criticism, the study of historical context has become topical. I would like to direct inquiry towards issues in material culture (such as food). Eating, drinking and literature are all intensely lived aspects of cultural history, part of what Braudel called 'the structures of everyday life'. Food and literature both involve ethical and aesthetic choices and patterns which are imagined and played out constantly. Questions of sympathy, humanitarianism, ecology, social change and even revolt mattered on a quotidian basis to the vegetarians. My aim has not been simply to record recipes, or cite instances of vegetarian argument; I have tried to detail the subcultural and counter-cultural structures of feeling in which vegetarianism was deployed. This was a period when nature, the body and consumption became highly charged political issues.

Some work has already been carried out to trace the development of discourses such as vegetarianism in the late eighteenth century. My subtitle is designed to draw attention to the most groundbreaking of these studies, Keith Thomas' *Man and the Natural World*. In adding to the existing work on the subject, I have tried to maintain a sense of four priorities about what kind of material I have been analysing, and how I interpret it. *Shelley and the Revolution in Taste* is not simply a collection of textual evidence about vegetarianism, but a discussion of this evidence in relation to its socio-historical contexts. Moreover, to understand the evidence involves not just reading vegetarian texts

I

mimetically (for their content), but also reading closely and figuratively, in order to talk about how figurative language constructs the body.

Why 'The Body and the Natural World'? This book attempts to be a work of 'green' cultural criticism, mapping different strands of culture in the 1790–1820 period under the aegis of the politics of the body in its environments. By green cultural criticism, I mean ways of showing how the body and its social and natural environments may be interrelated. The body, perceived through its consumption of food, is an interface between society and natural environment. Since this book is about the politics of nature, I have decided to stress the importance of the politics of the body.[1] Consider the rhetorical power of a language in which revolution could be linked to revulsion: if at the sight of tyrannical cruelty or tyrannical gluttony, one's very tastes rebelled. Such powers would be associated with that language's capacity to *naturalize* certain ethical norms.

My research straddles five traditions of cultural work. In literary studies of the Shelleys and Romanticism, I have found especially helpful Dawson's political reading of Shelley, Hogle's study of meaning-production through 'transference' and Leask's work on orientalism.[2] I have drawn upon the analysis of consumption in sociology, anthropology and intellectual history, exemplified by Appadurai's approach to 'the social life of things' and Bourdieu's work on modes of social distinction.[3] I have used the following contextual sources: the growing range of literature on food and drink in culture, in particular Drummond's and Wilbraham's history of English food, and Salaman's social history of the potato;[4] the 'wo/man and the natural world' tradition of texts on animal rights and vegetarianism, from the cultural history of Keith Thomas to the feminist work of Carol Adams;[5] and studies of the body in the eighteenth and nineteenth centuries (Foucault, Outram and Stafford).[6] Ecological theories, and the concepts developed by Deleuze and Guattari for understanding the social field in a post-Marxist, non-dualistic way, are used where necessary. The bibliography contains a full listing of all the authors named here.

This is no totalizing history; indeed I wish to explore particular cross-sections of 1790–1830 culture. I have employed a methodology of rich, deep contextualizing detail, inspired by Geertz's 'Thick Description',[7] and supported by the following words from *Anti-Oedipus*: 'Let us remember ... one of Marx's caveats: we cannot tell from the mere taste of wheat who grew it; the product gives us no hint as to the system and the relations of production.'[8] The relations of cultural production and consumption cannot be understood by the mere taste of food either. I want to show how the personal and the political are intertwined, in a way which takes account of how individual acts of consumption are always caught up in something larger.

My work is similar to John Barrell's remarkable *The Infection of Thomas De Quincey*, in that it tries to account for the psychic investment of the social field in the Romantic period. In other words, it tries to broaden our ideas about what role the psyche comes to play in social life, and the importance of social power in the life of the psyche. In *Material Culture and Mass Consumption*, Miller boldly linked 'personal' acts of consumption with the social field, through a politicized reading of the psychoanalysts Winnicott and Klein, and the behaviourist Piaget: 'The most interesting element in this analysis is, however, the complex nature of the mechanisms themselves, whose twists and cycles are able to capture a sense of dynamic interaction in a manner which may escape that vulgarized version of the dialectic [for example, versions of Hegelian or Marxist theories] which is commonly used to represent processes of this kind.'[9] While sceptical about the rather privatized psychoanalytic theorization of such projects, Miller and I share an interest in the machine-like intricacies, the 'twists and cycles', which such approaches suggest in a wider social context. The polis is recycled in the psyche.

I have chosen to call this introduction 'Prescriptions' to explain how figurative language works in many of the texts I have discussed. Prescriptive language is one of the central ways in which the body and society are linked together. Prescription, simply understood, is a way of doing things with words. Percy Shelley's pamphlet, *A Vindication of Natural Diet* (1813), the main text under discussion, ends with the following exhortations, in block capitals:

NEVER TAKE ANY SUBSTANCE INTO THE STOMACH THAT ONCE HAD LIFE.

DRINK NO LIQUID BUT WATER RESTORED TO ITS ORIGINAL PURITY BY DISTILLATION.[10]

The capitals interrupt a discursive flow: the essay has ceased to vindicate and enquire, and now *prescribes*. The discourse becomes a command to establish certain forms of consumption. The two sentences encapsulate the qualities of many of my textual sources. I am fascinated by such didactic forms, those now rather underrated rhetorics considered highly from Hesiod's *Works and Days* to Thomson's *The Seasons*.

How does didacticism work? By aspiring to a plateau of ideological conflict, it contests the very configurations of the body, thought, habit and morality. Shelley's pamphlet would have clashed quite explicitly with the various manuals on hunting (both prose and poetic) appearing in the period, which prescribed other forms of consumption of nature and property for a wealthy audience (Peter Beckford's and Somerville's spring to mind). Society's virtual models, its codes of virtues, are constantly contrived and revised in the didactic genre.

English literary study has been hesitant to discuss prescriptive language in anything more than a mimetic way. Other sorts of literary language (especially what we think of as Romantic poetry) have been read as exemplifications of pure figurative play, as far away as possible from the nuts and bolts of prescription. 'Rhetoric' has been 'returning' in English studies for over a decade; but which sort of rhetoric? I have tried to elaborate and challenge overtly textualist or deconstructive approaches, to stretch them until they touch the social field. Shelley's statements refuse to be 'merely' descriptive or 'purely' figurative. The archive of medical, literary and humanitarian texts is read primarily as exemplifying such a refusal. The texts are prescriptions: medical books quote didactic poetry, and Shelley quotes medical literature. One may place Shelley firmly in a tradition which revises the didacticism of the eighteenth century, despite his own self-proclaimed criticisms of the genre, and despite Romantic ideologies of anti-rhetoric.

Global flows of money, symbolism, happiness and misery may congregate in one's acts of consumption. Mapping the linkages of these acts involves a teasing-out of figurative streams which serve to activate prescriptive norms – in short, ideology. One eats ideology while consuming a McDonald's hamburger; and ideology is not just a matter of corporate image but of millions of cattle. Or in digesting a British 'Ploughman's Lunch', one is digesting ideology, for the Georgic myth of hearty labour figured in the cheese and Branston pickle is a marketing ploy.[11]

To study ideology is to examine how figuration meshes with prescription. Certain syntactical structures and anti-structures, such as ellipsis or *aporia*, or aversive rhetorics of disgust and distaste, are found to generate more than just images or embellishments, or an epistemological vacuum/plenitude (the thrills and spills of *mise-en-abîme*). The study of ideology is not limited to the 'history of ideas' or to deconstruction. Breakdowns like aporias or ellipses, as well as more positively-functional passages of description or citation, operate within a larger prescriptive network. When the doctor hands over a 'prescription', he enables our consumption of certain prestige-laden or 'enclaved' commodities (to use Kopytoff's term).[12] *Shelley and the Revolution in Taste* is about the prescriptive fashioning of consumers.

Vectors of prescriptive force in the discourses of food and diet set up and take apart boundaries, limits: between the stomach and society, politics and poetics,[13] nature and nurture, national and transnational commodity flows. How might one read a text like *A Vindication of Natural Diet*, which combines comparative mythology and anthropology, 'sociopathology', medicine, revolution, imperialism, orientalism, trade and literature, with questions about diet? With a certain bloody-minded and non-dualistic kind of literalism, I have traced relationships within those conglomerates of metastable physical and social states that we often call the body politic and the political body. These bodies are less monolithic organic unities than multiple processes.

It is necessary to stress just how material a concept ideology is. Tester's *Animals and Society* showed very well how limit-setting discourses on animal rights are an operator in specifically human political disputes: every hunt sabotage could be a potential *Animal Farm*-style allegory. But as my work on Shelley's *Swellfoot the Tyrant* shows (chapter 5), we would be begging the question if we refused to acknowledge the worm-tracks which link real animals to real dinner plates. These worm-tracks were created by productions, consumptions, and recordings. Recorded debates in the late eighteenth century between hierarchy and authority, monarchy and republicanism, despotic codes and disciplined axioms, involved discourses on nutrition and hygiene. These recordings were linked to consumption: the middle classes began to consume authoritarian structures by following their prudent vegetarian recipe books.

The worm-tracks pass through the lives and works of Percy, Harriet and Mary Shelley. My arrangement of material from their lives and works is thematic rather than chronological. The book moves from what may crudely be termed 'materials' to 'interpretations'; though 'materials' are really hardened interpretations, and the latter are materially determinate. The first three chapters show the cultural context of 1790–1820, the biographical evidence, and the literary texts which discuss the 'natural' or vegetarian diet. The last three chapters interpret Percy Shelley's prose on vegetarianism, the theme of intemperate consumption in the Shelley canon, and the broader questions of 'nature' and ecology.

The recent work of Thomas, Adams, Tester and Fiddes is part of a rapidly-growing field of interdisciplinary research into human relationships with animals and the 'natural' world, consumption, value and power. I would like *Shelley and the Revolution in Taste* to contribute to this field. Thomas' *Man and the Natural World* provided a treasure-trove of configurations between human culture and natural environments, suggesting that the period around the French Revolution marked a shift in European attitudes towards nature.[14] Tester's study of how human discourses about animal rights were expressive of political interests between humans paid special attention to the period exemplified by Rousseau and Shelley. Fiddes' *Meat* charted the shifts in the cultural value of the privileged, value-rich food, against which vegetarianism had to define itself, both counter-culturally and in more mainstream ways: 'The new ideology, in contrast to tradition, regards unrestrained domination of other creatures as a sign not of civilised elevation but of regrettable backwardness.'[15] Adams' powerful and pleasurable *The Sexual Politics of Meat* was a striking intervention in ideologies of consumption and gender. *Shelley and the Revolution in Taste* should develop the field in three ways: by offering more primary material, more literary and ideological interpretation, and more emphasis on the politics of the body.

There is no isolated causal relationship which will neatly describe why the data I have studied came into being. 'Food' is an ensemble of beliefs, texts, practices, materials. 'Vegetarianism' is an ensemble of such elements. My evidence is presented less as an object or a subject than as a terrain of conflict, a contested map. The study of food raises questions about aesthetics and economics, the natural and the cultural, the social, the psychic and the biological. There are *determinate but non-linear* relationships between these sets: 'fractal' relationships in which there is no single fundamental determinant but numerous attractors of material, social, textual and psychic tendencies.[16] As Massumi explains, the ' "random walk" ' which describes the proliferation of these determinants looks haphazard on one level, but on another it describes the '"cosmos"' or weaving-together of 'nature-culture ... monism in its other aspect'.[17]

This knowledge alters our understanding of the binary pairs like 'organic' and 'inorganic', 'nature' and 'culture', which we frequently use to describe the social and environmental aspects of the body. Recent ecocultural work on the body and society, and concepts of 'organic' and 'inorganic', have been influenced by Deleuze and Guattari's elaboration of multi-levelled, multi-causal relationships, and Bataille's concepts of 'general' and 'restricted' economy.[18] In chapter 4 I show how 'culture' is quite a naturalistic concept, but also how this naturalism does not abolish distinctions between nature and culture on another level (indeed, a certain dissimilarity is functional on both levels).

The Shelleys' ideas about food are not read as the sole determining factor of other ideas which they held. That tradition in the 'history of ideas' which searches for a primary cause in the social field, is highly problematic. I will consider my work to have succeeded if it manages to show, as if in slow motion, the doh-see-doh between the attractors listed above as opposing pairs (nature, culture ...). One might be tempted to call this analysis a kind of intellectual Lego rather than the Monopoly-games of aesthetics and economics, a sort of 'prosthetics' perhaps, that blithely considers desire to be immanent in the social field. If 'food' can be both subject and object, there is little point in using subjectivism or objectivism to describe it.

It should be noted that explosions of the categories of nature and culture are not new to anthropology. Since the 1970s, interpretive anthropology has sought to provide a contextualized analysis of practices and norms associated with the concept of 'culture'. The work of Mary Douglas has brilliantly shown how categories such as 'dirt' and 'cleanliness' may be culturally coded.[19] However, this method may loop us back to the 'substantialism' of 'culture', with its concomitant models of expressive or reflexive 'mediation'.[20] It is possible to modify Douglas' substantialist understanding of rituals, which seem at once both to be a symptom of society and to be a cause of society.[21] Dirt may be 'matter in the wrong place', but this begs the question of place. This substantialist thought resembles Shelley's root-and-blossom model of poetry, or his idea of vegetarianism as the cause and/or symptom of justice, and meat-eating as the cause and/or symptom of injustice. A mystical 'mediation' transubstantiates the substances of nature into the trans-substances of culture. These 'culturalist' modes of thought are ultimately part of my field of enquiry, rather than part of the analytical tool kit.

In writing the book, I found myself struggling towards revised ideas of culture and ecology. The playful Lego-method will not do for long. Cultural studies is not only the study of cultures, but also the study of 'Culture'. The struggle is urgent, given the racism, sexism and class oppression with which 'Culture' confronts us. In the wake of the Second World War, the Euro-American 'left' (this is a very fuzzy term) has developed various forms of culturalism in the wake of fascist ideology. For example, there is the cultural-nominalist approach, the rich and diverse examples of 'the linguistic turn'. Speak of the body, within the confines of this discourse, and one risks courting fascism. There is a politicized anxiety about speaking of the relation between totality and particularity within aesthetics and economics. The notion of totality has been criticized and substantially re-written in twentieth-century thought in response to totalitarian politics. But this reaction to the moment of fascism is in danger of discarding the very historical particularity and difference that it strives to celebrate in the present so-called 'condition of post-modernity'. Part of a progressive theory is a usable understanding of the past.

To understand the body is to understand how it was hijacked by fascist ideology and ignored or rejected (as a synecdoche for fascism) in left thinking for long enough to permit the widespread, popular and unchallenged adoption of beliefs associated with biotech, the 'Chicago gangster' theory of the selfish gene,[22] and the manipulation of birth control and population issues by the ruling class. 1790–1820 is a fraught arena of intellectual debate in relation to this subject, ever since the Frankfurt school's warning that there was a straight line between some of the period's theories and the death camps. However, if academics do not do their work, the banks and corporate machines, with their powerful stake in appropriating the history of technology and the body, will do it for us. There will be no way of answering back, only the cataloguing of the body amongst the vaulted treasures of cultural capital. This might not be the right way of handling questions of alienation in the Industrial Revolutionary period. In this sense I agree with Haraway that some understanding of science and technology is necessary, beyond the mere 'history of ideas' approaches developed in history-of-science institutions.[23]

I draw my inspiration from Percy Shelley, who was very actively and vigorously concerned with re-imagining the body. His ability to model society as a body and simultaneously as a machine has not been adequately accounted for. In chapter 4 I read his addition to the notes in *Queen Mab*, an allegory called *Falsehood and Vice*:

> Whilst monarchs laughed upon their thrones
> To hear a famished nation's groans,
> And hugged the wealth wrung from the woe
> That makes its eyes and veins o'erflow. (1)

Shelley describes precisely and beautifully a despotic machine which wrings wealth from the overflow of blood and tears. Wealth is itself a flow (wrung like droplets of water from a rag), which becomes a despotic fetish to embrace. The quotation displays Shelley's supreme gift for depicting society as a machine which processes flows, linking together the materiality of psychic and physical pain. The nation is a tortured body, bleeding and weeping and excreting wealth, its stomach emptied. Shelley himself is actively participating in a discourse which understands despotism and religion to be caught up in the logics of capitalism. This book explores how he responds to this understanding in terms of his approach to consumption, not simply through anti-capitalism (for example in the rage against polluting industry), but through the rhetoric of reformed and improved capitalism.

As for the writing which associates Shelley either with the supposedly quasi-postmodern discourse of 'Romanticism', or the equally trenchant claims for his debt to a rational Enlightenment, these arguments take place within already mapped-out and fetishistic domains of aesthetics and/or economics. Additionally, the kind of socialist or Marxist reading which places a strong emphasis on his propagandistic poetry loses a lot by refusing to read the perhaps more 'lyrical' poetry politically, and by refusing to read the so-called political poems 'poetically' (beyond a form of allusion-hunting). The poetics of food will provide important political data.

While studies of *Frankenstein* seem bound to mention something about the body, not enough attention has been paid to the body in the criticism of Percy Shelley.[24] Two reasons may be offered to explain this. Shelley's enthusiastic figuration of the mental (consider *Mont Blanc* or the preface to *Prometheus Unbound*) has been over-determined, elaborated and developed by critics, especially those concerned to present him as a coherent thinker. Moreover, these critics form part of a literary history which privileges what is taken to be 'the mental', in their continued use of concepts like genius, intentionality, and the canon as a colloquium of geniuses. There is a need in Shelley studies to discuss the interaction between the body, society and nature, in order to assess his place as an individual writer in this field. *Shelley and the Revolution in Taste* re-imagines the body in Shelley studies and emphasizes the Shelleys' interest in reforming the body.

In addition, the book seeks to show how both Mary and Percy were collaborating in re-imagining the body. While there is less textual evidence from Mary Shelley, it is possible to show how *Frankenstein* and *The Last Man* are caught up within the same programmatic reconfigurations of the body as found in Percy Shelley's writing. It is a lamentable fact of Shelley studies that the collaboration of these two writers has not been fully discussed. I have not sought to demonstrate that 'collaboration' was an idiosyncrasy in which Percy Shelley 'helped' to write *Frankenstein*, as a debatable reading of the manuscript evidence might show.[25] Rather, I have tried to reveal a shared intellectual climate between these two writers. This is especially significant insofar as Mary Shelley's work critiques the work of Percy Shelley, by putting the 'intellectual climate' into novelistic question.

This book treats the interaction between its themes as mediated through the representation of food and consumption. It examines the political significance of figurative language as it constructs the discourses of diet (vegetarianism, temperance, intoxication, famine). To speak of a 'discourse' of diet is to allow for the analysis of a consistent repertoire of images, narratives and focalizing techniques which the texts display, and for their place in the self-presentation of Shelley the radical reformer. It is also capable of accommodating a politicized sense of the ways in which institutions construct the individual and allow certain kinds of articulation. I analyse the devices which transform 'food' into the discipline of 'diet'. A wide variety of texts are discussed, from the medical to the literary, including recipe books, diaries, journals, periodicals, biographies, letters, tracts, textbooks, poems, plays and novels. All of these texts are found to contain figurative strategies that can be described as discourses of diet.

I have tried to avoid forms of individualistic or psychologizing reading which tempt researchers in food. Plotz's article about De Quincey and anorexia is stimulating, but it does not demonstrate the full range of responses to consumption in the literary text.[26] *Shelley and the Revolution in Taste* attempts to be a historicizing book. But it does not follow the familiar approach of Romantic historicist studies in the 1980s, in seeking significant *absences* and the transcendental as political refuge or solution. Instead, it seeks to alert the reader to significant figurative *presences*, representations of the body, in a manner closer to the groundbreaking work carried out in Renaissance studies since the late 1970s. The book also shares with contemporary work in cultural studies the sense of the importance of delineating a cultural practice in such a way as to place it in its economic, racial, gendered and class-based context, while it relies on the technique of close textual analysis proper to the discipline of English literary study. This is one of the first attempts to analyse the literary figuration of diet in a sustained way that goes beyond the citation of sources or the limited discussion of the Shelleys' writing on vegetarianism. I use 'theory' extensively, with two provisos: theory will be addressed when the evidence is ready, and evidence is often used to critique theory; thus there is no clear boundary line between text and context, 'evidence' and 'theory'.

The book thus rescues the theme of natural diet from its marginality in *critical* discourse and explains how it may be understood in ways which make it hard to dismiss as 'cranky'. It shies away from praising or accusing any of the individuals that it discusses, because the discourses under analysis, although programmatic, are not referred back to a single, self-present subject. Additionally, I have been somewhat literal in my readings (even *The Triumph of Life*, in its very moments of irony, may be read more materially and literally). On the whole I have avoided making comments about the marginality or centrality of this or any other theme in *the Shelleys'* discourse, seeking instead to deal with the interrelationship between themes: the natural diet does not explain all of their positions but is significantly related to many of them. Thus the book discusses the fields of revolutionary political representation (chapter 1), the hagiography and/or pathology of Shelley biography (chapter 2), the presence of poetry specifically about natural diet (chapter 3), the prose on diet as a means of naturalizing the idea of social reform (chapter 4), figures of intemperance as comments about tyranny and the status of figurative language (chapter 5), the poetry and prose treating the issue of famine as the articulation of different kinds of ecological agenda (chapter 6) and a list of posthumous publications of Shelley's prose on the natural diet (bibliography).

Shelley and the Revolution in Taste tries to find new kinds of 'empirical' evidence; to understand how this works in the 'figurative' production of the body through discourses of diet; and to tackle certain themes developed in sceptical or deconstructive thinking about Shelley (for example, the idea of 'disfiguration'). Its first half deals with evidence (historical, biographical and poetic); its second, with how to theorize the evidence (natural(istic) modes of discourse, the contrast between culture and luxury, and the discourse of sustained progress). A picture emerges of a Shelley committed to the body in its material relationship with its environment, both social and natural.

CHAPTER I

The rights of brutes

Look what a fine morning it is – Insects, Birds & Animals are all
enjoying existence.

> Mary Wollstonecraft, *Original Stories from Real Life*,
> frontispiece

A SMALL SECT OF BRAHMINS

What does it mean, to eat? Eating is not only biologically necessary,
but also culturally symbolic, and partakes in the social flow of
commodities. The opinions of so-called 'ecological' anthropology,
within which it was possible to assume that 'cannibals' ate meat
because they needed the protein, have now been surpassed.[1] The
production, circulation and representation of food provide ways of
understanding society.

Between 1790 and 1820 there was an interest in representing the
consumption of food as an element of social structure. Godwin's
Answer to Malthus (1820) compares the standard of living of the
labouring poor in the sixteenth century and the contemporary
period. By the act of Parliament 25 Henry VIII limited the price of
beef, veal, pork and mutton (named as the food of the poor). In the
seventeenth century the high price of bread was not of vital import to
the lower classes: they lived on other sorts of cheap food and occupied
the land. But now, they could hardly afford meat, while tea and
white bread had become necessities.[2]

This chapter describes the intellectual, political and literary
context in which it is possible to understand the Shelleys' writing
about diet. The growth of urban culture and the imperial economy,
and the language of rights that emerged in response to the French
Revolution, all bear upon this issue. The first section shows to what
extent groups of people practised particular forms of vegetarian diet

13

in (roughly) the 1790–1820 period (encompassing Shelley's life). The second section discusses the rhetoric used in writing about a vegetable or 'natural' diet in the period, while in the third section the relationship between questions of diet and radical politics is elaborated. The fourth section analyses examples of figurative language and graphic satire in the period, showing how diet came to be used in political language. A reading of two novels by Mary Shelley then demonstrates how discourses of consumption were developed and revised in figurative language.

Having become permeated with the laws of capital, food gained urgent kinds of political significance. A journeyman cotton spinner, addressing the public of Manchester in 1818, described his miserable diet of 'water gruel and oatcake broken into it, a little salt, and sometimes coloured with a little milk, together with a few potatoes, and a bit of bacon or fat for dinner'.[3] The potato was cultivated as a social stabilizer, especially after enclosure.[4] At the beginning of his career, Percy Shelley would have known about the successive crop failures that took place between 1809 and 1812.[5] The demand for fine white bread (especially in London) was a demand for an enhanced social identity, in response to a labouring-class sense of famine conditions.[6]

Materially, food was scarce for the poorer classes; symbolically certain kinds bore signs of prestige. William Lovett recalled a story of his uncle in the first decade of the nineteenth century:

> The first question when he came home at noon, was to ask his mistress what she had got for dinner. If it happened to be baked potatoes, pork, and pie-crust – a favourite dinner with him – Uncle Jeremy would kneel down and make a long grace over it; but if it was a dinner of fish and potatoes, Uncle Jeremy could never be induced to say grace; for he always persisted that 'God Almighty never ordained fish and potatoes for a working man's dinner.'[7]

According to Engels, the working-class diet was still extremely limited in 1844.[8] The foundation of co-ops may have promoted the purchase of 'pure and unadulterated articles of food'.[9]

Scarcity promoted adulteration: simulated abundance. Urbanization had led to new and complex chains of food production and distribution. 'Globalizing' studies of the diseases of London, such as Bateman's *Reports* (1819), discussed seasonal and environmental factors in order 'to refute an opinion, generally advanced by foreigners ... that most of the diseases of England are to be ascribed to the use of animal food, and malt-liquors, especially taken to repletion'.[10] Diet was a sensitive issue for those who profited from studying the rapid increase in urbanization. Bateman describes London as a militarized zone, like a permanent army camp where plague, fevers and dysentery are spread by wet and filth, where 'the increase in intemperance and vice' brought apoplexy, palsy and insanity.[11] Frederick Accum's *A Treatise on Adulterations of Food* (1820) delineated a relationship between different sorts of urban producer and retailer, including chemists who often supplied the raw materials (such as alum in the case of bread) for adulteration.[12] Through urbanized class division, food preparers became ignorant of these circulations of forgery.[13]

Accum's London is a maze in which origins are lost, to such an extent that: 'the traffic in adulterated commodities should find its way through so many circuitous channels, as to defy the most scrutinizing endeavour to trace it to its source'.[14] These metropolitan mazes brought about changes in consumption, producing whirlpools of deterioration in society: 'In reference to the deterioration of almost all the necessaries and comforts of existence, it may be justly observed, in a civil as well as a religious sense, that "*in the midst of life we are in death*".'[15] A popular ballad from around 1825 called 'London Adulterations' laments the condition described by Accum but with different emphases (an increased stress on how the consumer had been conned), sniffing at such items as PD, or pepper dust, and including meat in its list of adulterated products:

> The butcher puffs up his tough mutton like lamb,
> And oft for South Downs sells an old mountain ram;
> Bleeds poor worn-out cows to pass off for white veal,
> And richly deserves to die by his own steel. (Verse 7)[16]

Discourses of disease, poisoning, dissimulation and injustice were attracted to each other. While slaughterhouses were visited by the 'gently-bred' to drink blood, thought to be a specific against tuberculosis,[17] these discourses were steered towards writing on the rights of those who could not speak for themselves.

John Lawrence, a farmer, published *A Philosophical and Practical Treatise on Horses* (1796). He was disgusted by the sight of cattle being led into London under appalling conditions to be taken to Smithfield market for slaughter. Lawrence's liberal opinions also included anti-slavery and universal suffrage.[18] He specifically criticizes the wantonness, the lack of reason, in the suffering of Smithfield animals. Hume had questioned by what principles brute animals claim justice at human hands; but Lawrence's nature, however 'brute and indiscriminating', must *ipso facto* be subjected to reason, 'illumined and regulated by the reasoning faculty'.[19] But this subjection should not be violent. The issue of vivisection as a scientific tool is dovetailed into a revision of class society and personal identity:

It has been said that the world could not have either gold, sugar, or coals but at the expense of human blood and human liberty. The world in that case ought not to have either gold, sugar, or coals. The principle admits of no qualification. But the assertion was fallacious and unfounded; these comforts are all attainable by honest means, by voluntary and fairly remunerated industry.[20]

Lawrence emphasizes a voluntaristic kind of virtue, a secularized moral code which will redeem commodity production. Smithfield, once the site of Bartholomew fair, had become a different arena for the making and transgression of consumer and consumed.

Lawrence distinguishes (rather unsuccessfully) between his position and that of a significant group of others, people described in a quotation as 'saints' who 'were for / abolishing black-pudding / And eating nothing with the blood in': 'I am aware of a small sect of *Bramins* [sic] among us who are disposed to take a step beyond me.'[21] 'Bramins' were known as members of an Indian caste who abstained from meat, and vegetable eaters were often referred to as Brahmins. But who were these people in English society?

These were people for whom it was not economically necessary to eat vegetables but who had chosen to eat them, for reasons both medical and moral (and usually a mixture of both, not least because it is hard to make rigid distinctions in most contemporary medical texts). They were called Brahmins, Pythagoreans, eaters of a 'natural' diet; they were not yet called vegetarians.[22] Of the literary figures who wrote about natural diet in the period, about ten are known to have practised it. If we include those who wrote books and articles about vegetable diet, the number increases significantly (it probably doubles). If we include the literate market for a vegetable recipe book like Nicholson's *On Food* (1803),[23] or those who read *Vegetable Cookery* (1821) by the wife of Joseph Brotherton, who was a member of the church for three hundred vegetarian Swedenborgians, founded in Salford in 1809 by William Cowherd (Brotherton also wrote a teetotal tract in 1821),[24] the numbers of those interested in, writing about or practising a vegetable diet in the period seem large enough to merit a critical study. If one adds the emergent discourse of animal rights and the use of its figurative patterns in sources of political debate, the study becomes one of very large networks of significance in which ideological differences were signalled and disputed.

On Food illustrates the demographic spread of vegetable eating, of which the 'sect' Lawrence describes may be a small element, elevating the eating of vegetable food into an ideologically-coded form of self-presentation. *On Food* is clearly for a middle-class readership; it proposes the introduction of poor food in '*simple form*' for supposedly sophisticated people.[25] The book is marketed for an intellectually-cultured middle class who cannot afford luxuries: '*those who are prudent and economical* ... [the food] *may be valuable to many of scanty incomes, who desire to avoid the evils of want, or to make a reserve for the purchasing of books and other mental pleasures*'.[26] This sort of grading corresponds with Bourdieu's analysis of the *habitus* (or system of regulated improvisations) of middle-class intellectuals, perhaps living slightly above their means.[27] Enough of these were vegetarian in the early nineteenth century to justify the publication of *On Food*.[28] There is no easy means of distinguishing between middle-class and working-class styles of consumption along simplistic lines of 'aesthetics vs. morals'. Different kinds of morality and aesthetics were involved for both classes. The demand for fine white bread amongst the working class certainly contained discourses of habitual 'distinction', but also played upon the rhetoric of subsistence.

The general introduction of *On Food* stresses the importance of wholefood. Indeed, the entire chapter revolves around distinctions between 'simple' (equated with 'natural') and 'complex'.[29] Bread, for example, saps 'the nutritious properties of the gluten'; 'Nature unquestionably intended that man should use the whole of wheat as food.'[30] This fits a scheme of land economy: 'four times the quantity of ground is required to support an ox that it is necessary to support a man'.[31] But the desire for simplicity is not shared by the working class: 'the vulgar' have 'prejudices' for bread and 'farinacea' rather than whole-grain uses of the same plants.[32]

However, while not simple in one respect, the working class is too simple in another: 'Their whole system seems confined to baking the limb of an animal in an oven, as often as they can afford it, and when they cannot attain this supreme object, they live on bread and cheese.'[33] The workers are now accused of being clumsy, and *too* simple at making meals. This rudeness, however, links with their 'prejudices' for bread[34] since both are examples of simplistic uses of complexly-produced food. The representation of the working class is framed with that of the complexity and bad economy of animal food, which is 'among the causes that Britain is not able to raise grain for the supply of her inhabitants'.[35] The middle-class vegetarian diet is thus precisely the opposite of the working-class diet: a complex or sophisticated use of simple food. The return to nature in *On Food* circumvents the working-class *habitus*.

Thus within the group of vegetable eaters there was a distinction between upper and lower class in which food operated as a signifier. But in the so-called 'sect' there arises a more complex set of identifications and distinctions. The 'sect' presented itself in an extreme fashion as having gone beyond 'custom', symbolized by the threatening materiality of the visceral imagery employed in its rhetoric.[36]

The arguments of some Brahmins may have been notorious. In 1821 an article appeared in the *London Magazine* about a group of vegetable eaters. It was probably written by Thomas Love Peacock, a close acquaintance of at least some of them.[37] It reappeared in the first number of *The Medical Adviser*. Peacock would have known about the group in the early 1810s; his article is a witty lampoon of their means of self-presentation. But the piece was reprinted as the final article in the first edition of a new magazine designed to promote health among those who could not afford expensive books or doctors. This is evidence that the vegetable diet encouraged serious debates about distinctions between different uses to which it could be put.

The first volume of the collected issues of *The Medical Adviser* appeared in 1824.[38] Its purpose was to disseminate practical information about how the body should be managed in 'all parts of the empire'.[39] One aim was to dispense with quackery: the journal claims greater truth and accuracy, responding to a greater need for the proper articulation of the body in an expanding, increasingly industrialized imperialist economy.[40]

Issue 1 (6 December, 1823) contains a satirical piece on 'Animal and Vegetable Diet', criticizing Shelley's *A Vindication of Natural Diet* (1813). The occasion represented is a 'Dinner by the Amateurs of Vegetable Diet'.[41] In the chair is 'P. B. S': no guessing required there. Also present are 'Dr. L. [Lambe], Mr. R. the antiquarian

[Joseph Ritson], Sir J. S. [John 'Walking' Stewart], the Rev. P. [William Paley?[42]] and Mr. T. the Pythagorian [sic] philosopher [Taylor[43]], near him was Mr. G. [Godwin], Mr. H. [Henry Hunt] and Mr. L. H. [Leigh Hunt]'.[44] Leigh Hunt's status at this fictional gathering stresses the element of reformism in the defence of vegetable diet: he is 'not a vegetable man', but goes on to talk about 'the rights of petition and parliamentary reform'.[45] And after all, he had close connections with P. B. S.

'Mr Manchester Hunt' arrives 'to promote reform, if not in the country, at least in the constitution of [the citizens'] bodies'.[46] Henry Hunt, known as 'Orator' Hunt, was part of the radical reform movement in the early nineteenth century. He is in the article because of his invention of 'radical breakfast powder': 'Hunt sought to turn propaganda to his advantage by selling "radical breakfast powder"' ('a concoction based on roasted corn which was sold as a substitute for tea or coffee, and which was recommended to Radicals as a means of boycotting taxed articles').[47] This was a roasted grain breakfast that appeared long before the idea of breakfast cereal was promoted by vegetarians, and before the recommendation of coarse flour by the vegetarian Sylvester Graham (1794–1851).[48] Elsewhere in *The Medical Adviser* this idea is taken seriously.[49] Abstinence from taxed goods such as beer or sugar was also promoted by Cobbett and Southey to exert consumer pressure on the government and the slave trade respectively.[50] And on the other side, an 'alliance between Nonconformists and Utilitarians' promoted temperance as social control.[51]

Hunt's powder was advertised in *The Medusa* in 1820: 'Now that we are deprived of arms, the revenue is the only effectual manner in which we can overthrow the junto [sic] by whom we are so miserably enth[r]alled.'[52] There was some radical debate over Hunt's breakfast powder. The counter-cultural publisher Carlile tried it in the spring of 1820 and thought it was pleasant, but 'could not make a breakfast from either' this or another version which he tried.[53] It was not as good as coffee 'further than as a war upon revenue'.[54] He declares that 'a sprinkling of mustard and ginger' adds 'a great improvement to the flavour, and a wholesome addition as a pectoral or medical property. But', he continues:

I would beg to remind the industrious part of the people, that there are many grasses and herbs in this country that make an excellent tea if carefully gathered and dried. The common meadow hay is in my opinion preferable to the roasted grain, to make a beverage pleasant and nutritious, where the mind can be raised above the prejudice of habit. Those who love milk, butter, and cheese, need not feel a prejudice towards the use of grass or hay; whatever is nutritious in the former, is scarce any thing but a chemical solution of the latter.[55]

There is irony in Carlile's text which may derive from his understanding of Shelley's rhetoric of vegetarianism, based on ideas like *nature* and *habit*.

Peacock's article is full of rich observation. The vegetarians, described by *The Medical Adviser* article's epigraph as 'Lotophagi and men whose heads are not in the right places',[56] are lampooned for a kind of coy identification with the working and agricultural classes.[57] The linkage of a positive evaluation of thinness and high status, a relatively new phenomenon, is apparent: 'we have no superabundant flesh ... There is only a ring of thoughtful darkness around our eyes that speaks a true soul.'[58] Peacock ironically revises the orientalizing (carnivorous) exoticism of *Othello* i.iii.142–44: 'the cannibals that each other eat, / The Anthropophagi, and men whose heads / Do grow beneath their shoulders'.[59] 'Brahminism' could involve a domesticating consumption of the exotic: Shelley's *Laon and Cythna* shows to what extent the meal could become an orient (see chapter 3). Peacock shows how the Brahmins' lack of social realism threatens to disrupt civic life: if the 'Scotch and Irish' and the 'English peasantry' were invited to the 'Dinner', there would be a riot like 'a plague of locusts'.[60]

Shelley's *A Vindication of Natural Diet* is singled out for criticism as 'absurd and irrational'.[61] Its apocalypticism is parodied in the echo of the liturgical formula in 'As in Adam all die, so in Newton shall all eat cabbage.'[62] The apocalypse is coloured by 'natural state' or Golden Age philosophy, a return to the reign of Saturn in which there will be no property, no government, law or religion. This idealist politics is again satirized by a naturalistic discourse: the 'eulogism' on the natural state is disrupted by the 'natural effects' of an 'overwhelming shower of rain'.[63]

The article appears at the end of the first number and is intended to be a *tour de force*. It distinguishes between the class of its readers and the 'Amateurs' using skilful parody. The journal's appeal to a wider audience is clear, given the article on how to detect adulterated bread (an important issue, especially for the London working class),[64] and its use of popularizing rhetoric and illustration. The journal shares some of the rhetoric of 'nature' used by diet reformers. An article on food for 24 July, 1824 suggests the necessity of a balanced diet, but is aware that animal food alone is a health risk, and that too much cooking is dangerous – the public should heed the 'children of nature'.[65] The vegetarians in this period also seemed to value rawness above cookedness. A similar division is drawn between natural and artificial: the savages are healthy 'until the simplicity of their habits is intercepted by the adoption of the vices brought ... by the civilised invaders of their native forests'.[66] The Brahmins were a subculture within wider emergent discourses of health and nature.

The satire on vegetable diet was destined for a (possibly) labouring audience who would make a class distinction between themselves and the 'Amateurs'. While meat was too politically charged for Shelley to eat, it was too politically charged for the poorer classes *not* to eat.

THE CRY OF NATURE

How did the rhetoric of vegetable diet function? A clear example is provided by John Oswald's *The Cry of Nature* (1791).[67] Oswald was the son of an Edinburgh goldsmith.[68] He was made a lieutenant of the Black Watch, but left the army in 1783 because of the 'bloody farce' at Bednore.[69] He wrote for the *London Chronicle* and the *Political Herald and Review*, and later *The British Mercury*.[70] He became a member of the Jacobin club in Paris and was killed at La Vendée in 1793, having led the pikemen who formed the guard surrounding the guillotined King Louis. He attracted such public attention that he was mistaken for Napoleon.[71] The vegetarian writer and antiquarian Joseph Ritson suggests that he converted to Hinduism after spending two years wandering in India.[72] In *The Cry of Nature*, Hindu texts are quoted in translation in endnotes, and poetry quotations embellish the text. Oswald drew upon a tradition of orientalizing Indology, including Brahmin philosophy, exemplified in such figures as Sir William Jones, as well as a British literary canon.[73] He did not believe in metempsychosis (the Pythagorean doctrine of the reincarnation and transmigration of souls), but in the immortality of the body; he drank wine, and was an atheist.[74] He was a friend of General John 'Walking' Stewart,[75] who also wrote about humane consumption and was influenced by Hindu philosophy; they met at a party held by John Rickman for Tom Paine.[76] Oswald is represented in Wordsworth's *The Excursion*[77] and *The Borderers*, in the latter as a zealous and sinister figure: it is hinted that he uses deadly nightshade (*The Borderers* 1.i.44–46). Burke was alarmed by Oswald's writing after it was recommended to him in 1792.[78] In the House of Commons, in March 1793, he accused Oswald of spreading democracy. A novel by Shelley's cousin Thomas Medwin, entitled *Oswald and Edwin: an Oriental Sketch* (1820), tells the story of an Oswald who seeks nature in India like the Poet in Shelley's *Alastor*, and converts to Hinduism, practising abstinence and Yoga.[79] Section vii describes his vegetarianism:

> The Yogee's life – without the priest's pretence –
> Yet, though as hermit's pure, his simple feast,
> Unstained by blood of India's sacred beast:
> His strange conversion was but darkly guessed –
> His tenets only vague surmise at best.[80]

The narrator then wonders about the political motivation of Oswald's Brahminism.

Some of the writing about Oswald at the time dismissed his radicalism by pointing out the absurdity of his vegetarianism and atheism.[81] However, it is not that Oswald was a radical in spite of his vegetarianism, but that his vegetarianism was bound up with his radicalism. *The Cry of Nature* opens with the idea of 'just' legislation.[82] The first sections of the work develop conventional arguments for and against eating flesh, like comparative anatomy. But the central feature of the work is a critique of scientific rationalism, which uses the rhetoric of literalized anatomy or inverted demonstrative rhetoric involving the representation of cutting up a body.[83] One might call it *macellogia*, discourse about the shambles, about maceration (a kind of Smithfield contrablazon). The 'sons of *modern science*' do not see nature 'in the living loveliness of her works, but expect to meet her in the midst of obscurity and corruption', and:

interrogate trembling nature, who plunge into her maternal bosom the butcher knife and, in quest of... nefarious science, the fibres of agonizing animals, delight to scrutinize.[84]

Oswald appeals to the bowels of a carnivorous animal, 'fraught with mercy, and entwined with compassion'.[85] 'Nature' and 'science' were constantly and diversely questioned and revised by the sect of 'Brahmins'.

Here a dead body is brought into the text, the body of 'a playful fawn',[86] providing the frontispiece illustration by Gillray (unsigned; see figure 1), after a climactic figuration of dismemberment in which a series of rhetorical questions lead to a figurative murder: 'Glares in his eye-ball the lust of carnage? Does he [man] scent after the footsteps of his victim?'[87] The argument has been powerfully staged. The false 'rhetoric' of the scientists[88] is contrasted with the language of nature itself, which is represented as a cry, a rhetoric of non-rhetoric. There is an alternative interrogation:

O that man would interrogate his own heart! O that he would listen to the voice of nature! For powerfully she stirs within us; and, from the bottom of the human heart, with moving voice she pleads. Why, she cries, oh! why shouldst thou dip thy hand in the blood of thy fellow-creatures without cause?[89]

Oswald's 'O's are effectively echoed by nature's cry of 'oh!' If there are any precedents for Wordsworth's *The Tables Turned* ('We murder to dissect', 28), then surely this is one. Oswald proposes that humans have progressively deviated from a natural vegetarian state, from sacrifice to blatant butchery. Man has become anthropocentric, destroying himself and nature in the process: 'me the heaven-deputed despot of every creature that walks, or creeps, or swims, or flies in air, in earth, or in the waters which encompass the earth'.[90] Again, Oswald assumes the voice of another. He is attempting to take apart the grandiose and Biblical language of the despot, and to break open the despotic signifier which engenders 'me' and tyrannizes the other in the process, in order to substitute a more 'natural', and more 'humane', form of representation.[91] The echo of Genesis raises the question of the humane stewardship of others.

Oswald's directly political writing presents similar treatments of nature and figurative language. In *The Government of the People* (1793), Oswald sees voting for a government which does not directly represent the people as 'vox et praeterea [sic] nihil',[92] a voice and nothing besides. A natural representation would be non-metonymic, with no general or king or militia standing in for the people.[93] There are echoes of the language of *The Tempest*: 'the tottering fabric of the state'[94] is like 'The baseless fabric of this vision'.[95] Oswald misquotes Stephano to radical effect: 'and Trinculo and thyself shall be viceroys' (III.ii.108) becomes '"and I shall be viceroy over you"'.[96] *The Tempest* broaches the possibilities for revolt in a state whose fabric

Figure 1   Frontispiece illustration by Gillray (unsigned) for John Oswald's
The Cry of Nature (1791).

is so clearly purely figurative, and which rests so obviously on a previous state of nature where Caliban was ruler. This is a figurative inversion of colonial hegemony, in which the subaltern subject (the 'Caribee', or Caliban, whose name is a linguistic play on 'cannibal'), now gains control. Arguments about the colonies were already finding their way back home, as critiques of the imperialism of government and science. Caliban, on whose nature nurture could never stick, is here used as the advocate of a new kind of political nurture. Oswald's ideal assembly of the people would agree matters with an inarticulate, animal-like 'shout' or 'groan'.[97] To argue about a natural state is to make political judgments.

Oswald's *Review of the Constitution of Great Britain* (Paris, 1792) was originally delivered at a debate in Cornhill on Horne Tooke's petition on the right to reform. It contains a vivid metaphor in which John Bull (standing for the English people) is slaughtered by a corrupt government, eaten and stuffed with straw.[98] The image, found in Porphyry's *de Abstinentia* II.29–30, had been placed in the appendix to *The Cry of Nature* and compared with Pausanias' *Description of Greece* I.c24, in which a bullock is eaten, stuffed, and arranged with a plough 'as it were in act to till the ground'.[99] If Oswald's political texts were figured through food, then his dietary text is highly political. He justifies *The Cry of Nature* with an appeal to political reform, revising gospel language in a secular context:

when he [the author] considers the natural bias of the human heart to the side of mercy, and observes on all hands the barbarous governments of Europe giving way to a better system of things, he is inclined to hope that the day is beginning to approach when the growing sentiment of *peace and good-will towards men* will also embrace, in a wide circle of benevolence, the lower orders of life.[100]

The vegetable diet provided an image of social progress. In Oswald's play *The Humours of John Bull*, Mr Worthy, who like Oswald has just arrived from the East Indies, with his 'Hindoo' servant Tippo, reaches the inn belonging to Timothy Pimpleface:

Tim. Ay, sir, are you come from the East Indies? Then without doubt, you have seen the elephants, the rhinoceroses, and those savage cannibals, the Gintoos, who eat nothing but herbs, and entertain a most treasonable antipathy to roast beef, the glory of Old England. But pray, Sir, have you ever tasted the Nabob fish? It is, I'm told, most excellent eating.
Mr. Worthy. The Nabob, my friend, is a land-animal, very sweet indeed to eat, but sometimes rather hard to digest. But pray do conduct me to bed.[101]

Gillray was later to depict the revolutionary French as both cannibals
and vegetable eaters; here Pimpleface may simply be displaying the
insulting muddle-headedness indicative of a colonizing country (and
he has obviously been at the beef; a rather Shakespearean joke). His
remarks are a cue for a joke about the wealthy foreigners making
their fortune in India. But Oswald's sophisticated language shows
how diet may be socially constructed. The 'Gintoos' are demeaned as
'savage cannibals', despite the fact that they are vegetarian.
Pimpleface's stupidity is a cultural program for denigrating the
'other' with the whitewash of the signifier 'cannibal'.

    Henry Brougham's 1803 review of Joseph Ritson's *An Essay On
Abstinence from Animal Food* perceived revolutionary contexts for
Oswald's vegetarianism.[102] Oswald, 'Retaining his unparalleled
humanity of disposition, and abhorrence at the sight of animal blood,
this abstinent sage was the first who proposed to the Convention the
introduction of the pike, both for the use of the army and the mob.'[103]
Brougham continues by calling Oswald 'A maniac who fought the
massacres of Paris, and was zealous to avoid even the sight of blood:
a wretch who would not kill a tyger, but died unsated in his thirst for
human blood!'[104] Ritson declared in *Animal Food* that Oswald sent
his children out to forage in the gardens and forests in the suburbs of
Paris.[105] The contradictions in Oswald's beliefs and practices
demonstrate how cultural analysis should not involve plangent and
existentializing language about 'authenticity', however subtly-
coded, unless one wanted to court this kind of reaction.

    Brougham ridicules the vegetarian language that traces occulted
paths of commodity production: 'the oil which is wasted to illuminate
the midnight process [of writing?], is a damning proof of the long
protracted torments and inhuman butchery of the great leviathan,
the lord of the deep'.[106] Since man is inevitably carnivorous, 'From
the first to the last gasp of our lives' (since we breathe in thousands
of tiny creatures), meat is only 'an imperceptible voluntary addition'
to 'the catalogue of necessary enormities'.[107] In the 1790–1820
period, such an argument played dangerously between serious and
comic registers. Ritson's radicalism was associated with vegetarianism. His general preoccupation with roots was used in a caricature of
him writing incendiary prose amongst piles of root vegetables, with a
docile cow looking through the window, stepping on Percy's ballads
with open-toed sandals (see figure 2).[108]

    The discourse of vegetarianism creates waves of sympathy which

Figure 2   'A Vegetarian'. Caricature by J. Sayer of Joseph Ritson (published 1803).

overflow class, race and species limits or boundaries. A figurative code is generated in which an interaction is constructed between a voice (the cry of inarticulate nature) and a listener (the humane reformer who hears as it were the voice of their own humanity within the cry). Monboddo, Ritson, the Shelleys and others use this code in their construction of a reformist subject position. Through the rhetoric of the cry of nature, they present themselves as peaceful reformers revising Biblical, millennial language and classical representations of the Golden Age, along with anthropological research into the state of nature. The cry of nature was a way for reformers in positions of relative power to justify legislation for those humans as well as animals who were considered unable to do so for themselves.

'Humanity' in the period denotes both the non-sacred (non-Judaeo-Christian) study of culture (for example, classical literature), and sensibility or affection.[109] The play on 'humane' is very important in certain contemporary animal rights texts. Ritson's final chapter is called 'Of Humanity'. For Henry Crowe, 'Humanity' is 'a quality wholly acquired, and derived from mental, or rather moral culture. Hence savages, and uninstructed children scarcely know it; and for the same reason the lower classes are often lamentably deficient therein.'[110] Crowe articulates a certain paternalism available to those who used the concept. Erskine's magistrate must be able 'only to judge upon *hearing* from his own humane feelings', in a spontaneous perception of justice.[111] Young's *An Essay on Humanity to Animals* (1798) includes a prefatory *Ode to Humanity* by the Rev. C. Hoyle, and declares that 'it is our duty to cultivate humanity towards animals'.[112] This 'humanity' would 'undoubtedly tend to render us more humane towards mankind'.[113] Expressions of kindness amongst animals show that 'humanity' is a quality possessed equally by all animals, in a sense; but in particular, it links culture (defined as human frailty) to nature.[114] To be humane is to be refined and to accord with nature. Thus the human hears a humane voice within the silence of the animal about to be slain:

A humane man will never be able to take away the life of an animal, even by the easiest method, and for the purposes of food without pity and regret. There is a certain *mute eloquence* in the meek countenance and resigned manner of a sheep
        – that lays beneath the Knife,
    Looks up, and from her butcher begs her life,–
which far surpasses speech, and of which every heart must be sensible.[115]

Mute language is supplemented by the gaze of the spectator (and the passage stresses this with the 'There is ... '): humanity has something to do with this gaze beyond language. In the eighteenth century, the sublime discourse of nature's face was developed.[116] The idea of faciality as the generator of the 'humane' became very important for

Shelley, especially in the figurative scheme of *Queen Mab*. Young's use of the feminized lamb ('her ... her') is also important in comparison with Shelley's *A Refutation of Deism*.

One is tempted to consider the 'Brahmins' as so many peaceful flower children, with an aesthetics of beauty as the lack of harm, as innocence. Literary examples include the millenarian and aristocratic vegetarians in Mary Shelley's *The Last Man* (1826), the Poet in Percy Shelley's *Alastor* (1816), or the plea of the creature to be allowed to move to South America, with his mate, in *Frankenstein* (written 1816; published 1818). The creature is only a monster in his creator's eyes, and is really more like a hippy complaining to the older generation:

'If you consent, neither you nor any other human being shall ever see us again: I will go to the vast wilds of South America. My food is not that of man; I do not destroy the lamb and the kid, to glut my appetite; acorns and berries afford me sufficient nourishment. My companion will be of the same nature as myself, and will be content with the same fare. We shall make our bed of dried leaves; the sun will shine on us as on man, and will ripen our food. The picture I present to you is peaceful and human, and you must feel that you could deny it only in the wantonness of power and cruelty. Pitiless as you have been towards me, I now see compassion in your eyes; let me seize the favourable moment, and persuade you to promise what I so ardently desire.'[117]

Mary Shelley also plays upon the gaze in which the rhetoric of sympathy refers the sign back to the body.[118] The creature proposes to be a more accurate (more rational) representation of humanity than humanity itself. He re-imagines his body: the monster will be more human than man.

The possible analogy with flower children would be falsely conceived, however, since it ignores the element of rights language caught up in the struggle for representation in which the lower classes were also involved. Samuel Pratt's *Humanity: or, the Rights of Nature* (1788), shows how the discourse of natural diet can be caught up in the rhetoric against slavery (the central section opposes the peaceful Brahmins to the violent butchers of Europe). The debate on the Game Laws further shows how an intersection of discourses about class, animal rights and diet took place across a wide social range, from the proposals made by Lord Erskine (1809) to ban certain (lower class) blood sports to criticisms of the activities of the SSV (Society for the Suppression of Vice) in the radical journal *The*

Medusa. Moreover, if politics was being represented through the rights of brutes, then radical writers also had an interest in those rights themselves.

DIET AND RADICAL POLITICS

Parody is a good test of cultural dissemination. Thomas Taylor's *A Vindication of the Rights of Brutes* (1792) shows how other consumers regarded vegetarian diet as political.[119] Taylor (1758–1835) was educated at St Paul's School, studied mathematics, chemistry and Aristotle, and became a famous translator of Neoplatonic and neo-Pythagorean texts. De Valadi, a neo-Pythagorean *philosophe* from Paris, visited him between 1788 and 1789. Indeed, Shelley was acquainted with his work.[120] Taylor intended to ridicule Paine's *The Rights of Man* (1791–92), and his acquaintance Mary Wollstonecraft's *A Vindication of the Rights of Woman* (1792). His text is a *reductio ad absurdum*: if rights were allowed to the least rational of men and also to women, then animals (and ultimately, vegetables and minerals) must have rights by extension as possessing equal dignity and worth.[121] This is a version of the argument from marginal cases found in Porphyry's *On Abstinence from Animal Food*: a characteristic possessed by all human beings will not be possessed only by human beings.[122] (Porphyry was translated by Thomas Taylor.) It fitted into a late eighteenth-century debate about rationality as a criterion for justice: Rousseau had argued that sentience (Greek $\alpha \ddot{\iota} \sigma \theta \eta \sigma \iota s$) was enough. The principle of intimacy ($o \dot{\iota} \kappa \epsilon \dot{\iota} \omega \sigma \iota s$) discussed in classical literature as a means of determining the extent of justice could then be applied to animals, who after all were part of eighteenth-century natural theology's 'economy of nature'. The constellation of these issues was serious enough in the period under discussion to produce prosperous reformers such as William Thompson (1775–1833), who became a vegetarian and whose feminist *Appeal* was based upon the universality of human rights (and contained some anti-slavery passages).[123]

Taylor's mockery is levelled at the degree of abstraction he envisages as necessary to sustain a humanitarian argument. Thus he resembles Brougham, who laid a Burkean stress on the dangers of theory, associated with deviation from a socially-established normality. Distinctions break down: Wollstonecraft confuses 'beef for mutton',[124] and Taylor confuses social and natural-historical classes.

Aristotle had argued that as master or 'despot' is to slave, so soul is to body;[125] 'though almost every one is now convinced, that soul and body are only nominally distinguished from each other, and are essentially the same'.[126] Taylor understands that debates about the rights of animals involve discussions about categories of mind and matter or *hylê* and *technê*.[127] To re-conceive relationships between humans and the natural (animal) world is not only to re-imagine the body, but to decode the relation between despot and slave. Discourses of 'nature' tried to substitute immanence for the potentially despotic rule of idea over matter, which reproduces the despotic signifier of the tyrant.

Authoritative taxonomies are collapsing. Despite their differences, all beings are to be judged equal: Taylor asserts '*the equality of all things, with respect to their intrinsic and real dignity and worth*'.[128] Reason is no longer a category for judging difference: all animals possess some reason along with a distinct and particular quality (the lion's strength, the 'subtility of spinning in a spider'), but these two always add up to an equal 'worth'.[129] This erasure applies to language too, so that men are made to mutate into animals:

[tyrannical] distinctions indeed are so far from being natural, that the very words by which they are expressed, are evidently corruptions of more common, and less arbitrary appellations. Thus, for instance, the Greek word for a *king*, βασιλευς, is doubtless a corruption of βασιλικος, a basilisk;[130] and the English word nobility, is in like manner a corruption of the word mobility; just as *praying*, when it becomes social, is beyond all controversy a corruption of *braying*.[131]

The etymology of mutation accomplishes a sort of metamorphosis. Taylor would have known about Pythagoras in Ovid's *Metamorphoses* xv, where as the advocate of metempsychosis, he is the philosopher of shape-changes as well as of vegetarianism.

Taylor also satirically blurs reason into imagination. If animals are by definition not inanimate, and if 'every animated sensitive being possesses also a *phantasy*, as a kind of reason', then they should be respected.[132] The capacity of beings to imagine was one way in which Shelley defended his vegetarianism.[133] This universalizing criterion also applied to the politically-coded aspects of contemporary poetry about the imagination.

The possibility that others can imagine suggests the chance that they might speak. Taylor parodies a deconstruction of boundaries between 'cultured' and 'barbaric'. Gibbon's study of the inner collapse of the centralized Roman Empire and Monboddo's interest in primitive speech share this interest in the barbaric. 'Barbarians' are created in order to justify the treatment of the Other as inferior: in ancient Greece, for example, the 'barbarian' was invented in the context of the nationalist culture of Panhellenism formulated to strengthen allegiance in the Persian War.[134] Thinkers of the post-'Augustan' age were interested in this term. Sympathy and sociology could be extended to barbarians, but not powers of self-determination. Taylor is conscious of how 'Brahmin' discourse breaks down distinctions on one level, and retains the power of distinction on another. 'Barbarian' comes from the inarticulate stuttering which the alien culture is supposed to make instead of speech, a non-differentiated 'bar-bar-bar', an animal call. Taylor acknowledges the constellation of barbarian and animal language:

It is a true and Pythagoric opinion, that every soul participating sense and memory is rational, and is endued with speech as well internal as external, by means of which, animals apparently irrational confer with each other. But that the words they employ for this purpose should not be distinguished by us, is not to be wondered at, if we consider, that the discourse of many Barbarians is unintelligible to us, and that they appear to make use of indistinct vociferation, rather than rational speech.[135]

Humanitarianism supposes the non-differentiation of species, but, nevertheless, the capacity of all to differentiate (reason or imagine). Taylor refers to a Golden Age when in the quoted words of Pope 'Man walk'd with beast joint tenant of the shade.'[136] But humans fall from this happy state: 'we ... destroy many of them in theatrical sports, and in the barbarous exercise of the chase, by which means the *brutal* energies of our nature grow strong, and the savage desires encrease' (sic).[137] 'Brutal' suggests irrationality and inarticulacy.[138] 'Savage' suggests a primordial state ('of the forest').[139] What is happening? An element of differentiation persists, which judges man in accordance with 'lower' and 'higher' levels of being. This is an argument for animals which keeps them in their assigned place. Real savagery is not natural but the result of a fall into the flesh, an idea which Taylor's parody of Neoplatonism brings out: if we could abstain from even a vegetable diet, as well as animal food, 'stopping the flowing condition of our body, which like an ever-running stream, is continually rolling into the dark sea of matter, as into the abyss of non-entity, we could immediately be present with the best and most exalted natures, and rise to that condition of being, in which he, who is conjoined by an ineffable [unrepresentable] union with the deity, is himself a god'.[140] This figuration of flow is also characteristic (though its tinge of Behmenism is slightly mocking): the natural diet is instituted to limit a threatening flow of material, often represented as waste, pollution or miasma (moral pollution).

Taylor ironically suggests that justice towards animals resembles, or even generates, justice towards humans.[141] Justice and food may be related through thinking about appetite: thus 'the banquet of Pythagoras, is much more pleasant and desirable, than that of Socrates: for the latter of these affirmed, that hunger was the sauce of food; but Pythagoras asserted, that to injure no one, and to act justly, was the sweetest of all banquets'.[142] Taylor's statement about justice overcodes previous ideas in *The Rights of Brutes*: vegetarian arguments used in support of reasoning against cruelty to animals now become important in themselves (chapters iii, iv and v are devoted to abstinence from flesh). This could support the Burkean satire of revolutionists overfed with abstract theory.

The 1790s witnessed a number of publications on animal rights, argued with reference to vegetarianism. John Lawrence published *A Philosophical Treatise on Horses* between 1796 and 1798. In 1797 George Nicholson, who later edited *On Food*, published *On the Conduct of Man to Inferior Animals*. Public pressure had gathered enough pace for Thomas Lord Erskine (1750–1823) to make a speech in the House of Lords on 15 May 1809 on the second reading of the bill for preventing malicious and wanton cruelty to animals; the speech was published twice in the same year.[143] Erskine's position is that 'those reclaimed animals devoted to Man's use for food' may justly be killed.[144] Animals belong to an inhuman state of nature and in this respect should be 'kept down', and diet is the area in which they are re-figured or 'reclaimed' as part of a human sphere of culture. Sport, on the other hand, was in excess of this necessary destruction. Vegetarian writers could push the idea of sport to a limit at which it included consumption of animals: Erskine's arguments for animal rights were already based on 'the justest and tenderest consideration of the benevolent system of Nature'.[145] Erskine's speech was soon published by the vegetarian Richard Phillips (1767–1840), who also published Ritson's *Animal Food*. Phillips had been imprisoned for selling Paine's *The Rights of Man* in 1793. His vegetarianism was

commented on by Tom Moore.[146] Phillips also saw social implications
for vegetarian writing, and appended his *Golden Rules of Social
Philosophy* with arguments for vegetarianism, including a passage
denouncing animal sports.[147]

Meat was an enclaved marker of cultural value, used in the
ideology of John Bull and the Roast Beef of Old England. Wage
increases often led to consumption of meat, and *per capita* consumption
probably fell from 1790 to 1840.[148] Against this background Shelley's
promotion of a 'natural diet' seems an appeal to some ideal, hidden
England in the mind, a conceptual bonding with the poor. *The Black
Dwarf* for 3 September, 1817 contains a letter from a 'PETER PRY'
who claims, comically, to have found evidence of sedition.[149] This
'*Green Bag Correspondence*' turns out to be a lengthy poetic letter *From
a Potatoe to a Sirloin of Beef*:

> DEAR SIRLOIN, (For spite of the fashion and state
> Which has kept you from all your old comrades of late
> You are still *dear* to us,) I have taken my pen
> To implore you to visit our hovels again.
> ...
>
> Bad company ruins the best, and we see
> Your *high* friends have kept you from *Strawyard* and me;
> But we'll have you again, I pronounce with affiance
> In spite of the *gags*, and the *Holy alliance*!
> ...
>
> I'd a strong invitation my visage to show
> At a Spitalfields *soup party* some time ago;
> My brothers and sisters were all to go too,
> So I thought I should see something of you;
> Alas! I did not, but, as if to confound me
> *The bones of your ancestors* rattled around me!
> ...
>
> If you like just to come in the old fashioned mood
> To the cottage of industry, all well and good:
> Sam says if you *won't*, why he'll stick like a Cato,
> To Freedom, a crust, and
>   Your Friend, A POTATOE.   (1)

The reply from the Sirloin (presumably understood to be 'Sir Loin',
associating meat with status) in the same volume is just as acerbic:

> So my good friend Potato, if *friend* you must be,
> You had better return to your home d'ye see!

> From Brazil, I think it is said you was [sic] brought,
> To where with your ancient formality fraught,
> Go and teach humble slaves on your favour to dine,
> But never think more to approach a SIRLOIN.[150]

Similar comic language dealing with the issues of political power and famine, including the Green Bags, appear in Shelley's *Swellfoot the Tyrant* (1820).

The class division involved in the radical movements of the time is not to be underestimated. Shelley was not averse to putting down the 'aspiring philosophes' who were treated as feudal 'chattels' in the so-called 'republic of letters'.[151] Ritson's praise of the labouring diet coyly relates the upper to the lower classes, who were too poor to eat anything *but* vegetables.[152] The discourse of vegetarianism was by and large a specific ideological formation within a fairly elite grouping which included professionals and upper-class radical freethinkers. The discourse of *bread* would have been more familiar to artisans and others in the labouring-class hierarchy, but poets such as Ebeneezer Elliott would have had access to the works of Shelley (for their use of the figuration of bread, see the fifth chapter).[153] However, humanitarian and millenarian politics were not restricted to the 'Brahmin' sect.

In addition, political relationships were being expressed in terms familiar to animal rights writers. J. J. Brayfield wrote *The Mock Trial: a Parody* to draw attention to the case for blasphemous libel filed against the underground publisher Richard Carlile:

> O Priest-begotten Tyranny! what waste
> Thy cruel hands make in this fair creation,
> Treating Heaven's image, in thy fellow creature,
> Worse than the savage beast, or grazing herd!   (53–56)[154]

Carlile's paper *The Republican* also published 'REPUBLICAN IDEAS' reputedly '*written by a Citizen of Geneva*', which declared:

2. A society of men governed in an arbitrary manner, perfectly resembles a herd of cattle yoked for the service of their master. He feeds them that they may be in a condition to labour: he administers physic to them when sick, because it is in health alone that they can be of service to him; he fattens, in order to devour them; he cuts the skin of one into thongs to bind another to the plough.[155]

An image of conspicuous violence and consumption (found in the hunt, for example, or in animal husbandry) could suggest rhetorically that a structure had been set up in which the oppressed were cut off from any sort of redress: a cow could not answer a butcher back. It also suggested how class conflict established and brought into contradiction different planes of social activity that could not communicate with each other – Shelley's sleeping lions (*The Mask of Anarchy*, 368) could not be understood by the rulers if they spoke.[156] The politics of the body becomes important: if communication is hard, if not impossible, then mass action ('in unvanquishable number') is important. If the rulers have created a herd of human cattle, then the cattle can unite to prevent harm. But it was also designed to sting its readers into political articulacy: no one wanted to be a brute, an inarticulate member of another species. Part of the image's rhetorical power is that the animals end up being seen always-already to have had a human face.

The class division enacted by various kinds of animal rights activity, including vegetarianism, was clear to the politicized working class. Volume I of *The Medusa* contains a critique of the Society for the Suppression of Vice (which was active in the censorship of publishers like Carlile). It specifically attacks the SSV's position on animal rights, linking sport and food production together:

Nothing has disgusted us so much in the proceedings of this society as the controul [sic] which they exercise over the amusements of our fellow country-men. One of the specious titles under which this legal meanness is gratified, is, *Prevention of Cruelty to Animals*. Of cruelty to animals let the reader take the following specimens: – running an iron hook into the intestines of an animal; presenting this first animal to another as his food; and then pulling this second creature up, and suspending him by the barb in his stomach. Riding a horse till he drops, in order to see an innocent animal torn to pieces by dogs. Keeping a poor animal upright for many weeks, to communicate a peculiar hardness to his flesh. Making deep incisions into the flesh of another animal, while living, in order to render the muscles more firm. Now we fairly admit, that such abominable cruelties as these are worthy the interference of common humanity. But stop, gentle reader! these cruelties *are practised* by the society for the suppression of vice, not by the poor.

The first of these *cruelties* passes under the *mild name* of *angling*, and therefore there can be no harm in it, the more particularly as some of the society have the best preserved trout streams in England.

The next is *hunting*, and as all the poor people are excluded from this *innocent recreation*, it is not possible there can be any harm in hunting.

The next is a process for making *brawn*, a dish never tasted by the poor, and therefore not to be disturbed by the indictments.

And the fourth is, a mode of crimping *cod*.
All high-life cruelties, and so they cannot think of punishing these. O no! the real thing which calls forth their sympathy, and harrows up their souls, is, to see a number of artizans, by a relaxation from their labour, baiting a bull or a bear, while a man with ten thousand a year may worry a hare, a stag, or a fox, as much as he pleases! Any cruelty may be practised to gorge the stomach of the rich, but none to enliven the leisure hours of the poor.[157]

The list of cruelties echoes animal rights and vegetarian rhetoric, adding up to a kind of *macellogia*. The article recognizes the class basis of violence and morality concerning animals – the limits of concepts like sympathy.

It would be wrong, however, to say that animal rights were not an issue for working-class radicals. *The Medusa* itself pointed this out with its appeal to a 'common humanity'.[158] Shelley's vegetarianism was advocated by Carlile, who declared that many readers of the pirated *Queen Mab* supported the issue:

The last Note forms an essay of twenty-two pages, to encourage an abstinence from the use of animal food, and, to our knowledge, it has made a very great impression, upon that point, with many of its readers. Very powerful arguments can be brought forward on both sides of this question, but we hesitate not to say, that the laws of Nature and Necessity determine nothing regular on this point, but vary with climates and seasons. For ourselves we can say that we lean to the use of vegetable food in preference to animal, where its quantity and quality can be rendered sufficient to all the purposes of life and health.[159]

One can detect in Carlile's rhetoric of reasoned detachment a different tradition of food symbolism, not so much the laws of nature, but the capitalist 'laws' of supply and demand attacked in phenomena such as bread riots.[160] The most popular subject for anonymous letters of intimidation, that subgenre of protest literature, was the price of bread, grain and other foods, and practices such as the forestalling or monopolizing of food supply.[161]

For the working-class radical, hunger was a pressing, immediate problem as well as a way of representing political struggle. The consumption of meat and gaming were matters of class image, style and leisure. But for the upper-class radical, almost the reverse was true. It was vegetable diet, and opposition to bloodsports *in toto*, which were matters of presenting a radical image with one's leisured

Figure 3   Gillray, *Un Petit Souper à la Parisienne* (1792).

resources. Indeed, representing hunger was a way of discussing someone else's pressing concerns. This led to different stratifications, different emphases. What emerges from ruling-class writing on diet and cruelty is a preoccupation with the nature and naturalness of reform. For the working class, such issues may have followed logically from human political struggle, but they were not discourses in which fundamental problems were expressed, as they are in Shelley, for example. However, the evidence discourages generalizing distinctions between 'elite' and 'popular' uses of the discourses of consumption.

A CONSTITUTIONAL DISEASE

The debates about diet and the rights of brutes took place in a wider field of figurative language, argument and political difference. The field articulated relationships between the body and radical theory.

Figure 4   Gillray, *French Liberty and British Slavery* (1792).

A study of graphic satire in the period reveals a play upon a number of themes associated with death and food. Gillray's *Un Petit Souper à la Parisienne* (1792) is a powerful depiction of the French Revolutionists as libertines and cannibals (see figure 3). His *French Liberty and British Slavery* (1792) has been analysed as extremist and scatological,[162] but when seen as part of a culture in which the discourses of diet were a vital way of talking about the human body and human politics, it can be seen to bear a sophisticated message (see figure 4). The starved Frenchman is theoretically in Utopia: he makes a meal of the radical triumphs in abstract terms – he certainly cannot make a meal of his meagre vegetables.

The fat British John Bull, on the other hand, needs no theory: he is all body, his corpulence belying the complaints he makes about taxes. Read as a simple reactionary statement, the cartoon could mean: 'this is what revolutionary theory does for you'. The cartoon, however, also suggests that there is something about the British way of life, embodied in the constitution of John Bull, which does not need theory: it is of a piece, theory is unnecessary to its organic wholeness. John Bull tucking into beef is made to look more natural than the French Revolutionary's 'natural diet'. Nature was useful for reaction

in this respect, but it rendered representations of revolution problematic. For discussing the events as an outbreak of savagery meant
that British writers were preoccupied with representing the unrepre-
sented or those 'incapable' of representation (outside a hegemonic
sphere of articulated rational knowledge).[163] The preoccupation of
revolutionaries like Oswald, on the contrary, was to show that nature
could be considered articulate and that other ways of representing it
were divisive and based on class oppression.

Burke's *Reflections* (1790) constructs a figure of mystical bodily
participation in a naturalized state of society, rendering theory
otiose. Thus, 'What is the use of discussing a man's abstract right to
food and medicine? The question is upon the method of procuring
and administering them. In that deliberation I shall always advise to
call in the aid of the farmer and the physician, rather than the
professor of metaphysics.'[164] Burke conceives of the French Revolution as spawned by abstract theory. On the other hand, its
violence marks a sublime and terrifying excess of the body, what
Benjamin might have called the 'homogeneous empty time' of the
body over ways of representing it.[165] The spectacle of Versailles 'left
swimming in blood, polluted by massacre, and strewed with scattered
limbs and mutilated carcases' is enough to convince.[166] The idea that
this body is empty, unassimilable by culture, a piece of pure nature,
is simple to understand: it has always-already been appropriated by
the violence which horrifies Burke. This is why the benign body of the
English state must seem so mystical: if it is too material, it will fall into
the category of nature-to-be-dominated. The bodies of aristocrats at
Versailles would have been stripped of their oppressive instrumentality and radically demystified in the act of slaughter, according
to an account from the opposite political viewpoint.

Diet figures as a way of representing this degenerative 'return' to
a savage nature: 'the sufferings of monarchs make a delicious repast
to some sort of palates. There were reflexions which might serve to
keep this appetite within some bounds of temperance.'[167] Likewise,
theory can be comically depicted not as the body's starvation (or the
meagre/substantial opposition in play in the grasshoppers/cattle of
England image),[168] but as a perverse feast of paper: 'We have not
been drawn and trussed, in order that we may be filled, like stuffed
birds in a museum, with chaff and rags, and paltry, blurred shreds of
paper about the rights of man.'[169] The body of John Bull is one of
healthy masculine fullness and unthinking naturalness: 'In England

we have not yet been completely embowelled of our natural entrails;
we still feel within us ... those inbred sentiments which are ... the true
supporters of all liberal and manly morals.'[170] The Revolution
stripped symbolic meaning from the object (the mystical body of the
state), collapsing taxonomic differences: 'On this [revolutionary]
scheme of things, a king is but a man; a queen is but a woman; a
woman is but an animal; and an animal not of the highest order.'[171]
The animals, 'the hoofs of a swinish multitude', even get the upper
hand of Enlightenment theory whose class origins Burke is aware of
and which he tries to reinstate.[172] Brute and barbarian are equated,
as in Taylor, as dirty, 'gross, fierce, unintelligent and at the same
time, poor', beings whose 'humanity is savage and brutal'.[173] But
Burke also uses the discourse of animal rights, for the royalty's rights:
notice the use of 'creatures' in 'such treatment of any human
creatures must be shocking', and the subsequent fulminations upon
rank.[174] The bloody spectacle of the slaughtered clergy was staged in
order to excite 'an alacrity in hunting down to destruction an order
which, if it ought to exist at all, ought to exist not only in safety, but
in reverence. It was to stimulate their cannibal appetites (which one
would think had been gorged sufficiently) by variety and seasoning.'[175]

The constellation of diet, nature and rights had become increasingly acute throughout the eighteenth century.[176] At the close of the
seventeenth century, Thomas Tryon and his followers were advocating temperance and vegetarianism as a means towards prosperity
and vision. The republication of Roger Crab's *The English Hermite* in
1725 (first published 1655) displayed a renewed interest in ideas of
purity. Vegetable recipe books for the frugally-minded, like *Adam's
Luxury, and Eve's Cookery* (1744) were also published. But the
mythologizing brought to bear upon 'Peter the Wild Boy', taken to
the English court from the forests of Hanover, shows that discussions
of the natural and the primitive could be staged in discourse
associated with rights and liberties (though in the context of curiosity
and satire). These became more serious in later works like Paine's
Agrarian Justice.[177] Religious, philosophical and medical writing (for
example Cheyne, Hartley, Jenyns and Paley), and the literary
representation of hunting and killing for food as pernicious in writers
such as Thomson, Goldsmith, Blake and Cowper, provided ways of
showing how human behaviour could be mediated through temperance and non-violence.

A brief example from Blake's *Auguries of Innocence* (written between
1801 and 1805) demonstrates a developing sense of the cry of nature:

> The Game Cock clipt & armd for fight
> Does the Rising Sun affright.
> Every Wolf's and Lion's howl
> Raises from Hell a Human Soul.
> The wild deer wandering here & there
> Keeps the Human Soul from Care.
> The Lamb misusd breeds Public strife
> And yet forgives the Butcher's Knife.   (17)[178]

Compare his 'Proverbs of Hell' (*The Marriage of Heaven and Hell*): 'All
wholsom food is caught without a net or a trap. / Bring out number,
weight, & measure in a year of dearth' (13); 'The apple tree never
asks the beech how he shall grow, nor the lion the horse how he shall
take his prey' (50). Blake differentiates between the homogeneous
field of state production and violence, and the heterogeneous field of
the non-human world. He was concerned to represent the visionary
asceticism of Ezekiel and Isaiah in plate 12. *The Ghost of Abel*
(addressed to Byron), is about the politics of the trope of blood crying
for vengeance. 'The Fly' (in *Songs of Experience*) also seems dialec-
tically to question the politics of sympathy.

Rousseau was concerned with the politics of the body's economy,
its self-governed good housekeeping. The study of *Emile* (translated in
1763) shows how the vegetarian diet was used as an aspect of radical
self-presentation. *Emile* is about the 'natural' education of a child. It
was written at a time when the hegemonic organization of the
individual was becoming a matter of ideological concern in
Europe:[179] 'Among so many [scientific and literary] writings, which,
as it is pretended, have no other end than the public utility, that
which is of the most important use, the art of forming Man, is still
forgotten.'[180] Two places in *Emile* are discussed here as symptomatic
of a discourse about a natural state and diet: the beginning, and the
section on the child's food. Shelley probably read this text first hand
as well as through Ritson.[181]

Emile expresses anxiety about mankind: 'humanities' and
headaches were born at the same time. It is precisely the human
capacity to disfigure nature which creates this anxiety. The human
being seems in some way supplementary to nature. Culture, what
humans use to straddle their prematurity, is at once valued as
hegemony and berated as disfiguration:

everything degenerates in the hands of man. He forces a spot of ground to nourish the productions of a foreign soil; or a tree to bear fruit by the insition [sic] of another: he mixes and confounds climates, elements, seasons: he mutilates his dog, his horse, his slave: he inverts the nature of things, only to disfigure them: he is fond of deformity, and monstrous productions: he is pleased with nothing, as it is framed by nature, not even with man: we must break him to his mind, like a managed horse; we must fashion him to his taste, like the trees or plants of his garden.[182]

The problem is that 'Were it not for this culture, things would still be worse.'[183] Children, like plants, need education and culture, for 'Man in his natural state is all for himself; he is the numerical unit, or absolute integer, that refers only to himself, or to his likeness.'[184] Culture destroys this biological tyranny, but at the same time establishes a split ideology, for Rousseau wants both the natural, self-identical man and the disfigured, social man, the 'fractionary unit, who depends on the denominator, and whose value consists in his relation to the integer, namely, the body politic'.[185] If natural and cultural interests could coincide, a good society would result. Rousseau uses mathematical language to describe humans here. Mathematics is a language which is trying not to be a language, a language of pure representation. The equation '$x = y$' is supposed to represent x to y and y to x perfectly, through the medium of the equals sign. Rousseau reveals a contradiction between the body of capital (represented through the social as the 'natural' full body of the integer) and the technical machines used to discipline that body. Culture itself needs to partake of *laissez-faire*.

Rousseau conceptualizes the problem for the sort of society in which he lives as related to fitting individuals into concretely determined positions. There is an educational problem in a capitalist society 'where the ranks alone are continued, and the men keep continually changing [profession]'.[186] The creation of an integrated individual is thus at issue. Rousseau denigrates coercive child-rearing, in which the child's body is the property of the parent, to be moulded as she or he sees fit. The child should progress from being a slave and/or tyrant to being a citizen, for although the child's 'first ideas are those of empire and servitude', 'man is otherwise formed by nature'.[187] Education, for Rousseau, involves an element of *laissez-faire*. The return to 'nature' is based upon a deep distrust of social systems. Thus the Burkean anxiety about 'theory' is misplaced, since what is to become the dominant ideology is a 'theory of no-theory' ·

masking the extreme discipline of non-regal, non-feudal management plans; in a way, Burke should have been more wary of this regimenting, axiomatizing *anti-theory*.

Vegetarianism participates in this discourse of naturalness. Country women, writes Rousseau, eat more vegetables and less meat than those who live in town, and this is good for their offsprings' health.[188] Vegetables are more integral, more self-contained and non-contaminated than flesh: they do not 'swarm with worms'.[189] Milk is also considered a vegetable substance, forming 'an essential neutral salt', without 'the least tincture of a volatile alkali'.[190] In addition, 'The milk of herbivorous females is sweeter and wholesomer than that of the carnivorous', and 'farinaceous food produces more blood than flesh-meat does'.[191] Rousseau promotes the consumption of plain, unseasoned vegetable food (for seasoning is also a dangerous supplement).[192]

The discourse of the natural body is linked to a form of individualism, the capability of producing one's own, inevitably natural and correct, choices, when left to one's own devices. The citizen must beware of the corrupt and 'Populous' urban 'gulph' (like Accum's vortex), which consumes 'the human species' like flies swarming on diseased meat.[193] *Emile* presupposes that social liberty must be worked right through from the apparatuses which govern the proper distribution and expression of the child's desires. Correct diet is socially normative: 'Though we have the power of changing other substances into our own, the choice is not a matter of indifference: every thing is not a nutriment to man; and of those substances on which he may feed, there are some more proper for him than others.'[194] The body's tastes correspond to the state of nature exactly: 'Naturally speaking, man has no better physician than his own appetite.'[195] The way *taste* and *state* run into each other, conveniently as an anagram in the translation, can be felt in: 'The more we deviate from the state of nature, the more we lose our natural taste.'[196] The perfect society can be registered on the pulses of the body.

Rousseau's objection to unnatural taste is the same as his objection to artificial flights of linguistic fancy which distort the integral body and the law of nature: 'The most natural tastes ought also to be the most simple; for they are transformed with the greatest ease; whereas those which are raised and worked up by whim and fancy, assume such a form, as it is impossible to alter.'[197] Natural tastes cope with the fluid mobility of social life. Taste is the site of the relation of the senses to necessity and the body,[198] and thus 'the surest way to govern children, is by their belly'.[199] The eating of flesh engenders unhealthiness and bad 'temper'.

Emile continues with a long quotation from one of Plutarch's essays on vegetarianism. Rousseau considers it important, though he admits that it might seem a little out of place in the body of his text.[200] Actually, Plutarch arrives at a crucial point. Rousseau has just finished dealing with the outer aspects of the child and its rearing, what he calls 'the state of extraneous bodies'.[201] The passage through the stomach will eventually lead to the mind and heart. Vegetarianism is an essential rhetorical linkage in the proposal of modes of hegemonic (non-coercive) education. Plutarch's passage argues that the mangling of the animal body is a shock to human sensibility because it presents the internal organs opened up for public display.[202]

The second moment is a picture of economic consumption, and the consumption of economies. Rousseau's exemplary scene of instruction is a meal. Part of his passage on labour, money and wealth is the description of interrupting the child at a pompous dinner. While the so-called philosophers, 'inspired by generous wine, or perhaps by the fair ladies who sat next them, grew foolish in their talk, and acted the parts of children, my pupil sat philosophizing by himself, at one corner of the table'.[203] The question, 'how many hands do you imagine were employed in preparing this sumptuous exhibition?' is put to Emile.[204] To imagine hands is to restore the bodies that have been artificially excluded from the representation of the meal. The act of philosophical speculation uncovers disfiguration: 'With a judgment so sound and incorrupt, what must he think of our present luxury, when he comes to find that all the countries in the world have been ransacked, that twenty millions of hands perhaps have been a long time at work, and many thousands have perhaps lost their lives, and all this to present to him in great pomp at noon, what he will discharge himself of at night.'[205] This reading of the meal against the grain demonstrates that if a child is brought up naturally he or she is bound to be radical, thinking from roots. Moreover, the philosophizing eater perceives the barbarism that shadows civilization, the disfiguration which the spectacle of the feast renders unrepresentable. Emile 'is vastly fond of good fruit, good vegetables, good cream, and good people'.[206] *Emile* attempts to naturalize radical theory by rendering education a matter of unmediated contact with nature, and diet provides an important way of representing this naturalization.

By the time of the French Revolution, the discourses of diet had become effective ways of expressing its theme of more 'natural' (non-monarchical) forms of social representation. Thus Thomas Trotter was able to write *A View of the Nervous Temperament* (1807), which is both a medical treatise and a political discourse on the dangers of refined, artificial life. Burke's *A Letter to a Noble Lord* (1796) draws upon *macellogia*:

Is it not a singular phænomenon, that whilst the Sans culotte Carcase Butchers, and the Philosophers of the Shambles, are pricking their dotted lines upon his [their enemy's] hide, and like the print of the poor ox that we see in the shop windows at Charing Cross, alive as he is, and thinking no harm in the world, he is divided into rumps, and sirloins, and briskets, and into all sorts of pieces for roasting, boiling, and stewing, that all the while they are measuring *him*, his Grace is measuring *me*; is invidiously comparing the bounty of the Crown with the deserts of the defender of his order, and in the same moment fawning on those who have the knife half out of the sheath – poor innocent!

> Pleas'd to the last, he crops the flow'ry food,
> And licks the hand just rais'd to shed his blood. [207]

In addition, medical discourse was capable of depicting society as diseased. Beddoes' *Hygëia* proposed that 'A comparative physical census of the population' may lead to 'gradually and without disturbance removing that state-pestilence of polite luxury, which, although it parade in open day, and by the light of a thousand torches, contrives, unsuspectedly by the multitude, to mangle and destroy whatever it meets'.[208] Vegetarianism was one of a number of overlapping cultural segments which employed modern apparatuses of knowledge, such as the census or the sociopathological critique. Luxury was described as a form of disfiguration, of 'mangling', which distinguished the hierarchy of the upper classes.

A NATURAL SOCIETY

The concepts developed during this chapter now permit a reading of two literary texts, Mary Shelley's *Frankenstein* and *The Last Man*. This reading will highlight the political and figurative significance of consuming food. Despite the fact that she was not involved in the vegetarian circle of Shelley's early adult life, Mary Shelley's novels display an interest in representing a temperate diet. Her father's circle of friends since 1809 included John Frank Newton, whose work on natural diet influenced Percy Shelley. Moreover, Mary and Percy Shelley may have been collaborating between 1814 and 1816 on a collection of works revolving around themes already presented in *Queen Mab*. The sheer strength and vigour with which the themes involving food are presented in Mary Shelley's novels, and their allusiveness to the Godwin-Shelley circle (especially in *The Last Man*), suggest participation in an intellectual milieu.

Frankenstein is a modern Prometheus (this is the novel's subtitle). The old Prometheus gave humans language and fire for cooking. Percy Bysshe Shelley interpreted the myth as the story of the origin of flesh-eating – flesh has to be cooked to be palatable.[209] Cooking shares with language the myth of acculturation, insofar as cooking turns raw nature into culture.[210] Jonathan Parry has shown how food and eating provided the Brahmins with ways of 'conceptualising...the...circulation and transformation which maintain the cosmic and social orders', and *Frankenstein* also employs food in this way, describing the negotiation of the creature's body with the social and natural world.[211]

Frankenstein creates a monster who finds out about how good it is to cook flesh. His cooked offals supplement his diet of nuts, roots and acorns.[212] His body is made from dismembered corpses: he shares something with the offal he eats, at any rate. But he commenced his life eating berries and drinking water.[213] Diet becomes a way of expressing the difference between natural instincts and environmental influences (nature and nurture).[214] The creature is canny about the discourses of consumption: the dead hare which he leaves for Frankenstein to sustain him on the chase (book III) is a rather sick deconstruction of charity: the creature writes '"eat, and be refreshed"' on the bark of a tree.[215]

The questions and anxieties which preoccupy the narrative are based around notions of organicity and faciality: the poor creature looks inhuman with his dull eyes.[216] To what extent (echoing Rousseau) can society figure the human, or will it always disfigure in its botched attempt at representation? The creature has a face, but in Frankenstein's eyes it is inhuman. The face is inhuman; the gaze is what may impart a 'subjectivity or humanity'. Signs are referred back to the passion of the face: thus, whatever the creature says, he is ruined; a particularly painful figure in a discourse which must be read rather than seen (introducing far more pathos than the

numerous films of the novel).[217] For Frankenstein, the creature
deviates from a norm of faciality which is shared by the creature
himself. The pathos of the creature's Eve-like self-recognition amidst
nature (it is the first of the naturalized signs which he recognizes
spontaneously), stems from the universality of the 'humane' facial
code. There is nowhere to hide:

racism has never operated by exclusion... Racism operates by the de-
termination of degrees of deviance in relation to the White-Man face, which
endeavours to integrate nonconformity traits into increasingly eccentric and
backward waves... there is no exterior... There are only people who should
be like us and whose crime it is not to be.[218]

In the canon of texts on the natural diet, imitation and emulation
can be violent, as well as dissimulation and disguise (cookery and
language, but also the face). In Ovid's *Metamorphoses* xv, Pythagoras
(a founder of European vegetarian discourse), explains how human
emulation of the lion caused the first carnivorous violence, through
the Girardian 'mimetic violence' of the transferential gaze.[219] The
attempt to naturalize is also an attempt to distinguish once and for all
between simulation and dissimulation, between the despotic signifier
and a natural axiom. Additionally, the politics of sympathy is 'in
your face'. The creature's search for sympathetic kindness drives his
narrative forward.

Faciality is a predominant figure in the rhetoric which the Shelleys
associated with diet. Charity becomes institutionalized in gestures
like Laon's self-mutilation in canto v of Percy Shelley's *Laon and
Cythna*, where the whole body turns facial, something which gazes
and which attracts the gaze: micrological acts of kindness that
instantiate the 'natural' politics of *laissez-faire*. Percy Shelley was
concerned with the face as power-mask: Ozymandias, the branded
face of Leighton in *Charles I*, the face of the butcher in *Queen Mab* viii,
into which the lamb gazes.

The creature's cooking lessons are part of his education in an
environment where he is a Lockean blank sheet: compare the 'Peter
the Wild Boy' pamphlets of 1726 (including Defoe's *Mere Nature
Delineated*), or the thoughts of the linguistic researcher Lord Monboddo when he discovered Peter as a wild old man.[220] His education
generally consists of learning to articulate in a proper way: for like
Adam's Eden, the world is already there to be distinguished as
classified according to the English language and western natural

history.[221] However, this classification is skilfully blended into the natural sensations of the body: the creature learns to distinguish between the blackbird and the sparrow because of the felt difference between 'sweet' and 'harsh' notes.[222] The creature is practising the collection of empirical data and natural-historical analysis. Eighteenth-century notions of 'nature' and 'culture' turn their faces towards him spontaneously.

This figuration is part of the Shelleys' attempt to humanize radical notions of science and progress, like Percy's *A Vindication*. It is possible to find a contradiction in *Frankenstein* between 'art' and 'science'.[223] But such a reading cannot show how the creature is assembled potentially to be more humane than its maker, and how this Utopian 'technohumanism' is denied by the sublime horrors of Frankenstein's reactions and in his text (nested questionably between Walton's and the creature's).[224] This kind of analysis repeats a rather Frankensteinian reading of events, a dialogue between subject and object which has already alienated the abject creature.

Instead, it is necessary to show how the universalism of scientific progress is plugged into class politics through the figure of the artificial body. The creature in the state of nature is a potential *philosophe*, a 'rustic ... Newton' (*Queen Mab* v.137–43), but environmental conditioning oppresses this potential. For Percy Shelley, the oppressed working class were also suppressed *philosophes*, potential members of the new powerful class. The support of natural diet as quasi-*embourgeoisement* (along with other rituals of cleanliness) distinguishes the Shelleys' thinking from certain Marxist arguments about social change. Their program of nurtured nature is far more Rousseauist – a cultured numbers game: round off the barbarities of the aristocracy, round up the immiseration and indiscipline of the labourers. The creature is destined to become an ideal mockery of the upper-class reformist *habitus*.

As part of his continuing social degradation, the creature eats a labouring-class diet. He has a shepherd's breakfast of bread, cheese, milk and wine – he dislikes the wine.[225] When he finds a kennel to hide in, he eats bread and water.[226] He eats a worker's meal of cooked roots and plants from the meagre garden a little later.[227] He dare not show himself: his voice is like an animal's (more precisely an ass or a dog, a domesticated animal that surely deserves rights from its inclusion in a human sphere).[228] But he is not base or 'savage': he is against slaughter,[229] and he refuses to kill Felix – '"I could have torn him limb from limb, as the lion rends the antelope."[230] When William confronts him, the first thought that runs through the boy's head is that the monster is a cannibal (an '"ogre"' from the fairy tales).[231] This terrifying figure of otherness, however, is actually quite uncannily at home in a non-violent world.

The creature is made with a humane nature, but needs the right kind of nurture to sustain this. This was the message of upper-class reform as mediated through the discourses of diet. The creature observes the family near which he stays like a social historian whose methodology is naturalistic, based on sensations that are developed by judgment (nature and nurture again): noticing that they weep, and being 'deeply affected by it', he remarks upon their subsistence lifestyle as a cause: '"Their nourishment consisted entirely of the vegetables of their garden, and the milk of one cow."'[232] But the creature needs the nourishment of a radical self-image: '"perhaps, if my first introduction to humanity had been made by a young soldier, burning for glory and slaughter, I should have been imbued with different sensations"'.[233]

The creature is fashioned in the image of eighteenth-century ideas about man: a re-imagined body sprung from a scientific imagination. Mary Shelley's literary thought experiment poses a question: 'Is it possible to be moral in this context?' To which the answer should be: 'Yes, given the application of sympathy, or feelings of identity with other beings'. The configuration of sympathy affects the reader, through the narrative pattern of concentric facings and witnessings. The presentation of this argument is extremely sophisticated, since the narrative shows that the flashy, vitalist showman in Frankenstein the scientist cannot abide the autonomy of the life which has been created. It must be '"destroyed as a beast of prey"'.[234] The creature is hardly a beast of prey or a 'savage'. Through this linguistic act, Frankenstein asserts what Oswald would call his heaven-deputed despotism.

A process of what may be called 'alastorization' (or the manu-facture of avenging demons) takes place; Percy Shelley explored similar themes in *Alastor* (1816). The scientist and the creature become each others' avengers. The scientist should learn the discourse of the face, see the human within the dull eyes of the creature. Instead, Frankenstein constructs a redemption narrative for his own revenge, telling of how he is miraculously fed in the desert in his pursuit of the creature.[235] In contrast, the creature has learnt the Enlightenment's universalizing rhetoric only too well. His understanding of his own physical disfigurement (or deviant faciality) generates a sense of infinite debt to his creator (which is betrayed). Before the moment of alastorization, the creature offers the plan of natural nurture, feeding on fruits with his mate in the jungles of the New World. But the novel has advanced down the dark path of threat, debt and betrayal, and this rational, humane possibility is foreclosed. The creature speaks all the lines which the Godwin-Shelley circle would have adored, but he cannot be countenanced (faced) by Frankenstein, who has become life's impresario rather than its scientist. Like the other alastorizing narratives, *The Last Man*, *Alastor* and Coleridge's *The Rime of the Ancient Mariner*, *Frankenstein* forces attention to the cry of nature, to create a natural face in a humane landscape.

Mary Shelley remorselessly plays this thought experiment through to its conclusion. She sets up the reformist plan, deconstructs it, and finds the set of determinants which will render it hopeless, while framing the increasingly redemptive and Christianizing language of Frankenstein. The novel is not about the sin of presumption, the Promethean theft of fire (though it was certainly revised later to suggest this possible reading), but about the internal failure of a Promethean project, a demonstration of the conditions necessary for the construction of Condorcet's Utopian body. 'The Modern Prometheus' is laced with irony: Frankenstein is not materialist, not sympathetic, enough. He steals fire only to play God. Even the creature knows the naturalistic reformist codes better than him – the very codes by which he is condemned, but in the light of which, through figures of food and eating, he is partially vindicated.

Mary Shelley provides examples of anthropological understanding, and ideologies of reform, in *The Last Man* (1826), which show other sides to the issue, other sorts of class perspective. There has been no extensive discussion of diet in this novel.[236] *The Last Man* is set in a Utopian future where the major threat to the body is in the form of disease: a mindless epidemic irruption of nature. The epidemic makes for the novel's global focus. It is a tenet of recent 'deep ecology' that a Gaian earth could survive beyond the human species.[237] There are places in *The Last Man* where this attitude is expressed.[238] Experiments in 'global' figuration were attempted by Byron in *Darkness* (written 1816; published 1817; see chapter 6), and in the Last Man narratives of Campbell and Beddoes.

Cholera was considered to be a problem in the new world and far east which, through international trade and politics, threatened the old world. Epidemics were part of the deterritorialized flows of expanding mercantile capitalism (and not just a metaphor for it). Various forms of ecological apocalypticism represent a decoded flow of waste, disease or other miasmatic fluid: that is, a flow which is not the subject of a social act of overcoding. But Mary Shelley is careful not to declare that this is a moral judgment on the Utopia she represents. There is a certain paradoxical primitivism about the representation of the futuristic humane society, since the flow comes from without. The myth of an exterior decoded flow of waste which will engulf civilization (for example, a dangerous flow of money or ordure) is a pre-capitalist myth;[239] the capitalist version, ecology, states that humans themselves are responsible for the flow as a by-product of its very sources of production. All discourses about the natural are ecological, but some are more ecological than others. The suggestion that there are certain holes in the social body of *The Last Man*'s idealized community which allow the flow of disease, the 'intense germinal influx' of contagion to enter, is highly disturbing.[240] The novel allows the reintroduction of desire, movement, and social upheaval, into a system that had been considered static and millennial. Transnational flow eats away at the most rooted territory, even the purified space of Windsor. *The Last Man* is an allegory about the break-up of these upper-class spaces of self-presentation, despite their best attempt at blocking the gaps in the body through ascetic discipline.

In terms of narrative development, perhaps the only thing that can happen to the millennial paradise is its disfiguration, and an epidemic serves to stress the randomness of this process. Healthy naturalness is associated not entirely with the primitive, but also with refinement. The protagonist, Lionel Verney (his name is reminiscent of the vernal millennium of *Queen Mab* VIII), seems like a noble savage: in his adolescence he has a 'contempt for all that was not as wild and rude as myself... I was tall and athletic ... My skin was embrowned by the sun; my step was firm with conscious power. I feared no man, and loved none.'[241] He is contrasted with the aristocratic Shelleyan character, Adrian. Verney poaches in Adrian's grounds at Ullswater: 'I crept along by the fern, on my hands and knees, seeking the shadowy coverts of the underwood, while the birds awoke with unwelcome song above, and the fresh morning wind, playing among the boughs, made me suspect a footfall at each turn.'[242] Thus the so-called savage state is problematically noble: it reflects class conflicts, and these are expressed through the violence of poaching. The savage is not at home in nature because it does not belong to him. It, and he, must be re-imagined in order to counter this alienation.

Windsor was inhabited by Percy Shelley: during his experiments in natural diet with the Boinvilles he lived at Bracknell, to which Lionel travels, visiting the sick.[243] Adrian falls ill, and the Countess of Windsor, in response, 'hardly ate at all ... There is something fearful in one who can thus conquer the animal part of our nature, if the victory be not the effect of consummate virtue.'[244] Verney is wondering about the new ways of articulating the body which he has been introduced to. Adrian recovers and takes a country walk. He declares: '"O happy earth, and happy inhabitants of earth!"'[245] These lines are strikingly similar to the opening of *Queen Mab* IX: 'O happy Earth! Reality of Heaven!' (IX.1).[246] Adrian continues, showing that '"existence"' is not the end of being, but '"happiness"' is: '"The very sustaining of our animal machine is made delightful; and our sustenance, the fruits of the field, is painted with transcendent hues, endued with grateful odours, and palatable to our taste."'[247] He praises heaven, the earth and its creatures, and says: '"I thank God that I have lived! ... I am glad that I have loved, and have experienced sympathetic sorrow and joy with my fellow-creatures. I am glad now to feel the current of thought flow through my mind, as blood through the articulations of my frame."'[248] The circulation of nervous energy is the symptom of the Utopian body prefigured in Shelley's vegetarian prose. Here sickness and the decay of the body are mentioned: '"Oh, that death and sickness were banished from our earthly home! ... The choice is with us; let us will it, and our habitation becomes a paradise. For the will of man is omnipotent."'[249] Nature, for an aristocratic reformer, is not to be dominated but is, nevertheless, conceived as infinitely plastic.[250] To create Utopia is as simple as adjusting one's body to eat healthy vegetables instead of poisonous meat; the acuteness of the response becomes a metaphor for political change.

Vegetarianism is now allowed to leave the foreground of the narrative, once it has been established as the practice of the Utopian circle. It is mentioned at a couple of later points in the novel. Adrian is to be nominated for Protector, and one of the questions is '"Whether he ought to exchange his employment of plucking blackberries, and nursing wounded partridges in the forest, for the command of a nation?"'[251] It is important to note the sincerity of this question in the novel. Raymond says: '"I will go instantly to Adrian; and, if he inclines to consent, you will not destroy my labour by persuading him to return, and turn squirrel again in Windsor Forest."'[252] Windsor society is a millennial micro-climate. As in Percy Shelley's *Alastor*, the order of millennium and apocalypse (the plague) is reversed, contrary to the opinion that the novel presents the latter without the former.[253]

Verney gradually adjusts to the heady Utopian micro-climate of Windsor Castle. He does not want to leave, and takes up reading philosophy, history and poetry (in particular Sophocles and Shakespeare):

In the mean time, while I thus pampered myself with rich mental repasts, a peasant would have disdained my scanty fare, which I sometimes robbed from the squirrels of the forest.[254] I was, I own, often tempted to recur to the lawless feats of my boy-hood, and knock down the almost tame pheasants that perched upon the trees, and bent their bright eyes on me. But they were the property of Adrian, the nurslings of Idris; and so, although my imagination rendered sensual by privation, made me think that they would better become the spit in my kitchen, than the green leaves of the forest,
        Nathelesse, I checked my haughty will, and did not eat;
but supped upon sentiment, and dreamt vainly of 'such morsels sweet', as I might not waking attain.[255]

Verney does not spontaneously reject flesh, like the more-and-less-than-human monster in *Frankenstein*. The reader observes his appetite being acclimatized. This consumer code was class-specific, but still universalist: there is an appeal to a universal, essential humanity in the 'bright eyes' of the birds; compare the 'mute language' of the ecstasy experienced by the domestic circle.[256] Verney's ascetic retraining internalizes appetite as imagination, the capacity to dream. Desire as such becomes subjective while yet in contradiction with material conditions, which are felt as a constraint or discipline in which something is lacking. The programme of Verney's reform produces internalized nervous energy, and desire as lack: Brahminism for all – the cultural richness of withholding from one's passions.[257] Mary Shelley was an intelligent observer of contemporary forms of popular asceticism.

Vegetarianism is the hinge of an ideological elision: the perfect society is a natural (non-figurative) representation of natural (non-violent) relationships between living beings. Vegetarianism is also a shore against the body's decay (as for Percy Shelley). The ideal of a non-decaying body re-figures the sublime body of the Burkean state. Later in the novel, Verney contemplates the onward march of English power in the bodies of the Etonians:

Strange system! riddle of the Sphynx [sic] most awe-striking! that thus man remains, while we the individual pass away. Such is, to borrow the words of an eloquent and philosophic writer [Burke], 'the mode of existence decreed to a permanent body composed of transitory parts; wherein, by the disposition of a stupendous wisdom, moulding together the great mysterious incorporation of the human race, the whole, at one time, is never old, or middle-aged, or young, but, in a condition of unchangeable constancy, moves on through the varied terror of perpetual decay, fall, renovation and progression'.[258]

This body is threatened by cannibalistic violence similar to the threat of Jacobinism. The '"butchery"' of the plague[259] leads to a civil war which is represented as a mutual predatoriness: '"Cast away the hearts of tigers that burn in your breasts; throw down those tools of cruelty and hate"' says Adrian;[260] the 'impostor-prophet'[261] who exploits the plague conditions in France is called 'this merciless cannibal of souls'.[262] Adrian has become Protector at a time of increasing plague, an apt image both of the futility of political legislation and the appropriateness of grand humane gestures. Politics is transcended by care for the body. Idris' expectation of doom is like 'the vulture that fed on the heart of Prometheus': a resonant myth for the Shelleys indeed.[263]

Under the plague conditions, Lionel Verney regresses to a savage, predatory state. There are *Queen Mab*-like anxieties about the death of 'man, the lord, possessor, perceiver and recorder' of nature; 'Surely death is not death, and humanity not extinct; but merely passed into other shapes, unsubjected to our perceptions.'[264] Men die but Man must still exist. The consistent arch of *The Last Man*, built around representations of human relationships with nature, reaches an apex at the point where Burke's imaginary social body is invoked, as a preservation against death. Verney's human form is now alone:

I alone bore human features; I alone could give articulation to thought... [Verney compares himself to Robinson Crusoe]. He had fled from his fellows, and was transported with terror at the print of a human foot. I would have knelt down and worshipped the same. The wild and cruel Caribbee, the merciless Cannibal – or worse than these, the uncouth, brute, and remorseless veteran in the vices of civilization, would have been to me a beloved companion, a treasure most dearly prized... a human sympathy must link us forever.[265]

As in Oswald, the 'Cannibal' is providing ways of inverting social codes; the remorseless subaltern is being compared with the old, worn-out habits of the *ancien régime*. Mary Shelley sees how the culture of distinction, which Verney has so carefully cultivated at the Bracknell-like retreat earlier in the book, now counts for nothing. The decoded, deterritorialized and transnational flow (of disease) has undone this culture of distinction, and pared Verney down to the isolated social-contractor, the man in a state of nature exemplified by Rousseau and critiqued by Marx.

Comparative anthropology is now impossible, though Lionel recalls the 'politically correct' results (in a Shelleyan sense): the 'veteran in the vices of civilization' could have been a character in the first paragraph of the 'Essay on the Vegetable System' (1815). Verney's reflection in the mirror in a palace at Forli also regresses him: 'What wild-looking, unkempt, half-naked savage was that before me?'[266] Faciality, as in the first experiences of Frankenstein's creature, has been undone, and a primitive head has supplanted the redeeming face of 'humanity': the first come ironically last. With humans absent, relationships between animals cease to be valid. This is implied in: 'I saw many living creatures; oxen, and horses, and dogs, but there was no man among them.'[267] Domestic animals are now without a *domus*. The last and first man are the same, both ravaged by disease and death, while in the middle human beings can become the healthy recorders of nature. The novel articulates the contradictions inherent in the progressive humanism of thought amongst the radical middle and upper classes in the period of the Industrial and French Revolutions: confident about the universality of its claims, but anxious about the decoded flows of pollution that capitalism has released. While the natural diet intervenes to structure the purity, humanity and ideality of the radical body, for Mary Shelley it appears powerless to prevent that decoded flow.

In conclusion: there were many consumers of vegetable food in the 1790–1820 period, and their diets became politicized. The social attitudes and practices within and around the texts on vegetable diet negotiated between 'natural' ideologies, which tried to mediate culture and *laissez-faire* and present radical social change as peaceful and humane. Mary Shelley records the rich but provisional quality of such seemingly-grounded attitudes and practices, in the light of the expanding revolutions associated with industry, the French and American social struggles, and capitalism. We may now trace the Shelleys' lived participation in these discourses.

CHAPTER 2

The purer nutriment: diet and Shelley's biographies

> 'And if the spark with which Heaven lit my spirit
> Had been with purer nutriment supplied,
>
> 'Corruption would not now thus much inherit
> Of what was once Rousseau, – nor this disguise
> Stained that which ought to have disdained to wear it.'
>
> Shelley, *The Triumph of Life*, 201

MILTON'S HOSPITAL

A straightforward chronological discussion of Shelley's dietary attitudes and practices throughout his life has rarely been attempted before (apart from the work of Crook and Guiton). The studies of Shelley by those like Medwin, Hogg and Trelawny, who knew him, support the claim that vegetarianism was not confined in material and textual practice to Shelley's early years. Crook and Guiton try to show how Shelley's vegetarianism was medicinal: 'It is impossible that Shelley's reasons for becoming vegetarian were ethical alone, and that the hope of recovering his health did not affect his decision.'[1] This supports their claim that Shelley was battling with actual or suspected venereal disease. But a close study of contemporary texts reveals broader set of attitudes.

Shelley was clearly aware of the medicinal claims of a vegetable diet. However, critics have tended to assume that medicine and ideology are separable. This has tended to discredit the force of vegetarian arguments and any relation they might bear to other aspects of his thought and writing. The previous chapter showed that medicine and politics cannot be so easily separated.

The second aim of this chapter is to re-read the hagiography found in nineteenth-century biographies of Shelley. Diet was often used to portray a hermit-like poet who rose above material affairs. Both the

57

'hagiographic' and the 'pathological' styles of biographical presentation underplay the political and ideological content of Shelley's
interest in diet.

At the beginning of chapter 5 of *Shelley's Venomed Melody*, Crook
and Guiton cite Medwin's account of Shelley's walking round St
Bartholomew's hospital.[2] The dating of this account (somewhere
between 1811 and 1813) is unclear, and they state this in a footnote.[3]
Their purpose is to illustrate the kinds of health problem which
Shelley observed first-hand in his poverty-stricken loneliness, while
living at 15 Poland Street, after being sent down from Oxford in
1811. According to Medwin, Shelley wanted to become a doctor:

... he often told me he should have preferred [the medical profession] to all
others, as affording greater opportunities of alleviating the sufferings of
humanity. He walked [round] a hospital, and became familiar with death
in all its forms, – 'a lazar house, it was', – I have heard him quote the
passage –
>   wherein were laid
> Numbers of all diseased – all maladies
> Of ghastly spasm, or racking torture – qualms
> Of heart-sick agony – all feverish kinds;
and where
>   Despair
> Tended the sick, busiest from couch to couch.
And here, he told me, he himself expected it would have been his fate to
breathe his last. His wants were, indeed, few; he still continued, contrary to
the advice of his physician, his vegetable diet; for none but a Pythagorean
can tell with what a repugnance he who has once tried the system, reverts to
the use of animal food.[4]

What is interesting about the end of this passage, which Crook and
Guiton do not quote, is Medwin's movement from the quotation
from Milton's *Paradise Lost* xi, lines 479–90 to a discussion of Shelley's
vegetarianism.[5] This passage, a vision sent to Adam by Michael of the
fate of postlapsarian humanity, is quoted both in Shelley's *A
Vindication of Natural Diet* and in one of its major sources, Joseph
Ritson's *An Essay on Abstinence from Animal Food*.[6] Ritson himself states:
'For man to have a just and perspicuous idea of the bountys [sic] of
nature, he should visit hospitals, and not churches.'[7]

Shelley narrated his visit to St Bartholomew's 'years later' to
Medwin.[8] His vegetarianism did not date from 1811, in the strict
sense that he had not yet declared his adoption of the 'Pythagorean
system'. The date seems more like 1814–15, after Shelley's return

from his trip to Europe with Mary. Shelley's recollection of these lines from Milton make it obvious that he was familiar with the passage he quoted to such effect in *A Vindication*, when he related the story of the hospital to Medwin. Medwin's last sentence also reveals just how *unmedicinal* (and moral) he considered Shelley's vegetarianism to be. This is in no way to deny that the medical benefits of vegetarianism were well documented by contemporary vegetarian writers, including Shelley. Medwin's passage shows just how far into Shelley's life his thinking about vegetarianism continued, *and*, if as is very likely, Medwin's dating is muddled, how far vegetarianism was bound up with the important formative experiences of Shelley's life. The very elision and confusion of the passage provide rich information about the continuing importance of a vegetable diet for Shelley and those who knew him.

Two recent biographies of Shelley also misrepresent the ideological importance of his vegetarianism. William St Clair presupposes a distinction between the body and politics, and misunderstands the political significance of subcultures. Shelley's vegetarianism, the vegetarianism of the Newton-Boinville circle, and questions of diet in general, become laughable.[9] Rhetorically this is a weak strategy, because elsewhere vegetarianism is seen to be implicitly political, precisely insofar as it can be defined as left-wing, along with long hair, sensibility, feminism and radical *chic* (Mrs Boinville's red sash), belied by embarrassments such as the Newton-Boinville family connection with West Indian slave plantations.[10] St Clair's distinction between diets and political ways of life collapses under the primary evidence of the sincerity with which they are brought together from the mid-eighteenth to the early nineteenth centuries. The pulses of the body became politically normative for Rousseau; the history of the socially proper as the biologically proper had begun to be written.[11]

Richard Holmes' biography is less damning, but it suggests that Shelley's vegetarianism may well have been more medical than moral. Holmes reads Shelley's 'Essay on the Vegetable System of Diet' (1814–15) as an index of the 'quality of the talk among the Newton-Boinville set'.[12] This opinion is doubtful, considering the dating of the manuscript (*Shelley: the Pursuit* was written before Murray's dating). In Holmes' opinion, Shelley felt things with his stomach, and was in general very anxious about his body. He cites Shelley's early fear that he might have elephantiasis, and records his abdominal discomfort and the first of his 'minor spasms' which were felt at this time.[13] An asterisk footnote on the same page suggests that 'Shelley's increasing interest in vegetarianism was as much prompted by misplaced medical considerations as by ideological ones.' 'Vegetable System' is indeed concerned not so much with the consumed, and all the ethical and political judgments that this entails, but with the effects of a meat diet upon the consumer. But it is possible to read ethical and political thinking in Shelley's essay; it ends not on health but on humanitarianism.[14]

EARLY YEARS

David Lee Clark asserts that Shelley 'began a mild form of vegetable diet while at Oxford'.[15] He obtained his information about this from one of the major sources on Shelley at Oxford, the biography by Shelley's close friend Hogg, published in 1858. Shelley knew about vegetarian sects, and discussed with Hogg the difference between sacrifice and butchery.[16] Sacrifice was permissible, as it sanctified the slaughtered flesh, but the secular practice of butchery was impermissible as it left the flesh unsanctified. Corresponding ideas are found in the work of Oswald.

Critics who make a sharp division between an early rational atheist and a late devotee of the imagination have not taken this kind of thinking into account. Shelley was clearly not adopting a hard-line atheist stance at this period, insofar as his vegetarian ideology had traces of religious thought embedded within it. Shelley began to be interested in metempsychosis, and this became a feature of his entire *oeuvre*. At Oxford he had the chance to read Plato's *Phaedo*, but Medwin writes that he obtained the notion from Coleridge 'long before' he went up to Oxford, and that its influence can be seen in *The Wandering Jew*.[17] The idea is originally Pythagorean, and was one of the main reasons why meat was banned at Crotona: an animal may have a human soul inside it, or may have the potential to become human in a later cycle of existence. When reading for *Queen Mab* between late 1812 and early 1813, Shelley was determined to pursue Pythagorean ideas, as a request for 'Pythagoras' to Rickman makes clear.[18]

Hogg includes Pythagoreanism in his description of his and Shelley's ritual daily life at Oxford: 'The necessity of early rising was beneficial; like the Pythagoreans of old, we begin with the Gods...

To pass some minutes in society, yet in solemn silence, is like the Pythagorean initiation.'[19] Hogg may here be remembering a shared figurative language which enabled them to get through the ordeal of prayers. Shelley's humanitarianism is recorded in a later passage on a boy's cruelty to an ass in Bagley Wood.[20] His diet around this time is described as primarily vegetables, salads, pies, bread, fruit, cold water, tea, coffee and a little wine.[21] Hogg here begins his hagiographic description of Shelley's shame 'that his soul was in body', his 'virgin abstinence';[22] later he compares Shelley's life to that of 'an austere anchorite'.[23] His first meeting with Shelley was over dinner, where, characteristically, 'he ate little';[24] Shelley was not fond of 'the public dinner in the hall'.[25] After his expulsion, Hogg and Shelley ate meat: in Garden Court they had 'a comfortable dinner / Of steaks, and other Temple messes, / Which some neat-handed Phillis dresses'.[26] This Milton quotation is repeated in the parodic lines Hogg writes to Shelley about Dr Lambe (1765–1847; an advocate of vegetarianism as a cure for cancer) in April 1820.[27] It must have been a stock phrase of Hogg's which occurred to him on two separate occasions when he wanted to talk about Shelley's diet.

The religiosity of Medwin's account is greater than Hogg's. His description of Shelley's Italian mealtimes emphasizes a saintly other-worldliness:

[Shelley] generally had a book on the table by his side at dinner, if his abstemious meal could be called one. So little impression did that which contributes one of the main delights of ordinary mortals, make on him, that he sometimes asked, 'Mary, have I dined?' Wine he never drank; water, which as I have said is super-excellent at Pisa, being his chief beverage. Not but he was a lover of tea, calling himself sometimes humorously a *Théist*.[28]

Medwin states that 'He was an enemy to all sensuality ... his diet was that of a hermit.'[29] Both Hogg and Medwin use the natural diet as an element in their hagiography. But from a study of the evidence, differences between Hogg's and Medwin's approaches emerge. Basing his text on the somewhat sardonic Hogg, Medwin uses Shelley's diet to construct a far more ascetic, hermit-like Shelley, who though an atheist was religiose in habit. For Hogg, the natural diet was an element of Shelley's (and his own) fall into the ridiculous, and yet also a possible redeeming factor; for Medwin, this redemption has gone so far as to transfigure the person of Shelley. Somewhat later in his account, Medwin writes about Shelley's quasi-vegetarian diet in

Pisa: 'He was, as I have said, most abstemious in his diet, – utterly indifferent to the luxuries of the table, and, although he had been obliged *for his health* to discontinue his Pythagorean system, he still almost lived on bread, fruit, and vegetables. Wine, like Hazlitt, he never touched with his lips.'[30] Given that his diet was not strictly vegetarian at this point, or at least not for very long, Medwin's assertion that he had given it up makes little sense.

There are a number of dietary references in Shelley's radical reading list since his days at Eton with the inspiring, eccentric Dr Lind. In the *Phaedrus*, Plato discusses the medical teaching of Hippocrates, who appealed for a holistic study of body and soul to perfect medical *techné*. A comparison between diet and rhetoric is drawn. As rhetoric is the communication of the good to the soul via discourse, so medicine is the communication of health to the body via drugs and diet.[31] Shelley would have become aware of diet as a kind of discourse by reading the *Phaedrus*. Conversely, philosophy is here imagined in dietary terms. True *logos* is the bringing-together of doctrines (*synagogê*) into a single idea, which is then separated into elements classified according to *eidê*. This latter process (*diairesis*) must be 'natural' and must not disfigure any part (*meros*) of the whole, as a bad butcher would do.[32] Plato uses Hippocrates' medical work, *Regimen*, to illustrate the idea that food is not to be eaten arbitrarily but rationally and in accordance with what will benefit men. There is some evidence to suggest that Shelley was interested in finding classical sources on diet. A manuscript reference to Euripides' *Hippolytus* is discussed in chapter 4. The inside back cover of a miscellaneous notebook used over a long period, before and after Shelley's journey to Italy, contains the Greek quotation, '*Ἄτλαντες λεγονται οὐδεν ἔμθυχον σιτεσθαι οὐτ' ἐνυπνια ὁραν*' ('the Atlantes say that they do not eat anything which possesses a soul, and they do not dream').[33] Untroubled sleep was a goal of the natural diet. Shelley translated passages in Plato's *Republic* on medicine and diet.[34]

Two ideological areas present themselves for enquiry: perfectibilism and temperance. In 1811 Shelley had already been thinking along the perfectibilist lines which would eventually include a meatless diet. In a note to Miss Hitchener he wrote: 'I have long been convinced of the eventual omnipotence of mind over matter; adequacy of motive is sufficient to anything, & *my* golden age is when the present potence will become omnipotence: this will be the millenium [sic] of Xtians "when the lion shall lay down with the lamb".'[35] The tone of this passage combines a technologistic faith in the productive powers of human beings with a Golden-Age primitivism, a combination seen in many contemporary writers who use the figures of the natural diet. And Shelley is aware of the passage from Isaiah that later became important in *Queen Mab* VIII, which contains a section on natural diet.

Shelley was thinking about issues of economy and temperance around the time he got in touch with Godwin in early 1812. The *Declaration of Rights* states that 'Sobriety of body and mind is necessary to those who would be free; because, without sobriety a high sense of philanthropy cannot actuate the heart, nor cool and determined courage execute its dictates.'[36] Godwin had been suffering from fits from about 1800, and physicians such as Anthony Carlisle could find no cure.[37] In the middle of the first decade of the nineteenth century he gave up wine and, as a general rule, meat, for reasons of health, although he still served meat and drink to guests.[38] Later on, however, Hogg met him and wrote that 'according to my observation, [Godwin] always eat [sic] meat'.[39] Shelley was more interested in constructing a radical image through diet.

RADICAL CONSUMERS

In about March 1812, while living in Grafton Street, Dublin, Shelley and Harriet Westbrook, his first wife, became vegetarian. A letter from Harriet to their close friend Miss Hitchener of Saturday 14 March 1812 says:

> our living is different to those worldlings [preoccupied with 'worldly cares'] & you may or not adopt it as you think fit. You do not know that we have forsworn meat & adopted the Pithagorean [sic] system; about a fortnight has elapsed since the change and we do not find ourselves the worse for it. What do you think of it? many [lower case 'm' in *Letters*] say it is a very bad plan but as facts go before arguments we shall see whether the general opinion is true or false – we are delighted with it & think it the best thing in the world; as yet there is but little change of vegetable, but the time of year is coming on when there will be no deficiency.[40]

In the introduction to this letter, Harriet says that while living with her father, she 'looked with a fearful eye upon the vices of the great, & thought to myself 'twas better even to be a beggar or to be obliged to gain my bread with my needle than to be the inhabitant of those great houses when misery and famine howl around'.[41] The diet imagery is sustained: bread, famine, the 'system'. Harriet is clearly seeking the approval of a fellow radical thinker ('What do you think of it?') and is defensive of Percy's and her adoption of the diet as a matter of self-image. The issue must have been regarded with great importance, though with a degree of humour, for the very next morning Harriet wrote to their friend Mrs Nugent, from their address in Dublin: 'Mrs. Shelley's compts. to Mrs. Nugent, and expects the pleasure of her company to dinner, 5 O'clock, as a murdered chicken has been prepared for her repast.'[42]

Writing from Nantgwillt, in Radnorshire, one month later, on 16 April, Harriet recalls the journey back to Holyhead:

We did not eat anything for 36 hours all the time we were on board, and immediately began *upon meat*; you will think this very extraordinary, but Percy and my sister suffered so much by the voyage, and were so much weakened by the vegetable system, that had they still continued it would have been seeking a premature grave.[43]

Shelley's vegetarianism at this point seems to have little of the medical or self-preservatory about it, and the way in which Harriet underlines 'upon meat' indicates the kind of strong impression which it must have made upon Catherine Nugent. Harriet was later to continue her friendship with the Newtons, a vegetarian family who figured large in Shelley's early days in London, after he had left her for Mary. A letter from 23 Chapel Street of 5 June 1816 enquires after 'Mrs. Newton's illness' and offers to send fruit.[44]

The Shelleys returned from Ireland. In Cooke's Hotel, Albemarle Street, Shelley was annoying Hogg with his lack of attention to mealtimes. If Shelley were a woman, he might have been an early example of anorexia, though this kind of counter-factual is rather insensitive to feminist discourses on consumption.[45] Hogg claims that he did not eat mutton at table, often preferring to read aloud instead. Hogg and Harriet were obliged to eat crumpets between meals to compensate for meat which, when prepared, was 'detestable'.[46] Here is the point at which Hogg records Shelley's fondness for panada, bread soaked in water and brown sugar with nutmeg. Following a suggestion of Hogg's, he was excited to declare that in eating it he was lapping the blood of the slain, or supping the gore of murdered kings.[47] In daily practice Shelley was a politicized consumer, across a spectrum ranging from such statements to his habitual disdain for the social niceties of the meal.

1812–13 was very important for Shelley the radical consumer. He met John Frank Newton on 5 November 1812, and moved to Bracknell, to join a circle of radicals who practised the natural diet. Newton was a vegetarian, naturist and Zoroastrian.[48] He was part of Shelley's London circle centred around Godwin, and as the author of *The Return to Nature* (1811) was quoted and referred to in Shelley's *A Vindication*.[49] This text was finished in early November 1812, about four months prior to his completion of the notes to *Queen Mab*.[50] Vegetarianism was an independent issue which had occupied Shelley all year: misgivings led St Clair to describe him as a 'fanatic'.[51] He wrote to Hogg from Tan-yr-allt on 27 December 1812: 'I continue vegetable. Harriet means to be slightly animal until the arrival of Spring. – My health is much improved by it. tho [sic][52] partly perhaps by my removal from your nerve racking & spirit quelling metropolis.'[53] Indeed, popular vegetarianism arose partially from concern about the effects of urbanization. In a letter to Fanny Godwin of 10 December 1812, Shelley plays on the image of the pastoral grazer: 'I am one of those formidable & long clawed animals called a *Man*, & it is not until I have assured you that I am one of the most inoffensive of my species, that I live on vegetable food, & never bit since I was born that I venture to intrude myself on your attention.'[54]

Newton's family background can be sketched briefly. John Collins, a liberal planter on St Vincent, had a daughter, Cornelia, who married Newton (1767–1837), and another daughter, Harriet, who married into the de Boinville family (their son was called Alfred). James Marshal, Godwin's friend, travelled to St Vincent in 1784, and stayed with Collins. Godwin met Newton in 1809 (and Thomas Turner, who was associated with the Bracknell circle, in 1803). Shelley met Newton in November 1812 while collecting money in London for the Tremadoc embankment project. Hogg met him in Pimlico in the spring of 1813. Shelley's move to Bracknell introduced him to Peacock and Sir William Lawrence (1783–1867), a charismatic, progressive and radical doctor interested in social issues connected with heredity, who translated the section on 'Man' in Rees' groundbreaking *Cyclopaedia*.[55] Shelley witnessed Lawrence's marriage, at which the wife refused to take his surname.

In 1814 the Newtons moved to Hampshire, where Mrs Newton soon died. The Newtons and the Boinvilles cooled their relationship with Shelley after his elopement with Mary (since they were close

friends with Harriet).[56] Dr Lambe's daughter married Alfred, Mrs
Boinville's son, in 1818, the year in which the Newtons moved to
Weymouth. Thus Lambe, the Newtons, the Shelleys and the
Boinvilles were closely associated with the Godwins, Turner and
Lawrence.[57] It is also evident that since Mary Wollstonecraft Godwin
would have met Newton in 1809, her future collaboration with Percy
Shelley in the discourses of diet is therefore no surprise, given the
intensely intellectual atmosphere of the Godwin household.

Peacock provides a good description of John Frank Newton, whom
he met in the early autumn of 1813.[58] He was 'the absolute
impersonation of a single theory, or rather of two theories rolled into
one',[59] vegetarianism and Zoroastrian astrology. He appeared to
believe in what we nowadays call the age of Aquarius. The zodiac
could be seen as four cycles or compartments, in which the Fall and
rebirth of man could be traced. The Fall of man is represented as the
adoption of a flesh diet:

In the third compartment, the first entrance of evil into the system can be
typified by the change of celestial to terrestrial matter – Cancer into
Scorpio. Under this evil influence man became a hunter, Sagittarius the
Archer, and pursued the wild animals, typified by Capricorn. Then, with
animal food and cookery, came death into the world, and all our woe. But
in the fourth compartment, Dhanwantari or Aesculapius, Aquarius the
Waterman, arose from the sea, typified by Pisces the Fish, with a jug of pure
water and a bunch of fruit, and brought back the period of universal
happiness under Aries the Ram, whose benignant ascendancy was the
golden fleece of the Argonauts, and the true talisman of Oromazes.[60]

Shelley's interest in Zoroastrianism may have derived from
Newton's influence, and he is represented by Peacock at the start of
Nightmare Abbey as 'Mr Toobad, the Manichæan Millenarian'.[61] He
may also have inspired Peacock's unfinished Zoroastrian poem
Ahrimanes.

Newton is also clearly the model for 'Mr. Escot, the deteriorationist' in *Headlong Hall*.[62] Early in the novel, when the philosophers
are eating in the breakfast room, he declares ' "the use of animal food,
conjunctly with that of fire, to be one of the principal causes of the
present degeneracy of mankind" '.[63] This and his mention of
Prometheus shows that Peacock had a good understanding of the
material which Newton presented in *The Return to Nature*.[64] Mr Escot
is, like Newton, the impersonation of a theory; the fact that it is just
a *theory* is underlined in the moment at which he mentions the

Lotophagi and the 'Hindoos' while 'helping himself... to a slice of beef'.[65] Escot also uses animal imagery to describe the lot of humans, as was common for radicals in this period across all classes: '"The mass of mankind is composed of beasts of burden, mere clods, the tools of their superiors. By enlarging and complicating your machines [for example in factories], you degrade, not exalt, the human animals you employ to direct them... We divide men into herds like cattle."'[66] While the natural diet for both Shelley and Newton was bound up with gradual reform and quiet death, Peacock also skilfully registers the element of revolutionary fervour for violent change, redemption, sudden return to nature, a '"total and radical change"'.[67] The natural diet was a double-edged mode of self-presentation, since it could connote both peacefulness and the swift action of a medicinal corrective.

LONDON, BRACKNELL AND MARLOW

Hogg associates the spring of 1813 with Shelley's 'full and exact course' of vegetarianism.[68] He ate pulses, drank no alcohol,[69] and at Bracknell no eggs or butter were eaten by themselves, nor milk and cream.[70] Shellfish were also banned, as was cheese.[71] Hogg praises the 'artfully and scientifically arranged and disguised' vegetable food, a compliment which would not have gone down well with the advocators of a return to nature and an abandonment of culinary disguise.[72] There were plenty of sweets and confectionery, but no bread and butter or buttered toast.[73] Some members of the group advocated raw food, while others were anxious that additives did not corrupt the water supply.[74] The last point provides evidence that Lambe's work was being used as their vegetarian textbook, since his *Constitutional Diseases* blames an 'arsenical' compound in water as the source of chronic disease.[75]

Hogg is at his most ridiculing in this section of the *Life*, dismissing 'Joe' Ritson for his animal rights writing with a humorous shrug.[76] He recounts a lapse in Shelley's regimen involving a huge joint of boiled beef on a tiny table in a tiny inn.[77] The atmosphere at Bracknell had left him feeling excluded from the central life of the group: 'Sympathy is indispensable to a sentient being [this phrase could be part of a vegetarian argument], and, in order to sympathize with dull fellows, a certain amount of dulness is demanded.'[78]

From London, on 21 May 1813, Harriet wrote to Mrs Nugent: 'Mr. Ryan dines with us today. I give him meat, but we have all taken to the vegetable regimen again, which I shall not leave off, for I find myself so much better for it, that it would be very great injustice to eat flesh again.'[79] If interpreted strictly this means that at some point in 1813 (for Shelley had written to Hogg 'I continue vegetable' in December 1812) the Shelleys lapsed from a meatless diet. Thus St Clair's declaration of Shelley's fanaticism needs qualifying.[80] John Grove, Shelley's cousin, also dined with the Shelleys in May 1813.[81] He is known to have possessed a copy of *A Vindication*;[82] perhaps this is where he picked it up.[83]

Philosophical dinners were being held, and vegetable diet advocated, by Oswald's pantheist acquaintance John 'Walking' Stewart (1749–1822), whose *The Revelation of Nature* (1796?) promoted non-violence towards other creatures. There is little evidence that Robert Owen, Thomas 'Clio' Rickman, John Taylor, Thomas Taylor, Henry George Bohn and Thomas De Quincey heard any such arguments while attending Stewart's soirées on Sundays in Cockspur Street. De Quincey mentioned him in an article in *Tait's Magazine* on Wordsworth (1839).[84] However, while differing in sympathy for the French Revolution, Stewart shared with Shelley and Newton similar concepts of the select group of freethinkers, the role of reason and nature, and temperance. This strengthens the idea that attitudes to diet were class-based, and the product of emerging class interests in fields of knowledge established in the modern period. Indeed, Stewart was not a reactionary monarchist and he shared Newton's and Shelley's ideas about how civilization may lead to monopoly, luxury and class division.[85]

Godwin met Shelley in London again on 8 June 1813. Hogg met Godwin at the same time, and his second meeting provided another chance to ridicule vegetable diet:

He was stoutly maintaining, against several ladies, that hair and moss are the same substance, both growing in the same situation, and in precisely the same manner. His arguments were not successful ... I apprehend that the discussion arose out of consideration of vegetable diet, and that there is no essential difference between animal and vegetable substance.[86]

Hogg's sense of humour is not entirely indicative of a critical position. He takes care to say that Shelley's 'Pythagorean existence [and his friendship with the Newton-Boinville vegetarian group] ... was perhaps the prettiest and most pleasing portion of his poetical, philosophical, and lovely life'.[87] Cornelia Newton wrote to Hogg on 21 October 1813: 'I hope you will eat your Christmas Dinner with us – whether or not you continue one of the Holy or not for no change of Habits of such a nature can alter the esteem with which I subscribe myself / Your very sincere friend.'[88] The reference to 'the Holy' seems to be about natural diet, especially given the use of 'Habits'. Hogg had been put under pressure by his mother to mix with less radical company (and was at risk of being disinherited if he disobeyed). From his family's point of view, he was just as committed to the diet as his friend Shelley.[89] In fact, Hogg kept up a correspondence with Newton after Shelley's departure from the group.[90] The scathing passages in the *Life* reflect Hogg's ambivalent feelings and need to refashion his own past.

In order to reduce expenditure, Shelley moved to a house owned by Mrs Boinville at High Elms, Bracknell, in Berkshire.[91] Mrs Boinville was the wife of an *émigré* of the French Revolution, Jean-Baptiste Chastel de Boinville, a friend of Lafayette who died in February 1813 on the retreat from Moscow.[92] Later Shelley was to consider her 'the most admirable specimen of a human being I had ever seen', while fondly remembering her circle.[93]

Mrs Boinville was the vegetarian elder sister of Newton's wife. According to Peacock, 'At Bracknell, Shelley was surrounded by a numerous society, all in a great measure of his own opinions in relation to religion and politics, and the larger portion of them in relation to vegetable diet.'[94] In 1813 Shelley published *A Vindication*, after *Queen Mab*, as a revision of its vegetarian footnote.[95] The title is a significant echo of Mary Wollstonecraft's feminist text, highlighting the significance of rights language as the ability to embody just representation. Recent thinking has been inconclusive about whether *A Vindication* was either a piece of 'shrewd marketing strategy' for *Queen Mab* or a separate project.[96] The two pieces are clearly related in content but are approaching different audiences. *A Vindication* was published more openly, and by a medical bookseller (Callow), retaining the figurative density of *Queen Mab* but refracting its critique of tyranny, superstition and commerce through a lived, personal response to ethics, while emphasizing the code of radical self-presentation. *A Vindication* advocates the cultivation of the virtuous individual in accordance with the dance between virtue and politics in *Queen Mab*.

Hogg represented his position in the Newton-Boinville circle as an ironic outsider, sometimes participating with interest in the dietary experiments, while remaining skeptical. For example, he diverted himself with shooting game, perhaps while everybody else was off talking politics:

My way of gaining an appetite was in direct opposition to my mode of satisfying it. A striking incongruity – a patent contradiction; and such my existence – at once bloodthirsty and bloodless – would certainly have been, if I had taken up my line of feeding on the principles of Pythagoras or of the Brahmins, or perhaps upon any principles whatever.[97]

Hogg's attitude is similar to the more general one he adopts to 'The French revolutionists': they 'were eminently and conspicuously dogmatical; they could not bear contradiction'.[98] Hogg revels in it and wants to recruit Shelley to the same side: 'Shelley delighted in [contradiction].'[99] He maliciously relates how in the sale of Horne Tooke's library, a copy of Newton's *The Return to Nature* was sold to Canning for eighteen pence, uncut and hence unread, and that Newton tried to account favourably for this.[100] Tea appears to have been a light relief for Hogg under the circumstances: 'Tea was always most acceptable to me, particularly whilst I was a Pythagorean. Poor dear Pythagoras, with all his wisdom he did not know how to make himself a good cup of tea.'[101]

Some time later, between late October and November 1813, Shelley translated two essays by Plutarch on vegetarianism. At the time he was living at 36 Frederick Street, in Edinburgh. A letter postmarked 26 November 1813 is recorded in Hogg's biography, in which Shelley declares excitedly to his friend: 'I have translated the two Essays of Plutarch [περι σαρκοφαγιας, found in the *Moralia*], ... which we read together. They are very excellent. I intend to comment upon them, and to reason in my preface concerning the Orphic and Pythagoric system of diet.'[102] The 'preface' may be the short introduction to *A Refutation of Deism* (1814). It is also possible, although evidence is lacking, that Shelley was intending to produce an edition of the essays.

Shelley also writes of his time with Newton: 'My evenings will often be spent at the N[ewton]s, where, I presume, you are no infrequent visitor.'[103] Shelley indicates some knowledge of Orphic cults, which were related to Pythagorean cults. Orphism employed a Fall narrative to explain the importance of vegetable diet. There is a long history which links the imagining of a vegetarian future state in *Queen Mab* to the vegetarian redemption and return to a Golden Age in Orphism.[104] The idea of a poetic language of perfection, or 'Orphic song' is a strong feature of the Utopian ending of *Prometheus Unbound* (1818–19; published 1820). The Earth declares that man is 'one harmonious soul of many a soul, / Whose nature is its own divine controul' (IV.400–1), and that his language is:

> a perpetual Orphic song
> Which rules with Daedal harmony a throng
> Of thoughts and forms, which else senseless and shapeless were.
>
> (IV.415)

As Orpheus tamed animals, so language gives form to thought.

In mid-1814 Medwin noticed Shelley's bad health, caused by 'intense study, his strict Pythagorean system of diet, that by no means agreed with his constitution, and the immoderate use of laudanum', all factors which eventually caused him to leave London.[105] Hogg criticizes the use of vegetarian arguments in *A Refutation of Deism* (1814) with an alimentary joke: 'The subject of vegetable diet is brought in, dragged in, and in a crude, undigested manner.'[106] In his frustration, Hogg refutes Plutarch, Joseph Ritson and Lambe. He singles out Plutarch's point about the disgust we would feel if we had to kill an animal with our bare hands. Hogg associates this somewhat illogically with his study of comparative anatomy, which was also used to suggest that humans are not designed by nature to eat animals: 'You cannot cut down a fir tree with your teeth, and saw it into lengths with your nails. Therefore, says Plutarch, in spite of your axes and saws, you shall have no planks, no inch deals!'[107]

In the following year, when Mary began a new journal on 12 May, she wrote 'I begin a new journal with our regeneration.' Shelley added a humorous witch's recipe, strictly for carnivores: '*9 drops of human blood – 7 grains of gunpowder / 1/2 an oz. of putrified brain* [space] *13 mashed grave worms*'.[108] This sort of recipe, now a marker of a gothic or romance text, is based on the real formulae for regeneration used in the Middle Ages.[109] The connotations of human sacrifice and the eating of taboo areas of the body, such as the brain, appeal to non-vegetarian symbolic orders. Shelley's magic formula is obviously a joke in context, subtly commenting on Mary Shelley's assertion not of physical, but clearly *spiritual*, regeneration. It is plausible that 'Vegetable System' was part of a 'regeneration' of ideas and commitments which Shelley had shared with Harriet and wanted to transfer to Mary, reworking the notes to *Queen Mab*. When Claire left for Lynmouth in May 1815, Shelley advised her not to be corrupted by the world and not to eat any meat.[110]

1815 was a difficult year for Shelley: in June and July his chronic abdominal illness began.[111] He started to consult Sir William Lawrence, his Bracknell acquaintance and a radical materialist writer on evolution. In the first two weeks of September Peacock organized a boat trip, to reach the source of the Thames, a journey repeated in *Frankenstein*. Shelley's mood lifted and Peacock put it down to 'his diagnostic prescription of mutton chops'.[112] Vegetable consumption was not thought to be beneficial to the animal spirits. Peacock associates travelling and diet in his memoirs of Shelley:

His vegetable diet entered for something into his restlessness. When he was fixed in a place he adhered to his diet consistently and conscientiously, but it certainly did not agree with him; it made him weak and nervous, and exaggerated the sensitiveness of his imagination. Then arose those thick-coming fancies which almost invariably preceded his change of place.[113]

Peacock is one of several contemporaries who observe that veg-etarianism is related to illness, not to Shelley's need to be healthy.[114] The diet on the boat trip up the Thames made Shelley ill, in Peacock's estimation: 'He had been living chiefly on tea and bread and butter, drinking occasionally a sort of spurious lemonade, made of some powder in a box, which, as he was reading at the time the *Tale of a Tub*, he called *the powder of pimperlimpimp*.'[115]

Shelley was dissatisfied with himself, and rather introspective. He was visited by the Quaker Dr Pope of Staines. Holmes notes Shelley's 'natural reverence for eccentric doctors and sages, and the zealous, puritan cast to his own temperament'.[116] Hazlitt noticed and described this cast of mind with considerable accuracy and life: 'As is often observable in the case of religious enthusiasm, there is a slenderness of constitutional *stamina*, which renders the flesh no match for the spirit ... He strives to overturn all established creeds and systems: but this is in him an effect of constitution.'[117] There seems to be a subtle political judgment in Hazlitt's phrasing, in a passage that ostensibly is concerned with Shelley's looks and personality.

When Shelley returned in 1816 to London from his summer with Byron in Switzerland, he began to keep a record of the quantity of food he ate in grammes, a suitably French Revolutionary measure. An entry in Mary's journal in Shelley's hand reads: '*S. from this day determines to keep an account of how much food he eats*', converting ounces to grammes.[118] By Saturday 26 October he had eaten 22oz, and on Sunday he ate 24oz at '*L.*', '*D.*' and '*T.*' (lunch, dinner and tea). Shelley was not simply being abstemious, but was trying to consume in a disciplined and rational way. We now associate these traits with popular diet plans. Meanwhile, Hogg had renounced his diet but was still friendly with the circle in which he had been involved. Newton wrote to him on 6 February 1817: Newton's son Augustus 'suspects that among other odd things you, carnivorous as you are, have conveyed away in your pocket the mystic duck of the willow-bed, as you happily term it, for it is disappeared with you'.[119]

The following year he met the painter Benjamin Haydon. Haydon seems to have been impressed by Shelley's animal rights position. He records an instance, in January 1817, in which 'Shelley said he could not bear the inhumanity of Wordsworth in talking about the beauty of the shining trout as they lay after being caught, that he had such a horror of torturing animals it was impossible to express it.'[120] Shelley later expressed similar concerns to Hogg in October 1822 about botany: 'As to Botany how much more profitable & innocent an occupation is it than the absurd & unsophisticated diversion of killing birds – besides the ill taste of giving pain to sensitive animals, this amusement of shooting familiarises people with the society of inferiours & the gun & harsh habits belonging to these sort of pursuits.'[121] The class politics, the universalist humanitarianism, and the sense that 'harsh habits' make people more aggressive, were all present in his earlier vegetarian prose.

Haydon's autobiography of 1846 remembers an occasion at table on 20 November, 1817: 'I did not know what hectic, spare, weakly yet intellectual-looking creature it was, carving a bit of broccoli or cabbage on his plate, as if it had been the substantial wing of a chicken.'[122] 'Meat' and 'substance' are intimately connected. Shelley clearly irritated Haydon, and later in his diary he notes that the atheism in the notes to *Queen Mab* is 'intemperate, totally unworthy of a philosopher who lives on vegetables'.[123] The conversation at the dinner had been about Christianity. Haydon stated the orthodox position in terms of a hierarchy of nature ruled by 'something more': 'Unerring nature, I believe, requires something more than her own impulses.'[124] Haydon the Christian despised the secularization of redemptive codes. On the occasion of Shelley's death he wrote: 'There certainly is something in Shelley's death... The first time I ever saw him was at dinner. I could not think what little, delicate, feeble creature it was, eating vegetables only, when suddenly I was roused by hearing him say, "as to that detestable religion, the Christian religion".'[125]

The dinner was one of the many which introduced Shelley to Keats, who was rather disturbed by his new acquaintance. A letter to Leigh Hunt of 5 October 1817 asks, 'Does Mrs S-[helley] cut Bread and Butter as neatly as ever?'[126] Keats is responding to a neurotic precision that he observes in the Shelley household. As a poet of oral delights, who enjoyed mixing strange flavours in his mouth and on paper, he must have been anxious about the diet of Percy and Mary.[127] However, it was on the orders of Dr Lambe, Newton's acquaintance, that Keats left for Italy.[128]

Around the time that Keats became acquainted with the Shelleys, the family were undergoing some particularly difficult times. Mary's child Clara, born on 2 September 1817, 'had constant upsets from attempts to feed... [her] cow's milk'.[129] This was contrary to the advice of many vegetarian writers, such as Ritson, who all advocated mother's milk for the baby. At Christmas time that year, Shelley was in a despondent mood similar to his feelings during the boat-trip episode. A number of letters to Godwin declared that he was low in spirits and ill.[130] One of them states that he thinks he is consumptive and that he 'cannot persevere in the meat diet'.[131] The paragraph from which this comes suggests that he was offered not vegetables but *meat*, on this occasion, as medicinal (especially since it is called a 'diet'). A member of the household, probably Mary, perhaps on Godwin's advice, had possibly tried unsuccessfully to make Shelley eat meat for his own good. A letter from earlier in the year (30 June) to Leigh and Marianne Hunt declares:

Do not mention that I am unwell to your nephew; for the advocate of a new system of diet is held bound to be invulnerable by disease, in the same manner as the sectaries of a new system of religion are held to be more moral than other people, or as a reformed parliament must at least be assumed as the remedy of all political evils. No one will change the diet, adopt the religion, or reform parliament else.[132]

The cluster of associations (diet, morality, politics) is typical. This was the period of writing *Laon and Cythna*, a poem which exploits images of consumption and the natural diet as symbols of peaceful reform. For example, Laon hallucinates that he has been forced to eat fragments of his lover's body, an allegory of tyrannical oppression (compare cannibalism in *The Cenci*).

Horace Smith met Shelley at Marlow in 1817. His impressions are shot through with a familiar form of Shelley hagiography: 'Denying himself all luxuries, and scarcely ever tasting any other food than bread, vegetables, and water, this good Samaritan ...'.[133] He portrays diet as a form of *askesis* which deliberately dampens the influence of the ethical and political energy invested in it:

For several years Shelley had scrupulously refrained from the use of animal food, not upon the Pythagorean or Brahminical doctrine that such diet necessitates a wanton, and, therefore, a cruel destruction of God's creatures, but from an impression that to kill the native 'burghers of the wood, or tenants of the flood and sky', that we may chew their flesh and drink their blood, tends to fiercen and animalize both the slaughterer and devourer. This morbid sensibility, and the mistaken conclusion to which it led, did not permanently contemn him to an ascetical Lent; but he was ever jealous of his body, ever anxious to preserve the supremacy of his mind, ever solicitous to keep the temple pure and holy and undefiled by any taint of grossness that might debase the soul enshrined within it. Zealously devout and loyal was the worship that he tendered to the majesty of intellect.[134]

Nevertheless, Smith also recounts how Shelley rebuked two boys pelting a squirrel in the woods near Marlow.[135] He remembers how Shelley called animals '*brethren*. The phrase sounded strange to me, but I found that he had previously adopted it in that fine invocation commencing his poem of *Alastor*'.[136] 'Tenants' alludes to Pope's *Essay on Man* III.152 and to Thomson's *Spring* (part of *The Seasons*, 1726–30), where forest animals are described as 'gentle tenants of the shade' (789).[137] Liberty, rights, and property are shown to be connected in the natural world.

ITALY

The Shelley circle was also involved in the discourses of diet while in Italy. At the Gisbornes' house, the Casa Rica in the Via Genesi, in 1818, 'they were ... recommended to take advantage of the fresh vegetables and unseasonable strawberries with which Mary regaled Marianne and Leigh Hunt'.[138] On 25 February 1818 Shelley wrote to Peacock about refusing to allow a dog in the famous Grotto del Cane, to be 'exhibited in torture': the intoxicating fumes inside the earth were demonstrated by allowing a dog to be killed by them.[139] He was distressed by how 'the poor little animals stood moving their tails in a slow & dismal manner … a curlike emblem of voluntary servitude'.[140] Shelley translated the *Symposium*, Plato's famous philosophical drinking party, starting at the end of June, 1818.[141] The Italian sun could be a threat too. Shelley saw it as one of the primary tortures of the prisoners in the Doge's palace, using a culinary metaphor to describe them being 'roasted to death or madness'.[142] Shelley compared Michaelangelo's *Last Judgment* with Shakespeare's exploration of cannibalism in *Titus Andronicus*.[143] In 1821 he became interested in the story of Ugolino's incestuous cannibalism, found in *Inferno* xxxiii, translating it with Medwin and writing *The Tower of Famine*. Under the portico of the Temple of Jupiter one lunchtime, the Shelleys picnicked: 'we sate & pulled out our oranges & figs & bread & [? soil] apples (sorry fare you will say) & rested to eat'.[144] After writing in his tower at the Villa Valsovano in Livorno, he would come down and dine with Mary, after which they chatted and read, while eating grapes and figs.[145]

The intemperance of Rome, 'the new life with which it drenches the spirits even to intoxication',[146] was associated with its hierarchies and hypocrisies. The alcoholic image shows that it contradicted Shelley's desire for temperance. Italy was clearly a hothouse; when talking with Byron, Shelley sometimes felt as if under the influence of an intoxicating drug or drink.[147] On 6 April 1819, Shelley sent greetings to Mrs Boinville, via Peacock: 'I desire such remembrances to her as an exile & a *Pariah* may be permitted to address to an acknowledged member of the community of mankind.' But there is a note of sadness in this universal appeal: 'It was hardly possible for a person of the extreme subtlety & delicacy of Mrs. Boinville's understanding & affections to be quite sincere & constant.'[148] Perhaps Shelley's use of 'Pariah' here refers to Southey's Ladurlad, especially in the context of a letter to Peacock.[149] In the same letter he also asks after Newton. Newton had not forgotten Shelley, whom he mentioned to Hogg in a letter of 25 April 1818.[150] In a letter to Hogg on 30 April 1818, Shelley had remembered the Lambes: 'If you see Miss Lamb [sic], present my compts. … Remember me also to the Dr.'[151]

News of the Peterloo massacre in England that year made Shelley think about food in a less Elysian way. In a letter from Florence to John and Maria Gisborne of 6 November 1819, he wrote: 'I have deserted the odorous gardens of literature to journey across the great sandy desert of Politics; not, you may imagine, without the hope of finding some enchanted paradise.'[152] Shelley typically encodes his 'journey' through the spicy orientalism of Southey. The 'desert' raised questions of famine and bread (for example, in *The Mask of Anarchy*).[153] Bread partakes of a sacramental symbolism not found in vegetables; bread is a product of human labour, and was also considered the ideal foodstuff in western Europe for a very long while. It signified life, charity, justice, fulfilment: the connotations of 'Give us this day our daily bread' are very rich indeed.[154]

The desert could also be irrigated, imparadised. In 1820, at the Casa Frassi in Pisa, on the north-west side of the Lung d'Arno, Shelley met George William Tighe, an agriculturalist. He was so fascinated by 'Tatty' (so called because of his interest in root crops) that he kept notes on agriculture in the back of the same notebook in which he drafted the unfinished ballad about the starving mother, and *Ode to the West Wind*.[155]

Shelley remembered the Newton-Boinville set again. To Hogg, on 20 April 1820, he wrote: 'Do you ever see the Boinvilles now? Or Newton? If so, tell them, especially Mrs. Boinville, that I have not forgotten them. I wonder none of them stray to this Elysian climate, and, like the sailors of Ulysses, eat the lotus and remain as I have done.'[156] Shelley may have been responding negatively to the lack of such a radical group in Italy. His remarks also show the positive impression that was left by the group in which he began to establish a political identity, and echo the orientalizing consumption implied in Peacock's critique of 'Lotophagi' (see the first chapter). Hogg's reply, dated 21 April 1820, is worth quoting at length:

Newton I have not seen for a long time, he is still at Weymouth enjoying bloodless feasts. La Boinville is at some village in Hertfordshire with Alfred, who is learning the business of a farmer... A Poet's fancy may paint the widow with flowing [sic] tresses, occupied in tilling the earth, the innocent occupation of our first parents. Maimouni! Maimouni! [Shelley's word for her, an allusion to the witch in Southey's *Thalaba*, VIII.131–32, IX.172]... Dr. Lambe has turned his back upon this sanguinary city, and now lives at Kentish Town, on herbs and other country messes, which some Phillis, less neat-handed than Newton's, rudely dresses.[157]

Shelley later played upon his repertoire of food imagery in an 1821 letter to John Gisborne about *Epipsychidion*: 'As to real flesh & blood, you know that I do not deal in these articles, – you might as well go to a ginshop for a leg of mutton, as expect any thing human or earthly from me.'[158]

On 15 June Leigh Hunt wrote to the Shelleys at Leghorn, from Genoa, on his journey to visit them: '"I forgot to notice what Shelley says about his downfall from the angelic state. Does he mean his taking to veal cutlets, or that he has fallen in love with somebody who does not deserve it?"'[159] Hunt had written *Angling* (a piece against blood sport) in 1819; it appeared in the *Indicator* on 17 November of that year. Reiman declares that unlike the abstemious Shelley, 'Hunt continued to enjoy his meal, while averting his eyes from the kitchen and the butcher's shop.'[160] But his comment about the veal cutlets is more than a jibe.

Trelawny's first notes on Shelley in his *Records* state that he was using opium to drug himself in order to dull pain.[161] Shelley did not, however, appear to him to look debilitated: 'he always reminded me of a young Indian, strong-limbed and vigorous'.[162] This conforms with Medwin's description of his figure: 'He had ... a naturally good constitution, which he had impaired at one period of his life by an excessive use of opium, and a Pythagorean diet, which greatly emaciated his system and weakened his digestion.'[163]

Trelawny characterizes his relationship with the poet by describing how he admired a pastoral painting with its peaceful herbivorous wild animals: '"any carnivorous animal ... or a man with a gun"' would spoil it.[164] A Lausanne bookseller described *Queen Mab* to him in 1821 as forbidden fruit whose taste '"is crude, but well-flavoured; it requires a strong stomach to digest it"'.[165] His first meetings with Byron and Shelley involved the inevitable invitations to dine. Here is an early conversation, from around the beginning of 1822:

[BYRON]: Can't ask you to dine, for my dinner is soda-water and biscuits ...
TRE[LAWNY].: I promised the Shelleys. His banquet is less luxurious than yours – bread and unsophisticated water.
BYRON: The Snake [Shelley] neither eats nor drinks.
TRE.: I am not an air plant, and shall feed at the Locanda.[166]

Byron's diet was rather thin for cosmetic reasons: his 'terror of getting fat was so great that he reduced his diet to the point of absolute starvation'.[167] Byron would eat at a gulp 'a horrid mess of cold potatoes, rice, fish, or greens, deluged in vinegar'.[168] Shelley's professed reason for eating so little was pecuniary: he could only print his writing by '"stinting myself in food!"'[169] But he was famous for neglecting the body. When Trelawny rescued him from the Arno on the occasion of his first swimming lesson, Trelawny says that he declared: "'I always find the bottom of the well, and they say Truth lies there. In another minute I should have found it, and you would have found an empty shell. It is an easy way of getting rid of the body."'[170] Shelley's punning on his own name – shell: lyre [a stock classical poetic figure] :: Shelley: lyrical – suggests that he thought of his own body as a figure or figment. Shelley was not a strict vegetarian, if we assume his own appetite and intentions behind the cold meat, which Trelawny saw left uneaten with some bread in Shelley's reading room.[171] It may have been an attempt by Mary to drag his animal spirits up somewhat. But bread was 'literally his staff of life', and 'His drink was water, or milk if he could get it.'[172]

Trelawny also observed Shelley snacking 'only when hungry – and then like the birds, if he saw something edible lying about'.[173] Shelley avoided the ritual authority of the meal as much as possible: 'All fixed rules of feeding the Poet looked upon as ridiculous; he grazed when he was hungry, anywhere, at any time.'[174] Adams' study of vegetarianism suggests that the meal, with its central icon of the meat, the substance which hides the disfigurement which has produced it, is a focus for various sorts of conflict.[175] Trelawny's 'grazed' seems appropriate: Shelley was clearly modelling himself on the herbivore rather than the hunter-gatherer.

One day in Livorno, at about ten in the morning, Shelley and he were watching some children torturing lizards. Trelawny made the point that man is naturally cruel. The dialogue continued:

SHELLEY: He is in the process of training.
TRE: It is very slow.
SHELLEY: The animals that subsist on herbs are docile, the flesh-eaters are untameable.
TRE: In the tropics we can live on fruits, not in the north. The Brahmins live on grains and fruit and are docile, the flesh-eaters make serfs of them. Mrs Shelley says I am as eccentric as you; I wish I were as reasonable.[176]

The seasoned and somewhat cynical traveller and raconteur meets the consistent defender of the ethics of natural diet. Animals are related to vegetarianism in a context which relates colonialism to slavery. While eating fruit, Trelawny said '"The Muses might dine on this food"', to which Shelley replied, '"No; they live in the blue regions of the air."'[177] Political and poetic power are associated with consumption.

The representation of Shelley's death seems to be as preoccupied with the body as the representation of his life. Shelley had been consumed in the water: ' [His body ... was washed on the shore on the spot we were now at, dreadfully] mangled and disfigured by fish so that it was impossible to identify him by his person. '[178] Byron exclaimed, '"What *is* a *human* body! Why it might be the rotten [carcass of] carcase of a sheep for all I can distinguish!"', testifying to the prevalence of ideas about the status of the human body and the ethics of consumption which were exercising the minds of the community.[179]

The very least that can be drawn from primary sources, and biographies by those who knew Shelley, is that issues of diet were significant in his circle. Assuming that any biography is an imaginative reconstruction of events to suit certain needs of the biographer, the predominance of language associated with diet in Hogg, Peacock, Medwin and Trelawny demonstrates a will to fashion Shelley's life as a consumer. Letters and diaries suggest that Shelley attempted to construct a politicized lifestyle based on the natural diet between 1811 and 1817. The biographies suggest the recuperation of the ethical and ascetic aspects of this lifestyle into a redemptive hagiography (Medwin and Hogg), or of a critical pathology (Holmes and St Clair). A balanced assessment of Shelley's vegetarianism must negotiate between the medically unfit moral puritan, the *chic* radical, the humanitarian grazer, the introspective self-healer, the secular radical and near-New Ager, presented in accounts of his life. These presentations involved a wealth of sophisticated and complex figurative elaborations that also appeared in Shelley's poetry: how these may be described is the subject of the following chapter.

CHAPTER 3

In the face: the poetics of the natural diet

no longer now
He slays the lamb that looks him in the face,
And horribly devours his mangled flesh.

Shelley, *Queen Mab* VIII.211

INTRODUCTION

Shelley's imagining of the consuming self interpellates a *discourse* of diet, rather than a simple or gratuitous use of food imagery. This chapter discusses Shelley's poetic representation of vegetarianism in six poems, *Queen Mab*, *The Daemon of the World*, *Alastor*, *Laon and Cythna*, *Marenghi* and *Prometheus Unbound*. It analyses the relationship between consumption and Utopian vision in *Queen Mab*, employing the concept of the rhetoric of dismemberment (*macellogia*). *Alastor* is explored as a poetic revision of *Queen Mab*, a critique of Wordsworth, and a development of the figuration of 'nature'. The politicization of diet is explored in readings of *Laon and Cythna*, *Marenghi* and *Prometheus Unbound*.

The chapter confronts different aspects of the discourse of natural diet: faciality, violence as figuration, ascetic discipline, decoding (for example, the destruction of despotic hierarchies and boundaries between 'man' and 'the natural world'), and recoding (narratives of Fall, redemption and the Golden Age). Shelley's use of Isaiah, Pope and Southey is explored. Isaiah provided images of pastoral redemption and human reconciliation with the natural world. Pope set forth ways of elaborating a 'natural-state State' logic through discourses of the Golden Age and consumption. Southey was a figurative resource, which Shelley often politicizes or desacralizes further. Southey used food imagery in a vigorous record of popular

81

life.[1] Shelley deploys his orientalism (and the high-octane style), blending it with Isaiah.

Links between Shelley's vegetarianism and his poetry have been discussed briefly, but are mostly ignored.[2] It is clear from the last chapter that Shelley's natural diet was mainly ideological. Vegetarianism can be linked to other kinds of ideology, for example the 'Romantic' themes of sympathy and imagination. Radical writers wanted to extend the bounds of sympathy beyond expected or agreed limits. The idea of holistic imaginative sympathy with nature showed how tyranny, bloodshed and slavery may influence the *natural* as well as the *human* world. Moreover, if freedom can be established as natural, and tyranny as the imposition of men, then radical politics gains a powerful rhetorical tool.

There are misguided ways of interpreting relationships between diet and writing. Browning was influenced by his reading of Shelley to try a Pythagorean diet.[3] Work on Browning's early poetry suggests that his abstinence from flesh contributed to certain stylistic features. Stewart Holmes' view was that the 'verbal Alice's wonderland'[4] of *Sordello* was caused by a soft early life with plenty of books to read, leading to nervous disorder.[5] The young Browning's diet of bread and potatoes aided this disorder, just as 'Shelley's connection with the world of things was tenuous and unhappy.'[6] The content of Holmes' criticism is not figurative language but the apparently realistic reflection granted by a rationalistic model of scientific language. This is framed by a normative, rational concept of mental health and linguistic referentiality[7] at odds with an initial use of Jung.[8] Such forms of naive determinism should be avoided.

Shelley was aware of links between diet and poetry. Monocausal connections are limited: it would be hard to understand how diet affected poetry from a biographical point of view, for example, without getting caught up in ideas that were *already* representations of how diet might affect poetry. Shelley's decision to adopt a Pythagorean diet was based on a received climate of ideas about what effects it would have. To study his diet without reference to this climate would be reductionist. But we can at least discuss ways in which the representation of the body in figurative terms is determined by theories and assumptions about diet. Vegetarianism is a discourse in its own right, with its own sets of authorities, images, rhetorical devices and repertoires of data. It cannot be studied as if it were a piece of unmediated 'life', which somehow alters poetic writing. This is almost as simplistic as saying that a piece of dirt on the page could alter poetry. Vegetarianism itself is transformed by being written in poetry. Shelley's poetry distinctively and imaginatively re-figures his vegetarian ideas.

Shelley was not isolated in the period in the importance he attached to representing vegetarian diet in poetry. For example, we may examine the first description of Conrad in Byron's *The Corsair* (1814):

> his name on every shore
> Is framed and feared – they ask and know no more.
> With these he mingles not but to command;
> Few are his words, but keen his eye and hand.
> Ne'er seasons he with mirth their jovial mess,
> But they forgive his silence for success.
> Ne'er for his lip the purpling cup they fill,
> That goblet passes him untasted still –
> And for his fare – the rudest of his crew
> Would that, in turn, have passed untasted too;
> Earth's coarsest bread, the garden's homeliest roots,
> And scarce the summer luxury of fruits,
> His short repast in humbleness supply
> With all a hermit's board would scarce deny.
> But while he shuns the grosser joys of sense,
> His mind seems nourished by that abstinence,
> 'Steer to that shore!' – they sail. 'Do this!' – 'tis done.
> 'Now form and follow me!' – the spoil is won.
> Thus prompt his accents and his actions still,
> And all obey and few enquire his will.   (1.61)[9]

Consumption and language are related in a striking way here. A frugal diet is figuratively related to silence, as in Shelley. Vegetarianism is also described as a food for the mind in a way which echoes Shelley's description in *A Vindication*. The Corsair's silence, however, is a silence of control, of the disciplined consumer, not an eloquence of the consumed, a cry of nature. Indeed, the magic power which Conrad wields over words resembles the language of Count Cenci, whom Shelley represents as the incarnation of intemperate, grasping and violent appetite.

The vegetable diet of the pirate chief is portrayed for narrower reasons than it is in Shelley's writing. These reasons have to do with representing a disciplined and sensitive body: a variety of asceticism used to gain control over others.[10] Shelley was interested in asceticism as a way of re-imagining the body. But this asceticism is explicitly related to the ethics of peaceful and sympathetic relationships amongst humans and between humans and animals.

Queen Mab (1813)[11] is a sophisticated platonic fiction in which the soul of Ianthe leaves her body and is visited by the fairy Queen Mab, who imparts a vision of past, present and future, imagining Utopian and apocalyptic solutions for the social and moral evils which have plagued humans and thrown them into opposition with nature. In that fiction, one of the foreseen freedoms is the end of the eating of meat and its benefits for humankind. There is, however, also a series of representative sequences which employ discourses associated with diet.

In section VIII of *Queen Mab*, Shelley moves from a darkening description of religion and despotism which Ahasuerus, the Wandering Jew, embodied in his negative knowledge of reality, 'this phantasmal portraiture / Of wandering human thought' (VII.274), to the description of the future. How may such a shift be mediated? The Fairy Mab's unfolding of a future Utopia is already cast in imagery about eating: 'Time!... Render thou up thy half-devoured babes' (VIII.3). This image of revolutionary prophecy expressed as food being vomited up is strange and violent. Shelley repeats the concept in *Prometheus Unbound*, again at a crucial revolutionary moment: 'If the abysm / Could vomit forth its secrets', declares Demogorgon (II.iv.114).

Prophetic language and emblems of consumption are being associated. *Queen Mab* is structured as a series of disclosures figured as unveilings. Here, the unveiling of truth is alimentary. Language on the tongue is like food in the mouth. Dietary language gains significance as a particularly self-conscious linguistic device. Devouring is not simply a decorative rhetorical flower. Figures are used to comment on the nature of figurative language itself, a special feature of Shelley's discourses of consumption. The poetic significance of the consumer is not merely stated at the start of *Queen Mab* VIII, it is enacted. The figure of 'half-devoured babes' (5) stands for a use of figurative language as prophecy. Eating becomes the figure for a figure.

The representation of a new state involves a revolutionary violence at odds with the subsequent vision of universal peace and gradual change. The decoding acts of the 1790–1830 period were violent, but they seemed to be underscored by natural orders of representation. Shelley wants to reinscribe the recoded language of redemptive peace as fast as possible, since falsehood and vice also speak the discourse of violent unveiling. In the dialogue-poem *Falsehood and Vice*, which Shelley annexed to the notes to *Queen Mab*, Falsehood boasts, 'I have torn the robe / From baby truth's unsheltered form' (21). Lifting the veil is a feature of the radical Witch of Atlas, whom Shelley admired over the timidity of Wordsworth's Peter Bell. But here, truth is related to falsehood, change to violence, figuration to disfiguration. The visionary is itself vicious, violent, with the decoded, cynical violence of the new social axiomatics themselves, that gather and re-present the new masses, global and national flows of labour, capital, pollution. Into this contradictory gap between violence and peace, despotism and the logic of early capitalism, steps the redemptive discourse of natural diet, disciplining the ascetic body to cope with the violence of a decoded future.

The change from present to future that takes place is abrupt and unexplained. Food imagery here, and in the vegetarian section which soon follows, serves as a figure for a revolutionary shift in relations between subject and object. Since eating is the primary way in which the living body is sustained, it helps to create a dualism of eater and eaten which defines the eater as a subject: 'I am this because I eat that.' The priority of the Utopian diet in *Queen Mab*'s apocalyptic vision suggests a fundamental change in relationships between subject and object (eater and eaten). The cannibalistic violence of the prophetic disclosure contrasts with the peace of the region which is opened. Shelley is unsure of how to move from Ahasuerus to the Golden Age without an aggressive rhetorical shift. The shift is clearly troubling for a writer who in his prose about vegetarianism denounces the carnivorousness implicit in certain forms of rhetoric, for example in Christian symbolism.[12]

In part this relates to Shelley's anxiety over the topos of the Golden Age, expressed through the ambiguous figure of the child-devouring Kronos or Saturn, the presider over the Golden Age and father of the gods, whose Greek name was generally confused with *chronos*, the word for 'time'.[13] *Chronology*, the representation of changes occurring over time, is precisely Shelley's problem here. Are we moving backwards or forwards, with or without violence? To snatch a child from Kronos/Chronos' jaws suggests memory as much as prophecy (a re-membering of the half-eaten children), and Shelley had already used the image to this effect in *The Retrospect: Cwm Elan, 1812* (1812, 5–10).

The Golden Age is figured by Saturn, who devours his children; but the Golden Age was also the point in human history where human carnivorousness was unknown. The Golden Age may carry a wide variety of differing political charges, but it is generally used to explain the necessity for imperialist or statist politics. For example, the relatively 'conservative' Aphra Behn and Pope both use it, along with the 'radical' Shelley, to justify the control of the passions in a redemptive moment. The act of meat-eating inaugurates the onset of excessive and socially divisive patterns in the myth of the Golden Age. The Buddhist equivalent is an idyll in which the earth itself was eaten as a honey-sweet buttery substance (just as the earth spontaneously generated its own fruits in the European myth). The flow of karma eventually encouraged the earth's hardening, the onset of territoriality, and the threat of anarchy which led to the imposition of the despot.[14] The difference between the two maps of the idyllic, predespotic state lies in the difference between a distinctively-conceived Fall and the inevitable and constant dispersal of karma.

Shelley's future Golden Age excises Saturn, but he seems to return in the rhetoric which opens it up. How is it possible to re-imagine human relations with nature, to represent them afresh? The new imagining is bound up with Shelley's fascination for reflexivity: how to provide a reflective look that will re-establish humanity by mirroring nature more accurately. Shelley solicits narcissism as part of revolutionary energy in ways similar to some recent thought about corrupted relationships between humans and nature.[15]

Humanity and nature begin to be associated in the second lyrical stanza of section VIII:

> Love, freedom, health, had given
> Their ripeness to the manhood of its prime,
>   And all its pulses beat
> Symphonious to the planetary spheres:
>   Then dulcet music swelled
> Concordant with the life-strings of the soul.   (VIII.15)

The association happens twice. First, the earth has a 'manhood' (16). Southey's *Thalaba* is evoked: Thalaba opposes an antagonistic vision of mutual hatred ('"When to thy tent the venemous serpent creeps / Dost thou not crush the reptile?"', IX.148), with his vision of the mature '"Manhood of the World"' which has cast off vice (IX.150). Secondly, the earth and Ianthe's Spirit are seen to have grown so harmonious that they are one. Whose 'life-strings of the soul' (20) are being played upon in order to flow with 'feeling' (27) over 'the Spirit's human sympathies' (29)? It is obvious enough that the verse is recording a change in the entire globe. The rhetoric, however, delicately involves this with a change of human sympathy. The root-figure for the new age is Pythagoras' doctrine of the music of the spheres, specifically equated with the temperate harmony of the body (15, 17–18). 'Health' is an important third part of the tricolon for reasons that become clear later. The function of diet in Greek culture was to temper the body, both to the mind and to a proper relationship with animate nature. Pythagorean vegetarianism fitted into this scheme.[16]

On the rhetorical level we have moved from a purge (5) to a state of bodily equilibrium (17–18). A rhetoric of diet has enacted the move to a Golden Age. The earth's harmony with humanity is restated later (58–69). In the new growth animals forget their animality, and humans become more humane. Animals are imagined on the same level as man, as 'kindred' (78); man does not regress to a state of nature.[17] Nature is re-figured in the transformation of humanity, losing its ferocity of consumption and waste. This re-figured nature is represented through diet:

> And where the startled wilderness beheld
> A savage conqueror stained in kindred blood,
> A tigress sating with the flesh of lambs
> The unnatural famine of her toothless cubs,
> Whilst shouts and howlings through the desert rang,
> Sloping and smooth the daisy-spangled lawn,
> Offering sweet incense to the sun-rise, smiles
> To see a babe before his mother's door,
>> Sharing his morning's meal
>> With the green and golden basilisk
>> That comes to lick his feet. (77)

The violence of what Bataille would call the 'general economy' of predators is transmuted into the equilibrium of the 'restricted', narcissistic economy of nature. The empty or 'smooth' space of the desert has become the populated or 'striated' space of agrarian cultivation.[18] Earlier in the same stanza 'the shrill chirp of the green lizard's love / Broke on the sultry silentness alone' (72), to be replaced by a prospect of 'Cornfields and pastures and white cottages' (76). This is a revision of Southey's *Thalaba*, in which the Islamic orientalism of the scenery, with its description of the 'lizard's chirp' in the desert (IV.192) is disrupted by the 'occidentalism' of the mirage, 'Azure and yellow, like the beautiful fields / Of England' (IV.227). 'Culture' (from the Latin, *colo*, I cultivate), is being equated with England, and with an oasis. *Queen Mab* VIII is the figuration of an oasis (see the discussion of the ecological image of the green desert in chapter 6).

The quotation re-writes Biblical discourses about paradise.[19] The mutual look is shared between wilderness, tigress and the mythical basilisk, whose gaze no longer kills. The 'savage conqueror' (78) could be a human until we find out that it is an animal in the next line. 'Kindred' (78) supports this taxonomic breakdown. The lambs will appear again in the vegetarian passage. Food is no longer divisive and destructive but 'shared' in the emblematic image of the baby and the basilisk (84–87), a revision of Isaiah 11; the basilisk is a snake which in Greek mythology is said to kill with its gaze. This emblem recurs frequently in Shelley. The death-giving glance of the basilisk has been neutralized, and this anticipates the vegetarian couplet (VIII.211ff), 'no longer now / He [man] slays the lamb that looks him in the face'. To look in the face is to negotiate subjectivity: gazing and eating thus share a similar poetic function. Shelley's tame basilisk shows how subject-object relationships involving death and violence have been abolished.

Perhaps the most significant word is 'unnatural' (80). 'Unnatural famine' alludes to *Queen Mab*'s established scheme of human rebellion against nature, involving such figures as the poison tree. The phrase compresses Shelley's conception of the unnaturalness of a flesh diet and the imbalance between humanity and nature mythologized in Fall narratives like the myths of Eden and Prometheus.[20] To be natural is to be humane, now that humanity has been re-imagined. Humans will become more humane, more essentially human.

In representing this vital stage of his Utopian vision, Shelley significantly does not entirely rely on abstract logics of reform, but on ways of catching the reader's sympathy. This challenges a commonly-held assumption that the young Shelley undervalued the imagination. Scientific writing about diet was linked in the eighteenth century with a spiritual ethics of diet (for example in Thomson and Cheyne). The sympathy of Latitudinarian divines to the new science of sensation was related to the preaching of sermons on benevolence in the seventeenth century,[21] and by the eighteenth century, ideas that man would share paradise with the animals were seriously suggested, for example by Wesley.[22] This resulted in a particular kind of imaginative response to the natural world: a humanitarian critique of anthropocentrism. Humans were not entirely moved from the centre stage of a dominant relationship with animals, but the idea spread that it was more truly human, a more accurate representation of humanity, to modify the arbitrary exercise of power over animals.

These ideas are demonstrated at another level of the text. Ianthe's Spirit acts like a model of the reader inside the work, responding sympathetically to the rhetoric of *Queen Mab* (VIII.27–30). Cowper's Christian Utopianism in the vegetarian *Task* VI (759–817) inscribes a similar model. *The Task* VI is the result of growing confidence throughout the eighteenth century in using the discourses of diet to discuss humanitarian issues. Like Shelley's poem, *The Task* incorporates the sympathetic reader as the accurate reader:

> Scenes of accomplish'd bliss! which who can see,
> Though but in distant prospect, and not feel
> His soul refresh'd with foretaste of the joy?　　(VI.760)[23]

As in Shelley, the language of inner discipline beats social codes at their own game: no 'public praise' or 'refinement' is needed for those blessed with inner refinement, infinite debt to the truth (VI.906–1024).

The lion is introduced again some forty lines later:

> The lion now forgets to thirst for blood:
> There might you see him sporting in the sun
> Beside the dreadless kid; his claws are sheathed,
> His teeth are harmless, custom's force has made
> His nature as the nature of a lamb.　　(124)

The question of 'nature' (128) is raised again. The lion's nature is equated with that of its prey: it practically is a lamb. This revises Isaiah 11:6–9, in which domestic and wild animals, and the mythical cockatrice, are prophesied as living in harmony with each other and with man after the branch has grown from the Root of Jesse (Isaiah 11:1). This is one of the more important Biblical passages for vegetarian writers, suggesting a renewal of nature in parallel with the

renewal of humanity. It is a key to the note on vegetarianism, where
man and animals are equally 'depraved by his [human] dominion'.[24]
It is possible to compare Southey:

> The spotted prowler of the wild
> Lapt the cool water, and satiate from the [pelican's] nest,
> Guiltless of blood, withdrew.   (*Thalaba* v.129)[25]

The relationship of primitive humans with nature is then described
as having been wild but *not* 'natural'. The match between the
Utopian human mind and the nature whose 'renovation' (143) it
perceives (134–44) is contrasted with a primitive state in which man
was not only 'Fit compeer of the bears' (154) but also 'some abortion
of the earth' (153). Thomson's Virgilian description of primitive
barbarity where 'still the sad barbarian...mixed / With beasts of
prey' provided a model (*Autumn*, 57–59). This was apt, since it came
in a passage condemning the cruelty of hunting as a relic of barbarity,
thus appealing to Shelley's sense of how barbarity and luxury are
intertwined. Shelley's vegetarian diet is not a return to a Hobbesian
natural state, and is more radical than the rather simplistic 'return to
nature' practised by his friends, the naturist Newtons.[26] The hunter-
gatherer who eats 'the hardiest herb that braves the frost' (147) to
satisfy his 'meagre wants, but scantily fulfilled' (157) is a prey to
'famine', 'cold', 'toil' (160) and death; whereas a natural diet
should dispel these. Representations of primitive humans were
fundamental in the eighteenth-century debate about civilization.
Though meat is not specifically mentioned in Shelley's description of
primitive man (145–65), the wrath of nature, 'earth's revenge' on
'the infringers of her law' (163–64) is described, suggesting Shelley's
knowledge of vegetarian readings of mythology.[27]

The idea that humans represent a transgression of nature and are
themselves a kind of 'abortion' is found in Pope's *An Essay on Man*.
Shelley quotes the end of the passage about the Golden Age from
book III towards the beginning of *A Vindication* and the Note to *Queen
Mab*:

> But just disease to luxury succeeds,
> And every death its own avenger breeds;
> The fury passions from that blood began,
> And turn'd on man a fiercer savage – Man.[28]

Pope's 'circle of medical friends' at Bath in the winters of 1739–40
and 1742–43 included the vegetarian doctor, George Cheyne,

Arbuthnot (who published an explanation of the differences between meat and vegetable diets in 1732) and Hartley.[29] Pope had not 'disapproved' of animal sports in *Windsor-Forest*, but did contribute a paper to Richard Steele's *The Guardian* in 1713 which quoted Plutarch's *Moralia* XII, a classic piece of vegetarian writing, on humane killing.[30] Satires of Pope which represented him as 'a monkey dropping filth',[31] for example the frontispiece to *Pope Alexander's Supremacy and Infallibility Examin'd* (1729), may have rendered him sympathetic to animals.

Pope's own diet was not vegetarian, but he must have listened to Cheyne on the 'cooling' (vegetable) regimen. His eating habits are described by Mack as general frugality interrupted by excesses.[32] Despite a weak stomach, he was known to eat pigeon, fish and turkey.[33] In 1742 the mysterious 'Amica' wrote 'Mr. Pope's Supper', which 'stresses the Horatian simplicity of his diet, which on the occasion she has apparently heard about consisted of spinach, eggs, butter, bread, some cold fish, and Indian-Root [perhaps a sort of endive]'.[34] Vegetarianism appears in *An Essay on Man* (1733–34) as a topos which illustrates the fall of humanity from a perfect Golden Age, at first in a description of terrestrial ignorance of the celestial workings of fate: 'The lamb thy riot dooms to bleed to-day, / Had he thy Reason, would he skip and play?' (I.81). The hierarchical distinction between earthly and heavenly knowledge is repeated as a hierarchical division between man and beasts (113–18). Man appears 'To want the strength of bulls, the fur of bears' (I.176), as well as the wisdom of heaven. *An Essay on Man* tries to articulate the human place in an order that works according to propriety (I.79–80): 'Each beast, each insect, happy in its own; / Is Heav'n unkind to Man, and Man alone?' (I.185).

This order is based on the idea of a Neoplatonic plenitude, an organic whole:

> Nothing is foreign: Parts relate to whole;
> One all-extending all preserving Soul
> Connects each being, greatest with the least; ... (III.21)

Passages like this, along with the explicitly vegetarian work, were revised by Shelley in the radical *Queen Mab*. The human place in this order is in the middle. Pope criticizes anthropocentrism immediately after his description of the great chain of being (III.27–42):

> Has God, thou fool! work'd solely for thy good,
> Thy joy, thy pastime, thy attire, thy food?
> Who for thy table feeds the wanton fawn,
> For him as kindly spread the flow'ry lawn. (III.27)

But Pope's only stipulation is that man should not become the 'Tyrant' of nature (III.49–52). Man should be in the middle, but graciously so. This checking of human nature is again suggested to come from a providential source 'above' humanity, which treats all creatures alike in life and death. Thus, the vegetarian passages are balanced by passages about resignation to fate: 'The creature had his feast of life before; / Thou too must perish, when thy feast is o'er!' (III.69).

Vegetarianism performs a local or *topical* function within *An Essay on Man* as a whole, counterbalancing other poetic figures and *placing* man in relation to nature. Thomson's *The Seasons* shares this use of the vegetarian and anti-cruelty topos, to define a more liberal politics. In *Autumn*, shooting is criticized as barbaric (360–457), but fox-hunting is a noble, Centaurian feat which rids the land of vermin (458–501). In *Spring*, the Golden Age of perpetual ripening (317–35) gives way to the flow of the seasons, and to human ignorance of the powers of 'the wholesome herb' (378), while men grow worse than lions through their willed, conscious carnivorousness (342). The vegetarian passage modulates into a liberal British nationalist paean, suggesting how the ideology may be placed in a wider context. But Thomson points out that he only meant to 'touch / Light on the numbers of the Samian Sage [Pythagoras]' (372; perhaps a punning allusion to the number-theory involved in Pythagorean thought). *Autumn*'s descriptions of the happy English rural hearth-and-home happily picture the sizzling gammon. Shelley borrowed Pope's and Thomson's topical use of vegetarianism, and makes it more truly *Utopian*.

One should not consider *An Essay on Man* as unmediated philosophy, but as a figurative exercise in theodicy written to supplant *Paradise Lost*. In the third epistle, Pope advocates the justice of an ordered society: 'For forms of Government let fools contest; / Whate'er is best administered is best' (III.303). A state of society must thus resemble a state of nature in order to be just, which may explain why Pope is so dismissive about particular represented 'forms' of government: if representation came with the advent of man, then so did murder and anarchy. Thus the *Essay* declares itself a supplement

to nature which, it suggests, simply renders explicit a natural code:
'"Whatever is, IS RIGHT"' (1.294). The vegetarian passage is
employed as a *point de capiton* (in Lacanian language): the natural and
the social are beginning to be blended together:

> Nor think, in NATURE's STATE they blindly trod;
> The state of Nature was the reign of God:
> Self-love and Social at her birth began,
> Union the bond of all things, and of Man.
> Pride then was not; nor arts, that Pride to aid;
> Man walk'd with beast, joint tenant of the shade;
> The same his table, and the same his bed;
> Nor murder cloath'd him, and no murder fed.
> In the same temple, the resounding wood,
> All vocal beings hymn'd their equal God.
> The shrine with gore unstain'd, with gold undrest,
> Unbrib'd, unbloody, stood the blameless priest:
> Heav'n's attribute was Universal Care,
> And Man's prerogative to rule, but spare.
> Ah! how unlike the man of times to come!
> Of half that live the butcher and the tomb;
> Who, foe to Nature, hears the gen'ral groan,
> Murders their species, and betrays his own.
> But just disease to luxury succeeds,
> And ev'ry death its own avenger breeds;
> The fury-passions from that blood began,
> And turn'd on Man a fiercer savage, Man.   (III.147)

The passage skilfully adapts Plutarch, the Bible and Milton,
imagining human tyranny as self-replicating and therefore damaging
to the social order.[35] The purpose of *An Essay on Man* is to iron out the
violent feedback by equating the social with the natural order ('the
reign of God'), to temper nature to culture by tempering human
passions. A Fall from a vegetarian state of nature (imaged as things-
as-they-are) necessitates the imposition of a law that must nevertheless conform to nature. Shelley's revision of the *Essay* in *Queen
Mab* hinges on the status of the Fall narrative. Shelley's vegetarian
writing places paradise in the future and describes the natural not in
terms of things-as-they-are but as the process of eliciting what really
is (from the dissembling husk of man-made customs) in order to
produce what might be.

Two elements influenced Shelley's figurative language. The
vocalization of the cry of nature is depicted as a hymn, as if the state

of nature were always-already a state of paradise or heaven in which creatures continually praise the Lord. The state of nature as heaven, and the cry of nature, figure in *Queen Mab* VIII. Moreover, the line 'The shrine with gore unstain'd, with gold undrest', sets up a blood-and-gold figure (continued in the image of the 'Unbrib'd, unbloody' priest), which is used again and again. It is one of Shelley's constant images of alienation. Blood and gold are circulating commodities that sustain the economy (hence Shelley's critique of the slave trade); but they also 'stain' and pollute a primal goodness while providing artificial luxury (suggested by the dressing image, an example of figurative naturism). The flow of blood decodes the flow of gold, luxury is reversibly read as barbarism and economy as pollution or *miasma*.

The next passage in *Queen Mab* relates the themes of flesh and pain to the slave trade. In primitive states

> he [man] was changed with Christians for their gold,
> And dragged to distant isles, where to the sound
> Of the flesh-mangling scourge, he does the work
> Of all-polluting luxury and wealth
> ...
> Or he was led to legal butchery,
> To turn the worms beneath that burning sun,
> Where kings first leagued against the rights of men,
> And priests first traded with the name of God.   (177)

The use of 'mangling' (179), anticipating 213, 'And horribly devours his mangled flesh', and 'butchery' (183), ties the imagery to Shelley's thinking about diet.

Shelley's knowledge of the Della Cruscan poet, Samuel Jackson Pratt (1749–1814), now becomes relevant.[36] Pratt wrote under the pseudonym of 'Courtney Melmoth' and knew John Wolcot, who called himself 'Peter Pindar' and wrote some poetry about animals. Pratt was criticized by Byron in the original manuscript of *English Bards and Scotch Reviewers* (1809), but this section was omitted from publication.[37] In 1786 he published *The Triumph of Benevolence*, a poem celebrating the achievements of the vegetarian prison reformer John Howard. He discovered the cobbler poet Joseph Blacket (1786–1810).[38] *The Edinburgh Review* criticized his *Bread; or, the Poor* in 1802, especially its ideas about monopolies over food products causing poverty.[39] The similarity between the way in which slavery is treated in Pratt's poem *Humanity*, and its treatment in *Queen Mab*, suggests that Shelley was aware of more of his poetry than *Bread*, the text mentioned in his vegetarian writing. Moreover, there are links between Shelley's writing and poetry about the slave trade, often circulated amongst an upper-class audience.[40]

For Pratt and Shelley, the slave trade exemplified a domineering relationship between subject and object, man and nature. Just as the environment and animals can be turned into man's tool, so can other humans (in Aristotle a slave is *organon empsychon*, a tool with a soul).[41] In 1788 Pratt published *Humanity, or the Rights of Nature* (a telling title); the poem is a part of the growing literature about slavery, to which Cowper had contributed. Near the middle a claim is made for radical humanitarianism, using vegetarianism as its clinching theme:

> In polish'd arts unnumber'd virtues lie,
> But ah! unnumber'd vices they supply;
> Here, if they bloom with ev'ry gentler good,
> They are steep'd with more than savage blood;
> Here, with Refinement, if sweet Pity stands,
> There Luxury round them musters all her bands;
> 'Tis not enough that daily slaughter feeds,
> That the fish leaves its stream, the lamb its meads,
> That the reluctant ox is dragg'd along,
> And the bird ravish'd from its tender song
> ...
> 'Tis not enough, our appetites require
> That on their altars hecatombs expire;
> But cruel man, a savage in his power,
> Must heap fresh horrors on life's parting hour:
> Full many a being that bestows its breath,
> Must prove the pang that waits a *ling'ring* death,
> Here, close pent up, must gorge unwholesome food,
> There render drop by drop the smoking blood;
> The quiv'ring flesh improves as slow it dies,
> And Lux'ry sees th' augmented whiteness rise;
> Some creatures gash'd must feel the torturer's art,
> Writhe in their wounds, tho' sav'd each vital part.
> From the hard bruise the food more tender grows,
> And callous Lux'ry triumphs in the blows:
> Some, yet alive, to raging flames consign'd,
> By piercing shrieks must soothe our taste refin'd![42]

This is almost an inverted demonstrative rhetoric, or literalized *catachresis*: such is the clear concentration of words concerned with the destruction of the body. The violent language mimics the action

of the butcher by cutting up, reworking, metonymizing its contents:
it segments the actions into parts which do not bear an organic
relationship to the whole. The transformation of the animals in five
lines from 'being' to 'flesh', for example, is disjointing. *Macellogia*
makes the perverse alchemy of 'And Lux'ry sees th'augmented
whiteness rise' especially horrible: the art of making veal is the art of
purifying flesh, a peculiar purity which involves torture. The rhetoric
invites us to watch, or even to participate in, the slaughter of an
animal. In περι σαρκοφαγιας, Plutarch's point is that if we had to do
this ourselves then we would recoil with disgust, and only the social
division of labour masks this.[43]

Pratt then praises the 'Bramins [sic]'[44] who

> crop the living herbage as it grows,
> And quaff the living water as it flows,
> From the full herds, the milky banquet bear,
> And the kind herds repay with pastures fair.[45]

The use of 'living' opposes the Brahmin diet to flesh eating, which
has been seen as the art of death: Plutarch's *sarkophagos* can mean
flesh eater or tomb (hence the stomach). Christians are encouraged
by Hindu example to 'prove the *friends* not *tyrants* of the earth'.[46]
Thus Pratt attempts to separate luxury from vice, and as we shall
discover, Shelley tries to separate culture from vicious luxury in a still
more radically redemptive move. Now that the vegetarian discourse
is in place, the slaves travelling over 'Afric's dreadful sand' are
compared to oxen.[47] *Macellogia* has ensured that the trading of slaves
will be seen as a meat market. Vegetarianism is being used in
Humanity and *Queen Mab* VIII to convey an explicit political message,
not only about how humans should live with animals, but about how
they should live with each other. The connections found here serve to
explain Shelley's rhetoric of a 'bloodless victory' over inhumanity
(*Queen Mab* VIII.192). 'Bloodless' is an ambiguous word in Shelley,
denoting both 'lifeless' and 'without cruelty', but here it means that
the movement to a new age is one in which the destruction of the
body is avoided. 'Bloodless' is used again in *Alastor* to describe the
Poet's vegetarian diet.

The conclusion of section VIII contains the vegetarian passage upon
which Shelley's note expands:

> Here now the human being stands adorning
> This loveliest earth with taintless body and mind;

> Blest from his birth with all bland impulses,
> Which gently in his noble bosom wake
> All kindly passions and all pure desires.
>
> ...
>
> And man, once fleeting o'er the transient scene
> Swift as an unremembered vision, stands
> Immortal upon earth: no longer now
> He slays the lamb that looks him in the face,
> And horribly devours his mangled flesh,
> Which, still avenging nature's broken law,
> Kindled all putrid humours in his frame,
> All evil passions, and all vain belief,
> Hatred, despair, and loathing in his mind,
> The germs of misery, death, disease, and crime.
> No longer now the winged habitants,
> That in the woods their sweet lives sing away,
> Flee from the form of man; but gather round,
> And prune their sunny feathers on the hands
> Which little children stretch in friendly sport
> Towards these dreadless partners of their play.
> All things are void of terror: man has lost
> His terrible prerogative, and stands
> An equal amidst equals: happiness
> And science dawn, though late upon the earth;
> Peace cheers the mind, health renovates the frame. (198)

Vegetarianism extends through section IX, in descriptions of effects described in note 17: 'Mild was the slow necessity of death ... How vigorous the athletic form of age! ... How lovely the intrepid front of youth!' (IX.70) when 'The deadly germs of languor and disease / Died in the human frame' (62). The verbal structures developed here were used elsewhere in Shelley's work. For example, Asia questions Demogorgon about the nature of the universe in *Prometheus Unbound*: 'And who made terror, madness, crime, remorse ...' (II.iv.19). The association of crime, madness and disease is the most significant feature of *A Vindication*.

The passage is close to the essays on vegetarianism by Plutarch, which Shelley eventually translated to aid the note to *Queen Mab*, and Pope (the singing wood and the pollution are there). It is also clear that Shelley wants to assert the ethics of a fleshless diet *before* leading to a discussion of its medical benefits. Thirdly, the stress on the ethics of consumption resembles Rousseau. The look of the lamb establishes a connection between humans and animals. With great economy

Shelley opposes this to the difference between humans and animals
established in acts of killing and mangling. The *look* of sympathy is
contrasted with the *act* of horror. The idea that a look is itself not
quite an 'act' is brought out – the look establishes a connection with
the face that interrupts the act of murderous despotism. It is
represented as prior to an act of language, as a wordless cry of nature
preceding the dismembering rhetoric. The idea that nature expresses
itself with a 'silent eloquence' occurs in many places throughout
Queen Mab.[48] This figure has a dual significance: first, of natural codes
which do not require the mediation of human or divine signifying
systems; and secondly, the cry of brute nature. Shelley's *To Liberty*
(?1811–12) provides a clear example of how it was used in the
discourse of political agitation:

> OH, let not Liberty
> Silently perish! –
> May the groan and the sigh
> Yet the flame cherish!
> Till the voice to Nature's bursting heart given,
> Ascending loud and high,
> A world's indignant cry
> And, starting on his throne
> The tyrant grim and lone,
> Shall beat the deaf vault of Heaven.   (1)

The cry of nature is figured as the unmediated appeal to justice from
the passionate body of the world.[49]

Although Shelley sets his vegetarian Utopia in the future, the
rhetoric suggests that this is simply a fulfilment of what is already
present: the meek gaze of the innocent beast about to be slaughtered.
This gaze opens up something shared between potential killer and
potential victim, like the sympathetic bond between humanity and
nature remarked upon earlier. The vegetarian quotation draws
attention to an opposition between contemplation and carnivorousness:

> no longer now
> He slays the lamb that looks him in the face,
> And horribly devours his mangled flesh.   (211)

The mutual gaze makes each being dependently present to each
other, repeated in the joyous framing conclusion of the poem where
Ianthe, Henry and 'the bright beaming stars' gaze upon each other

(IX.236ff). This moment of faciality is also a moment of knowledge, opening up the epistemological domain of subject and object, verbally enforced by the echo of *Thalaba*. The eyes of the bird of wisdom, the Simorg, are described as having 'Unclosed', like Ianthe's (*Thalaba* IX.275); compare *Queen Mab* IX.234, 'Her veiny eyelids quietly unclosed.' Shelley's revision of relationships between subject and object has gone so far as to suggest an abolition of objects as such; he represents a Utopian intersubjectivity (the whole world has become a humane subject).[50] The vision suggests that it is the object-ness of the object which is at fault. To define a being as an object is to render it subject to 'me' – under 'my' control. A reformed world would contain no such objects, only an interpenetrating subjectivity, without (and here is the elision) getting rid of 'me', the reformed-reformist subject, so that 'I' will have literally to love others as 'myself'.

Recent work on Shelley's use of the language of reflection may now be supplemented.[51] Shelley's use of mirrors and gazing has been discussed as prefiguring the human-centred discourse of psycho-analysis.[52] The vegetarian passages in *Queen Mab* make Shelley's interest in reflection morally more assertive, and emblematic of a dynamic relationship. The 'in your face' look of the lamb recon-structs the potentially inhuman mask of faciality, *producing* a new kind of subject. Shelley reinscribes the sacred, since the passion which the face establishes is the passion of Christ (purified of vice), modulated into the passion of the lamb (the image of Christ), and of the butcher.

Vegetarianism, used concretely to enact the ideas of sympathy and imagination, reinforces Shelley's protestation to Hogg over *Queen Mab*: 'Reason is only an assemblage of our better feelings, passion considered under a peculiar mode of its operation.'[53] The rhetorical patterning of *Queen Mab* VIII, when viewed in the light of the discourses of diet, is remarkably unified and clear.

THE *ALASTOR* VOLUME

The Daemon of the World was included in the *Alastor* volume of 1816.[54] Along with *Superstition*, also appearing in that volume, it is a reduced selection of passages from *Queen Mab* which maintain its figurative structures, while sacrificing some of its explicit content. A larger version in two parts, written between September and December 1815

and tentatively entitled *The Queen of the Universe*, has been edited by
Cameron.[55] A different argument suggests that the second part, a
revision of *Queen Mab* VIII and IX, was omitted from the *Alastor* volume
for aesthetic reasons (it would have made the volume unshapely),
and that it can be considered as part II of *The Daemon of the World* since
it contains 'Daemon' rather than 'Queen' phraseology.[56] In what
Ingpen and Peck describe as the second (unpublished) part, Kronos
(319ff) and the basilisk (382) are both examples of recuperated
figures. Shelley chose to revise section VIII: this adumbrates the idea
that the discourse of natural diet could be considered to engage an
array of discourses about reform, nature and the human being's place
in the world, appearing as a condensation or synecdoche of those
discourses. In addition, the *Alastor* volume was prepared for a
specifically literary market and was Shelley's first major intervention
in that market. Thus *Queen Mab* VIII may have been considered by
Shelley as an encapsulation of the figurative scheme of the whole
poem. The presence of the quasi-vegetarian Poet in *Alastor* would
have overdetermined the adoption of a natural diet as a mode of
radical self-presentation in the volume, if part II of *Daemon* had been
published.

The changes from *Queen Mab* VIII to *Daemon* indicate Shelley's
increasing skill at synthesizing the discourses of natural history and
medicine with social critique – what could be called a 'sociopathology'. This project was proposed in *A Vindication* and the subsequent
'Vegetable System' (1815) extends the synthesis, including an
attention to stylistic modes. The violent apostrophes and vivid
Biblical allusions are replaced by a methodical middle style.[57] Here is
the vegetarian passage in *Daemon*:

> no longer now
> He slays the *beast* that *sports around his dwelling*
> *And horribly devours its* mangled flesh
> *Or drinks its vital blood, which like a stream*
> *Of poison thro' his fevered veins did flow*
> *Feeding a plague that secretly consumed*
> *His feeble* frame, and *kindling in his mind*
> Hatred, despair, *and fear and* vain belief,
> The germs of misery, death, disease and crime.
>
> (443; changes italicized)

By eliminating 'evil' ('All evil passions', *Queen Mab* VIII.216) and the
notion of the vengeance of 'nature's broken law' (VIII.214), and

developing the figure of bodily corruption leading to mental and moral corruption (and self-consumption), Shelley approaches a rational, secularized form of social critique. The intertwining of 'crime' and 'disease' progresses more logically than its antecedent in *Queen Mab* VIII. The animal is no longer specified or gendered. The 'beast' has less Christian overtones than the 'lamb'. 'The beast that sports around his dwelling' significantly sharpens and literally locates the sense of mutual identity in 'the lamb that looks him in the face', while emphasizing the power-relationship implicit in the concept of stewardship. Precisely insofar as the 'dwelling' is 'his' must man protect those whose being is determined at its margins, sporting around it. 'Dwelling' introduces a politicized notion of the environment as constructed home. Morality is more properly *economic* here: to do with the rules of the household. The image revises the vision of a Utopian hearth-and-home in the passage about the child playing with the basilisk (*Daemon* II.382). It is another attempt to show how it might be possible 'To taste on Earth the peace of Heaven' (*The Retrospect*, 56). Shelley had been reading Wordsworth's *Excursion* for *Alastor*, and may have enjoyed the contrast between that poem's hearth-and-home gothicism (more conservative in the 1810s than the 1790s), and his own orientalized vegetarian oasis.

The blood-drinking passage suggests a critique of the Eucharist and by extension a critique of consuming alcohol. The figurative relationship between 'kindling' and nutriment, continued from *Queen Mab* VIII (215), could be traced as far as the revisions made to *The Triumph of Life*, in Rousseau's analysis of his failure, in which 'nutriment' is substituted for 'flask' and 'oil' (201–2).[58] The secret consumption of the 'feeble frame' (a more direct description of chronic disease than *Queen Mab* VIII offers evidence that Shelley may have been more interested in Lambe at this period)[59] and the extended paratactic list of passions ('Hatred, despair...') are similar to a passage in 'Vegetable System', adding weight to the argument that this text was written in 1815.[60] The sense of chronological development in the extended image enacts a figurative process of digestion and corruption.

Shelley continued to develop his representations of the consumer. *Alastor; or the Spirit of Solitude* (1816) lucidly works through some of the figurative elements of *Queen Mab*. *Alastor* is a phenomenological reduction of the earlier *Queen Mab*, struggling to render (often critically) the 'feel' of some of the poetic figures and political ideologies employed there. Mab's 'magic car', whose main function is to 'move on' through the cosmos, becomes the shallop in which the lonely Poet is driven. The grand sweep and masque-like associations of 'The magic car moved on' acts like a refrain in *Queen Mab* (1.207, 237, 249) as Mab conducts Ianthe into deep space, towards the point at which theory can get an Archimedean purchase on practice.[61] But in *Alastor* 'The little boat / Still fled before the storm' (344), 'The boat fled on, – the boiling torrent drove, –' (358), 'The boat fled on / With unrelaxing speed' (365). This is a less empowering flight, reminiscent not so much of a courtly masque than of the boy Wordsworth's encounter with the natural sublime in the 'small Skiff' in *The Prelude* 1 (380). *Alastor* embodies the revolutionary spirit in *Queen Mab* and then conducts a thought-experiment, based on Shelley's encounter with Wordsworth's *The Excursion* (1814), to test how such an embodiment might succeed or fail.

A penetrating article by Crucefix claims that the poem 'is a portrait in negative of Shelley's belief that man must come to an awareness of the powers within himself, not those he thinks he perceives without'.[62] Crucefix reads *Alastor* as the narrator's project to heal the Poet in Wordsworthian terms: the Narrator 'takes the Visionary [Crucefix's word for the Poet] into the cavern of the mind', 'rehearsing *The Excursion*'s attempt to "heal" the Solitary's despondency'.[63] However, the increasing hostility of the landscape, noted by Crucefix,[64] seems anomalous if *Alastor*'s action occurs purely inside a human head. The Poet and his world appear at first ideal, millennial. How can decay occur if the initial elements are perfect? No critic of *Alastor* is happy to acknowledge the contrast between its descriptions of extreme introspection and the material horrors of slimy water, teeming animal life and the Poet's decaying body. Shelley's reading of *The Excursion* is ethically more engaged with Wordsworth in a sequence including the sonnet *To Wordsworth*, addressing him specifically as a 'Poet of Nature' (1), and *Peter Bell the Third*. *Alastor* also negotiates with Coleridge, Godwin and Southey.

Haydon's record of Shelley's reactions to *The Excursion* show how serious he was when he worried about the hypocrisy of a professed union with and simultaneous 'dominion' over nature, to use his word from the notes to *Queen Mab*.[65] Recent discussion of the relationship between Wordsworth and Shelley in *Alastor* is aware of Shelley's comments to Haydon, but is not prepared to follow the implications through closely.[66] Wordsworth's cavalier treatment of the non-human was mythologized as a benevolent reverence which repeated the representation of the relationship between God and man. Through the discourse of natural diet, Shelley had already thought out a subtle idea of nature, and man's place within it, which did not echo the predatory violence of other perspectives available to him, nor the dogmata of conventional religion.

It takes no Harold Bloom to realize why Shelley would want to revise Wordsworth. *The Excursion* explicitly tells of the fitness of the human mind for nature. The Preface famously promises that the poem will show:

> How exquisitely the individual Mind
> (And the progressive powers perhaps no less
> Of the whole species) to the external world
> Is fitted, (63)

and vice versa. Certain similarities betray Shelley's close involvement with the poem.[67] The use of nature as a retreat from the failure of the French Revolution (III.913–18) implies a respect echoed in lines about kindness to animals, which would have struck Shelley as paternalistic if they had remained in the final version (III.598ff).[68] However, Wordsworth's nature resembles Shelley's enough to challenge the younger poet. Nature's silent eloquence is stressed in book IV (405–15). The bleat of a lamb prompts the sage to stop speaking, and the solitude is honoured in reverential silence:

> Through consciousness that silence in such place
> Was best, the most affecting eloquence. (414)

The bleat of a lamb would have struck a chord in Shelley's imagination. Nature is supposed to be pleading silently with an eloquence beyond or before human language. For Wordsworth, however, nature compels reverent silence, whereas for Shelley, nature's silent eloquence compels a more concretely ethical withholding of dominion: the choice no longer to kill the lamb who looks with pathos into your face. Wordsworth was aware of the 'sober philosophy' topos involving food (IV.1035), used for example in Milton's *Comus* and *Elegia Sexta*. But he praises the eating of flesh by the family of the Priest (VII.164), by Oswald the shepherd (VII.740–57), and the Rousseauist natural boys who catch the trout in book VIII. The boys are first glimpsed as 'Keen anglers with unusual spoil elated' (VIII.550). Death, reverence and aesthetic sensibility are combined in a way which Shelley would have found macabre:

> And, verily, the silent creatures made
> A splendid sight, together thus exposed;
> Dead - but not sullied or deformed by death,
> That seemed to pity what he could not spare.   (VIII.568)

Haydon's dinner conversation records only the tip of the iceberg. Here was a poem meditating upon a match between mind and world which employed predatory language indicative of an earlier state of nature where the match *did not exist*. Part VI of *Peter Bell the Third* (1819) describes *The Excursion*'s trout again:

> In the death hues of agony
>   Lambently flashing from a fish,
> Now Peter felt amused to see
> Shades like a rainbow's rise and flee,
>   Mixed with a certain hungry wish.   (127)

This immediately precedes a passage about Wordsworth's political betrayal (132–36); the entire poem is about the Lake poet's descent into a hellish urban world of intemperance, food taxes and corruption. Food and drink carnivalize Shelley's rhetoric in the jaunty and ribald stanzas. Reverence is mixed with a rumbling stomach, the capacity to commune with nature predicated upon a Walrus-and-Carpenter style capacity to devour it. Shelley provides a note:

See the description of the beautiful colours produced during the agonising death of a number of trout, in the fourth part of a long poem in blank verse, published within a few years. That poem contains curious evidence of the gradual hardening of a strong but circumscribed sensibility; of the perversion of a penetrating but panic-stricken understanding. The author might have derived a lesson which he had probably forgotten from these sweet and sublime verses.

> This lesson, Shepherd, let us two divide
> Taught both by what she [Nature] shows and what conceals,
> Never to blend our pleasure or our pride
> With sorrow of the meanest thing that feels.[69]

This mockingly alliterative passage substitutes a more radical aesthetics, based upon sympathetic sensation, for the reverential colouring which turns the trout into stained-glass windows in the gothic church of *The Excursion*. The organism has been speared by the devilishly simple technology which Wordsworth's environmentally sound organic community celebrates: there is a rupture between 'organism' and 'organic'. Shelley's radical aesthetics tries to situate response in the body, in disgust and distaste at the perception of suffering; Wordsworth's aesthetic supports forms of alienation which he himself once strove to combat.

Shelley challenges *The Excursion* in *Alastor* by showing that a solitary wanderer does not match the world in any meaningfully ethical way: a hazy reverence is insufficient. The Poet's pursuit of 'Nature's most secret steps' (81) takes him into woodlands where one of the first things that we learn about him is concerned with 'bloodless' (guiltless, vegetable) food:

> he would linger long
> In lonesome vales, making the wild his home,
> Until the doves and squirrels would partake
> From his innocuous hand his bloodless food,
> Lured by the gentle meaning of his looks,
> And the wild antelope, that starts whene'er
> The dry leaf rustles in the brake, suspend
> Her timid steps to gaze upon a form
> More graceful than her own.   (98)[70]

The Orphic taming of the 'wild' repeats the sense of a 'Dwelling' in *Daemon*. Faciality is exploited in the central 'more graceful' human form and the sympathetic exchange of 'looks'. The imagination of the antelope is suggested by a view of the Poet from her perspective. His initial break with nature and flight into abstract knowledge comes in the verse paragraph immediately after the announcement of his vegetarianism (106–8ff).[71] The feeding of the forest animals is a concrete enactment of 'savage' wisdom ('of the forests'). The Poet's contact with the 'savage men' (primitive forest-dwellers) prefigures, in its play on innocent speech and looking, his contact with the animals: 'he has bought / With his sweet voice and eyes, from savage men, / His rest and food' (79). But the search for abstract knowledge severs the Poet from social contact, represented through the Arab maiden, who brings the Poet food but whose loving looks are not answered (129–39). Mutual acts of lingering, dwelling and consuming are undermined by rushing, uprooting and being consumed (by fatal desire). Unlike Coleridge's Ancient Mariner, he grows to dislike the populousness of nature, seen in the slimy and watery depths (213–15, 304–7).[72]

As the Poet dies, 'bloodless' begins to signify not humanitarianism but lack of humanity and a literal draining-away of contact with nature. 'Bloodless' is characteristic of Shelley's play with the ambiguity of language. The Poet addresses the source of the stream, imagining his own death as the time

> 'when stretched
> Upon thy flowers my bloodless limbs shall waste
> I' the passing wind!'   (512)

While he dies,

> the Poet's blood,
> That ever beat in mystic sympathy
> With nature's ebb and flow, grew feebler still.   (651)

The 'sympathy' is ironized by the physical decay of the body, brought on by the zeal of the mind. Death is figured as a predatory consumer:

> A rare and regal prey
> He hath prepared, prowling around the world;
> Glutted with which thou mayst repose.   (619)

Death reigns 'from the red field / Of slaughter, from the reeking hospital...' (614). The image of war as hunger resembles Byron's *Darkness*: 'And War, which for a moment was no more, / Did glut himself again', the vipers 'slain for food' (37). Byron is also concerned with a vision which is opened only to reveal emptiness, an ironic apocalypse of dehierarchization and desacralization (a 'sad' book of revelation). Milton's striking hospital image (*Paradise Lost*, XI.477–88), also associated with death, was available to Shelley through Ritson. Milton's vision of death was connected with the spawning of images (*Paradise Lost*, XI.466–69) and

> by intemperance more
> In meats and drinks which on earth shall bring
> Diseases dire, of which a monstrous crew
> Before thee [Adam] shall appear.   (XI.472)

The profusion of icons for the greedy gaze is paralleled by the fatal profusion of foodstuffs. Michael's prophecy of how death will be manifested in a fallen world is represented through ideas about intemperate diet and the corruption of the body. Shelley revises Milton's emphasis on iconoclasm and temperance.

The Poet in *Alastor* is a prey to violent, disfiguring death, the very thing his vegetable diet would have counteracted. His bond with nature has failed, his sympathy is empty. The tearing of the veil at the end of the poem contrasts with the shroud torn to reveal the future in *Queen Mab* VIII. It disjoins the Poet altogether from nature, preserving nothing. Clark associates Shelley's vegetarianism too easily with the idea that he espoused a primitivism in his youth which he later 'repudiated'.[73] *Queen Mab* VIII provides a complex and subtle movement from past to present to a transfigured Golden Age which is, of necessity, *not* a simple return to nature (Shelley is no 'deteriorationist', as Clark describes). *Alastor* develops the asceticism which *Queen Mab*'s espousal of virtue promotes.

Goldsmith's Hermit in *Edwin and Angelina* (1765) and Milton's epic poet in *Elegia Sexta*, translated by the humanitarian Cowper, are examples of the topos of vegetable diet connoting asceticism.[74] *Alastor* re-writes the canon and expresses anxieties about its author's status as a figure for political change. A wedding of humanity and nature, figured in the caring gaze between man and animal, contrasts with a disciplined pursuit of philosophical truth. The Poet's re-imagining of the body is ironic, an attempt to break out of the restrictive enclosure of what is identified in *Queen Mab* as unreformed nature into a new nature which is as empty as it is 'beyond' the first.[75]

Vegetarian diet is used as a signal in the larger framework of the poem, as in *Queen Mab* VIII, to usher in an apocalyptic vision of changed relationships between subject and object. If *Alastor* is an analogue of *Queen Mab*, as suggested previously, then this prolepsis is overdetermined. But unlike its predecessor, the benign apocalypse does not occur. The 'bloodless food' builds the reader's expectations, but the prolepsis is defeated thematically and linguistically (in the changed sense of 'bloodless'), in order to support Shelley's point about the solitude of the ascetic poet. 'When all / Is reft at once' (713) nature is not transfigured but *disfigured*.

The Poet has already reached a personal version of a millennial state, like Lionel Verney at the commencement of *The Last Man*. His mistake is a version of the Hegelian 'bad infinity': pursuing a vision in which he misrecognizes his own revolutionary desire.[76] The Poet is described as having already achieved the millennial state. But he proceeds to leap into vague and visionary generalizations of this state, although he has already arrived at his destination. *Alastor* is an analysis of how Wordsworth can start out as a 'poet of nature' and then deviate from this supposedly natural path, paradoxically by seeming to travel *further into* nature, rejecting revolutionary politics.

What sort of politics? *Alastor* is concerned with 'alastorization', vengeance carried out in the very pursuit of desire. Shelley's liberation from Wordsworth is a 'sad' liberation into asceticism. *Alastor* enacts the denoument of millennial theory – the lonely paranoiac, shunning the populous and the slimy, is driven to death by the ascetic discipline of the desire for desire ('Vision and Love!' 366). This is a tale of how the brightest hopes may feed upon themselves and generate despair. Hogle's reading of the poem plays upon themes of decoding, but relies too heavily on a monolithic opposition of *eros* and *thanatos* deriving from the late Freudian theories of desire-as-lack and castration. His reading, however, is a good place to commence the discussion of asceticism.[77]

Alastor presents a 'celibate machine':[78] at one node of this machine is the decoding process, the demythologization of hierarchies, the millennium and the life force. At the other is the axiomatic of ascetic desire (the kind of desire-as-lack which Hogle himself invests in), the death drive as Augustine's *amans amare* (the desire of desire, the poem's epigraph)[79] and the abstract aesthetics of 'vision and love' (compare the start of *Queen Mab* VIII, on 'love' and 'health'), the sense that the subject is master of a whole, but that this whole is nothing, stuck in the ante-natal tomb or womb. These nodes are narrativized, so that the journey of the scientist-artist into nature grows into the voyage in intensities on what Deleuze and Guattari would term the 'body without organs' of the ascetic.[80]

Alastor is hard to understand precisely because it throws down the gauntlet of understanding and decoding. It reads at once like a cautionary tale (this is where Worcoley will get you)[81] and an instruction manual, and it is exactly this sort of cynicism *and* spirituality (this decoded kind of spirituality) which makes of *Alastor* a desiring machine for late eighteenth- and early nineteenth-century British society, which decodes and axiomatizes, creating an ascetic self through strategies of emulation and simulation that do not rely upon the despotism of the signifier. To put it another way, the poem is a broken-down *Queen Mab* machine, a machine of humanistic technoprogress which encourages the reader to make it 'work' by making him or her 'work' along its own lines. This is how the reader is tormented by the *alastor* of the poem, in which the narrator is tormented by the *alastor* of the Poet, who is tormented by the *alastor* of his own bad infinity. Vengeance and self-torment are what drive Ladurlad in Southey's *The Curse of Kehama* to a stoicism that finally defeats the tyrant.

The plot turns around from Eden-as-life to show how it may become an Eden-in-death. The Poet starts out in a millennial state and moves to Dendera on the Upper Nile (the source of tyrannical codes such as the Zodiac); he moves to the vale of Kashmir (the point from which all races and creeds descended after the Ark was left on Mount Ararat by the Deluge); and ends in the Georgian Caucasus on the Chorasmian (Caspian) Sea, the projected spot of the Garden of Eden (projected according to the very decoding logics of the Enlightenment which Shelley invests in). Hogle comes close to an understanding of the Poet's asceticism in his sense of 'the grimly effective ways by which relational thinking [or radical transference] can recentre and restrict its own expansion using its own procedures and elements',[82] but he does not name it. The Poet retraces his steps towards paradise and then backwards to a Miltonic creation which is then reversed into an atheist Lucretian flux.[83] His voyage progressively decodes the spirituality with which the life commenced, the divinity of nature and the millennial (and vegetarian) state of bliss. But these two worlds are two poles of the same kind of machine. The Poet reconstructs or re-imagines his body as a lute, a body without organs whipped by the intensities of abstract nature's mechanisms (a kind of QED of the poem's own functioning).

The very irony and cynicism with which Shelley presents this process, the yearning for a redemptive elixir which is denied in the closing narrational passage, is part of the process of alastorization, the creation of the vengeful ascetic for whom desire is lack and the pursuit of desire a monstrous and decoded death drive. Hogle's reading could be extended by studying the hierarchies which the decoding process of transference still sets up, such as the populous and the slimy versus the individual and the clean. *Alastor* may be read as a dream-theatre, a presentation of Shelley's anxieties and sexual repressions, a critique of Wordsworth; but these readings invest in desire-as-lack. Freudian, deconstructive and intertextual readings, and Marxist readings which castigate the Poet's failure to connect with society as the cause of his downfall (the poem as self-present allegory), all fail to take into account the alastorization machine. The poem is a prescription, a guide-book rather than a theatre – a programme for the construction of an ascetic body. 'Bloodless food' straddles consumption-as-sharing and consumption-as-discipline.

The debate over revolution, death and killing is continued in *Laon and Cythna* (*The Revolt of Islam*, written 1817, published 1818).[84] Is revolutionary killing a matter of sacrifice or of butchery? When, if at all, is killing lawful? For John Oswald, sacrifice and butchery characterized two successive periods of human decline from a vegetarian natural state. Sacrifice implies a certain honour, while butchery implies a wilful disrespect for the body. Shakespeare's Roman plays strove to differentiate these terms, and Shelley renders more literal their *polis*-founding meals and vengeful cannibalisms in *Laon and Cythna*. Social anthropology has already speculated about the cultural reference of sacrifice as a deterrent to revolution, a 'violence outlet' typified by the Biblical story of Cain and Abel (a myth revised by Shelley).[85] But in *Laon and Cythna*, sacrifice itself is refigured.

The significance of vegetarianism in *Laon and Cythna* was noticed by J. T. Coleridge in *The Quarterly Review* (1819).[86] He declares that the poem represents a 'natural state' corrupted by 'kings ... legislators ... priests', his first criticism of Shelley's politics probably stemming from a misreading of *Queen Mab* or Shelley's reputation (the poem was not in wide circulation at the time, except perhaps in the radical underground).[87] Coleridge notices correctly that Shelley's rewriting of the Christian Fall narrative has an ecological orientation. The earth begins spontaneously bestowing its innocent pleasures, and ends unhealthy and harsh.[88] The main feature of this Fall, which Coleridge isolates with sarcasm, is diet: 'We have become a foul-feeding carnivorous race, are foolish enough to feel comfortable after the commission of sin ...'.[89] He singles out the revolutionary celebrations as 'A good deal of mummery ... of national fêtes, reasonable rites, altars of federation, &c. borrowed from that store-house of cast-off mummeries and abominations, the French rev-olution'.[90] One of the 'mummeries' is the vegetarian feast in canto v. Coleridge sees Shelley's revision of Wordsworth's discourse of nature, though he finds that Shelley corrupts the 'philosophy which comes pure and holy from his [Wordsworth's] pen'.[91] The reactionary critic was sensitive to how the symbolic relationship between humans and nature could be politicized.

Laon and Cythna treats bloody violence as an unnatural revolutionary principle. Shelley establishes the importance of the theme of blood at an early point. Human history is imaged as a near-Manichean conflict between forces of revolutionary struggle and oppression – the eagle and the serpent (i.viii). *Thalaba* is also preoccupied with Gnostic asceticism and dualism, exemplified in the antagonists' picture of the world as struggling powers: '"the same Earth / Bears fruit and poison; where the Camel finds / His fragrant food, the horned Viper there / Sucks in the juice of death"' (ix.147). Shelley distinguishes between these terms by rendering the anti-oppressive force the natural, life-preserving one. Whenever the revolutionaries encounter oppression, a dangerous temptation to use oppression's weapons – death, blood and 'dominion' – is presented. This conflict and temptation is crystallized in canto v. The force of oppression is emblematized among other things as poisonous food and miasmata (i.xxix.(253)).[92] Its conflict with humanity is 'a strife of blood' (*Laon and Cythna* i.xxxiii.(290)). This struggle is acted out on Laon's body in his imprisonment on the column 'With chains that eat into the flesh, alas!' (iii.xiv.(122)). The 'alas!' is well placed to register a cry of nature. On the column, Laon has to satisfy his hunger, and consumes himself (another allusion to *The Ancient Mariner*, 160):

> The uprest
> Of the third sun brought hunger – but the crust
> Which had been left, was to my craving breast
> Fuel, not food. I chewed the bitter dust,
> And bit my bloodless arm, and sucked the brazen dust.
>
> (iii.xxi.(185))

He also has nightmares about eating his sister and lover Cythna's flesh (iii.xxvi.(231)). Eating human flesh, and in the last resort one's own body, was characteristic in the representation of famine in Europe since the Middle Ages.[93] 'Representation' is significant here, since these activities are never directly recorded, but are ways of picturing the Other (races, classes, nations). Shelley had inherited this tradition. His placing of Laon's cannibalism within a dream-like state of feverish consciousness graphically represents Laon's point of utmost loss of self.

Burke's Jacobins were cannibals; so are Shelley's tyrants. Shelley uses food imagery as part of his revision of the revolutionary self. Later in *Laon and Cythna*, the famine and ecological disaster under the re-established despotism is represented through cannibalism:

> There was no corn – in the wide market-place
> All loathliest things, even human flesh, was sold;
> They weighed it in small scales – and many a face
> Was fixed in eager horror then.   (x.xix.(163))

Here is a compact example of the *macellogia* and faciality of Shelley's transgressive 'Smithfield Muse'. The predominance of (l) sounds in lines 164–65 is suggestive of the indiscriminate intermixture of flesh commodities. The 'small scales' reduce humanity, with horrific literalism, to disembodied numbers. Shelley was preoccupied with the figurative gutting and filleting of an essential humanity in such passages from *Queen Mab* as 'Even love is sold' (v.189) and 'The harmony and happiness of man / Yields to the wealth of nations' (v.79–80), a critique of the Mandevillian economics of Adam Smith.

Shelley uses visceral rhetoric as a marker of otherness, in order to establish the humanitarian credentials of revolutionary activity. After he has rescued him the hermit tells Laon: '"Perchance blood need not flow, if thou at length / Wouldst rise"' (iv.xviii.(154)). It is the guards of the tyrant whose food 'from infancy' has been 'Carnage and ruin' (iv.xxvi.(229–30)). The attackers of the revolutionary camp are

> Like rabid snakes, that sting some gentle child
> Who brings them food.   (v.vii.(55))

This alludes to *Queen Mab* viii (84–87), and associates the attackers not just with predatoriness but with poison. This is another revision of Isaiah's image of the basilisks, as is one of the sculptures around the Pyramid in the Golden City:

> A Woman sitting on a sculptured disk
> Of the broad earth, and feeding from one breast
> A human babe and a young basilisk.   (v.l.(442))

The sculpture represents the reconciliation of humanity with nature. The feminized humanity of suckling and even-handed nurturing is a paradigm of Shelleyan revolutionary success.

Shelley also plays with notions of temperance and intemperance: the moral measurement of consumption. Othman the tyrant is compared to a famine, embodied as an intemperate and bloodthirsty appetite (v.xxxi.(274–78)). In contrast, the 'gnawing fire' of revolutionary feeling consumes Laon's body, in an image of ascetic zeal (IV.xxix.(258)). The appetite of the revolutionary fire seems to consume the gross materiality of the body.

In canto v there arises the question of the justice of executing Othman. Laon assumes a Christ-like attitude with those who intend to kill him: '"Is there one who ne'er / In secret thought wished another's ill?"' (v.xxxiv.(298)). Laon is Christ-like in intervening upon the act of vengeance about to be carried out against the despot's soldiers who have been trapped (v.ix–xiii). He seems to short-circuit the feedback of wrath. This feedback was mediated through Cain-and-Abel stories in Pope and the seventeenth-century vegetarian, Tryon; Shelley also revises the Christian typology of the sacrificial lamb.

The appeal to sacrifice is encapsulated in microcosm at the moment when Laon uses his pierced body as a figure of sympathy and nature:

> The spear transfixed my arm that was uplifted
> In swift expostulation, and the blood
> Gushed round its point: I smiled, and – 'Oh! thou gifted
> With eloquence which shall not be withstood,
> Flow thus!' – I cried in joy, 'thou vital flood,
> Until my heart be dry, ere thus the cause
> For which thou wert aught worthy be subdued –
> Ah, ye are pale, – ye weep, – your passions pause, –
> 'Tis well! ye feel the truth of love's benignant laws.' (v.ix.(73))

This works in the same way as the silently eloquent look of the lamb in *Queen Mab* VIII or the creature's appeal to Frankenstein. In Psalm 50, God declares that He does not need the symbolization of piety in the sacrifice of animal flesh. In *Laon and Cythna*, humanity does not need the symbolization of zeal in the sacrifice of flesh. Laon's lines about his blood become a statement about representation, another figure about a figure involving blood and flesh.[94] Full communication between creatures does not need the symbolization of sympathy in words: sympathy can be felt on the pulses, it is written in the heart. Laon is re-imagining his body and the law in the cause of humanitarianism.

The revolutionaries decide not to bloody their hands. Here Cythna, now renamed Laone, sings a victory song. One of its verses is about animal sacrifice:

> 'My brethren, we are free! the fruits are glowing
> Beneath the stars, and the night winds are flowing
> O'er the ripe corn, the birds and beasts are dreaming –
> Never again may blood of bird or beast
> Stain with its venemous [sic] stream a human feast,
> To the pure skies in accusation steaming.
> Avenging poisons shall have ceased
> > To feed disease and fear and madness,
> > The dwellers of the earth and air
> > Shall throng around our steps in gladness
> > Seeking their food or refuge there.
> Our toil from thought all glorious forms shall cull,
> To make this Earth, our home, more beautiful,
> And Science, and her sister Poesy,
> Shall clothe in light the fields and cities of the free!'
>
> > > (v.li.verse 5 (523))

Vegetable food is announced in the opening lines as an aspect of the revolutionary vision. Like all good Shelleyan things, the fruit glows as if suffused with light. The animals are free to dream – to be subjects allowed to enjoy their own capacity for imagination, rather than objects of self-polluting human appetite. The verse rewrites Psalm 50: God does not desire or require a flesh and blood sacrifice, rather the inward sacrifice of the spirit (Psalms 50: 8–15).

The sacrifice of flesh is read as a corrupt symbol, a miasmatic marking, in 'Stain with its venemous [sic] stream a human feast'. The following line juxtaposes and contrasts a state of purity, 'the pure skies', with the perversion of a 'steaming' sacrifice: malignant flows of hot blood or poison are replaced by benign and harmonious flows. The vegetarian passage in Thomson's *Spring* shows how a feminized nature may be represented as a benign giver of flows:

> > > from her lap
> > She pours ten thousand delicacies, herbs
> > And fruits, as numerous as the drops of rain
> > Or beams that gave them birth.   (351)

The flows of an ecosystem are imagined producing 'delicacies' for consumption, challenging static, iconic representations. Similarly, the opening three lines of Cythna's song present a smooth, unified nature, the 'Beneath' and 'O'er' serving to unite sky and earth, the 'stars' and 'night winds' with the 'fruits' and 'ripe corn', an effect intensified by the chiasmatic patterning. This is continued in 'The dwellers of the earth and air / Shall throng around our steps in gladness', a revision of the *Essay on Man*: 'Man walk'd with beast, joint tenant of the shade' (III.152).

Vegetarianism is then discussed in its specific relation to human life. As in *Queen Mab* VIII, the benefits to health are described *after* a moral statement. Shelley rewrites the Cain and Abel myth, as the sacrifice of animal food may no longer be conceived as denoting an acceptable sacrificer. Another level of allusion deploys a Greek religious vocabulary of *miasma* (pollution) and *ate* (madness): disease and insanity are not merely clinical in resonance here. The following lines re-imagine human relationships with nature. The image of science and poetry dressing both fields and cities is a re-dressing of past disfigurings, and philosophy is associated with aesthetics: 'To make this Earth, our home, more beautiful'. The line repoliticizes Pope's line in *Essay on Criticism* (1711) about how true art is 'Nature to advantage dress'd' (297). The association of science with reform shows how little Shelley's ideology had changed in this particular context since *Queen Mab* VIII.227–28, and how the vegetarian passage was a working model for other poems.

There then follows 'the banquet of the free' (v.liv.(574)). It is a vegetarian feast to celebrate the revolutionary victory:

> Their feast was such as Earth, the general mother,
> Pours from her fairest bosom, when she smiles
> In the embrace of Autumn; – to each other
> As when some parent fondly reconciles
> Her warring children, she their wrath beguiles
> With her own sustenance; they relenting weep:
> Such was this Festival, which from their isles,
> And continents, and winds, and oceans deep,
> All shapes might throng to share, that fly, or walk, or creep.
>
> Might share in peace and innocence, for gore
> Or poison none this festal did pollute,
> But piled on high, an overflowing store
> Of pomegranates, and citrons, fairest fruit,
> Melons, and dates, and figs, and many a root
> Sweet and sustaining, and bright grapes ere yet
> Accursed fire their mild juice could transmute

Into a mortal bane, and brown corn set
In baskets; with pure streams their thirsting lips they wet.

(v.lv.(580))

This passage marks the apex of the poem's upward curve, the point at which revolutionary production (the clash of violence and sacrifice) becomes revolutionary consumption. The topically-described fruits orientalize the Golden City: compare the melon juice in *Thalaba* II.94–5, or the way in which water (not alcohol) and middle-eastern fruits are consumed in the Edenic bower-of-bliss at VI.36–41, or the dervish meal of a 'plain repast / Rice and fresh grapes, and at their feet there flowed / The brook of which they drank' (VIII.118–19). The emphasis on maternal reconciliation recalls the statue of the baby and basilisk. 'Poison' and 'pollute' suggest *miasma*, and the epithet 'Accursed fire' connotes the curse of Prometheus. Human stewardship of the earth and its creatures is hinted at in the echo of Genesis (588). The Golden Age is reconceived in an urban environment. Through adherence to nature's law, the civic culture is reformed. Shelley's use of orientalism as a critique of English politics (which he shared with others in the second 'Romantic' generation) is here explicitly related to the 'natural' consumption of vegetarianism.[95]

MARENGHI

Marenghi (1818; originally called 'Mazenghi' in the manuscript) is a fragmentary version of a story found in Sismondi's *Histoire des républiques italiennes du moyen age* (1808–18). The Florentines had besieged Pisa by famine (and not force; perhaps an element which intrigued Shelley). Pietro Marenghi was under a capital sentence from Florence. Having escaped to the mountains, however, he returned and set fire to one of the enemy galleys. Shelley did not finish the story, but the poem as it stands presents radical choice as a result of an Orphic consumption of nature.

Marenghi discusses the difference between revenge and radical action. Revenge is a game for those 'Who barter wrong for wrong, until the exchange / Ruins the merchants of such thriftless trade' (3). The Pisan feuds are represented as blood 'brimming' in 'a cup of sculptured gold' in a church (15–16); 'And reconciling factions wet their lips / With that dread wine' (20). The implication is that reconciliation is impossible, since the ritual 'sacrament' (17) is a bloody intoxicating drink. The subtlety of tyranny is presented, overthrowing the liberal spirit of Florence (stanzas vi–ix), with its cultural ancestry in Athens (vii): does '⟨that band / Of free and glorious brothers⟩' (23, deleted in the manuscript) 'gorge the sated tyrants' spoil?' (28). Political paradoxes are mediated through metaphors of drink and food. Thus one must untie the 'Good and ill like vines entangled' (49) and 'Divide the vintage ere thou drink' (51).

Marenghi's crime was so great that no one was allowed even to drink water with him (66–67). He wanders in the wild 'like a hunted beast' (70), feeding on

> globes of deep-red gold
> Which in the woods the strawberry-tree doth bear
> Suspended in their emerald atmosphere. (73)

Marenghi has been reduced to the animal-like status of primitive man described in *Queen Mab* VIII, amidst a nature which is 'overgrown' (78) and 'Deserted by the fever-stricken serf' (77), a pestilential wilderness endured only by 'things whose nature is at war with life' like snakes and 'Ill worms' (89–90). Two kinds of nature are presented: the benign nature hinted at in 'life' and the malign nature which turns back upon itself ('at war'). Soon this nature is to be transfigured (and so is Marenghi).

Marenghi lives in a murderer's cottage; the birds which eat the murderer's body die (98–99), suggesting a miasmatic plague. However, Marenghi's soul is virtuous, 'warring with decay' (104). He becomes an Orphic figure who tames the birds, amphibians and reptiles who talk and play with him in his 'silent time' (110).[96] He learns from nature: he 'Communed with the immeasurable world' (133), understanding how to 'read' (120) the path of the dawn. He 'felt his life beyond his limbs dilated, / Till his mind grew like that it contemplated' (134). This state of natural ecstasy awakens a sense of 'liberty' (129). Disease modulates into beauty through a correct reading of nature's signs. Now that he has become a true hermit, Marenghi's diet is described. Stanza XXV commemorates a renewed identity:

> His food was the wild fig and strawberry;
> The milky pine-nuts which the autumn blast
> Shakes into the tall grass; or such small fry

> As from the sea by winter storms are cast;
> And the coarse bulbs of iris-flowers he found
> Knotted in clumps under the spongy ground.   (136)

While not vegetarian, the 'fry' are not fished, only found once dead already. Marenghi's marginal consumption is the dovetail for an increasing sense of care and social consciousness (161). The return to nature becomes a means of returning to humanity: 'And so were kindled powers and thoughts which made / His solitude less dark' (142). The significance of 'kindling' has already been commented upon (see the section on *Daemon*). The rest of the poem is greatly corrected, but this stanza is hardly touched in the manuscript.[97]

Food imagery traces the movement from complexity to simplicity, from political irony and self-defeating violence to innocence and peace. In a state of despondency in Naples, often writing in solitude,[98] Shelley fashions himself as the political exile who can only be at best the shadow of a millennial future state. The individual's ascetic and sympathetic pact with nature is proleptic of social justice.

PROMETHEUS UNBOUND

Preparing to write his conclusion to Aeschylus' verse drama about the titan who was punished for stealing fire from the gods, Shelley asked Peacock about Cicero's opinion of Aeschylus: Cicero declares that Aeschylus' portrait of Prometheus shows that he was a Pythagorean.[99] *Prometheus Unbound* (written 1818–19; published 1820) is concerned with reform.[100] Its central image is Prometheus' tortured body, already discussed in *A Vindication*. Shelley is prepared to say that the liberation of Prometheus from the carnivorous torture he endures can be taken as figure for the reformation of both society and nature. Prometheus, the bringer of fire, cookery, language and medicine, is a figure for humanity itself, and, more specifically, for those humans in control of these discourses. In certain respects he is a ruling-class reformer: a powerful individual whose hegemonic status is a unique kind of 'burden' (the ring of Kipling associates this mode of hegemony with imperialism). Can the ruling class pull themselves up by their own bootstraps in this way? Prometheus' punishment seems almost to have become a part of his own body.[101] The drama shows how an ascetic kind of 'virtue', to use *Queen Mab*'s key ethical term, may be developed as a form of political resistance, reform and subversion.

In his opening speech, Prometheus himself uses some of the rhetoric which should now be familiar. He describes the eagle or vulture which tortures him daily:

> Heaven's winged hound, polluting from thy lips
> His beak in poison not his own, tears up
> My heart. (1.34)

The editors of the Norton anthology speculate that Shelley 'omits' Hercules' slaughter of 'the eagle (or vulture) that tortures Prometheus ... because, as III.ii had made clear, bloodshed was banished after the tyrant's fall'.[102] The vulture, a bird of pollution, is itself corrupted by the task which Jupiter the tyrant has forced it to perform, since it eats flesh. The image of a 'hound' associates the bird with the dogs who are the accoutrements of the despot (like the tyrant's guards in *Laon and Cythna*).

The Chorus of Furies describes the *miasma* and thirst which followed Prometheus' introduction of various arts, using Rousseau as an example of political figuration gone awry:

> The pale stars of the morn
> Shine on a misery, dire to be borne.
> Dost thou faint, mighty Titan? We laugh thee to scorn.
> Dost thou boast the clear knowledge thou waken'dst for man?
> Then was kindled within him a thirst which outran
> Those perishing waters; a thirst of fierce fever,
> Hope, love, doubt, desire, which consume him for ever.
>   One came forth of gentle worth
>   Smiling on the sanguine earth;
>   His works outlived him, like swift poison
>   Withering up truth, peace, and pity.
> Look! where round the wide horizon
>   Many a million-peopled city
> Vomits smoke in the bright air.
> Hark that outcry of despair!
> 'Tis his mild and gentle ghost
>   Wailing for the faith he kindled. (1.539)

Shelley was serious about thirst in 1813, when he adapted Newton's passage about Prometheus for *A Vindication*. The flows of desire and of polluted liquids are associated: in the original state of nature, humans survived on the liquid contained organically in fruits.[103] Desire and pollution, however, flow beyond and through the organism, and this flow needs to be contained to re-establish organic health.

The dietary metaphor continues through 'swift poison' and 'vomits', in a response to urbanization and fears about population growth. The (dis)figuration of human culture is part of the solution as well as part of the problem: this is another theme of *A Vindication*, and in both cases Prometheus stands for fallen humanity possessing the capacity for self-redemption. The passions which are 'kindled' (as in *Queen Mab*) act like poison but 'faith' is also kindled, so that the sufferings of the urban people (the present state of culture) foreshadow a millennial state. The sophistication of Shelley's dietary metaphor works against the position adopted by Baker that Shelley is no longer interested in what 'man puts, or does not put, into his stomach', and that the 1818 Prometheus has nothing to do with the 1813 Prometheus of *A Vindication*.[104]

In Act III Jupiter expresses a wish for 'Heaven's wine' (III.i.25–33). Those who are to exult with him in his power are supposed to be drunk: intemperance is associated with oppression. There is nothing inherently suspicious about the banquet, unless it is understood as an anti-masque. The tempting rhetoric of Jupiter's discourse of intoxicated ascension is reminiscent of Milton's masque, *Comus* (there are also echoes of the 'Amreeta Cup' episode in Southey's *The Curse of Kehama*). Rather than ascending in a despotic hierarchy, the rhetoric and action of Prometheus' liberation is one of descent, of a return (literally) to the full body of the earth. Jupiter's power has grown too arbitrary and must be tempered.

After Jupiter's deposition by Demogorgon, Ocean speaks to Apollo of the environmental-political change:

> Henceforth the fields of Heaven-reflecting sea
> Which are my realm, will heave, unstain'd with blood
> Beneath the uplifting winds, like plains of corn
> Swayed by the summer air.   (III.ii.18)

There will be no slavery, no more ships 'Tracking their path ... by blood and groans' (29). The agricultural image of 20–21 is echoed in the pastoral of 'wave-reflected flowers' (32) which replace 'the mingled voice / Of slavery and command' (30), and by the idea that the sea hungers for 'calm' in its 'unpastured' state (49). The lexical unity of earth and sea, whose allegorical figures tend to speak in images which each will find appropriate, is repeated elsewhere (c.f.

IV.346–48). The language of facial reflection is used again to depict the ways in which nature may be re-imagined in its relationship with culture. Nature hungers (to use Ocean's words) for the guidance of Promethean spirits of progressive humanism, the forward-thinking exploitation of productive resources. Shelley's agrarian image was materialized in his interest in ecological planning (see chapter 6).

The Earth, the ecosystem herself, celebrates the consumption of liberty:

> I hear, I feel;
> Thy [Prometheus'] lips are on me, and their touch runs down
> Even to the adamantine central gloom
> Along these marble nerves; 'tis life, 'tis joy,
> And, thro' my withered, old and icy frame
> The warmth of an immortal youth shoots down
> Circling. Henceforth the many children fair
> Folded in my sustaining arms; all plants,
> And creeping forms, and insects rainbow-winged,
> And birds, and beasts, and fish, and human shapes,
> Which drew disease and pain from my wan bosom,
> Draining the poison of despair, shall take
> And interchange sweet nutriment; to me
> Shall they become like sister-antelopes
> By one fair dam, snow white and swift as wind,
> Nursed among lilies near a brimming stream.
> The dew-mists of my sunless sleep shall float
> Under the stars like balm: night-folded flowers
> Shall suck unwithering hues in their repose:
> And men and beasts in happy dreams shall gather
> Strength for the coming day, and all its joy:
> And death shall be the last embrace of her
> Who takes the life she gave, even as a mother,
> Folding her child, says, 'Leave me not again.'   (III.iii.84)

Given the precedent of *Queen Mab* VIII, the 'human shapes' (93) are those which exclusively 'drew disease and pain from my [Earth's] wan bosom' (94), and 'the poison of despair' (95) renders the allusions more explicit. This figurative train is concluded by the 'sweet nutriment' (96; compare Rousseau, in *The Triumph of Life*, 202).[105] 'Men and beasts in happy dreams shall gather' (103) restates the right-to-imagination of animals in *Laon and Cythna*. The earth is youthful *and* maternal, as in *Queen Mab*, and is capable of speech, rendering the passionate play of faciality more explicit than in Shelley's didactic poem: the earth is kissed by Prometheus, and plays Ianthe *and* Henry. The earth's face is significant in a play preoccupied with 'facing' (for example, in Prometheus' address to Jupiter, re-articulated through the very Phantasm of Jupiter). The really new touch is the quasi-feminist 'sister-antelopes' (97). Antelopes typify innocent and defenceless (and thus fundamentally 'natural') nature in *A Refutation of Deism* and *Epipsychidion*.[106] The image can be traced back to the scene in *Thalaba* where a hunt is organized in which a deer and an antelope are slaughtered, employing a tame leopard ('The Ounce whose gums were warm in his prey...', IX.158–61).[107]

The antelope-image expands into a picture of nurturing, 'Nursed among lilies' (99). Even the flowers are eating: they 'suck unwithering hues' (102). This image of infantile bliss (echoed in the image of the dreaming Spirit of the Earth within the revolving orbs in Act IV) marks the reform as the unbinding of narcissistic energies, a remembering of the past and hence a 'return to nature'. The new world is a self-consuming cycle.

The absence of sacrifice is the culminating element in the description of the forthcoming Utopia:

> And those foul shapes, abhorred by god and man,
> Which, under many a name and many a form
> Strange, savage, ghastly, dark, and execrable
> Were Jupiter, the tyrant of the world;
> And which the nations, panic-stricken, served
> With blood, and hearts broken by long hope, and love
> Dragged to his altars soiled and garlandless,
> And slain amid men's unreclaiming tears,
> Flattering the thing they feared, which fear was hate,
> Frown, mouldering fast, o'er their abandoned shrines. (III.iv.180)

The image of propitiatory sacrifice, an example of what Horkheimer and Adorno called the 'mimetic' behaviour of primitive humans,[108] is concerned with a violent play of simulation and emulation (the projection of 'hate'). The phrase 'men's unreclaiming tears' perhaps alludes to Lucretius' demystifying account of the sacrifice of Iphigenia in *De rerum natura* (Artemis eventually relented and substituted a hind at the last moment). The hierarchized consumption of violence is associated with language (icons, forms and names).

Differences have been abolished, and man is 'Sceptreless, free, uncircumscribed, – but man' (194). In a figurative shift, culture and power become aspects of nature: man is without boundaries, 'Equal, unclassed, tribeless and nationless' (195) but has become autotelic, is

'King / Over himself' (196). An interior limit has been established which enables an unbounded play of self-determining subjects. Shelley's ascetic thinking is here developed further. The Third Fury tempts Prometheus to imagine that the flow of 'dread thought', miasmatic 'foul desire' and physical 'blood' will overwhelm the privatized limits of the self 'like a vain loud multitude' (1.483–91). Prometheus is trying to unbind whole populations of enslaved bodies, persons, desires and so on, but also to remain above the populous (compare the figuration of the populous in the darker poems, *Alastor* and *Marenghi*):

> Yet am I king over myself, and rule
> The torturing and conflicting throngs within,
> As Jove rules you when Hell grows mutinous.   (1.492)

The 'Orphic' regimentation of language delineated at IV.415 rules over throngs of psychosocial phenomena: Prometheus has mastered mastery.

The assertion of the very *value* of this concept of internal torture is the turning point in the first Act which banishes the Furies. Again, the Fury tempts Prometheus by suggesting that even if a scene of physical blood were admitted to the mind, in which desires and 'foul lies' over-rode the self 'As hooded ounces cling to the driven hind' (1.597–615; compare Southey's ounce), far 'Worse things' could be observed behind this scene: 'In each human heart terror survives / The ravin [prey] it has gorged...' (618ff). Prometheus answers: 'Thy words are like a cloud of winged snakes; / And yet, I pity those they torture not' (632), at which the Fury vanishes. Self-regimentation is positively wholesome, enabling Prometheus negatively to judge those who do not attain this internal mark. The problem becomes one of pathology: how is it possible to know when (and indeed, in a different sense, to be rational while) one is racked by such pain?

The visions of Act III of *Prometheus Unbound* are proleptic of the apocalyptic fourth Act, which revises the chronology of death and violence:

> Once the hungry Hours were hounds
>   Which chased the day like a bleeding deer,
> And it limped and stumbled with many wounds
>   Through the nightly dells of the desert year.

But now, oh, weave the mystic measure
    Of music, and dance, and shapes of light,
Let the Hours, and the spirits of might and pleasure,
    Like the clouds and sunbeams, unite.   (iv.73)

History itself is figured as an act of violence upon the body. The sophistication of the hunt image lies in the suggestion that the 'Hours' (the human measurement of time) and the 'Day' (the natural progress of time) were divided, but are now united. Shelley contrasts the empty desert and its nomad inhabitants with the stately (and statist) image of the measured hours and the 'spirits', united in a contradictory way, like clouds and sunbeams. Shelley's republican version of Pope's harmonious fusion of opposites blends nature and culture (day and hours), body and measurement, in a reign of peace.

The Golden Age is also refigured in *Prometheus Unbound*, in Asia's speech at ii.iv.32–109. The reign of Saturn was peaceful, 'the calm joy of flowers and living leaves' (36). But life-as-progress is absent from his reign, described as property, 'The birthright of their ['the earth's primal spirits', 35] being' (39), and imaged through science and technology, 'The skill which wields the elements' (40) and technologies of the self: 'Self-empire, and the majesty of love' (42). Prometheus as 'forethought', technology (a kind of mythopoeic television), gives to the spirits what was theirs already. The freedom thus granted to despotic power (Jupiter) established the next reign, but it is abused, releasing flows of 'famine', 'toil', 'disease', 'Strife, wounds, and ghastly death unseen before' which 'Fell' on 'the race of man' (49–52). Promethean vision 'tamed' fire, which obeyed 'like some beast of prey' (66), and smelted metals to produce money and weaponry, 'the slaves and signs of power' (69). But even these events were moments in a sequence of technological progress which outstripped their tyrannical swaddling clothes. An improving series of productions are listed: language, thought, science, art, medicine. Finally 'Disease drank and slept. Death grew like sleep' (86, the result of the explicitly *post-Promethean* natural diet advocated in Newton's *Return to Nature*). Shelley shows how culture may progress and be refined, as if from within.

It is now possible to reread the Kronos-allusions in *Queen Mab* viii as the snatching of a Golden Age from the jaws of a history which has consumed its promise. Shelley's use of figures associated with diet anticipates and appropriates such apocalyptic changes; he mobilizes what is often conceived as the recalcitrant operation of 'natural' instinct. The feast in *Laon and Cythna* is not merely an emblem but an *enactment* of changed relationships in/between society and nature. The feeding of the forest animals by the Poet in *Alastor* sets up the expectation of a reformist conclusion; the poem is structured around the withdrawal of such an expectation. *Prometheus Unbound* is a consummate elaboration of the discourses of consumption, faciality, measurement, and temperance (asceticism).

Shelley's discourses of diet enable the different organs of the body to exist in harmony rather than conflict. This harmony is expressed as a zero degree of passion, a state of peacefulness and coolness (as in the concept of the cooling vegetarian regimen). Passion has not been erased but tamed:

> Man, one harmonious Soul of many a soul
>> Whose nature is its own divine controul,
> Where all things flow to all, as rivers to the sea;
>> Familiar acts are beautiful through love;
>> Labour, and pain, and grief, in life's green grove
> Sport like tame beasts, none knew how gentle they could be!
>
> *(Prometheus Unbound,* iv.400).

Brain, heart, stomach, sense organs, nervous system, and the openings which connect these to kinship, familial, and state assemblages are joined together, through rhetorics of faciality, silent eloquence, and 'nature'. But this joining serves a specific purpose. Shelley's re-imagined social and psychic body resists the morselization of assemblages which sacrifice, butcher, create war, or engage in family- or kinship-disrupting acts of revenge. The model is dynamic and futuristic, designed to pioneer its way into the future, to sweat in the dark mine and wrest from it the gem of truth with which to decorate its 'paradise of peace' (*Queen Mab* viii.238). It attempts to enable a peaceful, reformist technological progress, and thus harnesses the warlike acts of vengeance into passions of self-discipline.

Shelley establishes the figurative resources for wars on pollution (both moral and physical), intoxicants, want, despotic violence itself. The rhetoric of internalized war is a familiar aspect of the 'modern' world and statist social models. *Queen Mab, Laon and Cythna* and *Prometheus Unbound* develop dialogues between figures of the body, vice and virtue, and urban/ecological renewal, deploying the idea of a 'natural' state (for example, the reform of the 'great city' observed by the Spirit of the Earth in *Prometheus Unbound* iii.iv.33–85). *Alastor* and *Marenghi* elaborate lines of flight or deterritorialization from the social body, which are then reincorporated and rechannelled, both in the transition from hermit to guerilla in *Marenghi*, and in the relative assessment of speeds and intensities of flight in *Alastor*'s thought experiment.

In his representations of the consumption (as well as production) of liberty, Shelley co-opts Milton, Pope, Cowper, Thomson, Pratt and Southey, while expanding and critiquing Wordsworth and Coleridge. He develops parallelisms between consumption and representation, general and restricted economy, nature and humanity, blood and gold. On a macrological level, he revises Biblical, classical and Hindu traditions. On a micrological level, the rhetorics of ecosystemic flow, *macellogia*, silent eloquence and faciality challenge the disfigurations of iconic language, disease and luxurious or carnivorous consumption.

It is still necessary to stress how prescriptions of diet plug body and society together. The figure of Demogorgon remains a puzzling feature of *Prometheus Unbound*. He deposes Jupiter, working like an immanence within the 'in your face' rhetoric of reforming sympathy and love. In him, the erotics of Shelley's poetry finds its motor, the figure of death appropriated from *Paradise Lost* (II.666–73): 'a mighty darkness / Filling the seat of power ... Ungazed upon and shapeless; neither limb, / Nor form, nor outline' (*Prometheus Unbound* II.iv.2–6). Demogorgon's facelessness is indicative of his axiomatic function: he goes under no direr name than eternity, and he speaks words of both peace and power at the close of the drama: to be 'joyous, beautiful and free' is 'Life, Joy, *Empire* and *Victory*!' (IV.577–78, my emphasis; compare *Queen Mab* VIII.232–34, about how reason and passion, now united, 'wield / The sceptre of a vast dominion' over the globe).

Demogorgon is symptomatic of Shelley's interest in something more than imagery – his concern for axioms, programmatic plans. Modelling society according to immanent axioms rather than overcoded figures is an element of societies that do not depend upon the hagiographic representation of the body of the despot, but on the unbinding and binding of flows of sympathy, technology, commodities, media and so on.[109] *Prometheus Unbound* does not support a mere outpouring of love as the source of reform; the flow of love is disciplined by an interior, 'imageless' limit (II.iv.116). The discourse of diet, for example, is no mere image of peaceful reform, but a device for producing peaceful subjects. The following chapter analyses the codes and axioms which generate their passionate faces and natural cries.

CHAPTER 4

Apollo in the jungle: healthy morals and the body beautiful

Unsophisticated instinct is invariably unerring; but to decide on the fitness of animal food, from the perverted appetites which its constrained adoption produces, is to make the criminal a judge of his own cause: – it is even worse, it is appealing to the infatuated drunkard in a question of the salubrity of brandy.

Shelley, *V, J* vi.9

And human hands first mimicked and then mocked,
With moulded limbs more lovely than its own,
The human form, till marble grew divine;
And mothers, gazing, drank the love men see
Reflected in their race, behold, and perish.
He told the hidden power of herbs and springs,
And Disease drank and slept. Death grew like sleep.

Shelley, *Prometheus Unbound*, ii.iv.80

INTRODUCTION

With the exemplification of Shelley's poetic figures of diet in mind, what are the networks which set up the grounding notions of 'aesthetics' and 'economics'? This chapter explores Shelley's vegetarian prose and its sources, analysing the implications that vegetarianism brings to bear upon the text and upon theories of writing and representation. It puts in play the concept of 'disfiguration', shorthand for the notion that the act of representing involves a degree of violence to the body of the thing represented (through masking, elision, incompleteness and so on); and that this violence can be traced in the letter of the resultant text as a mark or taint. The vegetarian writers who influenced Shelley were anxious that language should not be disfiguring, that it should mark without tainting. This anxiety suggests political implications about the representation of the body in society.

Disfiguration is countered by nature's silent eloquence. 'Silent eloquence' could be defined as the significant absence of language; but it could also be defined as an absence of language which in some way is itself a linguistic act, a pre- or super-linguistic language. It might even gesture towards something conceived as non-linguistic, an axiom rather than a code. The notion of 'silent eloquence' is a central feature of vegetarian language, in its insistence that non-human animals are 'speaking' without a perceived access to human language.[1] This kind of speech is privileged over other sorts of language associated with disfiguring representation and thus with violence. The most crucial word under discussion in the chapter is 'nature': the idea that there is something fundamental and not arbitrary or culturally produced about the universe and the beings which inhabit it. The writers analysed need to distinguish between two kinds of nature (predatory and peaceful), employing rhetorical slippages which are resolved using the notion of re-imagination.

Shelley wrote two essays on vegetarianism, one used as note 17 to *Queen Mab*, which was also published as a pamphlet called *A Vindication of Natural Diet*, and another, usually called 'On the Vegetable System of Diet' (1814–15). *A Refutation of Deism* (1814) is also discussed, as well as the unfinished piece on the Game Laws.

The chapter begins with a discussion of Shelley's reading of Plutarch and his four major vegetarian prose works, including an analysis of the theme of 'disfiguration' in three major poems. Then the works of Joseph Ritson and Monboddo, consulted by Shelley in writing the poem and notes which make up *Queen Mab*, are interpreted. There follows a reading of two other major sources, Lambe and Newton. The chapter tries to account for a number of different themes in Shelley's vegetarian prose: nature, humanity, cultural degeneration, sociopathology and social reform.

While studies by such writers as Cameron read these texts from a history-of-ideas standpoint, no study has attempted such a political and contextual reading of their figurative patterns as the one offered here. Hogle provides a brief but eloquent reading in *Shelley's Process*.[2] He shows how, in Ovid's *Metamorphoses* xv (the Pythagoras episode), emulative desire is set up by transference and how this leads to the violent simulation of the violence of others (Ovid's lions); Girard's 'mimetic desire' or my 'disfiguration'. Hogle invests in Shelley's own Utopian ideas and in doing so interprets desire as lack. Thus 'transference' is a valuable tool for seeing how Shelley's writing *decodes* the despotic signifier (of God, tyrant, man against woman, the ego, the carnivore) into a sequence of transferential flows. However, Hogle is unable to see how these decoded flows are then *axiomatized* (for example in the codes of temperance; put crudely, why is Shelley so nice to animals but so nasty to Irishmen?).[3] Polar thinking (rather than binarizing thinking) is employed in this chapter to show the ambiguities and complexities of the discourse of natural diet. Of the rhetorical strategies which Shelley's discourse employs, *elision* is the most significant. It seems appropriate to read in a way which will pay attention to this constant sliding back-and-forth between the apparent binary (but latent unit) of 'culture' and 'nature'. This kind of elision, far from generating a playful deconstructive scepticism, helps to produce a new kind of body. Neither 'left' culturalist readings (very broadly defined), nor deconstructive readings have shown how *aporia* can be productive in this way.

SHELLEY'S READING AND TRANSLATION OF PLUTARCH

Shelley's actual translations of Plutarch are not extant, but evidence of Shelley's interpretation of Plutarch can be found at the end of *Queen Mab*, note 17, where Shelley provides a montage of passages from περι σαρκοφαγιας.[4] These essays were part of a series which Plutarch delivered in his youth, possibly to a Boeotian audience.[5]

The first quotation can be translated:

You call serpents and panthers and lions savage [ἀγρίους, from the wilds], but you yourselves, by your own foul slaughters [μιαιφονειτε, 'you slaughter and generate *miasma*'], leave them no room to outdo you in cruelty; for their slaughter is their living [τροφη, 'bent'], yours is a mere appetite.[6]

This passage establishes a contrast between natural and unnatural diet. The connotations of *miaiphoneite*, 'pollute by slaughter', render parallels between body and soul, medicine and ethics, explicit. The second quotation presents both comparative anatomy and *macellogia*, exhorting the addressee to slay 'an ox with your fangs or a boar with your jaws, or tear a lamb or hare in bits. Fall upon it and eat it still living, as animals do.'[7] Shelley would also have encountered the figure at the beginning of Plutarch's first essay.[8] Plutarch's use of *pephukenai* (to be 'naturally' inclined or designed (to eat fish)) was also important for him.

The next quotation is fascinating. Shelley shortens a story about a Spartan who brings fish to an inn and asks the innkeeper to prepare it. The innkeeper asks for cheese, vinegar and oil, and the Spartan replies that if he had those, he would not have brought a fish.[9] Here *trophê* takes on a different meaning, not of a natural turn or bent but of a deviation, a turn *from* nature:

But we are so refined in our blood-letting [οὑτῶς ἐν τῷ μιαφονῷ τρυφῶμεν] that we term flesh a supplementary food [ὄψον το κρεας προσαγορευομεν] and then we need 'supplements' for the flesh itself, mixing oil, wine, honey, fish paste, vinegar, with Syrian and Arabian spices, as though we were really embalming a corpse for burial [ὥσπερ ὀντῶς νεκρον ἐνταφιαζοντες]. The fact is that meat is so softened and dissolved and, in a way, predigested that it is hard for digestion to cope with it, and if digestion loses the battle, the meats affect us with dreadful pains and malignant forms of indigestion.[10]

The idea that meat-eating is supplementary and, moreover, associated with dietary supplements which *disguise* death while *bringing out* flavour connects meat with (unnatural) representation. The logic of the supplement aids the idea that to eat flesh is to turn one's body into a tomb, a *sarkophagos*. The discourse of the supplement also affects the orientalized flow of spices across the integrity of the Roman imperial boundary. In *A Vindication*, 'sanguinary national disputes' are created through trade wars over 'those multitudinous articles of luxury' such as 'spices from India' or wines, dangerously supplemental commodities.[11] A politicized sense of what Derrida means by the *supplement* will be developed in the section on Shelley's sources, Lambe and Trotter. The final quotation, from Plutarch's second essay, demonstrates the progress from slaughtering 'wild' animals to slaughtering 'domestic' ones (like 'the well-behaved sheep'), to 'wars' and 'murder' amongst humans themselves.[12]

Many elements of Shelley's vegetarian writing exist in embryo in his selective reading of Plutarch. Shelley skilfully modifies these elements so that they form part of a generally Utopian discourse on diet that emphasizes the role of the political and symbolic order.[13]

QUEEN MAB NOTE 17 AND A VINDICATION OF NATURAL DIET

A Vindication of Natural Diet (1813), and note 17 to *Queen Mab*, begin by broaching the subject of 'nature' immediately: 'I hold that the depravity of the physical and moral nature of man originated in his unnatural habits of life.'[14] The opening paragraph then follows

Ritson's first chapter by discussing 'the origin of man'.[15] Shelley is concerned with the mythographical representations of the Fall included in 'nearly all religions':[16] the story 'that at some distant point man forsook the path of nature, and sacrificed the purity and happiness of his being to unnatural appetites'.[17] This is a near-anthropological approach to myth. The Eden story follows, along with Milton's representation of a hospital.[18] Shelley, who constantly converses with Milton in his writing, cannot help adding after the 'lazar-house' quotation: 'And how many thousands more might not be added to this frightful catalogue!'[19]

Thus nature and the unnatural are put in play. Shelley then follows Newton and tells the story of Prometheus.[20] The Eden story and this story are both read as 'allegorical'.[21] For vegetarianism acts as a master-code for interpreting all Fall narratives. Shelley discusses Hesiod and Horace who represent the Golden Age.[22] Newton also reads the vulture attacking Prometheus' liver as an allegory about alcoholic consumption. Shelley reads it as a punishment (by disease) for the invention of fire which disguises 'the horrors of the shambles'.[23] Vegetarianism not only reveals the 'plain ... language' within or behind (mythical) figurative language,[24] but also interprets meat production and consumption as modes of (dis)figuration: disease 'consumed his [Prometheus'] being in every shape of its loathsome and infinite variety, inducing the soul-quelling sinkings of premature and violent death'.[25] Food should not consume the consumer. Now 'natural' and 'unnatural' may be transposed into 'innocence' and 'vice': 'All vice arose from the ruin of healthful innocence.'[26] Shelley can then trace political oppression to the vices of the body. Since a meat diet induces 'the wanderings of exacerbated passion', it can bring about 'Tyranny, superstition, commerce, and inequality'.[27]

Shelley then quotes Newton on Prometheus *verbatim*.[28] He expands Newton's idea that thirst for water is unnatural if fruits are taken to contain as much water as a vegetarian would need. Shelley supposes that any 'culinary preparation', whether of meat or not, might exacerbate thirst.[29] It is not simply meat which is wrong for Shelley and Newton but cooking. The natural diet can at this point be read as a return to rawness, pre-cultural crudity.[30]

By now, nature and the unnatural, innocence and vice, health and disease, the raw and the cooked, the plain and the figurative (or disguised) are all in play. Thus a number of metaphorical connections

may be made. Society is a disease: 'Man, and the animals whom he
has infected with his society, or depraved by his dominion, are alone
diseased.'[31] Domestic, as opposed to wild, animals are corrupted and
diseased (Ritson provided examples).[32] Shelley is now writing not
only about human health (and moral hygiene), but also about the
social consequences of diet on entire species. Now language, what
differentiates humans from animals (though Shelley is careful to say
'fellow animals'), comes into the picture again: 'The supereminence
of man is like Satan's, a supereminence of pain; and the majority of
his species, doomed to penury, disease, and crime [a typically
Malthusian 'miasmatic tricolon'], have reason to curse the untoward
event, that by enabling him to communicate his sensations, raised
him above the level of his fellow animals.'[33] Shelley emphasizes
language as a near-contagious force of communication. Satan and
Prometheus both stand for the human race, and Shelley has not yet
quite worked out which one he prefers; he did so later in the preface
to *Prometheus Unbound*. The elision of species and society is another
way in which 'natural', fundamental errors are seen as the *root* of
human problems. Vegetarianism is, indeed, a *radical* discourse.

Vegetarianism involves two other kinds of radical language,
performing different tasks. One is transformative-magical: a key for
changing one's body (or nature). The other is conformative-
scientific: mapping representation perfectly onto the body (or
nature). The ideological effect of vegetarian rhetoric results from the
sliding together of these two languages: the suggestion arises that by
acting upon the body (or nature) so as to alter it we come to know it
as it really is. Vegetarian language is redeemed language, unlike
Promethean language, the language of cooking, which disguises and
disfigures. It *recalls* the body to an original state while ensuring that
no Fall can take place.[34] In Shelley it is a Utopian language: it does
not advocate a return to the past, but a return back to the future
which in some way is a perfect sublimation of an originary perfection.

At this point, Shelley opts for the conformative-scientific language:
'The whole of human science is comprised in one question: – How
can the advantages of intellect and civilisation, be reconciled with the
liberty and pure pleasures of natural life?'[35] Science is there to map
civilization perfectly onto nature: society will thus re-imagine nature
– recall a natural state while preserving social 'advantages'. The
phrase 'human science' could be read not only as 'the sum of all
sciences' but also as 'sociology' or 'psychology' at this period: as a

particular *kind* of object of scientific enquiry.[36] The idea that sociological knowledge is a naturalistic *and* improving discourse becomes important later in *A Vindication*.

Note 17 to *Queen Mab* follows with a paragraph omitted in *A Vindication* on 'other deviations from rectitude and nature': 'The mistakes cherished by society respecting the connection of the sexes'; 'the putrid atmosphere of crowded cities, the exhalations of chemical processes'; 'the muffling of our bodies in superfluous apparel' and 'the absurd treatment of infants'.[37] These points are more at home in the expansive atmosphere of *Queen Mab* and its notes, though all strive to differentiate between 'natural' and 'unnatural'. Vegetarianism engages issues of sexuality, urban ecology, industry, and the pathology of everyday life. Shelley's ominous note about 'exhalations' anticipates twentieth-century ecological thinking. These intersections of corporeal and corporate interests provoke questions of limiting and unlimiting flows (of population, libido, technology and industrial products). Shelley admired Henry Lawrence, author of *The Empire of the Nairs* (1811); Lawrence had remarked on how animals were free in love in a state of nature, and admired the 'simplicity' of the Indian dress at a festival on the banks of the Indus, describing the natives as 'naked, but purity is clothed in nakedness'.[38] Newton and his family were naturists.

From the general introduction of science, Shelley continues with comparative anatomy.[39] The biotechnological alteration of bulls into oxen and rams into wethers is then discussed as a degradation performed so that 'the flaccid fibre may offer a fainter resistance to rebellious [human] nature'.[40] This 'operation' is 'unnatural and inhuman' another rhetorical elision.[41] What made humans human a while before was language, associated with 'unnatural', artificial practices like cooking. Now it is *inhuman* to be 'unnatural'. This elision suggests that there is a genuine or original human nature, essentially good, but subsequently perverted. To be truly human is to be humane.

Shelley here cites Rees' *Cyclopaedia*.[42] In the article 'Man' William Lawrence proposes a prototype of anthropology, as the investigation of what falls out of the studies of the historian or the moralist, 'the description of species': the history of human 'notions of decency… honor [sic] and shame… the education of children and treatment of women', not 'inferior to the narratives of intrigue and treachery, of war, conquest and desolation, that compose general history'.[43]

Lawrence's proposal of a science of man is also a proposal for more dignified, reasoned modes of representation, not time-serving teleological narratives. *A Vindication* may be read as an early example of comparative anthropology, turning a discourse which was designed to account for New-World, non-Christian cultures, upon the culture which invented it.

A Vindication continues with an example of *macellogia* considerably stronger than the passage of Plutarch alluded to.[44] A rhetorical shift has also taken place. If everyone was a butcher, animal food would be considered disgusting. But we have moved from cookery (disguising the 'bloody juices and raw horror') to killing (revealing the raw): 'Let the advocate of animal food ... tear a living lamb with his teeth, and plunging his head into its vitals, slake his thirst with the steaming blood.' Corruption is no superficial gloss of vice but influences the material body itself.

Shelley then discusses comparative anatomy further, citing 'numerous instances' found in Ritson about domestic animals 'and even wood-pigeons' who were 'taught to live upon flesh, until they have loathed their natural aliment'.[45] Recent cases of BSE or 'mad cow disease' in Britain, caused by cows eating sheep's offal, bear out the relation between meat-consumption and disease. Rousseau's *Emile*, probably from the references in Ritson, is echoed concerning children: 'Young children evidently prefer pastry, oranges, apples, and other fruit, to the flesh of animals.'[46] The children figure as originary humans, naturally humane, pre-social yet embodying the potential best elements of civilization.

The next paragraph asks 'What is the cause of morbid action [tending towards death] in the animal system?'[47] Nature is exonerated – 'the unobscured sight of glorious nature' is not the cause.[48] Shelley is contrasting vision with fallen representation. 'Glorious nature' is open to the sight. Its corruption involves disguise, producing a 'sight of ... raw horror'.[49] The cause must be 'Something then wherein we differ from them ['the undiseased inhabitants of the forest']'.[50] Here the 'instinct' of a child should be trusted more than the 'reasoning' of an adult.[51]

How then is reason to be redeemed? By being naturalized. This is the content of the next paragraph, which Shelley considered so important that he cited it in 'Vegetable System'.[52] It begins with the vital enthymemic syllogism: 'Crime is madness. Madness is disease', a startling pair of sentences.[53] Its basis is 'Crime ... is disease' – crime is unnatural, following the linguistic play of the opening passages of *A Vindication*. But the most powerful effect is to naturalize reason by making 'madness' into a diseased, corrupt supplement of humanity.[54] This effect is most noticeable when the sentences are read as they should not be, backwards: 'Disease is madness. Madness is crime.' The two *is*'s are not functioning like a pure equals sign (=), though this is their ideological effect in a paragraph which adapts the language of 'human science'.[55] They transform a cultural 'perversion', crime, into a natural 'perversion', disease, via the ambiguous supplement of madness. Culture, the cooked, is a transgression of nature which also perverts nature, the raw. Reasoned science may stop this perversion but is itself an aspect of culture (Shelley is self-consciously explicit about this), which from its inception involved perverse disfigurings of nature. Prometheus *is* human nature, he 'represents the human race',[56] but he is also a dangerous *supplement* to it, giving language, cookery, animal food – disease and death – to humans. He is like 'madness', joining the two sentences through an *is* which is really performing a supplementary function. How Prometheus can think himself out of this madness became a preoccupation in *Prometheus Unbound*. Prometheus brought fire for cooking and also medicine. To turn culture into medicine is one of the significant prescriptions of *A Vindication*. Shelley introduces the idea of 'culture' (though unstated) as an always-already naturalized social body, to be eternally disciplined by the 'natural' and policed by reason.

Thus *A Vindication* is not simply advocating a 'return to nature' but a way of *naturalizing culture*. Naturalistic forms of representation (anthropology, quasi-sociology, medicine) are described as accurate representations of culture. These representations become ethical norms, likened to the caring attention of the gaze (rather than the dangerous disease of language). Human sciences are the path of humanity's return to a naturally good nature, which is another way of saying that human reflexivity is natural: *re-imagining the body*.

Crime is an excess of carnivorous passions: 'blood-shot eyes, and swollen veins'.[57] Shelley then coyly asserts that vegetarianism 'promises no Utopian advantages', though this is precisely its function.[58] It is said to go beyond representation, this time in an explicitly political sense: 'It is no mere reform of legislation ... it strikes at the root of all evil.'[59] One of the most eminently political aspects of natural diet is its claim to *transcend* politics. Of course the suppressed term here would be 'money' (the love of money as the root of all evil, 1 Timothy 6: 10). Later Shelley criticizes the injustices of food production and circulation in a system based on 'commerce'. This paragraph, however, is principally concerned with reason as both analysis and cure, an operation of temperate observation and virtuous behaviour. The body is the locus of an examination of a corrupt system of institutions which render it harmful to itself. Ultimately, sociology may be collapsed into physiology – another naturalization: 'Should ever a physician be born with the genius of Locke, I am persuaded that he might trace all bodily and mental derangements to our unnatural habits, as clearly as that philosopher has traced all knowledge to sensation.'[60] Disease, 'the root from which all vice and misery have too long overshadowed the globe, will [be laid] bare to the axe'.[61] 'Vice and misery' is a token of Shelley's engagement with Malthusian social theory. Shelley revises the rhetoric of vice and misery as natural afflictions in Malthus' *Essay on Population*, declaring them to be artificial, institutional afflictions. But he does so in the name of *naturalistic* forms of social representation. It would thus be simplistic to say that Shelley completely opposed Malthusian language.

Vegetarianism may be engaged in any social territory. Its effects can be demonstrated 'not alone by nations, but by small societies, families, and even individuals'.[62] There follows a highly charged passage on intemperance, politics and religion.[63] Vegetarianism is used to out-trope Christianity: an animal diet is the 'original and universal sin'.[64] Vegetarianism serves to limit flows (of desire, of currency) through nations or any of the other kinds of 'body' in which Shelley is interested. These limits are ambivalent. For example, mother nature, the 'bosom of the earth', opposes the full bodies of monopoly capitalism and tyranny, but this 'primitivism' is projected into the future. In this sense the natural diet does not only decode (as it decodes Christian Fall narratives), but also reterritorializes. It opens, unlimits, then delimits according to physiological, numerical axioms.

The next paragraph is medical, stressing the vegetable diet's renewal of the body: 'The very sense of being would then be a continued pleasure, such as we now feel it in some few and favoured moments of our youth.'[65] Shelley eloquently emphasizes the political and ecological aspects of diet: 'The monopolizing eater of animal flesh would no longer destroy his constitution [is there a deliberate play on words here?] by devouring an acre at a meal'; 'vegetable matter' would 'if gathered immediately from the bosom of the earth' provide 'ten times the sustenance' than the same food 'consumed in fattening the carcase of an ox'.[66] Vegetables stand for living nature, fresh, young, undiseased, while (domestic) animals are made to stand for dead nature, rotting, old and diseased. There is a sacred code behind this sentence: the idea that the flesh eater is a *sarkophagos*, an eater of death whose body is a tomb rather than a temple.[67]

Meat production is associated with wealth and privilege, and with 'commercial monopoly'.[68] Shelley finally strikes a note rung by others in the period: 'the use of animal flesh and fermented liquors, directly militates with this equality of the rights of man'.[69] Pratt's *Bread* (1803) and Shelley's experience on the Tremadoc embankment project are used to illustrate how vegetarianism may sustain a restricted, efficiency-driven, economy.[70]

Shelley then revises Trotter by seeing 'Animal flesh, in its effects on the human stomach' as analogous to a dram of alcohol.[71] Vegetables purge physical and moral excess: the scheme posits a closed, homeostatic model of the body, informed by cool reason and corrupted by hot passion. Vegetarianism is 'plain fare' for which the only 'sauce' is 'appetite'.[72] This is the second use of 'plain' (first used to describe the 'plain language' of myth interpreted as an allegory about diet).[73] The positive value placed upon *plain* resembles the recipe book *On Food*.

Shelley's linkage of psyche and polis, passion and revolution, was in earnest. It was a common topos to associate the English with 'beef and battles', as Byron puts it in *Don Juan* (II.clvi.1248). But in *A Vindication*, Robespierre and Napoleon are both criticized for excessive passion, and here the natural diet literally cools revolutionary fervour into reformist zeal. The intensity of passion may establish the despot: it is possible to invest a social field libidinally, and this investment may generate a desire for enslavement. Indeed in the rhetoric of natural diet, it seems inevitable that the social field is actually *constituted* through libidinal investments (I am here indebted to the insights offered by Deleuze and Guattari). It is nevertheless true that the discourses of domesticity and popular asceticism in both the Shelleys and Newton seek to close off and privatize this open perspective. The re-imagined body will not be disciplined by tyrants and tyrannical signs, but by internalized, private and abstract codes of health and justice. The flow of meat is associated with the flow of passion and with the tyrannical signifier. '"Muley Ismail"' and '"Nero"' are described as bloodhounds in Shelley's quotation, in the notes to *Queen Mab*, from a poem published in *The German Magazine* (1802).[74]

Meat is intimately connected with language, whether it is linked with the emergence of civilization and the death of natural innocence, or whether it is seen as sustaining a social economy, as a social discourse. To redeem language from its fallen state is to redeem the body cut up in the votive offering which founds the social order – to re-imagine the social body through its origins.[75] Meat and representation are born together: in *A Vindication* Prometheus invents the fire which becomes 'an expedient for screening from [man's] disgust the horrors of the shambles'.[76] From this derives 'Tyranny, superstition, commerce, and inequality'.[77] The domestic animals created for consumption are fake, unorganic, incapable of sustaining an autotelic life.[78] Meat is figured as monopoly in Shelley, the sign of power: it represents 'an acre at a meal'.[79] If England was vegetarian it would be 'organic', self-governing: its citizens would no longer 'depend on the caprices of foreign rulers';[80] in addition this newly autotelic society would not be subject to 'sanguinary national disputes'.[81] The meat industry is linked to the aristocracy, preventing a surge in peasant population by enclaving meat's circulation. In 'Vegetable System' Shelley emphasizes the opposition between naturalness and artifice, linking meat to artificial social rituals of 'ambition', 'slavery', 'imposture' and 'credulity'.[82] Meat underpins rituals of Christmas consumption, in which 'torture' renders up 'brawn for the gluttonous repasts with which Christians celebrate the anniversary of their Saviour's birth'.[83] Producing, consuming and recording food can either 'express' or 'disfigure' a natural order; in the latter respect they become metonymic of a social *disorder*.

DISFIGURED FIGURES IN SHELLEY'S POETRY

In the note on necessity in *Queen Mab*, Shelley criticizes the false incarnation of 'God' from 'metaphor' to 'real being', a parallel of the 'earthly monarch': 'God' is the despotic signifier.[84] In *Falsehood and Vice: a Dialogue*, which Shelley wrote in Dublin in 1812 and revised for *Queen Mab* a year later, Religion is said to be the daughter of Falsehood (49) who 'smothered Reason's babes in their birth' (50); Shelley resists the embodiment of God and the body of the monarch. This embodiment is associated with a deliberate mutilation of the innocent physical body, and with the imposition of a despotic signifier which overcodes the tyrant through 'God' and the priest. In contrast, nature's 'argument' is an infinite flow of 'silent eloquence' (*Queen Mab* VII.17–22).

Shelley thus links (false) representation with religion, and this in turn is associated with power and with the physical disfigurement of flesh. *Falsehood and Vice* describes the sadistic enjoyment of monarchs who disfigure the 'famished' body of the nation (1–4, quoted in the introduction). The natural diet provided powerful ways of discussing the violence of the symbolic systems of monarchy and religion, by rendering ethical language universal, and by making the Fall narrative terrestrial, secular and material. Three autobiographical examples of the anxiety provoked by a sense of figuration as *catachresis* or disfiguration are found in the *Letter to Maria Gisborne* (1820), *Epipsychidion* (1820–21) and *Adonais* (1821).[85]

In *Adonais* the narrator declares that he has 'gazed on Nature's naked loveliness' (275) and thus is hunted down like Actaeon (who gazed on Artemis), by his own thoughts, which 'Pursued, like raging hounds, their father and their prey' (279). Self-reflexiveness and violence ('father' and 'prey') are linked through a predatory image. Urania tells how beasts of prey fled at Adonais' presence (244–52). Urania is drawn upon by Milton and Wordsworth as a source of poetic inspiration. The narrator-as-Actaeon thus not only interrupts naked Nature with self-consciousness but also disfigures poetic language. Shelley follows last in the train following Urania:

> of that crew
> He came the last, neglected and apart;
> A herd-abandoned deer, struck by the hunter's dart.   (295)

Self-reflection is ironic, refusing to guarantee a fully-present self-image.[86] Representation as a form of predation is also ironic, since thought, to understand itself, pursues itself to destruction. These ideas are played with in the *Letter to Maria Gisborne*:

> If living winds the rapid clouds pursue,
> If hawks chase doves through the aethereal way,
> Huntsmen the innocent deer, and beasts their prey,
> Why should not we rouse with the spirit's blast
> Out of the forest of the pathless past
> These recollected pleasures?   (187)

Shelley rather comically asserts the rights of the chase associated with feudal power, by ironically presenting the freedom to explore one's own past as the license of an aristocrat to sport in his territory. The 'pleasures' have already been 'recollected', but they also need to be roused with violence. The paradox involved here echoes the opening paradox of a description of nature from which violence has been violently effaced ('Satiated with destroyed destruction', 41).[87] This sort of nature is associated with political oppression (35), since it contains the wreckage of past oppressive (and thus, for Shelley, inevitably failed) social orders. The self-reflexive figure of 'destroyed destruction' destroys itself. In contrast, the promise of a meeting with Maria draws upon images of past frugality in diet to elucidate the innocent intent of Shelley's self-presentation:

> how we often made
> Feasts for each other, where good will outweighed
> The frugal luxury of our country cheer;   (150)
>
> Though we eat little flesh and drink no wine
> Yet let's be merry: we'll have tea and toast;
> Custards for supper, and an endless host
> Of syllabubs and jellies and mince-pies,
> And other such lady-like luxuries, –
> Feasting on which we will philosophize!   (302)

The gendering of non-meat diet is obvious here, though perhaps in a different register from the gendering of nature in the vegetarian prose. Shelley criticizes Trotter's position on tea, 'The liquor doctors rail at' (88) in a sequence of lines which withhold the article until the final word, thus prompting an association with alcohol.[88] Shelley's excess is licensed as food for philosophy.

The following lines from *Epipsychidion* also betray a certain anxiety about representation (as a form of self-reflexivity) and its implication in violence:

> In many mortal forms I rashly sought
> The shadow of that idol of my thought.
> And some were fair – but beauty dies away:
> Others were wise – but honeyed words betray:
> And One was true – oh! why not true to me!
> Then, as a hunted deer that could not flee,
> I turned upon my thoughts, and stood at bay,
> Wounded and weak and panting.   (267)

Emilia Viviani, the addressee, is likened to an antelope (75): the antelope is a metonym for the kind of nature which Shelley desires to be recuperated by a reformed humanity. The passage about Shelley's self-reflexive act has become important in recent thinking about his inscription of figures about figures.[89] Elsewhere, however, self-reflexive figures appear as images of bodies in the text.

'VEGETABLE SYSTEM'

In the closing passage of *A Vindication* Shelley writes that it is 'custom' that turns 'poison into food'.[90] The 'Essay on the Vegetable System of Diet' (1815) starts with a general discussion of 'custom', developing *A Vindication*.[91] A common assumption is made that this essay was written after *A Vindication*. There is certainly less explicit dependence on Newton and Ritson in the main body of the text, which once suggested a 'redaction'.[92] Milton's hospital appears in another form,[93] but instead of directly quoting him Shelley quotes Southey, whom he had met, on the influence of drink and intemperance on the individual.[94] There are points of close similarity with *A Vindication*. A point about 'unnatural and inhuman' degradations of selective breeding repeats it *verbatim*.[95] The example of *macellogia* is also repeated, incorporating a note of silent eloquence in the 'inarticulate cries' of boiling lobsters.[96] The sentence 'Horses, sheep, oxen and even wood pidgeons [sic] have been taught to live upon flesh until they have loathed their natural aliment' is also repeated.[97]

Some textual evidence supports the idea that the essay was written in 1815. The 'Mary' in the manuscript[98] suggests that it was written after 1814, and besides, there are no manuscripts extant before that date.[99] There is a footnote omitted in the *Julian* edition to 'Hyppolytus [sic] 953'.[100] Euripides' *Hippolytus* 953 is about vegetable diet:

> set out thy paltry wares
> Of lifeless food: take Orpheus for thy king:
> Rave, worship vapourings of many a scroll.[101]

Orphism proscribed animal food. According to the Shelleys' reading-lists, Shelley read the works of Euripides in 1815, and *Hippolytus* (again?) in 1818.[102] The poem beginning 'Oh! there are spirits of the air' (1815) has a Greek epigraph from *Hippolytus*. The passage may have appealed to Shelley since an irate father is admonishing a reprobate son. There is also a quotation from Cicero's *De natura deorum* used in *A Refutation of Deism* (1814).[103] It is likely, given this evidence, that 'Vegetable System' was written between 1814 and 1815, possibly after *A Refutation of Deism*, and the use of *Hippolytus* inclines the date towards 1815. The Cicero quotation is also about a busybody God as a reflection of a busybody person, 'the hell which priests and beldams feign'.[104] Theosophus' point in *Deism* is about the unscrupulous atheist, who does not fear God taking care of everything who, being unscrupulous '*Iste non timeat...*'.[105] But deism itself is supported by the watchmaker mentality. Shelley is satirizing the neurotic God and the neurotic believer (resulting from torture and blindness to torture), by re-inflecting the quotation. Was Shelley intending to publish a collected series of essays, and is this evidence for it?

'Vegetable System' is shorter than *A Vindication*, but its sweep is more powerful. Political statements are swept up into the argument as often as possible. Shelley commences with a list of man's 'habitual ...perverse propensities'.[106] He imagines oppressive society as a version of brutal (violent and inarticulate) nature – a disfigured nature:

the narrow and malignant passions which have turned man against man, as a beast of blood [or prey], the unenlightened brutality of the multitude and the profligate selfishness of courts are *cherished* by errors which have been rendered venerable by antiquity and consecrated by custom.[107]

'Man against man' is an echo of Pope's *Essay on Man*. 'Cherished', with its suggestion of 'sustained' and 'nurtured', sets up a model in which investments in the physical world of the body are linked to libidinal investments in (or as) a social field. 'Scientific disquisition', as in *A Vindication*, comes to the rescue.[108]

Shelley again develops interrelationships between stomach and brain, science and politics, recycling the 'kindling' figure:

A popular objection which never fails to be opposed to every reasoning of this nature [that human morality and suffering are influenced by diet] is, that it is incorrect to ascribe such mighty effects to causes so comparatively trivial. Such nevertheless are the laws of the world which we inhabit. A spark well kindled will consume the most sumptuous palace.[109]

Milton's hospital is revised once again:

Hospitals are filled with a thousand screaming victims; the palaces of luxury and the hovels of indigence resound alike with the bitter wailings of disease, idiotism and madness grin and rave amongst us, and all these complicated calamities result from those unnatural habits of life to which the human race has addicted itself during innumerable ages of mistake and misery.[110]

Shelley gets his 'thousands' in where Milton had failed.[111] The hospitals are now the paradigms of society – they anticipate the palaces and hovels, informed by Shelley's model of sociology as physiology. Humans are imagined crying like animals: 'screaming', 'resound', 'bitter wailings', 'rave'. Rich and poor, tyrant and slave, are seen as 'victims' of the same disfiguration. This has already been prepared for by 'the unenlightened brutality of the multitude and the profligate selfishness of courts'.[112]

Shelley's later prose shows how he adapted this dual picture of social wrongs in many different contexts. Consider, for example, the alliance between despotic governments and a brutish populace at the end of 'On the Punishment of Death', or the combination in 'A Philosophical View of Reform' of 'popular systems of faith' and a 'superstructure of political and religious tyranny'.[113] The equation of luxury with barbarism is also a common pattern in Newton and Lambe. Shelley's social science of the body does to society epistemologically what disease does to it physiologically – levelling and equating classes, collapsing the social into the species ('the human race'), like the plague in Mary Shelley's *The Last Man*. This levelling pestilence is represented as an aspect of death in *Alastor*, where it appears at the end of the Poet's quest for ultimate knowledge. Shelley has to try to redeem the knowledge which reduces society to a diseased, screaming victim, so that reason can reform society. This may explain the final footnote in 'Vegetable System', which challenges Aristotle's physics and politics of *technê* and *physis*: 'The monstrous sophism that beasts are pure unfeeling machines and do not reason scarcely requires a confutation.'[114] There is a compact between man and the nature of which he is a part, including his relationship with other animals, that is broken by unthinking and oppressive regimes, and by oppressive beliefs that operate in parallel with these regimes, including the belief that animals possess no soul (Kant, Descartes, Aristotle). The maltreatment of all living bodies derives from these regimes and beliefs. A purely technological or mechanistic attitude towards nature will not do (here is Shelley's cry against industrial capitalism), since form is immanent in matter (as elaborated by Bruno and Spinoza).

From a study of the manuscript of 'Vegetable System' it is possible to perceive the emphasis placed by Shelley on the 'natural', including his commitment to a reasoned, sociopathological linguistic scheme (a form of naturalism). For example, he substitutes 'the faculties of the mind' for the vaguer 'energy of thought'.[115] He changes 'monstrous' dreams into 'portentous' ones.[116] To convince men of 'The speculative truths of moral science' means previously 'securing an ⟨undiseased⟩ / understanding, ⟨& a physical⟩ ⟨the advantage of a natural state⟩ / ⟨of body⟩'.[117] Shelley follows current medical thinking in his deleted sentence '⟨The impetuousness / of the animal appetites, which arises from unnatural excitability, & then extreme languor...⟩'.[118] William Smellie's *The Philosophy of Natural History* (1790, 1799) showed that 'vulgar and uninformed men, when pampered with a variety of animal food, are much more choleric, fierce, and cruel in their tempers than those who live chiefly on vegetables. Animal food heats the blood, and makes it circulate with rapidity.'[119] Shelley changes the 'imperfect' cries of animals into 'inarticulate' ones, following Monboddo (see the following section).[120] 'Complicated parts' provides a more scientific-sounding description of a human 'machine' than 'several parts'.[121]

The linguistic changes demonstrate Shelley's thoughtful understanding of the figuration of nature. Thus 'there are certain habits / which have a tendency to produce health' becomes 'a tendency to preserve health, and others / on the practice of which ⟨disease⟩ organic derangement inevitably ensues'.[122] The body is perfect in a natural state, needing only preservation to save it from a disfiguration of its parts: health is in no way added or even produced. Shelley deletes 'unnatural' before 'malady': 'the invasions of malady' are necessarily unnatural.[123] The 'indefinite extent of human life' becomes its 'natural term'.[124] Shelley may have borrowed the concept of human 'organization' from the surgeon, Abernethy (although, *contra* Abernethy, organization here explains life):[125] '⟨This is the consequence of diseased organization, which / results from unnatural habits of life⟩';[126] and 'conformation' (a more organic-sounding word) replaces 'anatomical economy', which sounds rather old-fashioned.[127] Shelley uses Abernethy elsewhere in 'Vegetable System'.[128]

A glance at the agonies which Shelley suffers while trying to define 'nature' as precisely as possible demonstrates his commitment: '⟨I am The use of The word unnatural nature in this enquiry / is to be justified⟩ By an unnatural habit ⟨I mean⟩ is to be understood such an habit / ⟨pernici pernicious & I esteem it such an habit⟩ ... '.[129] The subsequent passage about the wild boar (which is misread by Ingpen and Peck as 'bear')[130] and sheep relies on the idea of a 'natural state'.[131] The domestication of animals was criticized in Lambe's *Constitutional Diseases*.[132] 'Accustomed aliment' is changed to 'natural ⟨diet &⟩ aliment'.[133] The volcano, which is used as an example of the trivial effects of non-living nature compared with those of human vice, has little relevance to 'animated beings' rather than simply on 'the human species', the original phrase in the manuscript.[134]

The sentences about the volcano allude to a passage about an earthquake in Godwin's *Political Justice*, which occurs in the context of statements about the dangers of violent revolution.[135] A volcano or earthquake would consume or 'swallow up' far less lives than the 'ill passions' generated by fratricide. Shelley tempers political agitation, editing out fervour for change: less of the axe suddenly striking the poison tree (very much the tone of *A Vindication*). Sociopathology is directed against 'events ... affecting the welfare of society': hatred, murder, rape, massacres, revolutions; but 'tyranny' is deleted.[136] The deletions in the following are similar: 'war, in which men are ⟨paid⟩ / hired to mangle & murder their fellow beings, ⟨that tyrants⟩ / ⟨& courtiers may profit by⟩ the ⟨[?]⟩ by thousands'.[137] 'Vegetable System' promotes social reform within established structures to a greater extent than *A Vindication*.

A REFUTATION OF DEISM

A Refutation of Deism (1814)[138] continues Shelley's discussion of vegetarianism. This essay was perhaps an element in a book of papers including 'Vegetable System', extending *Queen Mab* and its notes in the context of Mary, to accompany work in the *Alastor* volume. The work intervenes in a debate about natural religion, at a time when to be called a deist connoted radical free thought. Shelley pushes the subversion of the authority of revealed religion by natural religion one stage further. Why choose religion at all, why not just nature?

Ideas associating religion and violence towards the body are introduced by the deist speaker, Theosophus: the Biblical Moses is 'An unnatural monster who sawed his fellow beings in sunder, harrowed them to fragments under harrows of iron, chopped them to pieces with axes and burned them in brick-kilns' for religious treachery.[139] God cannot be 'the benevolent author of this beautiful world' if he allows these disfigurings.[140] An author should wish to preserve his text intact. The rhetoric of *sparagmos*, the tearing of flesh, excites sympathy: Theosophus deplores 'the crucifixion of an innocent *being*',[141] mixing 'tyranny' furiously with 'anarchy' to describe the 'state of savageness' which produced it.[142]

Theosophus then confesses his deism, distinguishing it from atheism.[143] The Christian Eusebes refutes him, emphasizing the key point that 'Design must be proved before a designer can be inferred [the deist argument from design].'[144] The question of design broaches the subject of organic unity, which establishes in turn a discussion of the body. The 'design' of the body of an animal might help to focus the issue. Eusebes tries to relativize and humanize the idea of design or order, to remove God from the discussion of universal harmony. Of course this serves Shelley's own designs by making atheism the only consistent (though unspoken) alternative to both deism and Christianity, since to believe in a system proved to be purely arbitrary, especially in the context of a debate about organicity, would be unacceptable.

Vegetarianism significantly allows the debate to proceed more through imagery and the rhetoric of sympathy than cold argument.[145] Hogg's criticism that it is 'brought in, dragged in' attests to the way in which it functions precisely as an *ideological* coding of an intellectual debate.[146] Moreover, it shows how perceptions of the moral basis of actions arise in relationships between bodies interacting in a system or 'organization' which needs no external justifying force. This is a related idea, since it presupposes the effects on the reader of the language of bodily pain. Vegetarianism is the primary, most substantial way by which Eusebes humanizes ethics. The physical 'laws of attraction and repulsion'[147] are extended in relationship with the moral world, the exploitation of sympathy and disgust. Shelley places these humanizing words into the mouth of a Christian ironically, given the manifest hatred of Christian carnivorousness in *A Vindication* and 'Vegetable System'.

Eusebes challenges the fundamental question of nature. He focuses upon the material which may or may not be designed. The vegetarian argument helps to show that ideas about the 'order' or 'disorder' of nature are too abstract.[148] If the universe can be explained without the ordering authorship of God, then Christianity must be accepted as an arbitrary explanation: its justification is itself, not the 'order' of nature. That nature can be seen to be riddled with the unnatural: Eusebes first describes the 'gluttonous and unnatural appetite for the flesh of animals' working against the natural organization of the human stomach.[149] Shelley cites Cuvier and Rees as he had done in *A Vindication*.[150] Cuvier's teleological functionalism was predicated on a method-based, organic form of life science in which the status of God could become radically problematic.[151]

Eusebes' argument assumes that *nature* is an ideological term. It does not exist 'out there' but is constituted between beings, as a means of expressing their relationships. Thus 'it is a strange perversion of the understanding to argue that a certain sheep was created to be butchered and devoured by a certain individual of the human species', given the lessons of 'comparative anatomy'.[152] The naturalness of meat-eating is disproved using the naturalistic language of science: natural history, the writing of nature. Nature need have no author, but is a self-writing text which throws questions of ethical choice back upon humans.

A self-writing text is an unsustainable paradox. Shelley's skill lies in not making the reader pause too long upon this elision. Again, vegetarianism provides a way out. Shelley next introduces it in terms not of natural history but of sympathy. The pacing of these two moves is powerful, since sympathy functions well to erase differences between writing and writer, observed and observer. The paragraph about carnivorousness deconstructs the absoluteness of any particular ethical point of view, but also rhetorically underscores one of these points of view as inherently natural. The natural and the artificial, the tiger and the human butcher, are melted together:

A beautiful antelope panting under the fangs of a tiger, a defenceless ox, groaning beneath the butcher's axe, is a spectacle which instantly awakens compassion in a virtuous and unvitiated breast. Many there are, however, sufficiently hardened to the rebukes of justice and the precepts of humanity, as to regard the deliberate butchery of thousands of their species, as a theme of exultation and a source of honour, and to consider any failure in these remorseless enterprises as a defect in the system of things.[153]

The antelope becomes the synecdoche for 'this beautiful world'.[154] 'Unvitiated' suggests that vice is super-added to a natural perfection which is then destroyed: it is a supplement which disfigures natural inclinations towards compassion. The passage could be divided into words evoking givenness and words evoking arbitrariness: if 'hardened' and 'deliberate' connote the arbitrary, then 'instantly', the 'spectacle' itself, and by extension, 'the rebukes of justice and the precepts of humanity' suggest the given. Justice and 'humanity' are naturalized in a very subtle way. Justice sounds the rebuke which should be heard in the cry of the innocent animals. Thus by the end of the paragraph a political judgment is set up: a horrified reaction in the reader to war, expected by the phrase 'deliberate butchery', is as natural as the 'compulsion' described at the beginning. *It is natural to maintain these political ideas.* The final, relativistic sentence now seems flat: 'The criteria of order and disorder are as various as those things from whose opinions and feelings they result.'[155] But the naturalizing of 'humanity' through vegetarian rhetoric now falls into place behind this rationalist relativism. A deconstruction of Shelley's scepticism, asserting a groundless play of irony, would be in danger of ignoring this effect. Both Wasserman and Hogle (who interprets Shelley as toying with deism without embracing its monolithic arguments), ignore such figurations of the body.

The passage maps nature onto culture, as with 'Crime is madness. Madness is disease.'[156] In the larger structure of *A Refutation of Deism*, the movement from nature to culture here mimes the broader sweep from 'scientific' representations of nature to ethical representations, from natural history to social policy. It is clear that 'true' nature (non-violent, the model of 'true' civilization) has been feminized in the language which delineates it as 'defenceless' and 'beautiful'. The sexual politics of Shelley's writing about diet show how he wishes to correct the dominating instrumentality of reason. Feminized nature is always-already a victim of violence, so that to care for it is more an exercise in the protective stewardship of brotherly love than the coercive domination of a father or the radically different love of a sister.

Shelley was fond of expressing the highest love in brotherly terms, an issue which is now becoming important in feminism, for example in the work of MacCannell. Feminist discussion shows how Shelley's politics of sympathy for the natural is also implicated in violence: 'Pity would be no more, / If we did not make somebody poor.'[157] The discourse of faciality is a significant factor in this regime of the brother, which is in danger of preserving 'women', 'real tribal peoples' and 'real ecosystems...only in fantasmic fashion'.[158] Shelley's attitude of sympathy is evocative of a certain class position.

In conclusion, the self-forming organization of the body in *Deism* is used as an argument against tyrannical assemblages, and includes animals as subject to these tyrannies. In *Deism*, the concept of 'organization' becomes non-vitalist and non-theological. Organization may be explained according to teleological functionalism. Theosophus declares:

> The adaption of certain animals to certain climates, the relations borne to each other by animals and vegetables, and by different tribes of animals; the relation lastly, between man and the circumstances of his external situation are so many demonstrations of Deity.[159]

Compare Eusebes, who goes further: the fact that certain animals exist in certain climates 'results from the consentaneity of their frames to the circumstances of their situation'.[160] In order to refute Theosophus' anthropocentric criticism of the injustice of Christianity (and ironically to play into the hands of the atheist reformer), Eusebes says:

> This whole scheme of things might have been, according to our practical conceptions, more admirable and perfect. Poisons, earthquakes, disease, war, famine and venemous [sic] serpents; slavery and persecution are the consequences of certain causes, which according to human judgment might have been dispensed with an [sic; 'in'?] arranging the economy of the globe.[161]

Eusebes means this ironically but Shelley also invests in this. The notion of an economy of the globe, a homeostatic system of regulated flows (including flows of justice and war), has over-ridden any final, arbitrating signifier to which it could be referred.

SHELLEY ON THE GAME LAWS

Writing about game and using it as a metaphorical language became politically significant in the 1790–1820 period. Shelley's short essay on the Game Laws (1814?), found in a Mary Shelley notebook that contains writing on Christianity, contributes to this tradition. Shelley's first paragraph opens up a space for the interests of the weak and poor, which in turn, at the explicitly vegetarian end of the essay, opens up a space for the animal body.

'Game Laws' raises the issue of representation at once: 'It is said that the House of Commons, though not an actual, is a virtual representation of the people.'[162] This virtuality is bound up with power: 'Undoubtedly such cannot be the case. They actually and virtually at present represent none but the powerful and the rich.'[163]

Shelley is anxious about the violence which a 'deception' or 'shadow' (borrowing Platonic terminology) could exert. 'Actually and virtually' conveys how represented interests are bound up with material interests.

Shelley makes 'the laws... for the preservation of game'[164] a synecdoche for Parliamentary (mis)representation, enabling a distinction to be drawn between legislation for the powerful and morality. They 'bring home to this assembly... a charge of corrupting the tastes and morals sacrificing the lives... imprisoning the persons, and trampling upon the property of the inhabitants of the same country',[165] in the name of a practice (blood-sports) deemed to be timelessly immoral: 'a barbarous and bloody sport, from which every enlightened and amiable mind [contemplates with] shrinks in abhorrence and disgust'.[166] Shelley can thus elide two kinds of radical language: an attack on institutions in which there is 'a distinction of ranks';[167] and an attack on violence towards the 'natural' bodies of animals. The game laws can be condemned as immiserating conspicuous consumption, but also as a 'direct contravention' of the 'courage, generosity, and gentleness' afforded by surplus value and lacked by 'men chained to the soil'.[168] This surplus includes culture ('literature', 'philosophy' and 'the imitative arts').[169] Thus 'animals' can be equated with humans: 'one man enjoys all the productions of human art and industry without any exertion of his own, whilst another earns the right of seeing his wife and children famish before his eyes, by providing for the superfluous luxuries of the former'; 'Persons of great property nurture animals on their estates for the sake of destroying them... to grind the weak to the dust of the earth.'[170] 'Sport' can be read as an overcoding of 'superfluous luxuries', challenging a stably-maintained cultural heritage which Shelley elsewhere upholds as the soul of humankind. Something is rotten in British culture which finds a synecdoche in its treatment of the 'natural', figured as the bodies of the worker and his family and the game animals.

Vegetarianism is now used to clinch the argument:

When an ox or a sheep is put to death that their flesh may serve for human food the pang to the beast is sudden and unforeseen [unlike the 'tort[ure]' suffered by game animals, an observation found elsewhere in the period]. The necessity ⟨for⟩ of the action to the very existence of man is supposed to be indispensable. ⟨I am of the most inspired thinkers have ever disputed this necessity. But in theory no one has ever said that to destroy and mangle⟩.

But ⟨But to the destruction of game no⟩. The ⟨innocence⟩ justifiableness of such action flows directly from the right of self-preservation. Yet the ⟨framers⟩ authors of our common law forbid butchers to decide as jurymen on the life of a ⟨criminal⟩ man because he is familiar, however innocently, with the death of beasts. But how shall those men be considered who go forth not from necessity, not ⟨to⟩ for the preservation, but ⟨to⟩ for the insult and outrage of their fellowmen to the mangling of living beings. And the case is as widely different between the mode of death of an ox and a sheep, and ⟨that⟩ a pheasant, or a hare, or a deer as ⟨the former⟩ is the ⟨mostly for⟩ are the [.]¹⁷¹

The essay was left unfinished. The deletions in the opening half show that Shelley was about to become involved in a more complex vegetarian argument. The first deleted sentence ('I am of the most inspired thinkers ...') attests to knowledge of writers on vegetarianism. It is used *rhetorically* to differentiate degrees and kinds of violence (necessary and unnecessary, superfluous). The mere introduction of vegetarian language, however, suggests that all human violence against animals is unnecessary and thus *unnatural*. This gives rise to another *aporia* between morality and law: meat-eating is a morally sanctioned form of self-preservation, but the law will not allow a butcher to sit on a jury deciding on the life of another human being (because butchery is morally corrupting).

Shelley does not want to implicate himself in a difficult debate here, but the associations of unnaturalness can be read in the use of 'mangle' and 'mangling', echoes of the language of *Queen Mab* VIII. The change of 'innocence' for 'justifiableness' and 'framers' for 'authors' (one can put a frame round something which already exists), establishes a context of artifice, into which the disfigurement suggested by 'mangling' fits. 'Mangling' suggests the artificial and violent distortion of the body. However, to talk of 'mangling' collapses social oppression not only into physical violence, but into the 'brutal'. Culture has slid into nature: the upper classes let us down in their barbarity, not in their refinement. Perhaps one reason for the unfinished state of the essay is Shelley's inability to sustain a contrast between 'mangling' a sheep and mangling a pheasant or deer, given his own commitment to natural diet in practice. Alternatively, once reduced to 'mangling', one kind of social violence can be equated with another, thus weakening Shelley's argument about social division. The discourse of natural diet slides around these areas of class contradiction.

Shelley was aware of a working-class radical audience, and perhaps the specific politics of the SSV criticized in journals like *The Medusa*, and Erskine's speech on animal rights in the House of Lords. The essay suggests that meat production is favourably different from ruling-class sport; but also that gaming, when associated with the discourse of vegetarian diet, enacts a violence constituting a certain kind of subject (a tyrant), and that ruling-class practices of conspicuous consumption are complicit with this. Shelley attempts to embrace the supposedly inarticulate through the rhetoric of ruling-class reform. Elsewhere, Shelley is scathing of *working-class* sport and consumption (for example, drinking). A version of temperance squares with rhetorics both of reform and return-to-nature. It looks like the workers will not be enjoying themselves whether they are complying or reforming.

SHELLEY'S SOURCES: RITSON AND MONBODDO

Both Ritson and Newton draw on a large store of contextual detail, sharing a liking for the poetry of Milton and Thomson and an interest in the French radicals; but Ritson is far more eclectic, citing a vast array of sources from Rousseau to classical literature and post-Renaissance travel writing. Newton's project seems more modest in its combination of medical and moral justifications of vegetable diet. While Newton conforms more to an image of the faddish middle-class radical, Ritson had notable Jacobin sympathies and seems more outspoken. He liked to be known as 'Citizen Ritson',[172] claiming that the *sans culottes* took a stance against animal food, citing the example of the Hindu Jacobin John Oswald.[173] Ritson's radically literalist textual practices, which involved him in a dispute with Thomas Percy,[174] may also have been interpreted as part of his general radical concerns, especially insofar as he equated the body with language.[175] *Animal Food* is certainly a fine piece of radical antiquarianism, persuasive through the richness of its sources and the frequency of repetitive echoes.

Like *Queen Mab*, the structuring trope of *Animal Food* is catascopy, the distant prospect from which society and human life can powerfully be surveyed. While Shelley's fairy takes Ianthe's spirit to the edge of the universe, Ritson starts with the beginning of time, and presents less of an argument than an encyclopaedic amassing of different kinds of theory, theogony and theodicy.[176] Ritson quotes Diderot on the verso of the title page: 'Je n'ai pas la témerité de pretendre reformer le genre humain, mais assez de courage pour dire la vérité', epitomizing the value placed on rationalism. The thinker is imaged as withdrawing from the 'evidence' he employs, seeming simply to arrange it, face up. There is an ideological complicity between conformative and transformative languages here: 'Give me somewhere to stand and I will move the earth.'[177]

The silent eloquence of nature needs no figuration. It is revealed to the natural historian who looks upon it with an objective gaze. We can begin to see how Ritson's vegetarian rhetoric values literalism above figuration.

Ritson sets Occident against Orient, artificial against natural, civilized against primitive. These oppositions may be subsumed under the opposition between arbitrary language and silent eloquence. Ritson uses exoticized or marginalized cultures, for example Indian and Celtic, to critique contemporary England, stressing a 'natural state' theory of human nature, which emphasizes the artificiality of language.[178] This leads us to the crux of vegetarian rhetoric – the politics of disfiguration. Ritson's discussion of '*Genera*' leads him from the great chain of being to man's relation to apes, especially the orang-outang, an issue of interest to late eighteenth-century science.[179] Primate research revealed an ambiguity about language. Man's articulacy distinguishes him from apes, 'but this can be no solid objection to the present system [of cosmogony], as language is no more natural to man than to many other animals'.[180] Language may distinguish humans from animals, but it is also what distinguishes them from their 'natural', fundamental selves. Ritson develops these ideas in a series of unusually long footnotes, citing Buffon on the language of apes,[181] pygmies as liminal human-animals,[182] and Rousseau's position against language as a cultural marker of territory: 'there is no national language peculiar to man'.[183] Ritson's anxiety about this matter is visible in his attempt to defuse it in footnote form. *The Edinburgh Review* noted correctly that his first chapter attempts to show how unnatural (in the sense of refined, civilized) vegetarianism is, and that the second chapter is concerned to show how unnatural (in the sense of unrefined, savage), meat-eating is.[184] Is this simply illogical, or indicative of vegetarianism's interpellation of culture in nature?

In order to understand Ritson on this point it is necessary to study

Monboddo. The attack on Ritson in *The Edinburgh Review* criticized the first chapter of *Animal Food* as a crass summary of Monboddo,[185] referring to Ritson's use of his *Of the Origin and Progress of Language* (1773–92). This was ordered by Shelley as part of the reading list for *Queen Mab*.[186] Work has been carried out on the importance of Monboddo's theory of language for the early writings of Shelley, but the specific relationships in Monboddo's rhetoric between language, nature and diet may now be elucidated.[187]

Monboddo's political theory of language is concerned to describe man in a state of nature. The crucial chapters are 2 and 3 in Part I, book ii. Man has liminal status between wholly solitary and wholly gregarious animals.[188] Monboddo's comparison distinguishes between kingdoms and subsequently distinguishes between species. A division between enclosing sets (living beings) and within a subset (animate beings) is echoed later when Monboddo discusses man's fractionary nature.

First, the state of nature as a state of war (Hobbes) is rejected.[189] Man is declared to be naturally frugivorous: 'he only becomes an animal of prey by acquired habit'.[190] Evidence for this, disrupting habitual opinions and culinary practices, was constructed through orientalizing, imperialist discourse. But this discourse was soon folded into anxieties commonly held in the 'West'. As usual in narratives about this sort of experience, a self-confident anthropocentrism (and Eurocentrism) conquers physically but is troubled ideologically: hence the need to formulate arguments about a natural state. Monboddo relates a typical tale of wonder: '[when M. Bougainville] landed in the Malouine, or *Falkland islands*, as we call them, which are uninhabited, all the animals came about him and his men; the fouls perching upon their heads and shoulders, and the fourfooted animals running among their feet'.[191]

This narrative suggests that man has always-already been there before. Animal relations with humans are inbred, and not acquired through force of habit. Animals *expect* humans to be non-violent. This inbuilt harmony with brute creation (an intrinsic non-violence) does not need to be articulated in an active relationship established between creatures through 'habit'. In a long footnote on the Golden Age topos in Pausanias and Herodotus, Monboddo makes a telling remark about figurative language: all imaginative myths are based to some degree on historical realities occurring in nature.[192] Figurative language is being redeemed in the context of natural diet.

Man, however, is also cannibalistic; this derives from his lack of a 'natural propensity to society'.[193] Thus is born the need for a social contract, an arbitrary meeting of individuals, an idea related to philosophies supporting the French Revolution. This is 'a peculiarity that distinguishes us from every other land-animal, and sets us at a greater distance from our kind, than even the beasts of prey are from theirs'.[194] Man is the differential animal. Humans *are* articulated in a system (of classification), but emptily, by difference. In addition, this differential articulation is associated with violence and taboo consumption which makes humans worse than beasts of prey.[195] Man is naturally herbivorous but also cannibalistic, carnivorous and thus tending towards solitariness and lack of social being. Meat-eating is an extension of human cannibalism by implication, thus signifying the division of humans both outside and within their species.

The naturalness of man in a state of nature recedes before our eyes, no matter how vigorously Monboddo may compare man's 'amphibious' qualities to those of a beaver.[196] Monboddo discusses how language is not natural to man but a product of arbitrary, artificial reason (this is the project of book i). However, language can also be said to arise from cries emitted in a state of nature: 'In the beginning of his history he [Diodorus Siculus] says, that men at first lived dispersed, and subsisted upon the natural productions of the earth; that they had no use of speech, and uttered only inarticulate cries; but that having herded together, for fear ... of the wild beasts, they invented a language, and imposed names upon things.'[197] Onomatopoeia did not exist in 'barbarous nations', but 'inarticulate cries only that must have given rise to language ... language should be nothing but an improvement or refinement upon the natural cries of the animal'.[198]

Language seems both to divide and unite the animal and human, and the animal and rational spheres of human activity. The figurativeness of language (what makes it different from a cry) is at stake. How is Monboddo to redeem the argument? He deftly attempts this at the end of 1.ii.2. Eating vegetables and using articulate language are brought together at a further historical point, where man moves from a natural state into one of civil society, and at a higher level of human achievement, 'rational' rather than brutish.[199] This elides problems about the need to express or articulate a state of nature implied in the representation of man's virgin landing on the Malouine islands. Herding (associated with frugivorous animals, not predators) is equated with the 'political life' necessary to generate language.[200] Society is a re-imagination of a state of true human nature.[201]

Monboddo thus served Shelley not only with an explicit set of natural-historical insights into language, but with an implicit process of ideological construction which Shelley could have found in Ritson's *Animal Food* as well as his copy of *Language*. Just as Monboddo's process of construction can be seen in the limits, breaks and elisions which the text tries to surmount, so Shelley's problems lie at moments of transition between natural and social boundaries.

In *Animal Food*, Ritson wants to distinguish between two types of nature. The passage on language runs into an Erasmus Darwin-like description of nature as a 'system for the express purpose of [animals] preying upon each other'.[202] In *The Temple of Nature* Darwin describes the struggle for survival:

> In ocean's pearly haunts, the waves beneath
> Sits the grim monarch of insatiate Death;
> The shark rapacious with descending blow
> Darts on the scaly brood, that swims below;
> The crawling crocodiles, beneath that move,
> Arrest with rising jaw the tribes above;
> With monstrous gape sepulchral whales devour
> Shoals at a gulp, a million in an hour.
> – Air, earth, and ocean, to astonish'd day
> One scene of blood, one mighty tomb display!
> From Hunger's arm the shafts of Death are hurl'd,
> And one great Slaughter-house the warring world!
>
> (*The Temple of Nature*, IV.55–66)[203]

There is a bias against princely and priestly human power in the imagery, the 'grim monarch' the shark, and the 'sepulchral whales'. When he read it in 1811, Shelley may have considered this in a politicized context.[204] Nature is a violent, carnivorous restaurant which resembles, rather than contradicts, the violent excesses of society (compare Byron's *Don Juan*, II.lxvii.529: 'man is a carnivorous production, / And ... like the shark and tiger, must have prey'). And some of the patrons were not designed for human pleasure at all. For Ritson, following this observation, the plenitude of germs observed by microscopy decentres man – there are some creatures not designed for his use and benefit. This leads to the much-used Miltonic hospital (*Paradise Lost* XI.477–88).[205] Milton's passage comes after a warning

about (dietary) intemperance (XI.466–77) and before a description of
the paradox of idolatrous disfiguration (XI.515–25). Ritson's vegetarian rhetoric helps to construct a secular Milton, whose discourse
on temperance is connected with his iconoclastic criticism of images.
'Civilization' is thus associated both with unnatural language and
with the disfiguration of flesh, conceived as a drive towards death
which the politics of vegetarianism seeks to arrest with the promise of
an *imaginary* plenitude, nature consumed but not disfigured, whether
by language or by the knife. But Ritson persuades through elision,
declaring that a 'natural state' is a state of tameness or genuine
civilization, and dissociating this state from any kind of civilization.[206]
A strange doubling or short-circuiting takes place. There is *another*
nature, a model for a just society, of which vegetarianism is an
accurate representation. The imaginary plenitude revises the real,
threatening one by rendering nature tame for human benefit.

What to do to counteract the disease of language? Eat philosophy.
Vegetarianism is imaged as philosophical consumption. In Milton's
Comus, philosophy is the diet of the figurative, the 'vast excess' (770)
which Comus' rhetoric forces on its victims, reducing soul to body
(466). Philosophy is a use value without surplus, like the Lady's
'moderate and beseeming share' of 'Nature's full blessings' (766 ff.).
The Lady must resist Comus' fantasy of aesthetic control in which the
process of speech turns in on itself, a figurativeness 'in eternal restless
change / Self-fed, and self-consumed' (594). The diet of philosophy
will temper the figurative to the cognitive faculty, as Milton plays on
the meanings of 'temper':

> How charming is divine philosophy!
> Not harsh, and crabbed as dull fools suppose,
> But musical as is Apollo's lute,
> And a perpetual feast of nectared sweets,
> Where no crude surfeit reigns. (475)

In *Elegia Sexta*, some poetry is said to retain a correspondence with
carnality which makes the verse form itself double round: 'Carmen
amat Bacchus, carmina Bacchus amat' (14). Elegiac poets can eat
'convivia larga' (53) but epic poets, who practise a higher form,
require a vegetarian regimen (60); Shelley revises the Miltonic
discourse of temperance.

The rhetoric of the cry of nature involved both upper and lower classes in the 1790–1820 period. However, it is also possible to elucidate a struggle for representation within the discourse of natural diet in which the poorer classes had nothing to say.

The idea of a 'diet' suggests the Greek *diaitia*, which stood for a whole way of life (not just the eating of a type of food; in the early modern period, diet comprised the six non-naturals). The use of 'regimen' in authors as diverse as George Cheyne (earlier in the eighteenth century), John Frank Newton and Shelley demonstrates the construction of a *habitus*, a socially distinctive way of living. The key term in the construction of this way of life was *temperance*, fitting snugly between ethics and medicine. The voice of reason was inscribed within the cry of nature. In fact this is hardly a 'voice' within the cry, and is more like a code, an abstract logic of culture reduced to harmonious systems of numerical data. Here we must turn our attention from relationships between humans and animate nature to the human body and the codes which sought to measure it and govern it. The aesthetics of temperance are a measure of self-control. This is a response not so much to the inhumanity of urbanization and exploitation as to pollution, corruption, territorially-massed populations, upon which the disciplines of statistics and theories of population could be brought to bear. It is not so much an identification with the suffering and inarticulate as an order: clean up your act. The epigraph to Thomas Trotter's analysis of the nervous temperament, advocating a temperate diet (1807), is a quotation from *Macbeth* which is surely in part a warning to the Regency:

> Boundless intemperance
> In Nature is a tyranny: it hath been
> The untimely emptying of the happy throne,
> And fall of many kings.[207]

The theme of temperance cut across boundaries of political conflict: Shelley used the notion to criticize the excesses of Robespierre in *A Vindication*.[208] An emphasis on orderliness and sobriety is also to be found across the social range of radical writing. But the criteria of bodily harmony and perfection are rhetorical tools in a wider attempt to rationalize, justify and subject to scrutiny the living standards of urban citizens, notably the urban poor. To explain these criteria we need to move in the archive from an emphasis on cruelty to an emphasis on medicine, from animals to disease. There are many generic, thematic and political differences between the texts under discussion. But the tracing of a single theme unites them.

Trotter wishes to seek ways of disciplining the bodies of a literate class. *A View of the Nervous Temperament* contrasts modern artificiality with an ancestral savage naturalness. Modern artificiality breeds nervous disease, from 'wealth, luxury, indolence, and intemperance'.[209] In contrast, there was not enough time to develop 'delicacy of feeling' amongst the 'untutored and illiterate inhabitants of a forest'.[210] Artificial town life, providing a 'vortex of dissipation' for the idle, also provided an increasing amount of 'highly-seasoned dainties' which hastened the degeneration of a match between human and environment, and between labour needs and skills.[211]

Trotter needs to fit his treatment to his analysis of social classes. Treatment requires social discrimination, for 'He [the doctor] would not confound the complaint of the slim soft-fibred man-milliner with that of the firm and brawny ploughman.'[212] But such a discrimination is redeemed by looking at social distinctions in terms of *natural*, physical distinctions. Society is discussed disarmingly in terms of natural history (one may here compare the work of Beddoes). Trotter wants to draw up a new kind of social taxonomy, but the ideal man which he wants to create out of his system is modelled on a savage, a man in a state of nature, not in civil society. He therefore has a problem concerning the discourse of medicine in a state of society. As in Ritson, language plays a role in his notion of a lapse from an initially healthy uncivilized state to a subsequent, unhealthy civilized state. Trotter does not want to be involved with figures himself, but with the natural. This later leads him into complications with his model, and an attempt to emphasize that he does not want people really to return to a state prior to civil society.[213]

Trotter constructs an idealized male body gratified by the benefits which it gains from the world, this reciprocity providing a coherent and stable imaginary mirror image. His study of courtship in savage and modern culture allows a comparison between the non-tantalizing and sure 'return' of the savage male lover for his advances,[214] and the lacklustre performance of the modern man who 'like a knight errant in romance, must fight his way to a fortune'.[215] Trotter sexualizes diet by making some foods appropriate to the 'manly' savage way of living. Alcohol is strictly for the 'manikins' of the middle classes produced in the modern system, who need it to boost their rhetorical skill in bargaining.[216]

Trotter's methodology is not an isolated example. Though his politics were monarchist, his methods were developed by Shelley.[217] It is necessary to re-examine the paragraph in the middle of *A Vindication* which begins, 'Crime is madness. Madness is disease.'[218] If we were to turn Shelley's sociopathology upon himself, his text could be read as a symptom of literate, upper-class reformist desire.

The paragraph details the social consequences of diet. It bears a single footnote, a reference to Lambe's *Reports* on cancer adumbrating the sentence: 'Even common water, that apparently innoxious pabulum [note Shelley's high-flown early style], when corrupted by the filth of populous cities, is a deadly and insidious destroyer.'[219] Shelley brings in Lambe in response to the perceived pollutions of urbanization. The preceding sentence runs: 'arithmetic cannot enumerate, nor reason perhaps suspect, the multitudinous sources of disease in civilized life'.[220] Shelley's anxiety is that arithmetic and reason *should* be able to suspect and enumerate. The multitudes require the multitudes of statistics to discipline their vice and misery.

Dr William Lambe (1765–1847) was an acquaintance of Newton, who found relief from chronic asthma by adopting Lambe's vegetarian regimen.[221] He was well-respected as an anatomist and chemist.[222] *Reports on Cancer* (1809) suggests that two factors are responsible for chronic wasting illnesses like cancer. The migration from hot to cold climates necessitated the cooking of flesh in the absence of other sources of nourishment, leading to diminished sensibility (because meat is harder to digest and thus diverts nervous activity).[223] Additionally, 'watery liquids' were used as a 'substitute for the fruits and vegetable juices'.[224] Lambe advocated distilled or spring water (for example, he recommends Malvern) as a corrective.[225] The two factors showed how instinct or 'primal integrity' had been 'extinguished' in 'social man'.[226]

Lambe continued his research into vegetarianism in *Additional Reports on the Effects of a Peculiar Regimen in Cases of Cancer, Scrofula, Consumption, Asthma, and other Chronic Diseases* (1815). 'Chronic' is important: an acute disease may be seen as a more accidental occurrence, while a chronic one was a product of social environment, demanding a reasoned environmental enquiry. Thus chapter vii of *Additional Reports* is an analysis of social progress and a delineation of civilized and barbarous manners. Here figures of civilization reach their most critical intersection with a series of carefully patterned elisions which define a beautiful bodily norm and a reformist political agenda. My study of this chapter focuses upon a surprise discovery, the uncanny appearance of two Greek statues in the wilderness of the exotic world.

Lambe criticizes Beddoes, who had collected statistics from Aberdeenshire on what he called the 'wretched living' of the labouring poor. This consisted of vegetable food, 'abundant' because of 'the high state of cultivation of almost all European countries'. The 'labouring classes' ate it because it was cheap, children 'in easy circumstances' consumed it principally, and most others used 'a moderate portion ... two or three times a day'. Bodily defects were not considered by most to arise from 'the mode of living'. However:

if we examine the uncivilized races of mankind, we shall, perhaps, be led to form different conclusions. These whole tribes of men we consider as barbarians; and with reason, if we regard the knowledge of letters as the test of civilization. But many of them, being acquainted with agriculture and other useful arts, are so far as little barbarous as the mass of the population of Europe. Other tribes again are very imperfectly versed in that, or any other of the most necessary arts, and some are wholly ignorant of it, and almost all other useful knowledge.[227]

Vegetable food is associated with cultivation and 'the ... arts'. An aesthetics of diet is being elaborated which has as its paradigm the 'knowledge' of Europe. But while vegetables are associated with culture, and meat with the inarticulate barbarians, this culture is degraded in parts of Europe itself. Lambe attributes this to the imposition of an artificial and snobbish code of luxuries which are civilized in name only. The agenda he sets is for Europe to return to what constitutes its essence – the fact that it is a group of agricultural civilizations.

Lambe links the arts of peace with agriculture and enlightenment, and the arts of war with hunting, dependency, necessity and ignorance.[228] The costliness of animal food is part of the way in which 'persons in easy circumstances' exercise 'the silly vanity of distinguishing themselves from the hard working classes'.[229] Lambe here rhetorically abolishes the distinction, since class contradictions are not seen as structural elements of society but as an artificial gloss. 'Hard working' is delicately poised between moral and social categories: the labourers are not a class as such, just people who work hard.

The 'habit' of distinction 'must be considered to be one of the numerous relics of that antient barbarism, which ... still taints the manners of civilized nations'.[230] Barbarism returns, not as ignorance but as a disfiguring supplement of civilization. Representative language itself in its mode as silly vanity or supplementarity is the problem: Lambe wants to strip a culture's self-representation down to some harmonious essential signified. This would include 'cultivation of the earth' as the key and 'limit of improvement in the arts essential to the support of life ... if all mankind confined themselves for their support to the products supplied by the culture of the earth, war, with its attendant misery and horrors, might cease to be one of the scourges of the human race'.[231] This idea is ultimately derived from Plato's *Republic* and *Laws* and is remarkably similar to Shelley's treatment of similar themes.[232]

Dr Lambe certainly knows his way around the rhetoric. The cry of nature reappears in an exemplification of how 'habit and familiarity' soften 'scenes of blood' (the theatrical language is reminiscent of Burke): 'But look at a young child, who is told that the chicken, which it has fed and played with, is to be killed. Are not the tears it sheds, and the agonies it endures, the voice of nature itself crying within us, and pleading the cause of humanity.'[233] The voice of humanity is the voice of the other (child or animal), setting up a relationship with a listener which defines the humane as 'essence of human'.

However, in Lambe's distinction between 'artificial aids' to reason, the 'glimmering' of writings by 'sages' and 'obedience to the fixed and immutable laws of nature',[234] there is an element of nature which is not vocal (whether eloquent or inarticulate). This is a 'law' which enables the cry and the scene of blood to be staged. The opposition between cultural supplements and essentials (luxury and 'culture of the earth') is now reversed. The cry of nature is the articulation of a spontaneous essence, but this essence is enabled to be perceived by 'obedience' to a graven law. This obedience is redeemed and figures in a rhetorical scheme which seems to favour the operation of reason supposedly independent of imposed habits and hierarchies, expressing itself as a harmonious numerical code. The language of measurement (with or without Pythagorean overtones) suggests a correspondence of sign with thing. In that key Enlightenment text,

Outlines of an Historical View of the Progress of the Human Mind (1795), Condorcet envisions the universal language of the Tenth (Utopian) Epoch of history in which 'the sign might be known at the same instant with the object'.[235] The Tenth Epoch is also described as arresting the decay of the body, and it is the Pythagorean school which earlier forms Condorcet's paradigm for the progress of an autonomous scientific knowledge which might result in natural perfection.[236] Shelley, whose interest in Condorcet is well known, shared a similar interest in bodily perfection, and the scientism implicit in his use of the verb *to be* is intended as a form of perfect language, the essence of a cultural code: 'Crime is madness. Madness is disease' – and can now be analysed in scientific discourse which obeys and faithfully copies natural laws.

The over-riding discourse in the middle of Lambe's text is *physiognomy*. Recent work on Camper, Lavater and Gall, eighteenth- and early nineteenth-century physiognomists, has shown how useful both to later psychology and to the police was the Pythagorean/ Hippocratic mapping of the material body as symptom onto the character or mind of which it was thought to be an expression.[237] Most important was the idea that 'the line of demarcation between humanity and animality passes through man himself'.[238] Thus physiognomy could become a normative science in which the despised in humans could be labelled bestial or savage. Lambe is normative in just this way. While eschewing the Neoplatonic idea of a great chain of being, he is still able to differentiate between human and animal:

In his nobler part, his rational soul, man is distinguished from the whole tribe of animals by a boundary, which cannot be passed. It is only when man divests himself of his reason, and debases himself by brutal habits, that he renounces his just rank among created beings, and sinks himself below the level of the beasts [since in doing so he is not even guided by natural instinct].[239]

The moral descent can be traced in the figure of the body.

Lambe was interested in physiognomy. Note K to page 180 explains a distinction between the 'negro' and the 'European'. Lambe explicitly relates the shape of the body to diet: 'the form of the head and face, which distinguishes civilized nations, is produced in great measure by the cookery of their food'.[240] 'Negroes', on the other hand, have to chew a lot. The cutting-up of the body into binary oppositions (here the face would fall into the categories of 'high' and 'front' connoted as expressive of the soul), is a tradition traceable from Pythagoras through Aristotle.[241]

It is now possible to discuss the middle of chapter vii. 'Negro' was a floating racist signifier in the period. Joseph Ritson characterizes them at points as savage carnivores (indeed cannibals) and elsewhere as peaceful vegetable eaters, exemplary either of a savage or a natural (wild) state in the customary typology.[242] Types of human baseness or nobility, without refined trappings, are projected onto them. Ritson could not be accused of mere stupidity in his collection of contradictory data from the travellers' accounts he has read. Lambe's distinction between culture and savagery draws on works such as Symes' *Embassy to Ara*, Peron's *Voyages*, Dr Forster's *Observations* and Langsdorf's *Travels*. Thus: 'The inhabitants of the Andaman Islands (situated in the Indian Ocean) are described as the most uncivilized of the human race. They have the characteristic features of the negro.'[243] The association of civilization with bodily characteristics is consistent in the text. These societies do not eat vegetables, but shell fish, lizards, 'guanos', rats; they are constitutionally 'ill formed'.[244] Cook's second voyage to Tierra del Fuego provided evidence of how 'the deformity and stupidity of this race is due to their miserable diet'.[245] The Calmucks, according to Clarke's *Travels*, are ugly carnivorous savages: 'Such are pastoral manners', Lambe remarks ironically, 'naked and undisguised by the veil of pastoral refinement' (mocking a refined mode of European cultural production).[246]

Lambe is driven to naturalize social sanity, by which is meant both moral and physical cleanliness: the well-known phrase *mens sana in corpore sano* sums up Lambe's position. Thus 'a just bodily organisation is neither the object nor the consequence of intellectual culture. It is rather the gift of nature; which is saying, nearly, that it results from natural habits.'[247] The 'nearly' indicates another elision. A diseased or ill-formed body is a symptom of a corrupt or savage culture, but also now seems to be the generative *basis* of culture. This discourse of the symptom as both producer and product of cultural identity is itself symptomatic of a reformist ideology which cannot come to grips with the sources of its own power: Shelley's writing contains similar anxious slippages. Food discourse is useful for this kind of elision: it seems at once a natural product and necessary for survival, and a cultural artefact. Lambe uses Pope in support: 'See him from nature rising slow to art? / To copy Instinct then was

Reason's part.'[248] This quotation (*Essay on Man*, III.169) closely follows the section describing a vegetarian Golden Age.

Lambe turns his anthropological and physiognomic gaze upon the English (as Shelley does in *A Vindication*):

The great body of our English peasantry and the urban working class subsist almost wholly on vegetables and are perfectly well-nourished. The peasantry of Lancashire, and Cheshire, who live principally on potatoes and buttermilk, are celebrated as the handsomest race in England. Two or three millions of our fellow subjects in Ireland are supported the same way. On this subject it is said by Dr. Adam Smith, 'the chairmen, porters and coal heavers in London, and those unfortunate women who live by prostitution, the strongest men, and the most beautiful women perhaps in the British dominions, are said to be, the greater part of them, from the lower rank of people in Ireland, who are generally fed with this root (the potatoe). No food can afford a more decisive proof of the nourishing quality, or of its being peculiarly suitable to the health of the human constitution.'[249]

The vegetarianism of upper-class intellectuals was a form of radical self-presentation which could only make sense amongst themselves. If Shelley can be aligned with both Lambe and an avowed opponent such as Adam Smith on the issue of potato production, something strange happens to the professed universalism and egalitarianism of his rhetoric. Lambe's criteria here are not only health but also a rather abstract aesthetic of beauty: the look of the body as it hits the gaze, supported by the natural-historical discourse of 'race'. The discipline of a natural aesthetic standard overflows political boundaries. Lambe is not only concerned with the luxurious refinements of the wealthy, but the allocation of sustainable resources to a growing population of urban poor. This notably overlooks their demand for fine white bread, part of very different conceptions of the culture of nutrition, ways of signifying desirable living standards or shameful social degradation.

How is the criterion of beauty set up? By using two sculptures which could almost be the hallmark of high European culture: the Medici Venus and the Apollo Belvedere.[250] Tahitian 'natives' are observed to have a diet consisting mainly of vegetable food.[251] Physiognomically, '"The arms, hands, and fingers of some are so exquisitely delicate, that they would do honour to a Venus de Medicis."'[252] The following pages are remarkable, if only for their dense and lengthy footnotes full of measurements, in French feet and inches, of the bodily shape of a man from the island of Nukuhiva, a

Mau-ka-u called Mufau Taputakaua. This South Sea Islander was measured, according to Langsdorf, by Counsellor Tilesius, who took the observations to Gottingen, where Counsellor Blumenbach '"has studied so assiduously the natural history of man"':

'This latter compared the proportions with the Apollo of Belvedere, and found that those of that master piece of the finest ages of Grecian art, in which is combined every possible integer of manly beauty, corresponded exactly with our Mufau.'[253]

Down to the names, this could all have been from *The Glass Bead Game*; except that Hesse's vision of a Utopian game of abstract, fugue-like and ascetic disputation over the codes and ratios of cultural artefacts is supposed to take place in the future. To find a Greek statue in a Nukuhivan human body requires a deft technology of harmonic proportion which is itself the code for beauty. The Apollo is the exemplum of exemplars (Langsdorf dwells on this: it is a '"master piece"' of '"the finest ages"' of the finest European culture) and is itself a codified standard. The rhetoric of the passage chastises luxury with arithmetic, and defines beauty as 'integer'.[254] Blumenbach's theories of organic development included thinking about the influence of diet and the environment upon the body, in a tradition which Lambe was emulating somewhat. His writing contains similar figurative structures; moreover, the anecdote illustrates the magisterial power of the *naturalist* who has been brought in to measure the body according to a cultural standard.[255]

Just as the cry of nature is the cry of humanity audible in suffering creatures, so the scheme of European beauty is found in the abstracted form of a human in a comparative state of nature: the centre is found at the margins. This justifies Lambe's theory that the progress of culture should be a return to nature. Through Derrida's writing on the supplement in *Of Grammatology*, a racist discourse could be delineated in which the subaltern subject is filled with Pythagorean numbers:

the supplement supplements. It adds only to replace. It intervenes or insinuates itself *in-the-place-of*; if it fills, it is as if one fills a void. If it represents and makes an image, it is by the anterior default of a presence. Compensatory [*suppléant*] and vicarious, the supplement is an adjunct, a subaltern instance which *takes-(the)-place* [*tient-lieu*].[256]

Blumenbach performs his abstraction with brio; in the light of current thinking on colonialism, the brilliance of such a move is rather deathly. While Shelley seemed to have rid the discourse of natural diet of supplementarity, this move appears to reinstate it. The Pythagorean axiom is rather universalizing, but, it turns out, only in one direction: European 'culture'.

How strange to find a Greek sculpture on a distant Pacific island! As a friend of Newton, Lambe may have been moved to pursue integral beauty as a code of temperance. If it is a coincidence that the Medici Venus and the Apollo Belvedere are also found in Newton's *The Return to Nature* (1811), then the argument for a prevailing structure of feeling among these thinkers becomes even stronger. The Apollo paradigm was also used in Benjamin West's painting of an Indian warrior, referred to in Samuel Rogers' *Voyage of Columbus* (1809–12) and Reynolds' *Omai* (1775).[257]

For Newton, it is not so much the immorality of slaughtering animals, but the disfigurement of humans, that prompts the response of a natural diet. Newton reads the myths of Eden and Prometheus to show that in the 'perpetual spring' of the primitive state, man was not a prey to '*premature diseased death*'.[258] Thus 'all diseases, including deformity, are artificial'.[259] Newton's scheme demotes the sudden, the accidental, chance, decay, along with the artificial.[260] Originally humans enjoyed a state of bodily perfection, but in the present are merely inadequate representations of '*real*' humans.[261] Their bodies are stunted; however, this is not a result of intrinsic ill, but of consuming artificial supplements (meat and liquids not obtained from fruit, for example).[262]

The language of luxury resembles Lambe. Newton's image of parental control is centred on domestic nuclear families as a counter to urban dissipation: 'To those domestic parents, who, aware that temperance in enjoyment is the best warrant of its duration, feel how dangerous and how empty are all the feverous amusements of our assemblies, our dinners, and our theatres, compared with the genuine and tranquil pleasures of a happy little circle at home.'[263] The artifice of the theatre is 'feverous', like a disease.

Newton has to produce a model of bodily perfection which could be seen as the product of non-artificial temperance. He is anxious about the figurative as such: the artifices of modern life are described as those things which *disfigure* the body. Thus 'Real men' have never been 'depictured' in poetry or history for 'It is not man we have before us, but the wreak [sic] of man.'[264] But Newton has based his text on the analysis of Greek and Biblical myths as Fall narratives.

There had to be some state *from* which to fall. The people of the past were like the Apollo Belvedere or the Medici Venus.[265] Newton supplies a footnote which renders the art of the statues an imitation of nature, thus diminishing its figurative status as a supplement: 'The Apollo may very well have been a portrait as well as the Venus, which is suspected to have been so.'[266]

Newton's text is far less rigorously dependent on data than Lambe's and often lapses into whimsy. Nevertheless, it shares similar objectives. Whom does he use to exemplify the vigour imparted by vegetable food? The Irish immigrants in London.[267]

These dietary works respond not only to issues of human rights and medicine but also to perceptions of the increasing hazards of urbanization and capitalism. An aesthetic code defined the beauty of the body as an abstraction of high European culture, the perfect representation of nature. The code was also available both as a method of self-stylization, and as a tool of food production and demography. The reforms seemed not only peaceful but disciplined and temperate, an ideal model of the desirable modes of behaviour of the reformist members of subordinate classes. The move into an egalitarian future involved the reproduction of meanings concerning the body which were always-already inscribed in the beauty of number, form and proportion. Moreover, this reasoned approach was repeated at the level of methodology. The turning of an-thropological techniques upon the culture which invented them assumed the perfect and reasonable reproduction of this culture, and thus perhaps critiqued a teleological sense of History, while ensuring that what was doing rather well over there could also be made to say something quite interesting about over here. This produced bizarre juxtapositions of orientalist and hearth-and-home figures.

The discourse of natural diet analysed functions with the help of two ideological ellipses. First, the paradox of non-figurative rep-resentation, drawing on metaphors involving mathematics, science, 'silent eloquence' and natural modes of figuration, attempts to cancel the threat of disfiguration, language as a form of violence, culture as a dangerous supplement to nature, metaphors of hazard and decay. Secondly, the paradox that to choose a natural diet presupposes the mental set which it imparts (reason, delicacy of feeling, moral virtue, sympathy), attempts to represent social change as a return to some essential element of the existing state of affairs. How is it possible to convince a criminal, a drunkard, a meat-eater, a madman, embroiled in irrational passion to desist, or a society deluded by custom to lose its habits? Through these ellipses, the radical self is presented as having always been in the same place; it is perhaps 'truer' to itself in the act of self-presentation. With the natural subject in place, it is now possible to differentiate between 'culture' (conceived as a naturalized, ascetic social body), and 'luxury', and this is the subject of the next chapter.

CHAPTER 5

Intemperate figures: re-fining culture

Men uninfluenced by comprehensive principles of justice,
commit every species of intemperance.
Godwin, William, *Political Justice*, 116

For they thrive well whose garb of gore
Is Satan's choicest livery,
And they thrive well, who from the poor,
Have snatched the bread of penury,
And heap the houseless wanderer's store,
On the rank pile of luxury.
Shelley, *The Devil's Walk*, 94

INTRODUCTION

Shelley differentiated 'culture' from 'luxury' through representations of intemperance and viscerality, constantly associated with the
luxurious overcodings of the despot. The lists of words associated with
viscerality in the Shelley *Concordance* cover several columns.[1] Moreover, the representation of flesh is also taken as a figure for the
figurative itself. The visceral sublime of *The Assassins*, for example,
threatens the stable codes of meaning associated with a temperate
body. The body is redefined, its boundaries (*fines*) redrawn, through
the ways in which 'culture' serves to discipline 'nature', and by the
'naturalization' of 'culture'. Culture-nature is a square-dance which
eliminates the 'barbaric' or 'despotic' term of 'luxury'.

In works such as *The Cenci* (1819), Shelley wrote not only about
temperance but also about excess. The language of intemperance is
the language of tyranny. Shelley is uncompromisingly graphic: the
social system exists to provide sustenance for its rulers, and hence to
guarantee their continued existence of lordship over society. The
vivid and complex knot of imagery around this theme shows how the
rulers are blind to the horrors they inflict on the world they consume,

and like some form of life lower down the great chain of being are mere suckers and mouths.

Queen Mab provides the paradigmatic image of Shelley's intemperate tyrant. The King's power and his misery are figured by showing him at table:

> Now to the meal
> Of silence, grandeur, and excess, he drags
> His palled unwilling appetite. If gold,
> Gleaming around, and numerous viands culled
> From every clime, could force the loathing sense
> To overcome satiety, – if wealth
> The spring it draws from poisons not, – or vice,
> Unfeeling, stubborn vice, converteth not
> Its food to deadliest venom; then that king
> Is happy; and the peasant who fulfills
> His unforced task, when he returns at even,
> And by the blazing faggot meets again
> Her welcome for whom all his toil is sped,
> Tastes not a sweeter meal.
>   Behold him now
> Stretched on the gorgeous couch; his fevered brain
> Reels dizzily awhile: but ah! too soon
> The slumber of intemperance subsides,
> And conscience, that undying serpent, calls
> Her venomous brood to their nocturnal task.
> Listen! he speaks! oh! mark that frenzied eye –
> Oh! mark that deadly visage.
> [King.]   No cessation!
> Oh! must this last for ever! Awful death,
> I wish, yet fear to clasp thee! – Not one moment
> Of dreamless sleep! O dear and blessed peace!   (III.44)

The King has two aspects, an artificial one (his kingly aspect) and a natural one (an essential human nature revealed by the voice of conscience). The artificial aspect of the King intemperately oversteps the bounds of the natural: thus Mab concludes, 'all sufficing nature can chastise / Those who transgress her law' (III.82). To return to a more natural state of affairs, renouncing 'vice', would mark a political reform reflected in the happiness of the peasant at his meal (an almost Hegelian vision of the happy kingdom, the organic community). Shelley is, however, sophisticated in his double conditional ('If gold...or vice...'), since the rest of *Queen Mab* demonstrates that gold and vice cannot be reformed thus. The reader is to replace with a republican vision the proffered picture of an organic kingdom, for tyranny is essentially vicious. The language about vice converting its food to 'deadliest venom' is developed in the vegetarian passage in section VIII. The idea of 'numerous viands' 'culled / From every clime' is criticized in note 17 and *A Vindication*,[2] and is bound up with 'grandeur and excess': the monarchical nation cannot sustain itself, and the 'task' of the peasant cannot be 'unforced'. If 'viands' connotes animal food (which is not necessarily the case), then the 'gold... viands' passage is a typical 'gold and blood' figure, with animal food metonymic for the quintessential commodity (the commodity-form as alienation and death).

The image of the dyspeptic king whose 'brain / Reels dizzily' is a figure of corrupt passion turning round on itself, binding the monarch to his own artificiality: his appetite gorges but is 'unwilling'. The King wishes for the peace, quiet death and dreamless sleep (offered in the Shelley-Newton diet). But the fact that he is a King is precisely what prevents this ascetic reformation.

The representation of gore also provides a way of presenting disfiguration. 'To disfigure' used to mean 'to carve';[3] it literally means 'removing the appearance'. Appearance is bound up with faciality: the face, by metonymy, is the identity, the soul. 'No longer now / He slays the lamb that looks him in the face' (*Queen Mab* VIII.211) suggests an available principle of identity between human and animal. To take the face off the animal is one of the first things necessary for preparing a joint of meat: a mangled carcass does have a face (even if it is a head of lamb). Shelley had experimented with these aesthetics of horror in *St Irvyne* (1810). The ballad of Rosa's death and afterlife describes her form rising from her coffin:

> And her skeleton form the dead Nun rear'd,
>   Which dripp'd with the chill dew of hell.
>   In her half-eaten eyeballs two pale flames appear'd,
> And triumphant their gleam on the dark Monk glared.
>
> (stanza xvi)[4]

At the end of the tale, the devil bestows '"eternal life"' upon the evil Ginotti: 'On a sudden Ginotti's frame mouldered to a gigantic skeleton, yet two pale and ghastly flames glared in his eyeless sockets ... Yes, endless existence is thine, Ginotti – a dateless and hopeless eternity of horror.'[5]

'Disfiguration' maps the way in which figurative language constantly deconstructs stable identity, stripping the face off things.

De Man used Shelley as a fine example of this process.[6] Shelley's anxiety about, and exploitation of, figurative language is implicated in his representation of violence against the flesh. Shelley's use of gory figures in moral discourse involves a doubly figurative metaphor. If meat is a metaphor for disfiguration, and if this is the activity of figurative language in general, then meat is a figure of figures, a metaphor about metaphor. Gore serves as a *mise-en-abîme* in Shelley's writing, a mode in which the monodirectional status of the text is rendered problematic. Disfiguration was a mark of dystopia in the period's Last Man narratives. The attempt to create natural modes of social representation ('culture') is reversed in Byron's *Darkness*, in which a contrast is drawn between natural and man-made light, conceived as disfiguring light (22). The birth of the secular state, with its binding, 'mediating' cultures, is ironically figured as a culture of death. Asceticism-as-culture is a version of the desire of desire (see chapter 3).

The first section of the chapter deals with *The Assassins*, a work which articulates a contradiction between violent and peaceful representations of the body and the state of nature; the second section continues by analysing the ways in which Shelley's poetry uses intemperate figures to express political statements. This analysis raises the question of intemperance as a form of intoxication, and the following section discusses Shelley's ambivalent figuration of this theme. Shelley's representation of bread is then explored as an autonomous discourse which plays on meanings of refinement, but also as a paradigm of wholesome, simple culture which fits Shelley's social models of discipline and plainness. A reading of *The Cenci*, *Swellfoot the Tyrant* and *Charles I* explains their treatment of intemperance, flesh and violence.

THE ASSASSINS

Shelley records his adoption of vegetarianism at roughly the same time as his disavowal of Gothic and his introduction to Godwin (Ireland, 1812). His self-idealization represented his radical coming-of-age. Exploits in Ireland were his first major political interventions after being sent down from Oxford and losing the chance of becoming an MP.

Shelley used the language of temperance to assuage doubts sown by Godwin about the gory nature of his politics. In March 1812 he described the state of the Irish to Godwin: 'Intemperance and hard labour have reduced them to machines. The oyster that is washed and driven at the mercy of the tides appears to me an animal of almost equal elevation in the scale of intellectual being.'[7] Despite his egalitarian claims for the rights of animals, Shelley was not completely prepared to discount a hierarchy of being in which molluscs appeared to be slightly lower than Irishmen. This thought contrasts with the praise of Irish hardiness on the part of his colleagues, Lambe and Newton. Godwin quoted the statement in his anxious reply, along with Shelley's exclamation that they are 'one mass of animated filth!'.[8]

Godwin shares Shelley's judgment, but denies the Irish the opportunity to become enlightened: 'The people of Ireland have been for a series of years in a state of diseased activity; and, misjudging that you are, you talk of awakening them. They will rise up like Cadmon's seed of dragon's teeth, and their first act will be to destroy each other.'[9] Cadmon founded Thebes and made the five Spartoi or 'sown men' who survived the battle its first citizens, but was compelled to leave by Dionysus, after the slaughter of Pentheus by the Maenads. Cadmon was also famed for bringing the art of writing to Greece. Violence associated with legislation in a myth about the spread of revolutionary knowledge was too apt for Godwin to miss. Godwin's 'a state of diseased activity' might be picking up on Shelley's 'Intemperance', as well as suggesting perverse politics. Shelley became preoccupied with how to disseminate ideas about liberty without involving violence. His solution linked violence, tyranny and anarchic chaos with metaphors of intemperance (blood-drinking, cannibalism and so on): each can be seen as forms of excess over a 'natural' norm established as temperate and reasonable. This was paralleled by his professed adoption of rationalistic forms of poetic discourse which treated grand political topics, rather than the sensationalist forms of Romance.

The Assassins (1814) shows a maturing development in his understanding of the nature of politicized violence. However, it remains an ambiguous work which would have shocked a Godwinian reader. What seems to be at stake is not only violence as a theme in the story, but also the sensationalist representation of it in its Romance genre.

The Assassins is a short, unfinished, but fascinating work, written in 1814 while the Shelleys were travelling around Europe. This

'Fragment of a Romance' exploits the politics of disfiguration: Rome and Jerusalem are decadent and ruined powers, 'shattered fragments' of civilization;[10] within the holy city a small sect of Christians resembling Gnostics become notoriously subversive and threatening.[11] They flee to the Lebanon for peace and discover Bethzatanai, another disfigured city, but this time a product of 'genius' rather than 'tyrants... and slaves'.[12] Its ruins have been appropriated by nature. In this marginal world of 'strange... chaotic confusion and harrowing sublimity' all social codes are defamiliarized, and customary social judgments rejected.[13] The flight represents a return to nature, imagined through categories of wild and domestic: 'Hither came the tiger and the bear to contend for those once domestic animals who had forgotten the secure servitude of their ancestors.[14] No sound, when the famished beast of prey had retreated in despair from the awful desolation of this place.'[15]

The Assassins are Shelleyan products of love and reason, their sensual delight bonded to 'a keener and more exquisite perception of all that they [external things] contain of lovely and divine'.[16] Writing and law are naturalized and hence language is redeemed from its disfiguring civility: as the Assassins become more pantheistic their 'Perpetual... benevolence' is not 'the heartless and assumed kindness of commercial man, but the genuine virtue that has a legible superscription in every feature of the countenance, and every motion of the frame'.[17] The law is engraved in the body. They still strive to overthrow the government, and a food image describes the manner of the incorporation of law and ethics in oppressive Jerusalem society:

No longer would the worshippers of the God of Nature be indebted to a hundred hands for the accommodation of their simple wants. No longer would the poison of a diseased civilisation embrue their very nutriment with pestilence. They would no longer owe their very existence to the vices, the fears, and the follies of mankind.[18]

The notion that 'nutriment' could be made poisonous clearly derives from Shelley's vegetarian writing, suggesting that bad social relations are encapsulated in a system of food production. The 'hands' are reminiscent of Emile's educational meal: social 'vices' affect the very body of the citizen. Society is being judged in terms of (human) nature, explicit in the tricolon, 'the vices, the fears, and the follies of mankind'. The passage may thus directly refer to the adoption of a new kind of diet.

Overthrow is to be established, not through gradualist enlightenment, but through terroristic violence. The story takes a glutinous
delight in imagining the bodies of the Assassins' enemies reduced to
offal: 'How many holy liars and parasites, in solemn guise, would his
[the Assassin's] saviour arm...plunge in the cold charnel, that the
green and many-legged monsters of the slimy grave might eat off at
their leisure the lineaments of rooted malignity and detested cunning
...The Assassin would cater nobly for the eyeless worms of earth, and
the carrion fowls of heaven.'[19] The fate of the enemy is a form of
poetic justice, decoding the luxury of their lives to a miasmatic flow
of slime. Those in power, who use blood like money, will get the
brutal treatment they deserve: 'The respectable man – the smooth,
smiling, polished villain, whom all the city honours; whose very trade
is lies and murder; who buys his daily bread with the blood and tears
of men, would feed the ravens with his limbs.'[20] One kind of carrion
creature will be devoured by another. The writing suggests that
disfiguration is politically necessary.

Shelley is alluding to Shakespeare. *Hamlet* i.v.106–9 was the
precursor of 'smooth, smiling, polished villain' – the literary
language of revenge. *Hamlet* connects revenge with tyranny, and
tyranny is associated in early modern tragedy with the over-
consumption of one's fill. Significantly, Hamlet works himself up
through such sensational language to a murder which he does *not*
commit: this may be the direction of Shelley's story. One may detect
the ideological difficulty encountered in Shelley's rebellion against
his own class: revenge, as in *Hamlet*, is difficult when the people
involved are your close relations.

On the merits of assassination, the narrator writes 'Who hesitates
to destroy a venomous serpent, that has crept near his sleeping
friend...?'[21] However, Shelley's stock imagery rapidly regains
control: the Assassins' love makes their actions sleep 'like an imprisoned earthquake, or the lightning shafts that hang in the golden
clouds of evening'.[22] The move to supra-human natural effects from
the claustrophobia and slime of the previous passage sublimates the
violent revolutionary feelings which in true apocalyptic fashion will
have no truck with time: 'No Assassin would submissively temporize
with vice.'[23] Their espousal of 'active virtue' develops Shelley's
insistence on individual virtue and purity as a means to reform.[24]

One of the Assassins, Albedir, discovers a barely-living human in a
tree:

A naked human body was impaled on the broken branch. It was maimed and mangled horribly; every limb bent and bruised into frightful distortion, and exhibiting a breathing image of the most sickening mockery of life. A monstrous snake had scented its prey from among the mountains – and above hovered a hungry vulture.[25]

The proper reactions of horror and sympathy which Albedir undergoes are reactions described in Burke's aesthetic of the sublime. Burke considers the deformity of a mutilated body as a deviation from a central standard, the '*compleat, common form*' of nature.[26] Excess indicates a corrupt sublimity, an excess over the proper boundaries (*limina*) of nature. But 'maimed and mangled horribly' also has resonances with Shelley's vegetarian writing and its contexts: 'horribly' and 'mangled' appear specifically in the vegetarian lines from *Queen Mab* (VIII.213); also, compare Frankenstein's horror at 'The remains of the half-finished [female] creature ... I almost felt as if I had mangled the living flesh of a human being'.[27] The scene is also 'unnaturally' violent: the man is assailed by Shelley's favourite predators, snake and bird of prey.

The near-carcass is a 'mockery' of life, a false representation subverting Shelley's conception of a non-visceral body. Indeed, flesh becomes the figure of a figure: 'a breathing image of the most sickening mockery'. Disfiguration is re-enacted in the modulation from the 'breathing image', with its suggestion that a spirit lives within the artifice, to the 'sickening mockery', a show producing a 'gut reaction' in the spectator. Albedir's children are called Abdallah and Maimuna.[28] 'Maimuna' resembles Shelley's pet name for the vegetarian Mrs Boinville. The children are seen playing with a 'small snake' like the happy child in *Queen Mab* VIII.[29] These allusions and figurative patterns are made to clash with the language of carrion and violence in the story. They describe a revision of culture and of nature, a political allegory about luxury and purity. *The Assassins* may have been left unfinished because of the ideological contradiction inherent in the figuration of a 'virtuous' group's displaced and orientalized rhetoric of violent immediacy.[30]

FROZEN BLOOD AND BACCHANALS

In *The Retrospect* (1812),[31] Shelley reflects upon the pains of aristocracy. He plays delicately with suggestions of a nectar-like drink as an emblem for happiness: 'The casket of my unknown mind

... Imbibed no fleeting radiance there' (81–83). Aristocracy, un-tempered by a politics that committed him to another class, would place him in a position of isolation later (a theme Shelley developed in *Alastor*):

> A friendless solitude around.
> For who that might undaunted stand,
> The saviour of a sinking land,
> Would crawl, its ruthless tyrant's slave,
> And fatten upon Freedom's grave,
> Though doomed with her to perish, where
> The captive clasps abhorred despair.   (85)

The quotation suggests worms on carrion. Fatness and 'fleeting radiance' are contrasted: the transience of the nectar-like draught is opposed to the dull round of the imprisoning corporeality of 'freedom's grave'. Shelley's Pythagoreanism overdetermined the conditions in which a member of the gentry who had deliberately cut off the means of support found himself. The drinking of the mind's food, nectar or nepenthe, denotes Shelley's preferred identity; growing corpulent is a sign of what Shelley wants to reject.

Additionally, fatness is being associated with a visceral language which evokes images of creatures low on a Neoplatonic chain of being: 'crawl', 'slave', 'doomed... to perish'. This viscerality betrays the strength of feeling which *The Retrospect* evokes in its promotion of reformist politics. The aristocrat must self-consciously adopt a reformist identity against his or her own class interests. The use of food and diet in Shelley's poetry is thus not only explicitly political and moral with reference to vegetarianism, but is also used for representing the re-imagination of the ruling-class reformer.

This re-imagination involves an experience of transgressing the confines of one's situation. Liminal experience inaugurates *Queen Mab* in the idea that death is not an experience of non-life, but a positive experience akin to the dreaming sleep of Ianthe, in which her subtle body breaks the 'icy chains of custom' (I.127). Sleep is the precondition for the vision of *Queen Mab*: 'How wonderful is Death, / Death and his brother Sleep!' (I.1). Death-as-sleep is also achieved through a vegetarianism.[32] Wakefulness, revolution and fleshy horror are opposed to sleep, reform and peaceful fantasy. When God wakes up in the narrative of the Wandering Jew, 'From an eternity of idleness' (VII.106), he plants the upas tree (the poison tree) or 'tree of evil, so that he / Might eat and perish, and my soul procure / Wherewith to sate its malice' (110).[33] God is depicted as a tyrannical gourmand of evil waking up out of a stupor. God describes the Israelites to Ahasuerus as chosen to 'sate the lusts I planted in their heart', their conquering troops wading 'on the promised soil through woman's blood' (116–19). The subjection of woman is contingent upon the subjection of the environment, the 'promised soil', demonstrating Shelley's consistent association of non-Hobbesian nature with the female. A holy war is described as 'Scarce satiable by fate's last death-draught waged, / Drunk from the winepress of the Almighty's wrath' (217). The remains of a battle are seen as the threatening disfiguration of a culture; only the mangled corpses survive as a kind of visceral writing:

> No remnant of the exterminated faith
> Survived to tell its ruin, but the flesh,
> With putrid smoke poisoning the atmosphere,
> That rotted on the half-extinguished pile. (221)

A comparison is drawn between the aftermath of a battle and a sacrificial meal, with the smoke, as in *Cymbeline*, rising into heaven and God's nostrils (v.vi. 478–80). The mention of poisonous fumes looks forward both to the description of consuming poisonous flesh in VIII and the refusal of sacrifice in *Laon and Cythna*.

Cythna's vision of reform pits organic forces against religion and tyranny, depicted as frozen blood:

> 'Has not the whirlwind of our spirit driven
>   Truth's deathless germs to thought's remotest caves?
> Lo, Winter comes! – the grief of many graves,
>   The frost of death, the tempest and the sword,
>   The flood of tyranny, whose sanguine waves
> Stagnate like ice at Faith, the inchanter's word,
> And bind all human hearts in its repose abhorred.'
> (IX.xxiii (202ff))

Tyranny is a 'flood', an intemperate flux of royal desire, but 'Faith' causes those waves to 'stagnate' and clot, so that the (revolutionary) spirit is sunk in the *sarkophagos* of the body. The revolutionary impulse is represented as pure spirit, while tyranny is figured as a body which grows ever more stickily corporeal as the metaphors struggle to out-trope each other.

Shelley produced an emblematically consistent series of pictures of tyranny and rebellion which in their determinacy act almost as inserted figurative diagrams, though falling short of being full-blown examples of *ekphrasis*. The second stanza of his *Ode to Liberty* (1820), celebrating the Spanish liberal revolution, is modelled on Pope's *Essay on Man*: 'beasts warr'd on beasts, and worms on worms, / And men on men; each beast was a hell of storms' (29). These destructive *zeugmata* render mutual violence a product of oppression, whose effects are felt throughout nature. The *Ode* delineates the progress of the allegorical figure, Liberty, through the French Revolution:

> Thou heaven of earth! what spells could pall thee then,
>   In ominous eclipse? a thousand years
> Bred from the slime of deep oppression's den,
>   Dyed all thy liquid light with blood and tears,
> Till thy sweet stars could weep the stain away;
>   How like Bacchanals of blood
>   Round France, the ghastly vintage, stood
> Destruction's sceptred slaves, and Folly's mitred brood!   (166)

Liberty is implicated in violence, not through some internal, essential evil within it, but because of its *relationship* with power, described as the 'spells' which could 'pall' its light. Shelley is revising *Queen Mab*'s 'O happy Earth! Reality of Heaven!' (ix.1), and through this politicizes Satan's speech in praise of Eden in *Paradise Lost*: 'Thou heaven of earth!' (ix.99ff). The earth can be re-imagined as heaven, but liberty's ironic relationship with oppression, which 'Dyed all thy liquid light with blood and tears', stopped France from achieving it. The imagery of light and darkness, and the oppressive corporeality of the 'slime', 'blood and tears', modulates into an emblem of intemperance. France is imaged as a 'ghastly vintage' surrounded by the forces of oppression who are themselves oppressed by their own tyranny and priestcraft.

Other nations surrounding France were less developed, and contributed to its 'ominous eclipse'. Their forces are 'like Bacchanals of blood'. The Dionysian Bacchantes, celebrating orgies of intoxication, are ambiguously represented in Shelley. In a previous stanza, Rome is influenced by Athens like a wolf cub suckled on 'the milk of greatness' by a 'Cadmæan Maenad' (91–94), an allusion to Euripides' *Bacchae*.[34] This is one of the points at which Shelley represents suckling, as part of a figurative scheme of radical nurturance.[35] The Cadmæan Maenad is probably Agave, the leader of the Bacchantes who slaughtered the tyrant Pentheus. And 'Truth' is later represented as a 'mysterious wine' which creates a 'Wild Bacchanal' (200), in which German tyranny will be destroyed by the spirit of Arminius, the German liberator of antiquity.

The oppressors are unstable in the language of the *Ode*, their world is disfigural: they are themselves the victims of the Bacchic power with which they threaten France. Drinking wine and spilling blood are thus figuratively associated: they both confuse, negate or tear up an essentially natural identity. Later in the poem the word *king* is described: 'The sound has poison in it, 'tis the sperm / Of what makes life foul, cankerous, and abhorred' (222). A 'cankerous' life is life against itself, developing the representation of Napoleon as a tyrannical lord of misrule, an 'Anarch' (175). Here is another Golden Age/Fall narrative. A natural state of peaceful consumption is disrupted by the influx of an unnatural, tyrannizing violence whose rule undermines (natural) order.

Visceral language is used to debate those elements of ideological blockage (custom) and intemperate flow against which the upper-class reformer struggles, the ambiguous materiality of revolutionary violence, and the non-identity of unnatural forms of power. Viscerality also denotes the literal determinacy of material suffering, for example the 'woman's blood' in *Queen Mab* VII or the 'thousand years' of oppression which resists Utopia as the body resists the spirit. Shelley's figures of intoxicated consumption delineate historical ambiguities and complexities.

THE POLITICS OF ECSTASY AND DENIAL

Teetotalism was a tenet of *A Vindication*.[36] Trotter's *Essay on Drunkenness* (read in preparation for *A Vindication*) examines alcohol as a narcotic under the same heading as opium (in contrast with De Quincey, who distinguishes them).[37] To be drunk for Trotter is to pass upper and lower limits of human nature, 'from the purest perceptions of intellect... above the sphere of mortals... to a level with the brutes'.[38] Intoxication 'is [in the case of 'vinous spirit'] "delirium ferox"'.[39] Trotter delineates an extravagant spread of passions from the digestive to the nervous system, 'by sympathy, from thence to the *sensorium commune*, and the rest of the system'.[40] Drunkenness is associated with 'Obesity and fulness' which sinks the soul in the gross body.[41]

Alcohol 'constringes and hardens' the 'animal solid' when 'applied directly'; 'and suspends its progress towards putrefaction ... It coalesces the serum of the blood, and most of the secreted fluids'.[42] It renders the body more material, not more subtle. The drunk body resists natural putrefaction, but this culturally acquired, habit-forming superiority also consumes the body (culture in excess over nature, an intemperate figure). Thus drunk people in the first stages, excited, hot and flushed, need 'the cool [vegetarian] regimen'.[43] Drink is associated (somewhat naively) with figurative language. Poetry about Bacchus is delusive because it alludes to, an Arcadian era when fermentation was unknown.[44] Medical discourse, then, is a supplement to poetry (though anyone who read Trotter's extensive quotations would think that in his case it was the other way round). He introduces a physician-poet, Erasmus Darwin:

A modern British physician of great eminence, himself a poet, far above mediocrity, both in his medical and metrical works has held a language very different from Haller and Hoffmann [who advocate alcohol with classical quotations] ... He was no wine-bibber, and died lately about the age of seventy ... he was rather a gross eater, and made amends for the want of vinous stimulus, by consuming large quantities of animal food. The muse of Darwin therefore received no inspiration from Bacchus.[45]

Trotter was also concerned to provide a social account of alcohol abuse. The word 'alcoholism' did not yet exist, but Trotter helps to formulate a system of ideas in which it could exist.[46] He also established clear links between alcohol as a taxable item and power. A 'scarcity, bordering on famine' prompted temperance, but its conclusion led to the immediate production of 'poisonous spirits' from 'the first gift of Heaven, abundance of corn ... for the sake of taxation'.[47] Trotter also observes that different nations behave differently when drunk,[48] although the bodily effects of drink as observable by science apply to 'savages' and 'Christians' alike.[49] Drunkenness provides data for a sociopathological approach which explains relationships between nature and nurture.

Shelley uses drink in his poetry to adumbrate the intemperate exploitation of power. In *The Mask of Anarchy* (1819), Shelley represents the apocalyptic procession of an anarchic force of law (a disfiguring order), inspired by the recent massacre at Peterloo:

> And, with glorious triumph, they
> Rode thro' England, proud and gay,

> Drunk as with intoxication
> Of the wine of desolation.
>
> O'er fields and towns, from sea to sea,
> Past the Pageant swift and free,
> Tearing up and trampling down;
> Till they came to London town.   (46)

'Intoxication' is here an ecstasy of destruction. In response, the radicals are to 'Let' be, in Orphic manner, to resist passively. Stanzas lxxiii to lxxviii start with 'Let' (except for lxxiv, which contains a 'let'), declaring: do not meet the oppressors on their own terms. Thus, speaks the allegorical figure (probably the eloquent blood of the earth, 143–46), '"they will return with shame"' (352) and '"the blood thus shed will speak / In hot flushes on their cheek"' (354). Silent suffering, like Abel's blood, will speak louder than words. The ruling-class reformer gives voice to this passive victim, sounding within victimization the note of humanity. The Orphic pleasure of letting-be is advocated by the upper-class reformer who assumes that the beings to be liberated cannot speak up for themselves: he must bring their silence to meaningful fruition, making slaughter '"Eloquent, oracular"' (366).

In the first issue of *The Republican* the drunkenness of the Yeomanry Cavalry at Peterloo was contrasted with the deliberate abstinence of the demonstrators.[50] Temperance was also a way of avoiding taxes which would fill Treasury coffers on the purchase of drink, tea, tobacco and so on. Carlile writes:

I am convinced that much more might be done ['to curtail...the consumption...of any of the articles from which the Boroughmongers draw the means of prosecuting us'] through self-denial, or from principle; and as our fair country-women are entering so intrepidly into the cause of Reform, I wish to address myself equally to them. There can be no difficulty in selecting those articles which are taxed, a difficulty might arise to select one not taxed, however I shall be bold enough to say that malt and spiritous liquors, tea, tobacco, &c. are articles used in much profusion, I might say in waste, and for persons proffering principles of Reform to drink to intoxication is preposterous indeed, seeing that while they sacrifice at the altar of Bacchus, they are nerving the arms of tyranny.[51]

Shelley's two Irish pamphlets, *An Address, to the Irish People* (1812) and *Proposals for an Association* (1812), can be contrasted according to their treatment of the bodies of their expected readers. *An Address* risks condescension:

My warm-hearted friends who meet together to talk of the distresses of your countrymen, until social chat induces you to drink rather freely; as ye have felt passionately, so reason coolly. Nothing hasty can be lasting; lay up the money with which you usually purchase drunkenness and ill-health, to relieve the pains of your fellow-sufferers.[52]

The Galenic opposition of hot and 'cool' (still current in the eighteenth century) is politicized. There is a certain failure of address in 'drink rather freely'.[53] The pamphlet continues: 'Do not drink, do not play, do not spend any idle time ... Think, read, and talk' (a John Stewart-like maxim); 'Temperance, sobriety, charity, and independence will give you virtue.'[54] Re-imagining the bodies of the Irish poor carries an explicit class message: 'Before Government is done away with, we must reform ourselves. It is this work which I would earnestly recommend to you, O Irishmen, REFORM YOURSELVES.'[55] The *diaitia* or regulated way of life is proleptic of an ideal social state (compare *Queen Mab* VIII). Political success has been associated with physical discipline.

Jupiter's drink of nectar in *Prometheus Unbound* III.i is part of a hubristic anti-masque (III.i.25ff). But to drink nectar or dew is not figured as intoxicating in a negative sense. Thus *Wine of the Fairies* (nd) celebrates innocent pleasure: 'I am drunk with the honey wine / Of the moon-enfolded eglantine' (1).[56] The Moon describes her circuit of the earth in *Prometheus Unbound* IV as a Dionysian frenzy:

> I, a most enamoured maiden,
> ...
>
> Maniac-like around thee move
> Gazing, an insatiate bride,
> On thy form from every side
> Like a Mænad, round the cup
> Which Agave lifted up
> In the weird Cadmæan forest.   (IV.467)[57]

The image of Maenads dancing round a cup is similar to the image of the forces surrounding France in the *Ode to Liberty*, but here it appears to have a different, more positive value. *Rosalind and Helen: a Modern Eclogue*[58] presents the love of Lionel, a 'rich and nobly born' reformer (672),[59] through Orphic figures (902–92)[60] and an elaborate metaphor of intoxication, in which a nightingale's song is described as a wine which creates a 'world of extacy' (1124). Natural ecstasy falls into the figurative scheme created for the upper-class reformer, while drunkenness is an unnatural ecstasy which oppressors exploit and from which the oppressed should abstain. Lionel's poem about the '"banquet in hell"' (line 687), is clearly a political satire.

Shelley's translation of Euripides' *The Cyclops: a Satyric Drama* (1819) pits licensed against unlicensed excess, centred around figures of drinking and flesh-eating. The Greek satyr play unwound the tensions built up by tragedy with the portrayal of the lewd body. The chorus of satyrs represent erotic, unrepressed nature, and their entry (*parodos*, hence 'parody') comically resolves a potentially tragic plot.[61] The need to consume is the base of the plot of *Cyclops*. Perhaps Shelley was fascinated by Euripides' unusual use of *kreas* (used to signify 'the flesh of animals') as signifying 'human flesh'.[62] The chorus of satyrs are released by Ulysses and his men, having been enslaved by Polyphemus. The opposition between the satyrs' and the Cyclops' excess marks Shelley's ambiguous use of intoxication and intemperance. The satyrs celebrate collectively under the influence of Bacchus, but the Cyclops simply gets drunk.

Silenus notes the 'delight / Of Bacchic sports, sweet dance and melody' (28), describing how he is forced to stay indoors and feed the Cyclops 'some impious and abominable meal' (35) – of human flesh, it is later revealed. Ulysses gives Silenus the first drink he has tasted for a long time: 'Babai! Great Bacchus calls me forth to dance! / Joy! joy!' (149). The Cyclops interrupts the exchange of lambs for wine and prevents Ulysses' departure. He is hungry for milk, cheese and sheep's flesh (as Silenus anticipates at 115).

The Cyclops intemperately desires the man 'slaughtered' (223), 'broiled and seethed' (225). The Cyclops' language is Ritsonian: in his chapter on human sacrifice (as the consequence of animal food) Ritson describes how human flesh is 'toasted' and 'broiled',[63] mentioning the Cyclopes.[64] The Cyclops has recently eaten 'stags' and 'lions' (227), emblematic of masculine and predatory nature, thus contradicting Shelley's code of a peaceful, feminine natural ideal. Ulysses begs him to reconsider: 'Forego the lust of your jawbone; prefer / Pious Humanity to wicked will' (295). 'Humanity' is a significant translation of Euripides' play on εὐσεβές/δυσσεβίας (original text, 310–11), which strictly means 'piety'/'impiety' and refers to reverence for the gods, not an essential, intrinsic human nature.

The Cyclops offends against Greek guest-host culture, 'In the flesh of strangers [who should be welcomed as one's own] joying' (366). He is a self-serving 'lawless' (29) consumer:

> The wise man's only Jupiter is this,
> To eat and drink during his little day,
> And give himself no care.   (321)

Ulysses calls him a 'God-abandoned cook of hell' (388). The second Chorus is a luxurious example of *macellogia*:

> For your gaping gulph and your gullet wide
> The ravin is ready on every side;
> The limbs of the strangers are cooked and done,
>   There is boiled meat, and roast meat, and meat from the coal,
> You may chop it, and tear it, and gnash it for fun,
>   A hairy goat's skin contains the whole.   (343)

Ulysses describes this food as 'unnatural' (410, 702), translating ἀναισχυντον (original, 416), which normally means 'unmentionable' and is usually used of persons rather than things.[65] Ulysses makes the Cyclops drunk to take his revenge (by burning out his single eye). Polyphemus describes his state as immersion in the gross body, in contrast with the light tripping satyrs:

> Ha! ha! ha! I'm full of wine,
> Heavy with the joy divine,
> With the young feast oversated.
> Like a merchant-vessel freighted
> To the water's edge, my crop
> Is laden to the gullet's top.   (505)

The Cyclops is drunk with power, but the chorus wishes to be intoxicated with joy: 'Oh, I long to dance and revel / With sweet Bromius [Bacchus]' (624). The 'merchant-vessel' is germane, as the Cyclops in response to Ulysses' speech about humanity has already declared himself worshipper of money alone (301–31):

> As to the rest I care not. – When he [Jupiter] pours
> Rain from above, I have a close pavilion
> Under this rock, in which I lie supine,
> Feasting on a roast calf or some wild beast,
> And drinking pans of milk, and gloriously
> Emulating the thunder of high Heaven.   (307–12)

The wasteful scatology reinforces the uneconomic quality of the Cyclops (an over-freighted merchant ship). *The Cyclops* demonstrates the double-sided nature of Shelley's representation of intoxication: its intemperance and association with flesh-eating, and its permissible ecstasies.

BREAD AND BLOOD: THE 1819 VOLUME

Shelley's unpublished volume of radical writing including *The Mask of Anarchy* and 'A Philosophical View of Reform' (1819), tackles hunger throughout. He was competent enough with discourses of food to understand the different class registers and implications involved, concerned not only to re-imagine the body of the reformer, but to bring to political consciousness the starving body of the poor. Unfortunately Leigh Hunt did not reply to Shelley's request to publish this volume.

Shelley was aware that bread was an ideologically-coded food as well as an important staple. Successive crop failures from 1809 to 1812 had resulted in a tense political situation.[66] Food riots, often focused around the price of bread, were popular protests against the naturalized capitalist laws of supply and demand (see chapter 1). Bread was considered '*the* staff of life' in the eighteenth century. The 'growing preference for wheaten bread among all classes' was marked in London: 'White bread, like printed cotton-clothes, enabled the poor to challenge the wealthy's consumerist monopoly.'[67] It was a universal food, while meat implied status: 'The working-class housewife not only wanted to buy meat; she wanted to be seen shopping in the shambles.'[68] Urbanization, a rising population and 'broadening divisions between the agrarian and industrial section of the economy' had led to an increasing demand for food.[69] Shelley evoked a tradition of writing which takes bread as a sustaining provision for life itself.

Without bread comes death, the fate of the starving mother who approaches Parson Richards in Shelley's *Ballad.* The parson, 'Feeding his hound with bread' (2), guards an established order, with the dog a symbol of dominion over nature, including the 'woman ... with a babe at her breast' (5) (a characteristic emblem of liberty in Shelley). The woman is prepared to trade blood for bread:

> 'Give me a piece of that fine white bread,
>   I would give you some blood for it –
> Before I faint and my infant is dead –
>   O give me a little bit.'

> 'Give me bread – my hot bowels gnaw –
>   I'll tear down the garden gate,
> I'll fight with the dog, – I'll tear from his maw
>   The crust which he just has ate.'   (17, 41)

The poor, in Shelley's view, have little to exchange for hunger but their own bodies: the really effective means of reform in *The Mask of Anarchy* is mass protest, and bread symbolizes the 'mass'. One of the banners carried aloft during the Peterloo meeting called for 'No Corn Laws'. The demand for 'fine white bread' is about recognition as part of a culture: 'fine' means 'refined' – to eat coarse bread was to descend below an acceptable cultural line. The vegetarian recipe book *On Food* (1803) tries to persuade the middle-class audience to eat wholefoods like whole wheat while recognizing the problem of adulterated bread. To return to nature, to re-imagine the body, is a good idea, but some returns are more civilized than others, and some are cast in a language which different classes would not understand in the same ways.

While fineness is a mark of lifestyle (and the refined body an aspect of vegetarian *diaitia*) 'bread' itself is a sign of the very means to life. However, these means are not a piece of pure, raw nature. The pathos of the woman's speech comes from her readiness to exchange blood (another means to life) for fine bread, in the linguistic association of 'bread ... blood ... dead'. 'The means to life' is culture, refinement: the woman claims a share of this as well as the sustaining power of the food. Shelley understood that the poor classes would not decode the language of crudity or rawness in the same way as the wealthy classes. Bread was culture, inclusion in the common life lived through society's institutions, not rawness. The connotational cluster, essential-natural-humane, found in Shelley's representations of vegetarianism, is not there. The starving woman would willingly sacrifice her blood for inclusion in the cultural order, an idea that Shelley's vegetarian language seems designed to dispute.

Food as a means to life is employed in the rhetoric of *The Mask of Anarchy*. The allegorical figure who arises amidst the crowd distinguishes freedom from slavery, by delineating the means towards the sustenance of life. Slavery is defined:

> ''Tis to hunger for such diet
> As the rich man in his riot
> Casts to the fat dogs that lie
> Surfeiting beneath his eye.'   (172)

'Diet' captures the idea of a whole way of life: this is not just a question of sustenance. Like the *Ballad of the Starving Mother*, the lines request the attention of the labouring reader. The dog eating scraps is a figure of intemperate ('riot'), tyrannical and enclaved circulation. Even wild and domestic animals have a certain security of environment compared to the labourer ('"Asses, swine, have litter spread, / And with fitting food are fed"', 205). The '"savage"' (209) is brought in to reinforce the notion that the present system of distribution is wholly unnatural.

The first positive description of freedom involves bread:

> 'For the labourer thou art bread,
> And a comely table spread
> From his daily labour come
> To a neat and happy home.
>
> Thou art clothes, and fire, and food
> For the trampled multitude –
> No – in countries that are free
> Such starvation cannot be
> As in England now we see.' (221)

The image of culture is rooted in the antithetical vision of an organic community in *Queen Mab* iii. The emphasis on pleasure ('comely', 'neat and happy') marks this as a simply-worded and well-chosen rhetoric about cultural standards. 'Starvation' gains a significance beyond the Malthusian conception of famine (as starvation leading to death), connoting the attenuation of a standard, the degradation of a self-image. This is in accordance with a labouring-class conception of famine (as material *and* cultural loss), rather than the viscerally corporeal image promoted by charity institutions.

In the *Sonnet* on the state of England in 1819 Shelley politicizes the 'population check' of starvation by juxtaposing an image of uncultivated land, reminiscent of Peterloo: 'A people starved and stabbed in the untilled field' (7). Starvation becomes a matter of deliberate and active degradation: Malthusian politics as genocide. The field *should* be cultivated; nature is best when mediated through human nature. Bread figures in a densely-compacted image in *An Ode Written October 1819, before the Spaniards had Recovered their Liberty*, a popular song disguised as an ode (which did not appear in the 1819 volume, but with *Prometheus Unbound*), to deter unwelcome glances at the contents page. Here are the first lines:

> Arise, arise, arise!
> There is blood on the earth that denies ye bread;
> Be your wounds like eyes
> To weep for the dead, the dead, the dead. (1)

The second line is capable of a number of possible readings. The 'blood' is a metaphor for unjust suffering: blood which *prevents* corn from growing by choking the fecundity of nature. Alternatively, nature itself has been wounded and cannot be fertile. 'Blood' also suggests the oppression of ruling-class families. The verse continues with a baroque, rather Caroline, conceit about the politicization of mourning: to turn wounds into eyes is to turn suffering into insight, echoing Shelley's prose on Princess Charlotte (1817). The labourers are associated with the image of a wounded nature ('blood on the earth').

Shelley politicizes the lack of 'bread'. 'Famine' is linked with a sense of social injustice, a revolutionary potential in the contradiction between master and slave ('The slave and the tyrant are twin-born foes', 8):

> Wave, wave high the banner!
> When Freedom is riding to conquest by:
> Though the slaves which fan her
> Be famine and toil, giving sigh for sigh.   (15)

Those who famish are slaves (in the sense of line 8), but famine itself inspires the desire for liberty. This is a remarkably compact piece of Shelleyan theory (and it makes good verse).

Shelley omitted a final stanza[70] which in seven lines reworks the millennial vision of *Queen Mab* VIII, evoking a reconciliation amongst humans and nature:

> Gather, O gather,
> Foeman and friend in love and peace!
> Waves sleep together
> When the blasts that called them to battle, cease.
> For fangless Power grown tame and mild
> Is at play with Freedom's fearless child –
> The dove and the serpent reconciled!   (omitted)

'Fangless Power' recalls the lion who becomes a lamb; the sleep of the waves undoes violent death (compare *Laon and Cythna* v). Shelley probably wondered whether the rather self-contained coding of this stanza might not blunt the militant/evangelistic quality of the rest of the *Ode*, and its theory about the twin-born foes, although the final published stanza is an exhortation to 'Hide the blood-stains now' beneath crowns of leaves (31).

Shelley was concerned to promote reform through virtue, transfigured through the body's self-image. The poetry of 'bread', however, was a fresh and distinct kind of discourse that did not require the intricate revisions of the millennium which were carried out in Shelley's earlier work.

CULTURE AND LUXURY: *THE CENCI, SWELLFOOT THE TYRANT*
AND *CHARLES I*

Adams' study of the semiotics of food has shown how the slaughter of the animal is effaced or 'hushed up' (*The Cenci* i.i.i)[71] in the transformation from living animal to meat.[72] The first line of *The Cenci* asserts a linguistic *aporia* which is connected with violence: murder becomes metaphor. It connotes psychic violence in parallel with physical violence. Count Cenci's perspective is Hobbesian: the soul is an echo of the body.[73] Beatrice's silent eloquence is set against this.

The treatment of the relationship between violence and language in *The Cenci* shows how Shelley was involved in a debate about the nature of civilization.[74] Torture is criticized as a means of violently consuming forensic evidence, and the excessive lusts of the Count are described using the imagery of diet. The rape of Beatrice by her father promotes an analysis of the politics of language.[75] The rape figuratively relates gender, politics and consumption.

Beatrice gains control over the sympathy of the audience through her silence. Cenci's thaumaturgic use of language, in which words become deeds at a stroke, contradicts this silence. This thaumaturgy was known to Shelley as a form of incarnation: literally, the fleshing-out of a word, its embodiment or concrete enactment.[76] The Leavisite and New Critical schools have both criticized Shelley for not incarnating his ideas more concretely, and as 'incarnation' is their major token of praise (it is Shakespeare who is the model of 'incarnation' in one New Critical schema for all types of figurative language), Shelley has been demeaned.[77] A formalist reading of Shelley's prosody, such as William Keach's, shows how good Shelley was at incarnation. There were, however, ideological reasons for Shelley's difficulties: a link between incarnation and violence which was already pointed out in his vegetarian critique of the Eucharist and Christian iconography.[78] The bonds between Cenci and the

Church of Rome encode the links between injustice and violence against the body in the family and in society.

The preface to the play is anti-didactic, advocating moral learning through sympathy and antipathy and seeing all humans as fully human to the extent of their self-knowledge. *The Cenci* forces the audience to 'work out its solution, rather than imposing an authorial dogma'.[79] The problem is how to view the actions of Beatrice after the rape, notably in the Lady Macbeth-like murder of Cenci. But certain instructions for reading the play are inscribed in its use of the imagery of consumption. Its audiences' consumption, since it uses a 'judge with your own eyes' rhetorical patterning, is based on the rhetoric of faciality.

The Cenci widens the scope of sympathetic response and knowledge encoded by the rhetoric of dismemberment, initiating a debate about the social production of law, knowledge and violence. The most striking occurrence of consumption imagery in *The Cenci* is the banquet scene (I.iii), indebted to the tragic anti-banquets of *Macbeth* (III.iv) and *Timon of Athens* (III.vii). In Shakespeare as in Shelley, the sharing of food provides a dramatic analogue for the larger ethical structures in the plays. The meal is a ritual display of the protagonist's identity which, when it is disrupted in some way (the appearance of a ghost, the serving of inappropriate food like lukewarm water, or Cenci's boasting of the murder of his sons), precipitates the eventual downfall of the protagonist. The perversity of the celebration is an emblem of the adverse moral judgment of the protagonist.

The Count styles himself as a hermit returning from isolation. Hermit and tyrant are consistent Shelleyan figures for the temperate and intemperate archetypes:

> I have too long lived like an anchorite;
> ...
>
> But I do hope that you, my noble friends,
> Have shared the entertainment here,
> And heard the pious cause for which 'tis given,
> And we have pledged a health or two together,
> Will think me flesh and blood as well as you.　　(4)

But his schemes are transparent, since rather than presenting the self-sufficient identity of a true anchorite, the wish to display his power is manifested to excess: a conspicuous consumption of his identity after the parodic communal sharing of the meal. This desire to have power on display, constantly to be enacting it through the word-magic of self-fulfilling rhetoric, characterizes Cenci as a hateful tyrant. Torture and rape are forms of conspicuous consumption – the meal was arranged to honour the literal execution of Cenci's curse ('prayer') upon his sons (21–33). An explicit analogy between the aristocracy and Rome is drawn. Filling a bowl of wine, Cenci declares:

> Oh, thou bright wine, whose purple splendour leaps
> And bubbles gaily in this golden bowl
> Under the lamp-light, as my spirits do,
> To hear the death of my accursed sons!
> Could I believe thou wert their mingled blood,
> Then would I taste thee like a sacrament,
> And pledge with thee the mighty Devil in Hell;
> Who, if a father's curses, as men say,
> Climb with swift wings after their children's souls,
> And drag them from the very throne of Heaven,
> Now triumphs in my triumph! (77)

The opening lines mock the classical apostrophe to the amphora of wine. Intoxication takes one out of oneself. Cenci's violence is an ecstatic instance of non-identity; he drinks to steel his passion at the end of the scene. Cenci attempts to laud himself and make a virtue out of his self-deception.

In her panic before Cenci's rape, Beatrice declares to her step-mother Lucretia and her brother Bernardo:

> Oh! he has trampled me
> Under his feet, and made the blood stream down
> My pallid cheeks. And he has given us all
> Ditch-water, and the fever-stricken flesh
> Of buffaloes, and bade us eat or starve,
> And we have eaten. (II.i.64)

Beatrice's discourse is miasmatic: her use of food imagery is a figure for the breaking of taboos. Cenci has forced everyone intemperately to step over a threshold. Having been raped, Beatrice's body becomes a cloud of pollution (III.i.6–32), an ecstasy of clogged, thick materiality which the speaking subject literally stands beside:

> Do you know
> I thought I was that wretched Beatrice
> Men speak of, whom her father sometimes hales

> From hall to hall by the entangled hair;
> At others, pens up naked in damp cells
> Where scaly reptiles crawl, and starves her there,
> Till she will eat strange flesh.   (42)

This state of madness is micropolitical: Beatrice has been *forced* to eat taboo food.

Cenci's intemperance binds him to his self-deception, so that he will inevitably be slaughtered through Shelley's logic of consumption. Beatrice herself is implicated in the violence which rhetorically she tries to resist, again using a food metaphor, denying that:

> power is as a beast which grasps
> And loosens not: a snake whose look transmutes
> All things to guilt which is its nutriment.   (iv.iv.178)

During the trial scene, Beatrice still attempts to resist the literal Papal-familial-state machine whose 'look' marks and consumes the body. The machine perverts a benign relationship between humans and domesticated animals:

> Tortures! Turn
> The rack henceforth into a spinning-wheel!
> Torture your dog, that he may tell when last
> He lapped the blood his master shed.   (v.iii.61)

Beatrice responds to the Judge's demand for a truth that he believes may be elicited through violence: 'Let tortures strain the truth till it be white / As snow thrice-sifted by the frozen wind' (v.ii.169). One is reminded of the whitening of the butchered flesh in Pratt's *Humanity*. Marzio tries to put himself in Beatrice's place, using a hunting image: 'Bloodhounds, not men, glut yourselves well with me; / I will not give you that fine piece of nature / To rend and ruin' (v.ii.166). Torture is a method of consumption or glutting. Beatrice is here another example of feminized nature in Shelley's rhetoric of non-violence. The 'torture your dog' passage is apt, since *The Cenci* is concerned throughout with the disruption of the domestic. The act of domestication appropriates the boundary between culture and nature under the sign of violence. Beatrice is a 'fine piece of nature' who has already been ruined by an act of incest, a gross parody of domestication. Beatrice's point is that she must not be treated like a dog: to have a dog is to participate in a relationship where torture is already present, in the Shelleyan sense of the blunting and warping of its natural existence. Shelley is concerned with the problem of how to create non-violent legal, familial and domestic spaces.

Titus Andronicus is significant for *The Cenci*'s figuration of the body. When Lavinia is about to be raped, she pleads: 'The lion, moved with pity, did endure / To have his princely paws pared all away' (II.iii.151). This is revised in the section on the lion in *Queen Mab* (VIII.124ff). At the banquet in Shakespeare's play, Titus tells his daughter:

> Thou shalt not sigh, nor hold thy stumps to heaven,
> Nor wink, nor nod, nor kneel, nor make a sign,
> But I of these will wrest an alphabet,
> And by still practice learn to know thy meaning.   (III.ii.42)

The body and language are being associated in ways which Shelley developed in the figures of silent eloquence. At the end of *Titus Andronicus*, Saturninus eats pies made of the villains (v.ii, iii). Marcus speaks of Rome as a fragmented body:

> O, let me teach you how to knit again
> This scattered corn into one mutual sheaf,
> These broken limbs again into one body.   (v.iii.69)

There are, however, differences between *The Cenci*'s portrayal of the despotic overcoding of family, religion and state and *Titus Andronicus'* portrayal of *antisocial* violence in the figure of Saturninus (representing a corrupt 'Golden Age'). In the Roman plays in general, founding and re-founding acts of society are imaged as a feast whose overtones of cannibalism and eucharistic participation would have troubled Shelley. Shelley's vegetarian vision is not of a new society in this respect, but of a grounding and limiting of existing social flows based on axioms and principles rather than codes and symbols.

Oedipus Tyrannus; or, Swellfoot the Tyrant (1820) attempts to depict the political sufferings of another class.[80] *Swellfoot* articulates the political relations which emerge from dramatic action. Food is not only a 'content' element but also an expressive principle, providing ways of representing class relationships in speech, action and spectacle. Although its Spencean and Burkean contexts have been explored,[81] the play has never been given more than a humble place in the Shelley canon. It deals with famine and luxury. Much of the action is set in a grisly temple of Famine personified: '*built of thigh-*

bones and death's heads, and tiled with scalps' (I.i, opening stage direction);
'*The statue of the Goddess* [of famine], *a skeleton clothed in parti-coloured
rags, seated upon a heap of skulls and loaves intermingled* [and attended by
'*A number of exceedingly fat Priests in black garments arrayed on each side,
with marrow-bones and cleavers in their hands'*]' (II.ii, opening stage
direction).

The presence of pigs *and* humans in the cast suggests not only
prosopopoeia, but the establishment of a (political) relationship
between two *classes* of creature. This presence of farm-animals bred
for food along with humans opens up at least three levels of
interpretation. First, animals are represented voicing the opinions of
men: simple *prosopopoeia* adds an element of degradation to the
grotesque comedy (Greek satyr plays were supposed to have rowdy
animal choruses, and Aristophanic comedy certainly does: both are
conjectured models for *Swellfoot*). Secondly, this is overcoded so that
men *becoming* animals is itself significant: opening the possibility of
expressing social relationships biologically, and conversely, politi-
cizing the natural world. Thirdly, men are represented mangling
and butchering animals – and in the final comic reversal, animals
hunt down men. This third interpretative level shows how Shelley's
thinking about consumption had continued since his earlier life, in
the case of *Swellfoot* providing imagery which could be given a
number of figurative readings. Society is modelled as a farm; but the
monopolizing tendencies of the rich owners is shown to extend to the
power they wield over animals.

Swellfoot is another swaggering, incontinent and corpulent Shelley
villain. Through his worship of Famine (represented as a goddess) his
'nether promontories / Lie satisfied with layers of fat' (I.i.5). The
description of the Devil's suppers in *Peter Bell the Third* (IV.76–110) or
the figure of obesity in *The Devil's Walk* (1812),[82] and the viscerality
of *Similes for Two Political Characters* (1819) work along similar lines.
Swellfoot praises

> Kings and laurelled Emperors,
> Radical-butchers, Paper-money-millers,
> Bishops and deacons, and the entire army
> Of those fat martyrs to the persecution
> Of stifling turtle-soup, and brandy-devils.   (11)

This is the familiar dietary language of disgusting excess. To topple
him, must we suppose revolutionary revenge or reform (as the
epigraph asks)? To represent tyranny as a body suggests the former:

in the context of a satyr-play, a physical overthrow would be funnier than Swellfoot going on a diet. Indeed, *Swellfoot* allows Shelley to play more dangerously than normal with the discourses of diet.

The Chorus of Swine is the protagonist of *Swellfoot*. If Shelley can be seen to be interpreting Dionysian and Apollonian art prior to Nietzsche, as some critics have suggested,[83] then the Swine and Swellfoot show him interested in the necessary violence implicit in the imposition of Apollonian order on a disruptive Dionysian element which finally has its day. But the political nature of this 'necessary violence' means that this is not as easy as saying that Nature's chaos overrides culture's order. Shelley suggests that the body is constructed, produced and consumed in society. The Pigs are created for meat *within* culture. The Swine may be a grotesque multitude as in Burke[84] (and more specifically the labouring classes whose diet is potatoes and oatmeal, 1.i.27–28), but their triumph is not a triumph of life but a political rout.

Language is used to talk about food in *Swellfoot,* but in addition food is used to describe certain effects of language. In 1.i Dakry the Wizard harangues the Swine. Abstracts fill the lines of his speech. He describes the effects of pathos in rhetoric using visceral imagery which seems literally to enact his language-game in corporeal reality:

> and then I wept,
> With the pathos of my own eloquence,
> And every tear turned to a mill-stone, which
> Brained many a gaping Pig, and there was made
> A slough of blood and brains upon the place,
> Greased with the pounded bacon; round and round
> The millstones rolled, ploughing the pavement up,
> And hurling sucking-pigs into the air,
> With dust and stones. (336)

The visceral body is pinned under the Juggernaut of industrial tyranny (surely the connotation of the millstones), the alienation of the oppressed associated with a decoded flow of offal and gristle and blood: pathos as *ressentiment* which immiserates as it soothes. But the image is literally one of food production, of turning live pigs into dead bacon. In a far more sophisticated way than *Queen Mab*'s use of Juggernaut and machine imagery (which one suspects may be the source of Marx's image in *Das Kapital*),[85] Shelley articulates the worker's body as the functionary, the subject *and* the object of the capitalist machine (the Wizard is literally living off its products).

Eating is associated with appropriating material reality. Dietary metaphors are used in the description of Mammon's '"GREEN BAG"' (365), an allusion to the collection of incriminating evidence by the secret services in contemporary England and political scandals surrounding Queen Caroline's landing in England.[86] It is filled with poison which will register the effect of lies on the body of the liar through disfigurement. This corporealization of truth suggests comparisons with earlier non-democratic representations (compare *The Cenci*).[87] Shelley substituted the notion of cleanliness of conduct, the gaze of reason, for the bodily marking of violently coercive control. The aristocrats fabricate the idea that the Green Bag is like a medieval ordeal: its contents are 'the true test of guilt or innocence' (1.i.393) and will 'transform' the person to deformity (394) or cause him or her to be 'transfigured / into an angel' (396).

Description itself is used as rhetorical threat through the language about food. The fact that the Swine are potential meat underscores their political significance. When one of the Swine questions the greenness of the Green Bag (II.i.74–76), suspecting its contents to be poisonous, Purganax replies with a macabre version of the 'syllogism in grass':[88]

> Honourable swine,
> In piggish souls can prepossessions reign?
> Allow me to remind you, grass is green –
> All flesh is grass; – no bacon is but flesh –
> Ye are but bacon.   (76)

The verbs 'to be' in the sentence are performing ever more extravagantly metaphorical, *and* ever more violent, identifications. The implications for ecological understanding in this anti-logical 'syllogism' have recently been discussed; Shelley would have had reservations about this way of thinking.[89] These dubious metaphorical substitutions are repeated later when, after praising Famine, Laoctonos declares that 'Claret, somehow, / Puts me in mind of blood, and blood of claret!' (II.ii.35). The suggestiveness of figurative language is articulated as an intoxicated ecstasy of violence.[90]

Food provides a way of imaging politicized relationships between figurative language and violence in *Swellfoot*. Mammon sees political control as all very easy: just 'decimate some regiments' (1.i.106), forge some 'coin paper' (107) (again, a concurrence of blood and gold). It is all a question of figures (the numerical sense connoting an extreme arbitrariness), and of treating bodies as figures. This elision of the difference between an arbitrary system (paper money) and the bodies of men can also be expressed the other way round, so that paper money makes gold: gold will 'purge himself, / In emulation of her vestal whiteness' (109). The aristocrats are by implication sucking the blood and excrement out of John Bull like the animals they use to spy on Iona, the Gadfly, the Leech and the Rat.

Swellfoot details the celibate, 'purged' body of paper coin, and the excessive body of capital (a cynical use of 'vestal whiteness'), in contrast with the 'bilious face' of gold. Drunkards (1.i.113) are depicted in control of an oppressively puritanical order. A capitalist system simply substitutes another form of control: the meaningless and hypocritical purity of 'virgin' capital for the lewd (and now devalued, purged) 'face' of gold (the face of the sovereign or despot). Aristocratic power is decoded as capital's full body: the 'new aristocracy' of which *A Vindication* and 'A Philosophical View of Reform' speak.

The Swine demand better conditions from Swellfoot:

> Now if your Majesty would have our bristles
>   To bind your mortar with, or fill our colons
> With rich blood, or make brawn out of our gristles,
>   In policy – ask else your royal Solons –
> You ought to give us hog-wash and clean straw,
> And sties well thatched; besides, it is the law! (64)

In response Swellfoot calls Moses the sow-gelder and Zephaniah the pig-butcher. The 'brute' to be killed by Zephaniah is 'overfed' (84). Zephaniah complains that the pig is sick (86–89): 'We shall find five pints of hydatids [cysts] in's liver' (87). Swellfoot insists that he can be used 'instead of riot money' (90) when the troops will 'relish carrion' (93) 'after a day / Of butchering' (92–93). This sophisticated circulation of meat even finds a place for excrements: the pigs are worth 'skin and bones, and some few hairs for mortar' (39).

The part played by faciality in the revision of the body of the coin can be used to interpret the function of the ascetic, 'cultured' diet. The natural diet resists the tyrannical 'face' (the lamb looking like Christ into the butcher's face). In addition, however, it re-encodes capital's full body by tempering the circulation of value and the flow of miasma, creating yet more power, immanent capital, true patriotism. It operates both as a decoding process which decodes a hierarchy, and as an axiomatic (a Pythagorean 'golden rule'), which releases the decoded flows along rigid channels.

The bodily plenitude resulting from the farmyard/slaughterhouse model raises some political problems at the end of the play, when the overthrow of Swellfoot must be *embodied* by Iona's throwing of the Bag over his head. She has just been praying for reform rather than civil war:

> The earth did never mean her foizon
> For those who crown life's cup with poison
> Of fanatic rage and meaningless revenge.   (II.ii.93)

But civil war is practically what happens, in a gleefully-enacted carnival: the 'holiday' atmosphere is explicit (125). It is as if the play's figurative language were linked to a certain triumphalism at odds with a reformist, 'bloodless' message. The contents of the bag turn Swellfoot and the court into '*a number of filthy and ugly animals*' (II.ii, stage direction). These animals are then hunted down by a Pig whose body has been transfigured back into John Bull, on whose back rides the spurred Iona:

> Hoa! hoa! tallyho! tallyho! ho! ho!
> Come, let us hunt these ugly badgers down,
> These stinking foxes, these devouring otters,
> These hares, these wolves, these anything but men.
> Hey, for a whipper-in! my loyal pigs,
> Now let your noses be as keen as beagles',
> Your steps as swift as greyhounds', and your cries
> More dulcet and symphonious than the bells
> Of village-towers, on sunshine holiday;
> Wake all the dewy woods with jangling music.
> Give them no law (are they not beasts of blood?)
> But such as they gave you.   (117)

The figure derives from the Medieval topos of the *monde renversé*, in which animals are depicted hunting men.[91] The Swine must return to an aristocratic form in order to defeat aristocracy: the image is somewhat self-defeating.[92] The final chorus (of Iona and the Swine together) is a muddier version of the psychedelics of *Prometheus Unbound* IV, with its exhilarating dance of reforming desire. In a different register, the same formal components yield strangely similar messages: we are not riding through villages and towns but through bogs and fens, just as the characters in *Prometheus Unbound* ride into an uncharted, non-cultured nature (131–40). The tyrants are chased off England's farm like vermin, and disfiguration is undone. Shelley is taking a political risk by using figurative language about nature and the body. Shelley's millennial, carnivalesque poetry attempts to revise the conservatism of the world turned upside down, the *adynaton*. Instead of a comment on the immaturity of contemporary times, the *adynaton* (of which the revision of Isaiah in *Queen Mab* VIII is an example) becomes Utopian. But the image of a lion lying down with a lamb is different from that of a hunted creature becoming the hunter.

At the end of *Swellfoot*, the food rises up against its consumer: the abysm of England literally vomits forth its secrets (continuing the parallel with *Prometheus*). The licentious moment of overthrow must at some point be regulated, however, and set to work. The no-spaces of pollution, the bogs through which the pigs travel, the decoded flow of poison which literally decodes the tyrants, issuing from the Green Bag, are brought into play. The secret evidence contained in the Green Bag is an occult knowledge of society which could shake it to its foundations, but only when released upon the right people. The happy monastic asceticism of Shelley's millennium is not yet in place.

Shelley evidently had swine on his mind between 1819 and 1820, while writing 'On the Devil, and Devils'. His grotesquely comic treatment of the body and food bears resemblances to *Swellfoot*:

What became of the Devils after the death of the pigs [in the Gadarene Swine episode of the gospels], whether they passed into the fish [on hurling themselves over the cliff], and then by digestion, through the stomach, into the brain of the Gadarene Ichthyophagists [fish-eaters];...I should be anxious to know whether any half-starved Jew picked up these pigs, and sold them at the market of Gadara, and what effect the bacon of a demoniac pig, who had killed himself, produced upon the consumers...If I were a pig herd I would make any [space] rather than that [to jump off a cliff], to a master renowned for subtility of penetration, and extent and variety of experience.

Among the theories concerning the condition of Devils, some have applied to the Pythagorean hypothesis, but in such a manner as to pervert that hypothesis, from motives of humanity, into an excuse for cruel tyranny. They suppose that the bodies of animals, and especially domestic animals, are animated by devils, and that the tyranny exercised over these unfortunate beings by man is an unconscious piece of retaliation over the beings who betrayed them into a state of reprobation. On this theory Lord Erskine's Act might have been entitled 'An Act for the better protection of Devils'. How devils inhabit the bodies of men is not explained.[93]

This little-known passage shows that Shelley formed a critical opinion of Erskine. The 'Pythagorean hypothesis' is the theory of metempsychosis, and those who have 'applied' it would include (in a grotesque irony) anyone who exercises cruelty to animals. Shelley conveys a sophisticated notion of the projection of hatred onto animals. He understands Lord Erskine's speech to be about power-relationships between humans and animals. The comic discussion about eating possessed bacon shows Shelley's interest in meat as poison.

The passage is from a comically sceptical series of improbable questions about relationships between spirit and matter. God and the Devil have already been lambasted in a grandiose image of cruelty to animals, including producing veal calves, 'whipping pigs to death' (mentioned by Ritson),[94] vivisection and 'cooking': they are like 'a troop of idle dirty boys baiting a cat', with 'that very disinterested love of tormenting and annoying which is seldom observed on earth'.[95] Shelley is suggesting (here comically, elsewhere in earnest), that there is a straight line from lobster boiling to Christian state despotism. The passage about the swine simply pushes the thinking to a grotesque conclusion. The representation of the 'half-starved Jew' parallels *Swellfoot*'s representation of the inextricable linkage of greed, hunger and (political) violence, and it is implicated in the same kinds of problematic discourses of the carnivalesque which helped to construct Medieval anti-semitism.[96] As noted elsewhere, issues of ethnicity are intricated in the discourses of diet.

Charles I (1818–22) employs emblems of disfiguration as a way of representing revolutionary politics. The seventeenth century was remembered in the debate about the French Revolution. Medwin's hagiography of Shelley was keen to stress the poet's dislike of the beheading of the king.[97] But in the text as it stands another disfigured character emerges: Alexander Leighton. His face has been branded and thus disfigured, in a sense his 'true face' has been torn off. Leighton (1568–1649) was fined, degraded from holy orders, pilloried and whipped (twice), had both ears and nostrils cut off, and his face branded with 'S. S.' ('sower of sedition'), for publishing *Sion's Plea* (1628); he was then imprisoned for life.[98] The relationship between disfigurement and the violence which it generates suggests that the oppressed cannot pull themselves up by their own bootstraps as exemplary humanitarian reformers.

The opening of the play shows that the supposed harmony and aesthetic pleasure of Charles' regime masks a disfiguring violence. The masque of the Inns of Court simply makes 'Hell' briefly resemble 'Heaven' for the Citizens who open the play (1.5). The Second Citizen declares:

> Eight years are gone,
> And they seem hours, since in this populous street
> I trod on grass made green by summer's rain,
> For the red plague kept state within that palace
> Where now that vanity reigns. In nine years more
> The roots will be refreshed with civil blood. (1.6)

The Citizen evokes a certain revolutionary nostalgia through his memory of nature. The natural scene is opposed to the artificial 'vanity' of Charles' rule. Noticing the Archbishop, he remarks:

> Rather say the Pope:
> London will be soon his Rome: he walks
> As if he trod upon the heads of men:
> He looks elate, drunken with blood and gold; –
> Beside him moves the Babylonian woman
> Invisibly, and with her as his shadow,
> Mitred adulterer! he is joined in sin,
> Which turns Heaven's milk of mercy to revenge. (1.58)

To tread ground is to assert one's presence in an environment. Three kinds of treading have already been imagined: the procession of the masque, the nostalgic treading on the green grass, and the treading on the heads of men by the Archbishop. The turf of England has been staked out by those who have no claim to possess it, including the Archbishop, a figure of intemperance, 'drunken with blood and gold' (as opposed to the mild milk of heaven). This bloodthirstiness is reproduced lower down in the 'lewd and papist drunkards' (1.96) who dance around the Maypole on the Sabbath, like 'A man who thus twice crucifies his God' (101).

The regime is symbolized by the masque which affects the seamless aesthetic beauty and order described by the Youth (1.137–49). The Second Citizen disrupts this order by introducing another 'nature': the aristocracy are

> Nobles, and sons of nobles, patentees,
> Monopolists, and stewards of this poor farm,
> On whose lean sheep sit the prophetic crows. (1.151)

This image is sophisticated in its additional suggestion of a social division which splits society into two sections: the rulers who luxuriously monopolize what is really only a 'poor farm' (bad culture) and the ruled, who live in a squalid nature ('her cold hard bosom', I.162). Culture and nature are intemperately divided. The Youth appropriates the Second Citizen's vision of two halves of a torn whole:

> 'Tis but
> The anti-masque, and serves as discords do
> In sweetest music. Who would love May flowers
> If they succeeded not to Winter's flaw ...   (I.174)

This recurrent image now questions the ambiguity of a natural perspective. The Youth pictures a cyclic (Catholic) nature; the Puritan's version is of a nature burnt out by society, a realm not of flowers but of 'disease', 'shame', 'famine' and 'want' (I.163–64).[99] The two characters arrive at an altercation over the ideology of nature which the Second Citizen begins to articulate: 'I and thou –' (I. 179). The scene ends abruptly without resolving the conflict: the pair are simply pushed aside by a Marshalman directing the flow of the masque. Shelley 'places' the language of the disfigured within a larger social context which questions its efficacy. He is wrestling with his own aesthetic discourses, trying to situate politically the themes of nature, beauty, 'appearance' and 'inner truth'.

However, the argument in favour of the Second Citizen has already been weighed by the disfigured figure of Leighton. The symbolic order of the masque is offset by this sudden intrusion: the King's power is articulated not only through pageantry but also through violence. Leighton himself images the violence done to him as a kind of articulation:

> I *was* Leighton: what
> I *am* thou seest. And yet turn thine eyes,
> And with thy memory look upon thy friend's mind,
> Which is unchanged, and where is written deep
> The sentence of my judge.
> *Third Citizen.* Are these the marks with which
> Laud thinks to improve the image of his Maker
> Stamped on the face of man? Curses upon him,
> The impious tyrant!   (I.88)

Through the rhetoric of silent eloquence (the voice of the same within difference), Leighton reclaims a kind of identity beyond physical (dis)figuration. Laud thinks that he can overwrite the law of God, inscribed on the very body of man. It is a strong image of extreme ugliness and horror in the midst of aestheticized pomp: every 'cultural document' can be read as a 'record of barbarism'.[100] Shelley's *A Vindication* supplies a similar reading of violence within civilization (difference within the order of the same): 'luxury is the forerunner of a barbarism scarce capable of cure'.[101] The political difference between Shelley and Benjamin lies in the difference between a document and a forerunner.

Shelley mobilizes discourses of difference as a politicized effect of signification in a graphic, sardonic, satirical register. Writing about intemperance and viscerality focuses issues of power, class, nature and change. Shelley draws upon Romance, Greek drama, Shakespeare and popular Medieval traditions, producing not only figures of intemperate consumers but also self-reflexive, intemperate, linguistic figures. The flows of blood, gold, miasma and desire, the succession of wrath and the progress of the seasons, set up dialogues between revolution and reform. Such corporeal flows are used to insist upon the refinement of culture according to principles which evoke 'nature' as a tool of distinction.

Shelley's dramas are about the proper management of spaces in which the body is articulated: the spaces of domestic, urban, agrarian, parliamentary and state power. The management of the body in national and global spaces was a feature of Shelley's ecology, examined in the final chapter. Shelley's use of intemperate figures supports his attempt to distinguish between luxury and culture. The notion of the poet as a culture-manager was elaborated in the 1790–1820 period. It was no longer a question of what Wordsworth's *Essay, Supplementary to the Preface* (1815), called the 'passive sense of the human body', *taste*,[102] but of a *power* embodied by the poet,[103] which renders the 'discovery' of the 'Man of Science' 'palpably material'. A similar mode of expression occurs in Shelley's 'Defence of Poetry' (1821): 'we have eaten more than we can digest',[104] refers to the uncontrolled development of the productive forces against the cultural lag in the early, expansive Industrial Revolution. The figure of digestion connotes not the outward registration of the sense of taste, but the deep inward processes of assimilation, growth, in other words *culture*, straddling the luxury and want, anarchy and despotism which flow from the intemperate or 'unmitigated exercise of the calculating faculty'.[105]

Shelley's anti-capitalism only went so far. The point was not to vomit up the newly-eaten food of industry, but to digest it: the redemption of the calculating faculty was the celebration of techno-humanism through the concept of culture. 'Technohumanism' may be defined in the formula: industry plus culture equals pleasurable progress.[106] How might one sustain this progress? 'Thinking-about-sustaining-an-environment-for-progress': ecology.

CHAPTER 6

Sustaining natures: Shelley and ecocriticism

Malthus is a very clever man, & the world would be a great
gainer if it would seriously take his lessons into consideration –
if it were capable of attending seriously to any thing but mischief
– but what on earth does he mean by some of his inferences!

(Shelley, *L* II.43)

The rich *grind* the poor into abjectness & then complain that
they are abject. – They goad them to famine and hang them if
they steal a loaf.

(*L* I.271)

INTRODUCTION

Of all the words discussed in this book, 'nature' is the most fraught
with conflict, and it is obviously in the field of definitions of nature
that ecology is contested. This chapter closes the book and opens out
further ways of articulating the body, the city and capitalism through
food. It accounts for developments in ecological writing, including
the new prose on 'Romantic ecology'. If the Shelleys and their circle
speak to us of waste and flow, populations and poison, the dangers
and benefits of capitalism, the corruptions of a certain kind of
'materialism' and the reform which will green the desert and sustain
life for all, then may they be considered to be speaking ecologically,
and with what sort of dialect?

The first section discusses the discourse of famine in Shelley's
debate with Malthus. Since the contemporary arguments about
famine and population are so vigorous, it seems an apt beginning. To
focus on famine may help to ground further discussions of ecology in
the 'politics of the body'. The analysis of representations of famine
in Shelley's poetry in the following section shows how Shelley strives
to reconfigure 'nature', to re-politicize it by emphasizing miasmatic
flows (both material and moral). The next two sections can thus

develop the notions of Romantic ecology from a grounding in Shelley's imagining of famine, renewal and sustainability. The central question here is, 'what place do ecologies occupy in capitalist society?' Shelley's place within modernity must be scrutinized.

In conclusion, how may we map the relationships between Romanticism, the Enlightenment, postmodernism? It has been commonly assumed in recent academic debates that Romanticism (of which Shelley is taken to be a part) is anti-Enlightenment, and that ecology is also, to a certain extent, anti-Enlightenment. These concepts carry very serious ideological cargo (for example, anti-fascism). Shelley's use of writers from Monboddo to Malthus in his figuration of the body can hardly be described as a blatant anti-Enlightenment strategy. Is it necessary for an anti-capitalist discourse, such as ecology or the Romantic critique of alienation, to oppose capitalism to its roots? While he is usually hailed as a proto-Marxist thinker, Shelley seems to be criticizing industry and capitalism while he invests in the very naturalistic modes of representation and distribution of bodies that maintain the machines of industry and commerce.

As capitalism drains the earth's resources, it is necessary to think about the status of the earth lest we fall into a slough of blood and soil politics. But the futurism of the pure ascetic body may also be a danger. There may be fascisizing (recoding and reterritorializing) tendencies within any of the discourses produced by the capitalist social machine. The problem must be analyzed squarely rather than by shoring one discourse against another (a product of the very fetishizing and abstracting process which generates the problem). Aware of this, the conclusion raises general questions about the project of the book as a whole.

THE POETICS OF FAMINE: SHELLEY AND MALTHUS

Shelley's vegetarian prose discusses famine explicitly.[1] Questions of *diaitia* (the culture of diet) and *sustenance* (the means to life) cut across more political boundaries than one might assume. Shelley criticizes Malthus with objections in part derived from his support of Godwinian ideas about the perfectibility of man (explicitly attacked by Malthus). Malthus, however, provided a figurative framework through which Shelley could think ecologically. Indeed, Godwin's

Answer to Malthus had been praised ambiguously as 'a dry but clever book, with decent interspersions of cant and sophistry'.[2] Malthus' naturalism is used for 'conservative' ends, Shelley's for 'radical' ends.

The *Essay on Population* (1798) reduces politics to the discussion of the gross, material body. Populousness itself is a threat to social stability. Populousness is related directly to 'the means of subsistence',[3] whereby improvements in material culture jeopardize society. Society is a process in which groups try to pull themselves up by their own bootstraps through progressively successful means of subsistence.[4] This narrative of progression is supported by the idea, expressed figuratively through Milton, that a savage paradise is lost fortunately to the gain of nomadic shepherding societies: '"The World was all before them where to chuse."'[5] There is a gap between this expression and the figuration of misery and vice which Malthus regards as checking populations.

Malthus' vision is grimly 'realistic' – his use of Miltonic figurative language is exceptional.[6] Unlike Pratt, who idealizes his peasants in *Bread*, Malthus writes about stunted bodies: 'The sons and daughters of peasants will not be found such rosy cherubs in real life, as they are described in romances.'[7] Political idealisms such as poor relief do not work either: giving more money to labourers 'would not increase the quantity of meat in the country',[8] for the resulting competition would cause price increases.[9] Meat is used as an index of wealth and spending power and, in its necessary circulation amongst the already-wealthy, of political power.

Malthus maps his syntax onto capitalist paradigms. His transposition of sociology onto the natural history of the body was enabled by the emergence of a class whose sole function was to produce more of itself: its numbers were economically manageable through the convenient operation of hunger and death, perceived as naturally occurring constants. The stunted labourers, since they have no control over the means of production, 'must at all events be reduced to live upon the hardest fare, and in the smallest quantity'; 'a part of the society must necessarily feel a difficulty of living'.[10] The labourers are figured precisely as immiserated childbearers – the proletariat (*proles*, 'childbearing'). Malthus' prose subtly eschews figurative language and rhetorical flourishes in favour of a descriptive realism which can yield prescriptive sentences: 'must' is felt as logical axiom rather than a despotic command. Like Shelley's vegetarian prose,

Malthus is concerned with *natural* representation, but for different political ends.

Food is a particularly helpful element of Malthus' axiomatics, since it seems more 'natural' than other commodities. There is a difference in kind between food and manufactured commodities: demand can outstrip a necessarily discreet maximum quantity of food in one nation.[11] Malthus glides over the artificially-produced territoriality of this model of food production, based on power over the land on which it grows. Shelley's writing on food reveals an opposite tendency: the representation of food production and consumption through institutions, whether cultural ('habit', 'custom') or corporate (monopolies).

Food seems to slip over into natural categories through disease. The 'cleanliness' which 'expelled' the plague from London could be counteracted by 'unwholesome and insufficient food', which Malthus ranks in the same class as 'sickly seasons' and 'epidemics'.[12] Shelley's discussion of food and disease perceives a morally-warped *culture* to be the main cause. In Malthus' case, it is precisely his naturalism which leads him to regard famine as an apolitical phenomenon:

The vices of mankind are active and able ministers of depopulation. They are the precursors in the great army of destruction ... But should they fail in this war of extermination, sickly seasons, epidemics, pestilence, and plague, advance in terrific array, and sweep off their thousands and ten thousands. Should success be still incomplete; gigantic inresitable [sic] famine stalks in the rear, and with one mighty blow, levels the population with the food of the world.[13]

Shelley's vegetarian subculture emphasizes food choice, and shows how famine is derived from political oppression. Malthus' rhetoric makes famine seem inevitable, non-human, 'natural', placing its iron fist in the velvet glove of food resources.

Condorcet's outline of the progress and perfectibility of human-kind[14] provides Malthus with the opportunity to point out the failure of such Enlightenment thinking to cope with the French Revolution:

To see the human mind in one of the most enlightened nations of the world, and after a lapse of some thousand years, debased by such a fermentation of disgusting passions, of fear, cruelty, malice, revenge, ambition, madness, and folly, as would have disgraced the most *savage* nation in the most *barbarous* age, must have been such a shock to his ideas, of the necessary and inevitable progress of the human mind.[15]

This repeats Burke's point about Condorcet and the swinish multitude. The revolution was a return to a savage natural state which Malthus outlines as the most miserable primitive conditions of humanity. Condorcet's perfectibilism, predicting a distant era when population will exceed the means of subsistence, is denied by Malthus ironically by asserting its presence: it 'has long since arrived;... this necessary oscillation, this constantly subsisting cause of periodical misery, has existed ever since we have had any histories of mankind'.[16] This is the politics of crisis management, supported by the idea that this crisis has been a permanent 'thermodynamic' condition.

Condorcet's idea of man's 'organic perfectibility'[17] which also occurs in Shelley's vegetarian writing, is a biological absurdity for Malthus. Since the laws of nature are constant, there are limits to the selection of attributes: one could not breed sheep with a head and legs which were 'evanescent'.[18] The body's determinacy may be as yet undefined, but it is not 'unlimited' or 'indefinite'.[19] Shelley's vegetarianism modifies Condorcet and Godwin with ideas which resemble Malthus: declaring *human* bodily perfectibility, but also asserting the right to organic determinacy of the *animal* body. Shelley isolates the breeding of domestic animals for meat consumption as an example of the injustice of man towards the natural world. But Shelley refines Malthus: the horror from a Shelleyan perspective of Malthus' speculation on the etiolated limbs of animals is that it *has* occurred. Where Malthus uses this macabre example in an argument against amelioration, Shelley uses it in an argument against disfiguration.

The natural and necessary, figured as the gross and determinate body, win out over the artificial and human (for example the falsely sympathetic gesture of the Poor Laws). Malthus criticizes Godwinian egalitarianism using the culture of limits:

Man cannot live in the midst of plenty. All cannot share alike the bounties of nature. Were there no established administration of property, every man would be obliged to guard with force his little store... Every individual mind would be under a constant anxiety about corporal support.[20]

Godwin's Utopia is imagined: there is no 'war' or 'contention', no 'Unwholesome trades' or overcrowded cities.[21] Malthus envisages the moral improvement of humankind, coupled with a living pattern of small towns, hamlets and farmhouses, where all men are 'equal', everyone shares in agricultural labour and the same population exists as in the present. A predominantly vegetarian regime, supported by the morality of frugal economy, sustains 'health, strength, and spirits'.[22] But the lifting of monopolizing restrictions on marriage envisioned by Godwin would nullify these better conditions within thirty years.[23] Malthus sees vegetarianism on a national scale as the only expediency in this case:

The only chance of success would be the ploughing up all the grazing countries, and putting an end almost entirely to the use of animal food. Yet a part of this scheme might defeat itself. The soil of England will not produce much without dressing; and cattle seem to be necessary to make that species of manure, which best suits the land. In China, it is said, that the soil in some of the provinces is so fertile, as to produce two crops of rice in the year without dressing. None of the lands in England will answer to this description.[24]

Vegetarianism (as an economic, 'frugal' expedient rather than a humanitarian choice) is thus considered twice to support the Godwinian thought-experiment. It is defeated by Malthus' sense of natural determinacy and is ultimately used as a straw target. Malthus' theories of nutrition have been discussed recently by Gallagher.[25] She argues successfully that Malthus shows how meat and livestock as unproductive labour oppresses the working-class body. She fails, however, to draw attention to Malthus' wholehearted support of the enclaving of meat: it is economically sound that the poor are so immiserated. Though he may *seem* to be shedding tears of sympathy for the starving, Malthus is unsympathetic to working-class politics.

Shelley's critique of Malthus is often bound up with diet:

they ['well-meaning persons'] would tell me not to make people happy, for fear of overstocking the world, and to permit those who found dishes placed before them on the table of partial nature, to enjoy their superfluities in quietness, though millions of wretches crowded around but to pick a morsel, which morsel was still refused to the prayers of agonizing famine.[26]

Shelley attacks the notion of a 'partial nature', intending to politicize famine: 'temporal *and* eternal evil' exist,[27] but hunger is seen as a political phenomenon:

Are we to be told that these [vices – 'war, vice, and misery', a verbal echo of Malthus] are remedyless, because the earth would, in case of their remedy, be overstocked? That the rich are still to glut ... and that the poor are to pay with their blood, their labor [sic], their happiness, and their innocence, for the crimes and mistakes which the hereditary monopolists of earth commit? Rare sophism![28]

The Malthusian tricolon of 'war, vice, and misery' is a stock Shelleyan figuration of social wrong. 'Disease', 'famine' and 'crime' are practically interchangeable terms, a 'miasmatic tricolon' which describes the evil consequences flowing from an unjust social order. For Shelley, Malthus pits the miasmatic flow against the flow of population in a ruthlessly oppositional way which seeks to reproduce the callous inattention of *laissez-faire* economics. Shelley dialogically engages with the tricolon: he was not entirely immune to the naturalism of *laissez-faire* arguments (for example, consider the influence of Rousseau). We have seen how Shelley seems to produce similar versions of Malthus' argument that significant political action involves limiting flows, in parallel with the discourse of management plans sketched by him and Adam Smith. Malthus has been reappropriated by ecologies: references were made to him at the 1992 MLA seminar on Green Romanticism (and his grim collusion with so-called postmodernity). Ecologies themselves are an aspect of what has been named 'the age of limits'.[29]

Proposals anticipates *Queen Mab* viii, in the figurative and Messianic language which Shelley uses to speak to his philanthropist audience. Catholic Emancipation 'is the fore-ground of a picture, in the dimness of whose distance, I behold the lion lay down with the lamb, and the infant play with the basilisk'.[30] Isaiah was clearly on Shelley's mind. So was Jesus: 'The tree is to be judged of by its fruit'.[31] A repertoire of fruit and blossom imagery[32] is contrasted with figures of cannibalism: 'The aristocracy of Ireland suck the veins of its inhabitants and consume the blood in England.'[33] This image is repeated in *Song to the Men of England* (1819), verse two. Shelley uses 'monopolizers' to suggest a maleficent circulation of goods,[34] a feature shared by his vegetarian writing. He understood diet in terms of the ways in which circulation creates networks of power. Vegetarianism is part of philanthropic ideology, bursting the bounds of human perceptions and concerns 'till their country becomes the world, and their family the sensitive creation'.[35] This is another example of the 'concentric' thinking of animal rights.

Shelley perceived the limits of philanthropy in 1812: 'No man has a right to monopolise [sic] more than he can enjoy; what the rich give to the poor, whilst millions are starving, is not a perfect favour, but an imperfect right.'[36] The danger is that philanthropy could traverse the entire world and leave it just as it was: what is really needed is institutional change. This partially explains why 'nature' is such a hotly-debated term. Malthus sees famine as an inevitable process of nature, not as being in any way constructed by social oppression. The philanthropist has the global vision to conceptualize oppression, but the way in which he or she engages with the problem could foster an attitude which saw the task as simply one of redressing an imbalance in a timeless, 'natural' system. Nature was an ideological battle-ground for ruling-class reformers.

There is a fascinating sentence in *Proposals* which compares Malthus to someone who finds fault with the 'order' of spring 'because winter must come'.[37] Shelley then declares:

Do we not see that the laws of nature perpetually act by disorganization and reproduction, each alternately becoming cause and effect. The analysis that we can draw from physical to moral topics are of all others the most striking.[38]

The sliding from 'physical' to 'moral' has been prepared for figuratively by the Biblical language. Nature could be seen not as timeless, but as a dynamic movement of 'disorganization and reproduction'. The line from *Ode to the West Wind* (1819) echoes this: 'If Winter comes, can spring be far behind?' (70). Nature, like the social order of which it is an analogue, may be conceived as a machine which 'works' better through breakdown. To speak of 'nature' at all in this context concedes something against a social-constructivist definition of famine. If famine is winter, then perhaps all one has to do is sit around and wait for spring. Still, Shelley's engagement with Malthus was neither clear-cut nor philosophical, but discursive and political. The context of the passage asserts that 'nature' implies 'human nature' and that merely biological 're-production' should not be considered a direct cause of human misery.

Shelley was aware that the body may be articulated in culture, but also that it resists culture. Thus he writes in the *Address*:

the lower classes must waste their lives and liberty to furnish means for their oppressors to oppress them yet more terribly ... the poor must give in taxes what would save them and their families from hunger and cold ... they ... do this to furnish further means of their own abjectness and misery ... There is an outcry raised against amendment; it is called innovation and condemned by many unthinking people who have a good fire and plenty to eat and drink.[39]

The workers' bodies are hijacked to produce goods which they will never enjoy. Diet imagery enables Shelley to demonstrate the cruel irony that the very pleasure whose creation immiserates the working class stops the ruling class from noticing the misery. Shelley gives the example of British victories in India: the working class at home is dominated by imperialism as well as the conquered nation, since it must waste its blood and labour for 'money and food' to conquer the other country.[40] This is an intemperate, incontinent system. In opposition, the Irish must practise temperate self-organization: drinking becomes thinking.

In 'A Philosophical View of Reform' (1819–20), Shelley employs his own dead-pan literalism. The 'new aristocracy' of bankers and others[41] overburdens the poor man's body since labour is worth a half of what it was:[42] 'They eat less bread, wear worse clothes, are more ignorant, immoral, miserable and desperate'; 'the labouring classes, when they cannot get food for their labour, are impelled to take it by force'.[43] Malthus believes that their sole pleasures in marriage and sex must 'be obliterated', because 'hunger and the suppressed revenge of hunger has stamped the ferocity of want like the mark of Cain upon their countenance ... the last tie by which Nature holds them to benignant earth whose plenty is garnered up in the strongholds of their tyrants, is to be divided'.[44] The Cain metaphor associates hunger with the despotic signifier. Society is disfigured or unnatural: one must reshape it according to natural virtues.

The mismanagement of the 'benignant earth' soon became an issue in which the Irish Famine was the focus. A letter in *The Republican* from 'J. Greenacre' on a paper entitled *Famine in Ireland*, circulated by the Southwark committee for establishing a fund for the Irish famine, declares that while the 'God of Nature' is 'munificent and bountiful',[45] the Irish are the victims of political and religious misgovernment.[46] In 'A Philosophical View of Reform' Shelley shows that he does not have to be a culturalist to oppose Malthus, emphasizing the materiality of the body: 'the rich are to be permitted as many mouths to consume the products of the labour of the poor as they please'.[47]

COMMERCE AND MIASMA

Shelley's early representation of famine was sustained throughout his works. *Zeinab and Kathema* (1810–11) exploits the miasmatic tricolon.[48] Kathema visits England and becomes disillusioned, comparing it with his home in 'Cashmire's vale' (92):

> There flowers and fruits are ever fair and ripe,
>   Autumn there mingles with the bloom of spring,
> And forms unpinched by frost or hunger's gripe
>   A natural veil o'er natural spirits fling, –
> Here woe on all but wealth has set its foot.
> Famine, disease and crime even Wealth's proud gates pollute. (97)

These last three elements all disfigure a natural order. The following stanza laments 'Unquiet death and premature decay, / Youth tottering on the crutches of old age ... Madness and passion ... And souls that well become such miserable frames' (103). The disfiguring sufferings which might be remedied by a natural diet are listed. Famine, disease and crime are not natural, they are the negation of nature – culture or 'Art' construed as tyrannical habit or custom: 'These are the bribes which Art to man has given, / To yield his taintless nature to her sway' (109). In *A Vindication* disease and crime are equivalent (as is madness): they are the registration on the body of a disfiguring order of power (for example a tyranny). Famine, like crime, is thus also a form of disease – a state which is not socially meaningful or functional, but a cankering of a naturally benevolent nature. The socially meaningful is figured as a product of a 'natural' order and opposed to the meaningless, anarchic authority of tyranny.

Kathema selects famine as if it were a *symptom*. It is an anomaly in a social order which is assumed to be just and perfect. Like a disease or a crime it can be used as evidence by a reformer of the pathological tendencies of society. 'Globalizing' urban studies by Beddoes and Bateman were mapping populations and classes in terms of disease, and these maps could be moralized. Abernethy's medical studies were indebted to a theory of the symptom in which inflammations of the brain could be observed in the dysfunction of some other part of the body (one of the main arguments which Shelley employed in 'Vegetable System').[49] Shelley musters the seemingly hideous, monstrous invasion of alien nature in the form of famine or disease, as an expression of an oppressive social order. He desired a society which did away with the tendency towards symptom as such, natural

diet being part of this project: a society without structural contradictions (capital/labour, for example).[50] Disease as a symptom of
oppression reveals the contradictions within an apparent universalism. Shelley substitutes a Utopian form of universalism which seeks to
negate contradictions, for example the model of benign exploitation
at the end of *Queen Mab* VIII (technohumanism, wresting the gem of
truth from the dark mine to decorate a paradise of peace). The
language of the symptom is indicative of a reformist ideology which
cannot come to grips with the sources of its own power.

Bodily disfigurement is a symptom of intemperance and injustice.
Mab describes the ruined (probably Mayan) civilizations thus in
part II:

> Spirit! ten thousand years
> Have scarcely past away,
> Since, in the waste where now the savage drinks
> His enemy's blood, and aping Europe's sons,
> Wakes the unholy song of war,
> Arose a stately city.   (II.182)

The city is preferred to the savage state: in Shelley's rather anarchist
critique, the savage is a product of (and potential inherent in)
European power ('aping Europe's sons'). The cannibal 'apes'
Europe, simulating the warlike and bestial qualities of another
culture. Oppression again is shown to generate a debased form of
mimesis; this is no simple regression. The change is seen as disfiguring
a natural environment:

> Once peace and freedom blest
> The cultivated plain:
> But wealth, that curse of man,
> Blighted the bud of its prosperity.   (II.202)

'Blest' is expressively opposed to 'Blighted', as are the 'curse' and
the 'bud'. The production of 'wealth' or capital has an effect which
may be compared to a disease which causes the crops to fail.

In section III (the description of tyranny) the persistence of hunger
is linked to 'unnatural' despotism (III.103). 'Custom' reproduces
power (98) through the masochistic consent of the famished (99–106).
The starving family which Shelley depicts relies upon a nature that
is not adequately tended for their need: the 'cultivated plain' (II.203)
is opposed to 'earth's unpitying bosom' (105). The earth can only be
a good mother if it is enabled to be so. Vice turns the earth into a

'thorny wilderness' (III.125). Hunger is represented as the fault of unequal distribution. Thus the aristocratic 'drones' (III.109) are set in contradiction with 'the starved hind' (III.110), the manual agricultural labourer, who 'For them compels the stubborn glebe to yield / Its unshared harvests' (III.111). This is another example of the deer as an image of an oppressed female nature (here in opposition to the useless male drones).

Section V (on commerce) contains *Queen Mab*'s major discourse on famine. Despotism alone was not responsible for famine; capitalist axiomatics could reproduce it too. In III the King's own intemperate body is oppressive. But in section V, commerce is discussed as a systematic form of intemperance, deprivation and anarchic circulation:

> Commerce! beneath whose poison-breathing shade
> No solitary virtue dares to spring;
> But poverty and wealth with equal hand
> Scatter their withering curses, and unfold
> The doors of premature and violent death,
> To pining famine and full-fed disease,
> To all that shares the lot of human life,
> Which poisoned body and soul, scarce drags the chain,
> That lengthens as it goes and clanks behind.   (V.44).

The paratactic construction ('poverty and wealth ... famine and ... disease'), the images of the poison tree's scattered leaves, and the lengthening chain express the sense of malign circulation. As in *Zeinab and Kathema*, famine is linked with disease and premature, violent death. While it is tempting to read implicit references to meat production into this passage (especially 'poisoned, body and soul'), the language here does not directly adumbrate this. Shelley carefully and characteristically extends the effects of commerce to cultivated and domesticated nature: not only all humans but 'all that shares the lot of human life' will be 'poisoned'. Shelley's vegetarian texts crystallize certain images employed here.[51]

Famine is represented as a goad for the reproduction of power rather than just as a by-product: it is a symptom which aggravates its conditions. Labourers are described as 'the slaves by force or famine driven, / Beneath a vulgar master' (V.72). The 'vulgar master' is surely the new aristocracy of wealth which Shelley berates in *A Vindication*.[52] The quotation's context describes workers as 'Scarce living pullies of a dead machine' (76). As discussed earlier, the problem for Shelley's cultural program was to humanize the industrial and technological machines of the existing society (techno-humanism). What is the solution? Shelley appeals to virtue, the perfect 'germ' in human potential (147) that could foreshadow a general reform. In the verse paragraph, famine is described as an aspect of a bodily and spiritual imperfection which, if cleansed, 'Might imitate and equal' (166) the 'high being, of cloudless brain' (154) who could die a slow and natural death (147–66). A certain Romantic pastoralism is negotiated in the image of the urban environment in which this imperfect body is placed:

> every slave now dragging through the filth
> Of some corrupted city his sad life,
> Pining with famine, swoln with luxury. (159)

The phrase suggests that what is at stake is an impure body-image: famine is not just a question of starvation but of being too thin. Shelley makes another appeal to a certain state of bodily well-being *and* aesthetic balance. The starving body is represented from the position of an onlooker standing in for a judgmental symbolic code. In this vision, nature (the otherness which silently but eloquently judges inhumanity) and conscience (an internalized ethical system) are one and the same. Shelley's attempt to represent the famished body thus seems to emanate from a 'natural' ethical perspective – the view from Mab's palace is its emblem. *Queen Mab*'s super-imposition of extremely generalizing language and localized figures of microscopic detail suggests that the body bears the symptoms of political effects.

GREENING THE DESERT: FAMINE AND A 'ROMANTIC ECOLOGY'?

The idea of a specifically 'Romantic Ecology' was recently discussed by Bate. Certain 'historicist' readings of Wordsworth may be criticized in terms of the violence they do to the poems: conserving nature is here an aegis for conserving a certain type of poetry and a certain reading of it. To criticize 'new historicist' writing by reformulating and re-presenting the way poetic ideologies of place are built around these issues is to redress a balance, to perform a conservationist ecology of reading ('conservative' with a small c).[53] Secondly, if a radical shift of direction is acceptable, then we could start with the textual evidence that Shelley was involved in various sorts of 'ecological' writing, often more radical than Wordsworth's poetics of place. 'Green' may be presented as an alternative to 'red' and 'blue', 'left' and 'right'; but ecology (more properly, ecologies) may be permeated with 'left' *and* 'right' thinking. Not only the *poetics* of place, but the *politics* of place (left and right sides of a liberal-democratic assembly), lack the dynamism inherent in the best ecologies. Moreover, the appeal of ecocriticism to science must be questioned constantly; perhaps we need an 'ecography' to challenge the impersonal logics of restricted economy.

There is an uneasy and unresolved contradiction between green Romantic anti-capitalism and forms of asocial reverence for nature, brought together under the sign of a return to nature.[54] Romantic ecology may recycle themes available to both Wordsworth and Shelley: preservation, redemption, transformation and sustainability. Wordsworth seems to be involved more with preservation and redemption than the last two. Shelley presents a complex pattern of redemption narratives, transformative discourses and discourses on sustainability. Shelley wrote about how an environment of suitable niches for each species is important for survival.[55] His prose on the natural diet considers sustainability.[56] Both instances show 'eco-systemic' thinking: the ecosystem may be defined as the closed terrestrial circulation of energy (ultimately, sunlight). A non-suitable niche would cause a 'waste' of energy.

Ecologies have analogues in poetry of the late eighteenth and early nineteenth centuries. Byron's *Darkness* provides a *Dunciad*-like picture of social degradation, demonstrating an ecological consciousness of famine as the death of nature and of cultural, political order. Energy sustaining the ecosystem (light) is the basis of Byron's model of an interconnecting and politically self-sustaining world. *Darkness* figures the consequences of an onslaught of negativity, anticipating Mary Shelley's *The Last Man*. Consumption is brought into play:

> a meal was bought
> With blood, and each sate sullenly apart
> Gorging himself in gloom: no love was left;
> All earth was but one thought – and that was death,
> Immediate and inglorious; and the pang
> Of famine fed upon all entrails – men
> Died, and their bones were tombless as their flesh;
> The meagre by the meagre were devoured,
> Even dogs assail'd their masters.   (39)

'Famine' writes 'Fiend' on the brows (69; a revision of the mark of Cain). The obverse world of darkness can sustain neither a social nor a natural economy:

> The world was void,
> The populous and the powerful – was a lump,
> Seasonless, herbless, treeless, manless, lifeless –
> A lump of death – a chaos of hard clay.
> The rivers, lakes, and ocean all stood still,
> And nothing stirred within their silent depths;
> Ships sailorless lay rotting on the sea,
> And their masts fell down piecemeal.   (69)

Environmentalism is only one of a *variety* of ecological responses to poems like this. While Byron shows how materially and spiritually *dependent* societies are on a determinate flow of energy, Wordsworth's writing on places as regions, environmental horizons, involves a natural supernaturalism (Abrams' remarkable phrase remains invaluable), which may be closer to the Heideggerian aspect of ecological writing, an uneasy mixture of environmentalism (conservation) and 'deep green' philosophy (ultimately derived from myths of the fallenness of humankind). Shelley struggles with Fall narratives precisely insofar as he wants to rewrite them. Differences emerge in his emphasis not on passive reverence, but active imparadising: how to turn the desert into a paradise, and his interest in food resources and the language of eating itself (as a microcosm of an active relationship between humans and nature). Here he may seem closer to the Hegelian element in ecological theory, or 'social ecology'. Culture is the negation of nature, but the negation of this negation is not a return to nature but a reconception of society. There are complexities within Shelley's 'ecological' position, differences between globalizing management axiomatics, nationalism and the figuration of 'dwelling' (for instance in *The Daemon of the World*).

It is true that poetry about 'nature' is also about the representation of human nature. Shelley's response to Wordsworth was that he was not 'natural' enough, not a 'Poet of Nature' but of supernature. Shelley's concern for nature was linked to his concern for the rights of humanity (a concern which the sonnet *To Wordsworth* recognizes in that poet's earlier achievements). He was engaged in ways of representing the renewal of the earth at the hands of a just society.

Famine was a logical topic for Shelley, since it seems to be a natural crisis which implicates a socio-cultural crisis. The reality of

the famine situations in England around 1795 and 1800 has been
hotly contested by historians.[57] Radical literary circles around the
time were convinced that there was a problem: Joseph Ritson, for
example, voiced an opinion.[58] It can be argued that there were 'few
attempts ... by popular radicals to exploit civil disorder ... [and] few
identifications of a populist democratic presence' by the establishment.[59] But the length and scope of the crisis finally led to its
'exploitation by democrats'.[60] Difficulties in ascertaining the historical reality of the situation stem in part from a misrecognition of
what counts as famine: is it primarily a case of starvation leading to
death, or a degradation in the standards and quality of life of a
particular class? *Want, Famine, and Mortality* appeared in *The Black
Dwarf*:

> What marks with sadness ev'ry eye?
> What blench'd the cheek that just went by?
> What gen'ral gloom the nation shades?
> 'Tis famine's reign the land pervades.
>
> Sweet labour once employed each hand,
> Contentment spread throughout the land;
> Industry's plenteous store was seen,
> And health, and every joy serene.
>
> What adverse fate destroys our life?
> Are nature's laws with man at strife?
> Or is it man's delirious sway,
> Destroys our wealth, and wastes our lives away?[61]

This poem is part of the debate over whether nature or society is
responsible for the sufferings of the poor. The representation of a past
Golden Age of labour and bodily health suggests that social
oppression is responsible. The political ecology of famine would have
been familiar to Shelley: Pratt had shown how a natural idyll of
economy of nature is linked to social idylls of sustainable commodity
flow. Shelley's interest in Pratt's poem, *Bread*, his use of the 'green
desert' topos and his response to experiments in 'social ecology' open
themselves to ecocriticism.

Shelley read Pratt's *Bread* (1802), using it in note 17 to *Queen Mab*
and *A Vindication* to exemplify the difficulties of self-sufficiency for the
working-class and agricultural labourers. Pratt develops a quasi-
sociological analysis of the poor, while opposing their simple, natural
idyll to the luxurious exploitation of the rich. Pratt, like Shelley,

states the danger of anarchy in tyranny: power should 'sustain' its 'advantage' with 'liberal modesty' rather than monopolization.[62] His ideal society is based on a temperance which will render the tyrant's appetite an unnecessary anomaly: it will be based on 'Content', 'Neatness', 'Hope', 'Frugality' and 'Œconomy': methodized organization.[63]

Britain is fertile but 'Half of our unfed Britons pining stand',[64] because of the monopolizing of 'One tyrant husbandman' in each local community,[65] the 'farmer-sportsman'[66] who sees:

> the smoking viands, costly wine,
> And fragments that might all their [poor] households dine,
> Yet not one meal their fainting hearts to cheer,
> But unsubstantial roots, and meagre beer.[67]

He goes drunk to bed, 'his body swill'd'.[68] His gross body is set against the poor body, refined by circumstances on its diet of, amongst other things, strawberries and currants (resembling Shelley's list of vegetables in *A Vindication*).[69] The intemperate king in *Queen Mab* III also eats 'viands' and totters to bed and bad dreams. If this is a direct source for Shelley's passage, then the 'viands' in section III are more likely to be meat than anything else. Man is associated with innocent herbivores, as in Monboddo:

> O MAN PRESERVE THYSELF in time of need!
> In awful characters so stands the deed:
> For this the lamb has bled, the fawn has fought,
> And set the tyrant of the woods at naught;
> The timid hare upon the wolf has sprung,
> While deep-ton'd howlings thro' the forest rung.[70]

The tyrant, however, is carnivorous, a 'gaunt lion', and autophagous, for 'his own flesh in agony [he] devours'.[71] He is a kind of parasite: 'A TRAITOR IN EACH TYRANT LIES.'[72] Rich farmers are shown as intemperate in their tyranny. Pratt records an anecdote about their dipping bank bills and 'other property' into wine, 'soaked and sopped in wine, like rusks in chocolate', in a grotesque parody of the Eucharistic meal.[73]

An anonymous poem was published in 1793 entitled *An Address, in Verse, to the Author of the Poetical and Philosophical Essay on the French Revolution*. The author it attacks is a certain 'C***T**Y'.[74] Since Pratt used the pseudonym 'Courtney Melmoth', it is certain that he is the addressee of these anti-revolutionary remarks. One of the *topoi* which he or she attacks is that in which the 'general presence' of 'liberty' 'bids the desert bloom'.[75] Liberty, the personification of a relationship between humans, is described transforming nature. For Pratt it is not that 'nature', in a culturalism which considers it to be merely part of human discourse, was always already 'human' and could then be depersonified to stand for what is outside the social order – an ideology which employs nature as society's way of washing its hands of itself. To talk about human relationships with the natural world is not necessarily to espouse this kind of culturalism.[76] This becomes obvious if a field is opened in literary study to examine the poetics of famine. Pratt's *A Poetical and Philosophical Essay on the French Revolution*, a critique of Burke, is aware of the class basis of food circulation.

The topos of the desert which becomes a paradise occurs frequently in Shelley. *Queen Mab* VIII–IX is a clear paradigm of this topos:

> Those deserts of immeasurable sand,
> Whose age-collected fervours scarce allowed
> A bird to live, a blade of grass to spring,
> Where the shrill chirp of the green lizard's love
> Broke on the sultry silentness alone,
> Now teem with countless rills and shady woods,
> Cornfields and pastures and white cottages.   (VIII.70)

Shelley envisions nature as rendered fertile for consumption, and as a safe environment to live in. The desert is politicized in *Laon and Cythna*. The oppressive regime leads to a famine and plague which kills the fish, birds, insects and livestock; the land is poisoned (x.xiv–xv). The counter-revolution is represented as an ecological as well as a political disaster (xvii–xviii):

> the scattered flocks and herds
> Who had survived the wild beasts' hungry chace [sic]
> Died moaning, each upon the other's face
> In helpless agony gazing; round the City
> All night, the lean hyænas their sad case
> Like starving infants wailed; a woeful ditty!
> And many a mother wept, pierced with unnatural pity.
>   (x.xv.(129))

The configuration of the maternal, the infant, and the animals, under the sign of the weeping agonized face, engages with Shelley's discourse of faciality and humanity. The flocks look each other in the face just as the lamb looks at the slaughterer in the face. Compare the Earth's description of the miasmatic effects of Prometheus' curse, 'When plague had fallen on man, and beast, and worm, / And Famine; and black blight on herb and tree' (*Prometheus Unbound*, 1.152–86, 172–73 quoted here). The Earth's 'breast' is a face which grows 'wan' and 'dry / With grief' (176–77), like eyes which have been weeping.

Ozymandias (1817; published 1818) describes a past tyranny visible in the present only as a desert. The desert represents a wild (inhuman) nature which, following the law of necessity, claims back for itself the follies of even the proudest tyrant (*Queen Mab* 11.134–61). The political judgment in *Ozymandias* is ironic. It is not so much that the tyrant created the wilderness. Rather, the desert is a sign of the lack of benign culture (including agriculture). Culture in *Ozymandias* is present only as a series of empty gestures: the very speech of the 'traveller' (1), the 'legs of stone' without a trunk (2), the 'shattered visage' of the tyrant (4). The tyrant is disfigured just as the statements in the poem seem to be hopeless, formal gesticulations in a wilderness. The most urgent irony is the inscription on the pedestal of the statue: '"My name is Ozymandias, king of kings, / Look on my works, ye mighty, and despair!"' (10–11). A tyrannical lesson to other tyrants has become a democratic lesson. The act of marking itself becomes a gesture of death in the traveller's phrase for how the tyrant's passions are visible in stone, 'stamped on these lifeless things' (7; compare *Charles I*, 1.94). The verbs of placing suggest a lack of anything so supportive as an environment: 'stand' (3), 'remains' (12), 'survive' (7). The desert sands perform the operation which should have been enacted by levelling movements of social reform. But Shelleyan reform, far from producing the smooth space of a desert, produces the striated space of an agricultural state, an oasis culture. The traveller's description of 'The lone and level sands' (14) expresses both solitude and desolation, both associated with tyranny in *Queen Mab*. In *Ozymandias*, a sharp separation between nature and culture makes both of them unproductive. They are two halves of a torn whole which Shelley's ecography attempts to unite.

Desert and paradise are opposing figurative possibilities in *Hellas: a Lyrical Drama* (1821; published 1822), a poem about the Greek revolution.[77] The Chorus speaks with anticipation: 'Let Freedom leave, where'er she flies, / A Desert, or a Paradise' (90). Paradise

then becomes a dream negated by Turkish rule and Christianity
(226):

> Our hills and seas and streams
> Dispeopled of their dreams,
> Their waters turned to blood, their dew to tears,
> Wailed for the golden years.   (235)

The second line powerfully suggests a close relationship between
person and environment ('Our' place). The hills and seas and
streams are without 'dreams': how can an environment dream? For
Shelley humans are the mind, the self-awareness, of nature, borne out
in 'Dispeopled'.[78] The dreams are like people in that human ideals
are what create the environment as a place fit for inhabitation. The
'golden years' are the age of Saturn in which humans enjoyed a
primitive and spontaneous relationship with natural fecundity.

The Turkish tyranny is described as creating a wilderness of
unmanageable nature which feeds back on tyrannical power:

> 'The vultures and the dogs, your pensioners tame,
> Are overgorged; but, like oppressors, still
> They crave the relic of Destruction's feast;
> The exhalations and the thirsty winds
> Are sick with blood; the dew is foul with death;
> Heaven's light is quenched in slaughter: Thus where'er
> Upon your camps, cities, or towers, or fleets,
> The obscene birds the reeking remnants cast
> Of these dead limbs, – upon your streams and mountains,
> Upon your fields, your gardens, and your house-tops,
> Where'er the winds shall creep, or the clouds fly,
> Or the dews fall, or the angry sun look down
> With poison'd light – Famine and Pestilence,
> And Panic, shall wage war on our [Greek] side!
> Nature from all her boundaries is moved
> Against ye: Time has found ye light as foam.'   (427)

Tyranny (associated with predatory animals, poison and disease) is
an excess over nature which will eventually be consumed by this
excess. Genesis is perverted in the image of creeping, flying pestilence:
tyranny decodes the economy of 'nature' into a threatening flow of
pollution.[79] A benevolent, egalitarian economy would set internal
limits on flows. The oscillation between a sense of natural necessity
and the need for human agency in accomplishing liberty's aims
marks an ambiguity within Shelley's green desert. Like John Bull's

reactionaries, the Moslems conversing here see their downfall as the violent irruption of nature.

The oscillation is figuratively resolved later in *Hellas*: 'Let the tyrants rule the desert they have made; / Let the free possess the paradise they claim' (1008). In the closing triumph of liberty, Venus, 'Love's folding star' (1029) is described suspended above the ocean 'Between Kingless continents sinless as Eden' (1047). The 'folding star' enacts a basic 'ecological' vision of nature, fundamentally 'sane' and quite dualistic, anthropocentric.[80] The universe is homely, *oiko*-logical, guiding the flocks home at the right time so that they can remain under human appropriation (and be eaten at the right time); a universe of prudence. Paradise and human virtue are opposed to the rule of kings. The figure negates the blemish of sin as a human-created mark upon nature: in this sense Shelley shares the redemptive scheme of the 'deep' ecologists. However, kingdom and nation are opposed to 'Kingless continents'. The earth is a non-hierarchical system in this image (ecology is not necessarily about blind respect for 'natural' hierarchies). The dream of paradise can return ('The golden years return', 1061) in the twilight vision. Shelley's note on the final Chorus exploits the imagery of millennium associated with *Queen Mab* VIII:

It will remind the reader, 'magno nec proximus intervallo' of Isaiah and Virgil, whose ardent spirits, overleaping the actual reign of evil which we endure and bewail, already saw the possible and perhaps approaching state of society in which the 'lion shall lie down with the lamb', and 'omnis feret omnia tellus'. Let these great names be my authority and excuse.[81]

SOCIAL ECOLOGY AND SUSTAINABILITY

Shelley was not only interested in providing visions of the green desert; he wanted to test its political efficacy. The *Ode to Liberty* (1820) explores the possibility of an earth renewed to bear more sustenance. The idea is placed as a question in stanza xvii, discussing relationships between humanity and technology:

> He who taught man to vanquish whatsoever
>   Can be between the cradle and the grave
> Crowned him the King of Life. O vain endeavour!
>   If on his own high will a willing slave,
> He has enthroned the oppression and the oppressor.
>   What if earth can clothe and feed

> Amplest millions at their need,
> And power in thought be as the tree within the seed?
> O, what if Art, an ardent intercessor,
> Diving on fiery wings to Nature's throne,
> Checks the great mother stooping to caress her,
> And cries: Give me, thy child, dominion
> Over all height and depth? if Life can breed
> New wants, and wealth from those who toil and groan
> Rend of thy gifts and hers a thousandfold for one.   (241)

'Amplest' is an apt register of a vision of earth filled to capacity, a Godwinian ideal of human development.[82] Shelley was probably reading the *Answer to Malthus* while writing the *Ode*. The lines condense powerful thinking about how sustainable growth is rendered pointless by political oppression. Godwin promotes the idea that just political institutions would enable it.[83]

The earth (or Nature) is depicted as self-sufficient: Art (a figure for human culture or ingenuity as a whole) is obliged to be the child of Nature – a natural reproduction of the earth (picking up the association of 'child'). The lines are concerned with the relationship between nature and culture. Now another sort of reproduction is introduced: 'Life can breed / New wants.' The concept of reproduction becomes problematic: the triumph of Life may be the negation of Liberty, since it is the triumph of reproduction, not only of images or signs (*pace* de Man) but also of bodies. The stanza raises the question of a potentially endless supply checked by a potentially limitless demand. A political dilemma arises in which the criterion of *temperance* must figure. Human 'art' must be tempered to fit the resources of the 'nature' from which it springs, inducing the 'natural' tendency towards health, innocence and liberty. A purely technological solution (the 'power of thought') is not enough. It would create an inflation of 'Life' over both 'Nature' and 'Art' ('a thousandfold for one'). This image of the law of diminishing returns seems opposed to the capitalist economics of expansion; the mercantile figure makes it explicit. This stanza is not an abstractly sceptical riposte to other notions of liberty in the *Ode*, but a statement of the need to think carefully about the idea. If science was the sister of poetry for Shelley (as in *Laon and Cythna* v), then the issue of human subsistence was one area in which both must interact. Again, Shelley is arguing for technohumanism: industry plus culture equals pleasurable progress.

Shelley was committed to a particular *kind* of politics of the environment. He was not interested in a dualistic philosophy which separated society from nature, nor a conservationist philosophy which preserved things as they were under the present system of society (environmentalism). There are nuances of his vegetarian prose and certain aspects of *Queen Mab* which suggest that he might have favoured a reductionism which 'dissolves society *into* nature'.[84] But while he launched a critique of certain social institutions as 'unnatural', he did not provide a sweeping, generalized critique of humanity or institutions as such – the so-called 'deep', anti-humanist or biocentric version of ecology.[85] Shelley falls more squarely into a position currently defined as social ecology, though he does not anticipate it in a continuity of the 'history of ideas' presented in a Whiggish reading of history. His interest in a tradition of philosophical anarchism allies him with its leading contemporary exponent, Murray Bookchin.[86] Social ecology proposes 'that major ecological problems have their roots in social problems'.[87] These problems are products of hierarchical structures (monarchy-tyranny, aristocracy, religion).

Pratt's *Bread* grapples with issues such as food distribution and social justice which are now debated in social ecology. A footnote in *A Vindication* mentions it:

It has come under the author's experience, that some of the workmen on an embankment in North Wales, who, in consequence of the inability of the proprietor to pay them, seldom received their wages, have supported large families by cultivating small spots of sterile ground by moonlight. In the notes to Pratt's poem, 'Bread, or the Poor', is an account of an industrious labourer, who, by working in a small garden, before and after his day's task, attained to an enviable state of independence.[88]

Shelley comments wryly on the politics of social ecology. It seems that this experiment in community fell within established capitalist schemes of production and thus could be carried out at the margins. Shelley was, however, convinced that such experiments were valuable, as his dedication to the Tremadoc embankment project (from which he gleaned this information) demonstrates.

In 1812 Percy and Harriet arrived at Tremadoc in Caernarvon-shire, an experiment in community carried out under the aegis of William Alexander Madocks, a Foxite Whig MP who had allied with Burdett, Cartwright and Cobbett and was a founder member of the Hampden Clubs. The central project in which Madocks' town (named after him) was occupied on the Shelleys' arrival was to build a grand cob across the sea mouth and to 'reclaim and cultivate' the estuary.[89] After a hard winter, the embankment was breached on 14 February 1813, and Madocks slid ever closer to bankruptcy. The difficulties which the project faced may have acted as a catalyst for the break-in to Shelley's house which induced him to leave Wales.

Shelley helped this project as a fundraiser, canvassing in Sussex without much success, and faring better in London. In Tremadoc he had to follow up promised payments from gentry and local farmers. This grew difficult since he sided with the workers (who were attempting collective bargaining and strikes) against the quarry owner, Robert Leeson, a hard-line Tory, son of an Irish landowner and admirer of Wellington. Shelley's sympathy for the Luddite risings during the winter of 1812–13 cannot have endeared him to the capitalists.[90] Leeson eventually received a copy of one of Shelley's Irish pamphlets distributed to John Williams, one of the overseers. John Williams proposed that Shelley give a speech supporting the project at a meeting with the Corporation of Beaumaris. His name headed the bill on the evening of the meeting, 29 September 1812. His enthusiastic tone was captured by the North Wales Gazette for 1 October 1812, whose report wandered into the first person:

The Embankment at Tremadoc is one of the noblest works of human power – it is an exhibition of human nature as it appears in its noblest and most natural shape – benevolence – it saves, it does not destroy. Yes! the unfruitful sea once rolled where human beings now live and earn their honest livelihood. Cast a look round these islands, through the perspective of these times – behold famine driving millions even to madness; and own how excellent, how glorious, is the work which will give no less than three thousand souls the means of competence.[91]

Shelley's uses 'natural' (as in his vegetarian prose) to describe a desirable state of human nature. He proposes a social solution to 'famine' – which is here associated with social deprivation and an expensive shortage of the means of subsistence, rather than Malthusian natural checks on population. De Waal's social anthropology has shown how famine is not considered so much as starvation leading to death amongst those who are affected (this tends to be the view of the onlookers), but as poverty and loss of social identity (see chapter 1).

Shelley's position was also defined more rigorously by class. The Tremadoc anecdote fits into *A Vindication* in a paragraph about social effects. The aristocracy, whose taste for flesh is purely a matter of 'luxury',[92] are supported by a peasantry who do not enjoy this luxury:

The peasant cannot gratify these fashionable cravings without leaving his family to starve. Without disease and war, those sweeping curtailers of population, pasturage would include a waste too great to be afforded. The labour requisite to support a family is far lighter [here is the footnote] than is usually supposed. The peasantry work, not only for themselves, but for the aristocracy, the army, and the manufacturers.[93]

The final sentence understands class division. But the sentence about 'waste' seems insensitive given the loss of common land since enclosure. Shelley's garden-scheme is a Napoleonic wartime economy: the worker-cultivated gardens sustain capitalist production against the forces of anti-production (such as the military); this technique was advocated again during the Second World War.[94] But perhaps the wartime economy of 'Victory Gardens' could fruitfully outlast a war?

These austerity measures may not have appealed to the working class. The necessity of monocultures based on fast-growing and nutritious crops like the potato was a matter of urgency to ruling-class reformers, but of insult to lower-class reformers. Globalizing management plans for the environment were being formulated by dominant thinkers, destroying the spatial boundaries of enclosure farming. The current figuration of 'depopulated' flows of information by the American company, Geographic Information Systems (GIS), has been discussed as a further development of the technologies of land management predicted by Marx, in which the full body of capital appropriates the very spaces which previously had been intensely localized; in such a development, flow replaces space, and what Virilio calls 'chronopolitics' replaces geopolitics.[95] Salaman describes the potato's introduction in the eighteenth century as part of a scheme of 'organized pauperism'.[96] But Shelley's Malthusianism perhaps only appears by default. The only reason that the peasantry are not starving to death is the social structure which introduces disease and war to check population. Shelley prefers an 'agricultural' system[97] to the 'pasturage' system. An unjust social order based on hierarchies creates a wasteful system of food production. 'Waste' suggests the wilderness of the desert as a product of the intemperance of power. Shelley's programme is for a system without waste; the cultural full body, 'the spirit of the nation', will become agri-cultural.[98]

The agricultural theorist Tighe provided Shelley with a wealth of scientific information, chemical, biological and statistical. The notebook in which Shelley wrote *Ode to the West Wind* is also full of agricultural notes dating from this period. George William Tighe had set up house with Lady Margaret Mountcashell at the Casa Silva in Pisa. Lady Mountcashell had changed her name to Mrs Mason – more appropriate for a radical, and also the name of the adult instructor in *Original Stories* by her governess, Wollstonecraft. Mrs Mason was a feminist member of the United Irishmen who had published works for Godwin's Juvenile Library, and attended the famous trial of Hardy, Horne Tooke and Thelwall.

Tighe and Mrs Mason inspired Shelley with a new-found sense of radicalism when he met them in 1820. Tighe encouraged him to read Davy's lectures on agricultural chemistry (1813). Davy had dis-covered electrolysis as a means of decomposing substances like earth metals to their elements. Shelley had read his *Elements of Chemical Philosophy* at Lynmouth in 1812, and Mary read it in 1816. Tighe also urged Shelley to study Malthus. Shelley borrowed Henry Reveley's encyclopaedia and was seen by Claire walking through the streets of Pisa reading it; perhaps he was 'gathering population statistics'.[99] He ordered Godwin's *Answer to Malthus* from Peacock around this time.[100] The 'Philosophical View of Reform' and *Ode to Liberty* were written with Tighe in mind. On 13 April, 1820, Shelley wrote to John and Maria Gisborne: 'I have been thinking & talking & reading Agriculture this last week.'[101]

Shelley took notes from Davy's *Elements of Agricultural Chemistry* at the back of the 1820 notebook.[102] He was very interested in exactly how vegetable life was formed, at one point employing a scientific metaphor: 'The earth is the laboratory in which the nutriment of vegetables is prepared.'[103] Methods of extracting sugar from plants are also carefully documented.[104] It was considered at the time that the so-called 'saccharine' element in vegetable food was what rendered it particularly nourishing. Shelley was clearly still interested in vegetable diet. The opening pages of the notebook form a 'Prose fragment on milk and potato production'.[105] Tokoo assumes that this starts on page four, but from the look of the calculations on pages two and three, and what seems to be a drawing of a field, Shelley's notes may be more extensive than this.[106] The notes discuss the relative production of food under different food production systems, the 'dairy' and the 'potatoe'.[107] According to Shelley's calculations, the proportion of potatoes yielded in the system far outstripped any milk, butter or meat produced by the same land in the dairy system.[108] Agriculturalism may be understood along with the natural diet (as a potentially global diet for a small planet), as a management plan within advancing capitalism. Capitalist economies necessitate techniques of mass observation and dietary restructuring. The natural diet and the discourse about potatoes can be seen as two poles ('personal' and 'collective') of the same attractor.

An objection to the idea of associating Shelley with ecological thought was recently made.[109] Dawson's thoughtful critique of Bate leads into a discussion of Shelley's use of Godwin's arguments about the necessity of extending human dominion, his employment of the language of monarchy to celebrate republicanism, his dualist conception of reason and passion and what Dawson sees as his inheritance of the 'murderous dialectic of Enlightenment' described by Horkheimer and Adorno as exploiting and dominating nature.

It is unclear whether Dawson understands the links between Godwin, agricultural reform and the politics of social ecology, or the critique of instrumentality and domination of nature through figures of 'silent eloquence' and the cry of nature. Additionally, it is not simply a matter of reason and passion, but of mind and matter. Shelley celebrates the omnipotence of mind over matter in *Queen Mab* at the end of the vegetarian section (VIII.235–36). Is the idea of an omnipotent mind necessarily at odds with an ecological perspective? Vegetarianism is a transformative practice, rendering matter permeable by mind, replacing the circulation of blood with the circulation of nervous energy. Shelley's figuration of the green desert is not about preservation, but is, like his vegetarianism, a matter of self-presentation, and also of Utopian exploitation, a sort of humanist ecology. Ecological concepts need not be anti-humanist.

Enlightenment thought may not necessarily be murderous (and if it is, is it any more murderous than the postmodern dissemination of Reaganomics?). There are lines which lead not only from the Enlightenment but from 'Romanticism', modernism and postmodernism to the fascist death camps. Hitler, after all, was a vegetarian, but this is where he differs from Nietzsche and agrees with Wagner. Vegetarianism is not, however, as Horkheimer and Adorno declare, one of the dangerous half-truths which necessarily adumbrate fascism. And ecologies are not necessarily fascistic either, although there is the *possibility* of reconstituting the politics of blood and soil. Epistemological finger-pointing about half-truths and dialectics is not enough of an anti-fascist exercise; it may be implicated in the abstract aesthetics and economics that take us to 'race' and 'culture' in the first place. Discourses are contestable and internally contradictory: there are many vegetarianisms, many ecologies.

CONCLUSION

Shelley's writing is full of references to food and eating which formed a meaningful and coherent ideological framework, based on the attempt to represent the 'natural' and the 'human' amongst upper-class reformers and intellectuals in the 1790–1820 period. The Shelleys (Harriet, Mary and Percy) collaborated in formulating discourses of diet in collective, politicized ways. They elaborated complex and ambivalent embodiments of 'nature', 'culture', 'miasma', faciality, dismemberment, constructing sophisticated and politicized corporeal maps. Percy Shelley's prose on the natural diet may be read as part of a wider politics of the body: in its response to revolutionary passions, its elaboration of techniques of sociopathological analysis, its decoding and re-encoding of Golden Age and Fall narratives; and its programmatic, illocutionary construction of a new body, a new sense of culture and nature. His deployment of figures of intemperance and the grotesque establishes modes of deviance, both from 'above' and 'below' in the social order, which help to set up norms of non-luxurious culture. Culture is conceived as a homeostatic system in which the bodies of the earth and of the human labourer are not misappropriated but are productively welded to the technologically advancing and culturally-smoothed wheels of a progressive, reformist capitalism.

It is now possible to think about figurality in Shelley by examining the issue as part of a larger cultural study. Figurality must be thought through the prescriptive discourses which delimit the consumer. Shelley's anxieties about figurative language were caught up in anxieties about the disfigurement and decay of the body and the need to present political reform as natural, peaceful and humane. His capacity for scepticism and figurative sophistication, engaged by contemporary theories about deconstruction, must now be seen to be qualified by a profound yearning for a mode of self-reflection which is universal but closed (the ability to gaze into the lamb's face as much as Ianthe's, faciality as the figure of figures), for a state of innocence within the disfiguration of the sentimental; a violent desire for peace articulated in triumphalist and millennial programmes of active virtue. These desires were not simply personal lacks or psychic phantasy. The gendering of diets is clear, from Trotter's effeminate middle classes to attacks on certain kinds of left effeminacy by writers like Orwell or St Clair. The race-ing of diets is also clear in the texts discussed in chapter 4. Questions of race and gender in Shelley's revolution in taste cut across boundaries of public and private, disabling the privatization of consumption which another kind of study of psyche and polis might highlight.

It will now be difficult to dispute the continuing significance of *Queen Mab*, both poetically *and* politically, or the significance of a text such as *Swellfoot the Tyrant*. It will also be difficult to sustain arguments that Shelley's politics faded or became cynical, or that he moved from 'materialism' to 'idealism' in a straightforward way, given the consistency of his figuration of the body, and its implications in theories of social reform, of which the 'natural diet' is a symptom. Shelley's atheism may now be read as actually rather theistic, since it involves the recoding of Christian redemption in the body itself. Even as he participates in Holbachian materialism, he strives to reincorporate Isaiah. And even as he gestures towards Southey, Wordsworth, Byron, Keats, he appropriates Milton, Pope and Thomson.

Contemporary ecologies can be related to Shelley's appropriation of Malthusian axiomatics, his discourse of the symptom and sociopathology, and his interest in 'social ecology'. As well as placing the Shelleys in late twentieth-century debate, it is also necessary to understand them in the context of earlier modernities. Shelley's serious scientific and medical concern over the body was involved in a wider social configuration of purity, temperance and discipline, as well as radical reform. Both these configurations are bound up with post-enclosure agriculture, increasing industrialization and urbanization, and the need for literary and upper classes to distinguish themselves from others. Shelley was able both to identify with, and to differentiate himself from, the working classes. The elaboration of secular codes of social redemption involved replicating the natural within and beyond the social, in the corrupted or vicious body or in the state of nature. A culture of limits was created in arguments about sustainability.

In studying how this culture was created, I have shown how Bourdieu's categories of distinction ought to be nuanced. Bourdieu shows how middle-class distinctions are abstractly-aesthetic, while working-class distinctions are articulated in a moral register. The culture of vegetarianism between 1790 and 1820 was such that the middle-class aesthetic was not entirely 'abstract' but 'moral', though it involved rhetorics of bodily discipline and abstract concepts of bodily beauty. Chronic diseases such as cancer helped to model 'chronic' cultures of moralized self-analysis and care. The working-class mode of distinction was actually rather aestheticized in the demand for 'fine' white bread, though bread connoted a substance for which one would offer one's life.

In addition, Appadurai's analysis of 'luxury goods' may be modified. In *The Social Life of Things*, he declares that these goods are not to be contrasted with necessities but defined 'as goods whose principal use is *rhetorical* and *social*, goods that are simply *incarnated signs*', giving as examples 'pepper in cuisine, silk in dress, jewels in adornment, and relics in worship'. Luxury goods are not a stable essence, and Appadurai acknowledges that there is nothing inherently luxurious about a content-substance like pepper or meat. I would add that there is nothing given about what kinds of sign can be incarnated, either. Certain expressive social assemblages designate 'luxury' and other categories: mere vegetables may become '*incarnated signs*' for a class of consumer who could afford 'better', but chooses to eat as a vegetarian. Appadurai's semiotics is here rather formalist; following Hjemslev's linguistics, I suggest that the planes of 'content' and 'expression' are arbitrary parallel flows, so that the 'humble' vegetable could be designated differently in different social configurations. The sign can also be incarnated in a 'non-luxurious' commodity (by anti-luxurious vegetarians, for example), and thus *non-luxurious* commodities also demonstrate 'a high degree of linkage of their consumption to body, person, and personality'.[110]

Mary Shelley's position on science and the body was sophisticated. To elaborate perhaps somewhat tritely on the 'horror' aesthetic in *Frankenstein* is a process which might reduce the reading to the familial (if not Oedipal), individualist perception of a sexually-charged text: for instance, the rather patronizing idea that in terms of the body the novel is an adolescent story about sexual propriety, a *schaeurroman*. It is possible suggestively to read the creature's request to travel to South America as an example of a sexualized but also political Fall/redemption narrative: it 'expects its father to save it through a restoration of the garden; that is, through the fabrication of a heterosexual mate, through its completion in a finished whole, a city and cosmos'.[111] Such a reading, however, cannot trace *continuities* between the Enlightenment thinking in which the creature and the Shelleys invest, and 'postmodern' forms of 'biopolitics'.[112] The Enlightenment inscribed its own forms of critique of the concept of technological progress. The use of archaizing as well as futuristic narratives, the use of holism and fragmentation, in *Frankenstein* and *The Last Man*, predates the contradiction within late twentieth-century discourse between ecofeminism (and Gaian politics) and manifestos for cyborgs. Haraway herself points out that sociobiology draws upon the myth of Prometheus, since forethought is 'an optimal result for a communications science'.[113]

However, while it is worth taking into account the theoretical differences between my model of 'sociopathology' and sociobiology, how different is this use of a myth from the perfectibilism-within-secular-limits advocated in the Shelleys' stories of the modern Prometheus? Haraway cannot delineate how the re-imagined Promethean body may differ from, say, the monarchical body, since her notion of social control is based on 'domination' rather than the axiomatized exploitation of resources. These axioms were mythologized as technohumanism. The view that Prometheus encodes 'liberation through domination' was surpassed in *Prometheus Unbound*.[114]

Haraway invests in the always-already naturalized concept of 'culture', and culture as the fabrication of a social field, omitting a mapping of consumption. She would find it hard to demonstrate effectively how the assemblages which set up such a notion are themselves looped back into the myth of Prometheus. In writing about consumption and figuration, I hope that I have *not* subverted her powerful attempt to provide a materialist analysis of the body in society. I hope that I have established a more rigorous kind of materialism. Studies of consumption are riddled with problems of fetishizing history as a commodity, betraying Benjamin's valuable dictum that one should muddy the waters of one's object as much as possible. De Certeau has shown how everyday practices (such as eating) both 'exacerbate' and 'disrupt' our logics. Power is both 'destabilized' and 'entailed' in 'practices of consumption'. The critic should be sensitive to 'conflicting realities at work in any instant of Modernity'.[115] Studying consumption in a fetishistic way is not salvific, just as 'literature' and 'culture' are not salvific.

The discussion of diet and health raises the question of the importance of discussing vegetarianism in relation to the contemporary religioning of health; as Ross remarks, 'health has replaced sexuality as the new privileged discourse of bodily truth and inner essence'.[116] This is a reversion to a discursive formation which was generated during early modernity, including the current trend for criticizing drugs and 'big science' medical technologies in favour of nutritional approaches, for example in New Agisms. However, the relatively high status of nutrition in eighteenth- and nineteenth-century medicine (because of the perceived relationship between drugs and quackery), suggests differences between the present and the past. Smith's *Sure Guide in Sickness and Health* (1776) is not a New Age document.

The New Age religion of health shows how the notion of 'secularization' (the hobbyhorse of secular humanistic studies) is problematic. Some criticism of the body in the French Revolutionary period, for example by Outram, has been limited to the extent that it discusses the changes in terms of a radical phase of secularization. Regicide is read as a dethronement both of the King and of (religious) symbolism as such. But Fall-and-redemption narratives persisted in discourses which are often quite 'radical' and overtly non-theistic, within the reformist rhetoric of the 1790–1820 period. Decapitation and cannibalism may be considered as anti-symbols which release threatening decoded flows (of capital, pollution, people ...). Thus a certain kind of revolutionary asceticism may be accounted for, which resists both the tyrant and the multitudinous flows (whose visceral materiality and whose counter-symbolic qualities Burke himself noted).

The social field may be psychically invested in different ways; what occurred in the discourses centred around the alimentary and nervous systems in the period was certainly not a draining-out of sacred meaning. In fact, the sacred codes of religious asceticism become immanent rather than transcendent in the period. Religion hardly waned, but the new phenomenon was how asceticism began to be mass marketed. It is surprising how popular the vegetable diet became during the period. It had been practised and written about by a number of writers in the late seventeenth century (for example, Thomas Tryon), using parallel figures and themes: the limitation of flows and the proper circulation of nourishment as a means to psychic and material wealth and so on. Between 1790 and 1820, however, the body beautiful as articulated by dietary discourse became available to a wider market. New Agism is another form of asceticism for the masses; but it is also related to global management plans for populations and the environment. Boundaries between the body, society and nature are permeated with the global, anarchic flows that are defined, limited and productively 'unbound' in a period of advancing industrial growth. The Christian cardinal virtue of 'temperance' has a long life in other forms, as it begins to define interior limits to aid the *disciplined* expansion of industry beyond its exterior limits.

At one extreme of that complex entity, vegetarian discourse, is a representation of sensual and intellectual bliss and benign contact with nature; at the other is a discourse of purity, cleanliness and order. Figurative language (for example, figures of viscerality) is exploited at both ends of this ideological chain, which is held together through forms of representation which promise to record the natural and social worlds more accurately and in a secular way (anthropology, sociopathology). Figurative patterns are generated, in which the subject of urban industrial society is pulled up by his or her own bootstraps into a reformed world, through discourses which both decode and redeem.

This backward and forward motion, of modernizing and archaizing, guilt-tripping and bootstrapping, is typical of the ways in which the body is brought into line in the new age of urbanized, industrial production. Both these motions, however, are caught up within a universalizing rhetoric which brooks no contradictions. The planes of earth and society are evened-out in order that the 'centre' may be found at the 'margins' (see chapter 4). The universalizing reformism of the moment of modernity gathers all the codes which distribute and represent bodies, and organizes them according to axiomatics such as number, utility, sustainability. The body and society are being conceived as homoeostatic systems in which flows of capital, code, pollution and passion are regulated: a matter of asceticism for all, Brahminism for all. 'Naturalization', the recurring theme of ideological studies, has been modified. Instead of understanding it simply as an appeal to universal, timeless values, it can now be interpreted in some instances as a call to channel or embody certain speeds or flows: to progress infinitely into a futuristic, higher nature, to boldly go where no man has gone before (as *Star Trek* voices it). A 'sustainable' nature is related to how a mediating vector of temperance sustains these embodied speeds (or basic vectors).

The discourse of natural diet may be modelled as a magnet, with two poles which distribute power. Asceticism is an *interior limit*, like the inner force of a magnet, which allows for the expansion of exterior social limits. Both poles of the discourse magnetize blocs of flow and code. At one end is the series of concentric rings of human families and the natural world; at the other, the ranking of progressive orders of deviance from 'sameness'. The discourse decodes differences between class, race, and gender, but at the same time it is class-, race- and gender-specific. Humanitarianism and 'white [middle class] man's burdenism' are being born together.

The vegetarian body experienced a dual process of identification with the oppressed (the natural world, dominated by technologies of tyranny, animals, the working class), and differentiation from the oppressed (ultimately a redemptive justification of dominant interests, for example the need for technological exploitation of the earth's resources). (Dis)figuring language was imaged as despotism: the tyrant (dis)figures. Thus the cry of nature is not to be converted into a signifier but is a desire for justice, an axiom to be sought after. Natural diet and animal rights do not seek to bring into representation but to turn the law into an axiom. The poetic and political justice of the naturalistic axiom is that the animals cannot vote, that the workers are disenfranchised even if they can. The politics of the body and the natural world remain a consuming problem.

Notes

INTRODUCTION: PRESCRIPTIONS

1 See A. Ross, *Strange Weather*, 191.
2 I also benefited from the work of Chase, Curran, Derrida, Jacobs, Keach, McGann, Rajan and many others.
3 Bataille, Baudrillard, Miller, Porter and Taussig have all provided widely differing approaches to this matter.
4 See M. Douglas, 'Eschewing the Fat: Food Faddism in the Light of Global Famine', *Times Literary Supplement* (30 July 1993), 3–4. In addition, I have found the writing of Douglas, Jeanneret and Spencer to have been especially helpful.
5 Also, see Barkas, Hargrove, Smith and Tester.
6 For further examples, see the writings of Butler, Desmond, Gallagher, Scarry, and Turner.
7 C. Geertz, *The Interpretation of Cultures*, 3–30.
8 G. Deleuze and F. Guattari, *Anti-Oedipus*, 24.
9 D. Miller, *Material Culture and Mass Consumption*, 93.
10 *V, J* vi.18.
11 A Channel 4 film made this clear in the mid-1980s.
12 See A. Appadurai, ed., *The Social Life of Things*, 22.
13 Here the Bakhtinian work of Stallybrass and White has been helpful.
14 K. Thomas, *Man and the Natural World*, 295–96.
15 N. Fiddes, *Meat*, 117. Cf. the discussion of Elias on the shift from public to private carving of meat (99–101).
16 See B. Massumi, *A User's Guide to Capitalism and Schizophrenia*, 13, 23, 42–45 (a critique of Saussurean linguistics as a tool for cultural analysis), 52, 64–65 (on strange attractors), 68.
17 Ibid. 23.
18 See M. DeLanda, 'Nonorganic Life', and D. Sagan, 'Metametazoa: Biology and Multiplicity' in J. Crary and S. Kwinter, eds., *Incorporations*, 129–67, 362–85.
19 M. Douglas, *Purity and Danger*.
20 See F. Jameson, *Prison House*, vi.
21 J. Kristeva, *Powers of Horror*, 66. Kristeva has worked on her own theories

of how desire may instantiate the social field, but I do not share her dependence on Oedipal models of the 'symbolic order' in, as it were 'the last instance', however stimulating her discussion of a pre-Oedipal flow of pulsions, the 'semiotic', may be.

22 My thanks to Andrew Ross for suggesting this phrase.
23 D. J. Haraway's, *Simians, Cyborgs, and Women* would probably describe 'prosthetics' as cultural studies for cyborgs.
24 Some encouragement is offered in J. Whale and S. Copley, eds., *Beyond Romanticism*.
25 For a recent discussion, see M. H., Huet, *Monstrous Imagination*, and Anne Mellor's critique, in *The New York Times Book Review* (25 April 1993), 7.
26 J. Plotz, 'On Guilt Considered as One of the Fine Arts: De Quincey's Criminal Imagination', *The Wordsworth Circle*, XIX: 2 (Spring 1988), 83–88.

I THE RIGHTS OF BRUTES

1 For an anthology of views on ecology, anthropology and nutrition, see N. W. Jerome, R. F. Kandel, and G. H. Pelto, eds., *Nutritional Anthropology*.
2 William Godwin, *Of Population*, 490–92.
3 *The Black Dwarf*, II.623.
4 R. N. Salaman, *Potato*.
5 M. H. Scrivener, *Radical Shelley*, 18.
6 See De Waal, 'Conceptions of Famine', in M. Chapman and H. Macbeth, eds., *Food for Humanity*, 24.
7 William Lovett, *Life*, 6–7.
8 F. Engels, *The Condition of the Working Class in England*, 104–9.
9 William Lovett, *Life*, 45.
10 Thomas Bateman, *Reports on the Diseases of London*, 11–12.
11 Ibid. 12–13, 21–22.
12 Frederick Accum, *Adulterations*, 4.
13 Ibid. 5–12.
14 Ibid. 13.
15 Ibid. 30.
16 See R. Palmer, *A Touch of the Times*, 175–78.
17 R. Tannahill, *Food in History*, 292.
18 E. B. Nicholson, *The Rights of an Animal*, 75.
19 Ibid. 89.
20 Ibid. 91.
21 Ibid. 83.
22 *OED*, 'vegetarian', A.sb.1.a. The first citation is for 1839; The Vegetarian Society was formed in 1847.
23 Nicholson also published *The Life of Benjamin Franklin* in his *Miscellany*:

it contains a section on Franklin's vegetable diet, influenced by the seventeenth-century Behmenist Thomas Tryon (5–12).

24 See Thomas, *Man and the Natural World*, 296. The Vegetarian Society had close connections with this church: see W. E. A. and E. Axon, *Vegetarian Society*, 4. Also, see Joseph Brotherton, *The First Teetotal Tract*.

25 G. Nicholson, *On Food*, i.

26 Ibid. i.

27 P. Bourdieu, *Distinction*, 179–208; for a discussion of the concept of *habitus*, see P. Bourdieu, *Practice*, 72–95.

28 G. Nicholson, *On Food*, ii.

29 Ibid. 4–5.

30 Ibid. 11. This accords with Shelley's position in *V* (*J* vi.13; the reference is to 'simpler habits').

31 Ibid. 3.

32 Ibid. 11.

33 Ibid. 4.

34 Ibid. 11.

35 Ibid. 10.

36 See Bourdieu, *Practice*, 76.

37 K. N. Cameron, *The Young Shelley*, 378.

38 *The Medical Adviser*, ed. Alexander Burnett, M. D., 1 (1824).

39 Ibid. 1.i.

40 For example, the opening article on the tread-mill (1.1–4).

41 Ibid. 1.13.

42 See William Paley, *Principles*, 593–95.

43 Alexander Thomson's *Memoirs of a Pythagorean* seems a tempting solution, but a further reference to 'Mr. T. the platonist' (1.16) makes the choice of Thomas Taylor inevitable (see the section, 'Diet and Radical Politics'). Thomson's work employs transmigration as a plot device.

44 *The Medical Adviser*, 1.14. See chapter 2 for a discussion of Leigh Hunt's essay on angling.

45 Ibid. 1.13.

46 Ibid. 1.14.

47 E. P Thompson, *English Working Class*, 686.

48 J. H. Kellogg, the inventor of cornflakes, advocated fasting, vegetarian diet and exercises at his Battle Creek Sanitarium in the early twentieth century. See T. C. Boyle, *The Road to Wellville*.

49 E.g. *The Medical Adviser*, 1.53–54, 368.

50 Thompson, *English Working Class*, 814.

51 Ibid. 812.

52 *The Medusa; or, Penny Politician*, 1 (1820), 360.

53 *The Republican*, vi (May–December 1822), 12.

54 Ibid. vi.12.

55 Ibid. vi. 12.

56 *The Medical Adviser*, 1.13.

57 Ibid. i.13.

58 Ibid. i.16.

59 All references to William Shakespeare are from S. Wells and G. Taylor, eds., *Complete Works*.

60 *The Medical Adviser*, i.13.

61 Ibid. i.13; see *V, J* vi.3–20.

62 Ibid. i.16.

63 Ibid. i.16.

64 Ibid. ii.379.

65 Ibid. ii.83.

66 Ibid. ii.83.

67 See D. V. Erdman, *Commerce*, 90.

68 Ibid. 13.

69 Ibid. 27.

70 Ibid. 34; the edition for November 1785 contains an article on the Brahmins (34, footnote 1).

71 A. Liu, *Wordsworth*, 525.

72 Joseph Ritson, *Animal Food*, 199.

73 Jones also wrote *The Palace of Fortune* whose chariot-figure, along with Southey's use of similar figures in his epics, influenced Percy Shelley's *Queen Mab*. For a discussion of Shelley and orientalism, see N. Leask, *British Romantic Writers and the East*, 68–169. There is no mention of the popular forms of orientalism embodied in 'Brahmin' diet.

74 Henry Redhead Yorke, *Letters from France*, 160–63.

75 Erdman, *Commerce*, 118–19.

76 Ibid. 32.

77 The 1806 *Excursion* refers to an Oswald who is 'a sympathetic... leader of military volunteers... opposed to the shooting of animals' (ibid. 3); all references to William Wordsworth are from E. de Selincourt, E. and H. Darbyshire, eds., *Poetical Works*.

78 Erdman, *Commerce*, 4.

79 Leask, *British Romantic Writers and the East*, 160–61. Medwin based his work on his experiences in India.

80 Thomas Medwin, *Oswald and Edwin*, 8.

81 Erdman, *Commerce*, 7–8.

82 John Oswald, *Cry*, 1.

83 See chapter 3 for a more complete literary discussion.

84 Oswald, *Cry*, 31–33.

85 Ibid. 33.

86 Ibid. 36.

87 Ibid. 35.

88 Ibid. 38.

89 Ibid. 38–39.

90 Ibid. 77.

91 For a discussion of the despotic signifier, see Deleuze and Guattari, *Anti-Oedipus*, especially the section, 'The Barbarian Despotic Machine'

(192–200), and 'Barbarian or Imperial Representation' (200–17), especially 206 (on 'biunivocalization').

92 John Oswald, *The Government of the People*, 5.
93 Ibid. 6.
94 Ibid. 8.
95 Shakespeare, *The Tempest*, iv.i.151.
96 Oswald, *Government*, 9.
97 Ibid. 11.
98 Erdman, *Commerce*, 99.
99 Oswald, *Cry*, 143, 146.
100 Ibid. ii, my emphasis.
101 John Oswald, *Poems* (np).
102 W. E. Houghton, ed., *Wellesley Index*, 1.432.
103 *The Edinburgh Review*, ii.134.
104 Ibid. ii.134.
105 Ritson, *Animal Food*, 200.
106 *The Edinburgh Review*, ii.132; we are now more inclined to think highly of the whale.
107 Ibid. ii.130.
108 The cartoon contains a bill of fare for 'Sour Crout [sic]', 'Horse Beans', 'Nettle Soup' and 'Creamed Leeks'.
109 *OED*, 'humanity', 1.1.b, ii.3.b., 4.
110 Henry Crowe, *Zoophilos*, 5.
111 Thomas Erskine, *Cruelty to Animals*, 20; see iii, 1.
112 Thomas Young, *Humanity to Animals*, 7. Young was a Fellow of Trinity College, Cambridge.
113 Ibid. 7.
114 Ibid. 51–55.
115 Ibid. 130–31, my emphasis. The passage of poetry is a misquotation of John Dryden, *Of the Pythagorean Philosophy* (a translation of book xv of Ovid's *Metamorphoses*), 686–87: 'Deaf to the Calf that lies beneath the knife, / Looks up, and from her Butcher begs her Life'; all references to Dryden are from J. Kinsley, ed., *Poems*, vol. iv.
116 See F. Ferguson, 'In Search of the Natural Sublime: The Face on the Forest Floor', *Solitude and the Sublime*, 129–45.
117 Mary Wollstonecraft Shelley, *Frankenstein*, 142; see the section, 'A Natural Society'.
118 Cf. 94: the reader is asked to sympathize with him, just as he senses connections between beings. For a discussion of faciality and language, see G. Deleuze and F. Guattari, *A Thousand Plateaus*, 167.
119 The book was also published in Boston, Mass., 1795.
120 Shelley ordered Taylor's translation of Pausanias' *The Description of Greece*, in July or August 1817 (*L* 1.548–49).
121 This argument is beginning not even to be humorous at its extremes (such is the size of an epistemic shift). Mineral rights is seriously advocated by the proponents of 'nuclear guardianship'.

122 See D. A. Dombrowski, 'Vegetarianism and the Argument from Marginal Cases in Porphyry', *Journal of the History of Ideas*, XLV:1 (January-March 1984), 141–43.

123 William Thompson, iii.

124 Thomas Taylor, *Brutes*, 15.

125 Ibid. v.

126 Ibid. vi.

127 Arguments about nature in the period under discussion were still by and large within Aristotelian concepts of *technê* and *physis*. Recently, the idea of 'appropriation' has been challenged in terms of a critique of these concepts. See J. Ely, 'Anarchism and Animism', in J. Clark, ed., *Renewing the Earth*, 49–65.

128 Taylor, *Brutes*, 10.

129 Ibid. 13.

130 The basilisk also appears in Shelley's *Queen Mab* VIII.86 as a symbol of threatening nature, borrowed from Isaiah (see chapter 3).

131 Taylor, *Brutes*, 16–17.

132 Ibid. 30.

133 See the discussion of *Laon and Cythna* (*The Revolt of Islam*) in chapter 3.

134 See E. Hall, *Inventing the Barbarian*.

135 Taylor, *Brutes*, 20–21. Chapter vi is concerned with the language of animals.

136 Ibid. 20; the quotation is from Pope's *An Essay on Man* (1733–34), III.152; see Alexander Pope, *Poems*, ed. J. Butt. Cf. 37 (Hesiod's *Works and Days*).

137 Ibid. 29, my emphasis.

138 *OED*, 'brutal', A.adj.2a, b.

139 *OED*, 'savage', A.adj.1, 5.

140 Taylor, *Brutes*, 73–74.

141 Ibid. 34–35.

142 Ibid. 35. For Socrates on hunger as the true sauce of appetite, see Xenophon, *Memorabilia*, 49 I.iii.5. The idea is also famous in Cervantes, Langland, Taverner and Erasmus.

143 The bill was passed in the House of Lords but not in the House of Commons.

144 Ibid. 9.

145 Ibid. 4.

146 Thomas Moore, *Memoirs*, IV.296 (both Phillips and his daughter 'telling well for this Pythagorean diet'). *DNB* describes this as 'ridicule' ('Phillips, Sir Richard').

147 Richard Phillips, *Golden Rules*, 347–56, especially 354–55. *Golden Rules* is a conduct-book for an entire society. Turning the duties of politics into ethical virtues, Phillips presents advice for Sovereign Princes, Legislators, Electors, Bankers and so on. The preface is an address to Simon Bolivar, the South American liberator (iii–viii).

148 Thompson, *English Working Class*, 349.

149 *The Black Dwarf*, 1.511.

150 Ibid. 1.588.

151 I. McCalman, *Radical Underworld*, 85. It is ironic that George Cannon, one of the aspirers, helped to make Shelley famous (81).

152 Ritson, *Animal Food*, 77–78.

153 For the work of Ebeneezer Elliot, for example the *Corn Law Rhymes* (1831), see P. Schecker, ed., *An Anthology of Chartist Poetry*.

154 *The Republican*, 1 (27 August 1819–7 January 1820), 206–8.

155 Ibid. 1.213.

156 See M. P. T. Leahy, *Against Liberation*, especially 137–39; Leahy's argument applies Wittgenstein to this question, who also wondered whether a lion could talk.

157 *The Medusa*, 1.18–19.

158 Ibid. 1.19.

159 *The Republican*, v (January–May 1822), 148.

160 Thompson, *English Working Class*, 68.

161 E. P Thompson, 'The Crime of Anonymity', in D. Hay, P. Linebaugh, J. G. Rule, E. P. Thompson, and C. Winslow, eds., *Albion's Fatal Tree*, 260.

162 R. Paulson, *Representations of Revolution*, 185, 200.

163 See Liu, *Wordsworth*, 140–48.

164 Edmund Burke, *Reflections*, 89–90.

165 W. Benjamin, 'Theses on the Philosophy of History', in *Illuminations*, 266.

166 Burke, *Reflections*, 106.

167 Ibid. 107.

168 Ibid. 126–27.

169 Ibid. 128. Compare the gruesome image of the character murdered with his own radical texts in Peter Greenaway's film, *The Cook, the Thief, His Wife, and Her Lover*.

170 Ibid. 128.

171 Ibid. 114.

172 Ibid. 117.

173 Ibid. 118.

174 Ibid. 110.

175 Ibid. 210.

176 It is unfortunate that there is not enough space to discuss the matters raised here more fully. A number of seventeenth- and eighteenth-century texts are listed in the bibliography.

177 See Thomas Paine, *Agrarian Justice*, 3.

178 William Blake, *Writings*, ed. G. E. Bentley, 2 vols.

179 T. Eagleton, *The Ideology of the Aesthetic*, 13–30.

180 Jean-Jacques Rousseau, *Emilius*, 1.ii.

181 See the refutation of D. L. Clark (and, by implication, Cameron), in E. Duffy, *Rousseau in England*, 90–91. It is unclear which edition of *Emile* Shelley used.

182 Rousseau, *Emilius*, I.1.
183 Ibid. I.1.
184 Ibid. 1.3, 6.
185 Ibid. 1.6.
186 Ibid. 1.10.
187 Ibid. 1.22–23.
188 Ibid. 1.40.
189 Ibid. 1.40.
190 Ibid. 1.40–41.
191 Ibid. 1.41.
192 Ibid. 1.206.
193 Ibid. 1.43.
194 Ibid. 1.205.
195 Ibid. 1.205.
196 Ibid. 1.205.
197 Ibid. 1.206.
198 Ibid. 1.207.
199 Ibid. 1.208. The passage on the child's 'indifference' to 'flesh-meat' was cited in *V* (1.210).
200 Ibid. 1.214.
201 Ibid. 1.205.
202 Ibid. 1.211.
203 Ibid. 1.278.
204 Ibid. 1.278.
205 Ibid. 1.278.
206 Ibid. 1.280.
207 Edmund Burke, *A Letter from the Right Honourable Edmund Burke to a Noble Lord*, 69; the quotation is from Pope, *An Essay on Man*, 1.83–84.
208 Thomas Beddoes, *Hygëia*, 79.
209 *V, J* VI.6.
210 C. Lévi-Strauss, *The Raw and the Cooked*, 336, 338.
211 J. Parry, 'Death and Digestion: the Symbolism of Food and Eating in North Indian Mortuary Rites', *Man* xx:4 (December 1985), 612–30 (612 quoted here).
212 Mary Shelley, *Frankenstein*, 100.
213 Ibid. 98.
214 Thinkers tend to prefer either environmental or hereditary-instinctive models of behaviour; for a fuller discussion see the section 'Could People be Blank Paper?' in M. Midgley, *Beast and Man*, 19–24.
215 Mary Shelley, *Frankenstein*, 202.
216 Ibid. 52.
217 See Deleuze and Guattari, *A Thousand Plateaus*, 170–71.
218 Ibid. 178.
219 See J. E. Hogle, *Shelley's Process*, 92–93.
220 See chapter 4; also, see James Burnet, (Lord Monboddo), 'Lord Monboddo's Account of Peter the Wild Boy, formerly brought from the

Woods of Germany', *The Gentleman's Magazine and Historical Chronicle,* LV (1785), 113–14.

221 Mary Shelley, *Frankenstein,* 99.
222 Ibid. 99.
223 A. Ronell, *The Telephone Book,* 191–200, 'The Televisual Metaphysics: Frankenstein-AGB-Hölderlin'; also, 202, 432. For a different approach, see M. Butler, 'The First *Frankenstein* and Radical Science', *The Times Literary Supplement* (9 April 1993), 12–14.
224 The term is inspired by Ross, *Strange Weather,* 70: a discussion of Buckminster Fuller's 'spaceship Earth', completely denigrated in the anti-modernism of deep ecology.
225 Mary Shelley, *Frankenstein,* 101.
226 Ibid. 102.
227 Ibid. 104; c.f. 106.
228 Ibid. 110.
229 Ibid. 125.
230 Ibid. 131; see the discussion of Shelley's *A Refutation of Deism* in chapter 4 for a precedent for the lion and antelope image.
231 Ibid. 139.
232 Ibid. 106.
233 Ibid. 125.
234 Ibid. 197.
235 Ibid. 201.
236 Critics have commented on vegetarianism in *Frankenstein.* See C. Adams, 'Frankenstein's Vegetarian Monster', *The Sexual Politics of Meat,* 108–19.
237 See W. I. Thompson 'Gaia and the Politics of Life: a Program for the Nineties', in W. I. Thompson, ed., *Gaia,* 209–13.
238 Mary Shelley, *The Last Man,* II.240–42, 245, III.1–3.
239 See Deleuze and Guattari, 'The Primitive Territorial Machine', *Anti-Oedipus,* 153.
240 Ibid. 176.
241 Mary Shelley, *The Last Man,* I.22–23.
242 Ibid. I.37–38.
243 Ibid. II.214.
244 Ibid. I.148.
245 Ibid. I.151.
246 In II.120–21 the astronomer Merrival repeats the idea suggested in the notes to *Queen Mab* that the earth's pole will coincide with the ecliptic, thus generating a universal spring (*J* I.143).
247 Ibid. I.152.
248 Ibid. I.153–54.
249 Ibid. I. 155; the happy humans are depicted 'Sleeping thus under the beneficent eye of heaven' – compare the restful state imagined in *Queen Mab* VIII and IX (in VIII it is explicitly a function of a natural diet, which renders death less violent and more like sleep).

250 C.f. *Queen Mab* v.134–35, VIII.235–36.
251 Mary Shelley, *The Last Man*, I.195.
252 Ibid. I.197.
253 M. D. Paley, 'Mary Shelley's *The Last Man*: Apocalypse without Millenium [sic]', *Keats-Shelley Review* IV(1989), 1–25.
254 There is a parallel here with the Poet in Percy Shelley's *Alastor*, 100–1.
255 Mary Shelley, *The Last Man* , I.160.
256 Ibid. I.163.
257 See I.163: Adrian and Idris find Lionel in his cottage, 'Curius-like, feasting on sorry fruits for supper'. Curius Dentatus was a consul of the third century BC who was famous for austere living; see *The Oxford Companion to Classical Literature*, 162.
258 Mary Shelley, *The Last Man*, II.139. The quotation is from Burke, *Reflections*, 48.
259 Ibid. II.302.
260 Ibid. II.303.
261 Ibid. III.162.
262 Ibid. III.166.
263 Ibid. II.306.
264 Ibid. III.224.
265 Ibid. III.304.
266 Ibid. III.318.
267 Ibid. III.305.

2 THE PURER NUTRIMENT: DIET AND SHELLEY'S BIOGRAPHIES

1 N. Crook and D. Guiton, *Shelley's Venomed Melody*, 76.
2 Ibid. 69.
3 Ibid. 240.
4 Thomas Medwin, *Life*, I.224–25. H. Buxton Forman's edition adds *crede expertum* (in brackets after 'none but a Pythagorean can tell...' (136).
5 All references to Milton are from A. Fowler, ed., *Paradise Lost* and J. Carey, ed., *Complete Shorter Poems*.
6 *V, J* VI.5 (c.f. the notes to *Queen Mab*, *J* I.157–58); Ritson, 39.
7 Ritson, *Animal Food*, 39.
8 Crook and Guiton, *Shelley's Venomed Melody*, 69.
9 W. St Clair, *The Godwins and the Shelleys*, 260, 261, 337, 338.
10 Ibid. 263, 264.
11 Cf. T. Clark, *Embodying Revolution*, 45.
12 R. Holmes, *Pursuit*, 220.
13 Ibid. 220.
14 'VSys', *J* VI.343–44.
15 D. L. Clark, 'The Date and Source of Shelley's "A Vindication of Natural Diet"', *Studies in Philology* XXXVI (1939), 70.
16 Medwin, *Life*, I.124–26; c.f. Thomas Jefferson Hogg, *Life*, I.128–29.

17 Ibid. I.133.
18 *L* I.344; Pythagoras is not himself the author of any extant works, though Shelley may have been referring to an edition of Iamblichus' *Golden Verses*. He mentions transmigration in a letter to Elizabeth Hitchener (25 July 1811): see *L* I.124.
19 Hogg, *Life*, I.91.
20 Ibid. I.120–22.
21 Ibid. I.130–31.
22 Ibid. I.131.
23 Ibid. I.245.
24 Ibid. I.52.
25 Ibid. I.85.
26 Ibid. I.302. Hogg's quotation is from Milton, *L'Allegro* (1631?): 'Of herbs, and other country messes, / Which the neat-handed Phillis dresses' (85–86). Some lines later, stories are mentioned of 'How Faëry Mab the junkets eat' (102); junkets are cream cheeses. This is obviously a clever allusion to Shelley's time spent writing *Queen Mab* and associating with Mrs Boinville.
27 *L* II.187–88.
28 Medwin, *Life*, II.47.
29 Ibid. II.355.
30 Ibid. II.240, my emphasis.
31 See W. D. Smith, *The Hippocratic Tradition*, 45.
32 Plato, *Phaedrus*, 265e; see Smith, *The Hippocratic Tradition*, 46–47.
33 Bodleian MS Shelley Adds. e.12, inside back cover. I am indebted to Timothy Webb for noticing this quotation.
34 *J* VII.262–63.
35 Ibid. I.152.
36 Shelley, *Declaration of Rights*, *J* v.275; this pamphlet was printed but not attributed to Shelley on the title page.
37 St Clair, *The Godwins and the Shelleys*, 260.
38 Ibid. 261.
39 Hogg, *Life*, II.447.
40 *L* I.274–75.
41 Ibid. I.273.
42 Harriet Shelley, *Letters*, 4.
43 Ibid. 6.
44 *L* I.476–77.
45 For ways in which Shelley fits the *habitus* of the urban literary class in his abstemiousness and irregular consumption, see Thomas Trotter, *Nervous Temperament*, 37–39.
46 Hogg, *Life*, II.322.
47 Ibid. II.320–22.
48 Holmes, *Pursuit*, 174.
49 *V*, *J* VI.6–7, 13, 17.

50 Clark, D. L., 'Date and Sources', 71.
51 St Clair, *The Godwins and the Shelleys*, 337.
52 The word is not capitalized.
53 *L* i.347; Shelley anticipates Nietzsche's description of urban 'Schlacht-häuser und Garküchen des Geistes' in *Also Spracht Zarathustra*; F. Nietzsche, *Werke*, III.425.
54 Ibid. I.337.
55 The sociopathology suggested in Lawrence's approach will become important in the discussion of vegetarianism in chapter 4.
56 K. N. Cameron, ed., *Shelley and his Circle 1773–1822*, III.277.
57 Ibid. III.254–59.
58 Thomas Love Peacock, *Works*, VII.517.
59 Ibid. VIII.71; c.f. Thomas Love Peacock, *Memoirs*, 30.
60 Ibid. VIII.72–73; c.f. Peacock, *Memoirs*, 31–32.
61 Thomas Love Peacock, *Nightmare Abbey* in *Works*, III.11; John Oswald refers to the vegetarianism of the Zoroastrians in *Cry* 83, 166–67 (quoting St Augustine's *de moribus Manichaeorum*).
62 Ibid. I.8.
63 Ibid. I.15–16.
64 Peacock describes Escot's feeling of love in heart and brain as like Ladurlad (the protagonist of Southey's *The Curse of Kehama*); this poem is alluded to in 'VSys' ('like Ladurlad', Bodleian MS Shelley Adds. c.4, 267v): the idea of using Ladurlad as an example of wayward passion may have been a topic of conversation at Bracknell.
65 Peacock, *Works*, I.18.
66 Ibid. I.34–35.
67 Ibid. I.103.
68 Hogg, *Life*, II.414.
69 Ibid. II.414–15.
70 Ibid. II.419–20: this means that Shelley's diet at this stage was lacto-ovo vegetarian, with some gestures towards veganism.
71 Ibid. II.420.
72 Ibid. II.420.
73 Ibid. II.420.
74 Ibid. II.422–24.
75 William Lambe, *Constitutional Diseases*, 41–46.
76 Hogg, *Life*, II.425.
77 Ibid. II.426.
78 Ibid. II.432.
79 *L* 1.368.
80 St Clair, *The Godwins and the Shelleys*, 337.
81 *L* 1.167.
82 See *J* VI.347.
83 See Medwin, *Life*, 1.184 for an account of Shelley's vegetarianism in July 1813.

84 Leask, *British Romantic Writers and the East*, 178.
85 See John Stewart, *Opus Maximum*, 190–92.
86 Hogg, *Life*, II.451.
87 Ibid. II.414.
88 Cameron, ed., *Shelley and his Circle*, III.253–54.
89 See the letters from the Rev. William Terrot to Hogg in Thomas Jefferson Hogg, *The Athenians*, 22–23, 24–25.
90 Ibid. 44–45.
91 Holmes, *Pursuit*, 216.
92 Ibid. 217.
93 *L* II.92.
94 Peacock, *Memoirs*, 29.
95 *V, J* VI. 347 (editorial note).
96 S. C. Behrendt, *Shelley and his Audiences*, 89.
97 Hogg, *Life*, II.469–70.
98 Ibid. II.405.
99 Ibid. II.405.
100 Ibid. II.433–35; this is probably untrue. See Cameron, *The Young Shelley*, 378–79.
101 Ibid. II.448.
102 *L* I.380 (c.f. Hogg, *Life*, II.480–82); Shelley also declares that he has been reading Cicero's philosophical writing: *De natura deorum* is quoted in 'VSys', making this text likely to have been written after November 1813.
103 Ibid. I.380.
104 See R. Parker, *Miasma*, 302.
105 Medwin, *Life*, I.213.
106 Hogg, *Life*, II.485.
107 Ibid. II.487.
108 Mary Shelley, *Journals*, I.79–80; italics in this edition denote Percy Shelley's own hand.
109 See P. Camporesi, *Bread of Dreams*, chapter 3, 'Sacred and Profane Cannibalism' (40–55).
110 St Clair, *The Godwins and the Shelleys*, 400. Contrast the later prescription, 'Take care of yourself... especially abstaining from all sorts of fruit' (*L* II.314).
111 Holmes, *Pursuit*, 286.
112 Ibid. 294.
113 Peacock, *Works*, VIII.80.
114 Ibid. VIII.80–81.
115 Ibid. VIII.99.
116 Holmes, *Pursuit*, 297.
117 William Hazlitt, *Complete Works*, VIII.148–49 ('On Paradox and Commonplace').
118 Mary Shelley, *Journals*, I.142.

119 D. H. Reiman, ed., *Shelley and His Circle*, v.97.
120 Benjamin Robert Haydon, *Diary*, II.89; the passage of Wordsworth is *The Excursion*, VIII.558–69.
121 *L* II.361.
122 Benjamin Robert Haydon, *Autobiography*, I.253.
123 Haydon, *Diary*, II.157.
124 Ibid. II.157.
125 Ibid. II.372–73; the date is 5 August, 1822.
126 John Keats, *Letters*, I.140.
127 See P. Conrad, *Everyman History*, 435.
128 *L* II.15, footnote 6, 188 (about Lambe). De Almeida's recent study of Keats' relationship to the medical discourses of his time shows no knowledge of Lambe, or of the possibility of reading the figuration of diet in his texts in association with these discourses.
129 Holmes, *Pursuit*, 376.
130 E.g. *L* I.570, 572–73.
131 Ibid. I.573.
132 *L* I.543.
133 A. H. Beavan, *James and Horace Smith*, 169.
134 Ibid. 170–71.
135 Ibid. 171.
136 Ibid. 172; here Smith quotes the first 14 lines of *Alastor*.
137 All references to James Thomson are from *Complete Poetical Works*, ed. J. Sambrook.
138 Holmes, *Pursuit*, 423.
139 *L* II.78; c.f. Peacock, *Memoirs*, 170.
140 Ibid. II.191.
141 Holmes, *Pursuit*, 429.
142 *L* II.42.
143 Holmes, *Pursuit*, 479.
144 *L* II.73.
145 Ibid. II.114.
146 Shelley, preface to *Prometheus Unbound*, *J* II.172.
147 Holmes, *Pursuit*, 449.
148 *L* II.92.
149 *The Curse of Kehama* is about a power-crazed and degenerate Brahman, who curses the peasant pariah Ladurlad. Ladurlad is thus exiled from both society and nature (the elements, time, food and drink, sickness, death, sleep), but develops a stoical fortitude, 'An agony represt' (VIII.118).
150 *L* II.68, footnote 2.
151 Ibid. II.15.
152 Ibid. II.150.
153 With Reiman, I prefer to suggest the double meaning of 'mask' (the poem is entitled *Masque* in *J*).

154 See Camporesi, *Bread of Dreams*, 10, 120.

155 Holmes, *Pursuit*, 576; c.f. Bodleian MS Shelley Adds. e.6.

156 *L* II.187.

157 Ibid. II.187–88. 'Maimouni' (Hogg's word for Southey's Maimuna), is a sick joke, probably more on Hogg's (revisionist) part. Having spellbound Thalaba, Maimuna asks the 'She Bear' who has just entered with 'prey in her bloody mouth' to eat him; but 'the She Bear fawned on Thalaba / And quietly licked his hand' (*Thalaba* VIII.131–32; cf. the basilisk licking the child's feet in *Queen Mab* VIII). The Spirit and Maimuna take Thalaba in a car to Mohareb (whom Thalaba had cast into hell); an inversion of *Queen Mab*. Hogg may be reviling the days he spent with Shelley at Bracknell. Maimuma commences as an evil witch, but then repents at the moment of death; Thalaba buries her in the snow.

158 *L*, II.363.

159 Edmund Blunden, *Leigh Hunt*, 169.

160 Reiman, ed., *Shelley and His Circle*, VI.1075–80.

161 Edward John Trelawny, *Records*, I.ix–x.

162 Ibid. I.x.

163 Medwin, *Life*, II.343–44.

164 Trelawny, *Records*, I.xiv.

165 Ibid. I.3.

166 Ibid. I.34.

167 Ibid. I.74.

168 Ibid. I.76.

169 Ibid. I.82.

170 Ibid. I.90–91.

171 Ibid. I.94.

172 Ibid. I.94.

173 Ibid. I.94. C.f. I.140–41, I.161: Shelley ate dry bread and grapes while reading philosophy.

174 Ibid. I.120.

175 Adams, *The Sexual Politics of Meat*, 47–48.

176 Trelawny, *Records*, I.111–12.

177 Ibid. I.116.

178 Mary Shelley, *Journals*, I.422; the square brackets denote a holograph draft by Trelawny.

179 Ibid. I.423; the phrase in square brackets was deleted; this passage is Trelawny's holograph draft.

3 IN THE FACE: THE POETICS OF THE NATURAL DIET

1 Southey, *Thalaba*, 1.25: '"The corn matured not for the food of man, / The wells and fountains failed"' (cf. the ecological disaster discussed in the section on *Laon and Cythna*).

2 The best examples in literary critical discourse to date are Cameron's chapter 'Men and Vegetables' in *The Young Shelley*, and C. Grabo, *The Magic Plant*, 114–15 (a cursory reading of *Queen Mab* VIII).

3 F. A. Pottle, *Shelley and Browning*, 17, 22, 28.

4 S. W. Holmes, 'Browning: Semantic Stutterer', *PMLA* lx (1945), 231–55.

5 Ibid. 245.

6 Ibid. 251.

7 Ibid. 243–44, 254.

8 Ibid. 231.

9 All references to Byron are from *Poetical Works*, ed. J. McGann.

10 See M. Vitale, 'The Domesticated Heroine in Byron's *Corsair* and William Hone's Prose Adaption', *Literature and History* x (1984), 76–78.

11 Shelley, *Queen Mab; a Philosophical Poem. With Notes* (London: printed by P. B. Shelley, 1813).

12 'VSys', *J* VI.340.

13 See P. Dawson, *The Unacknowledged Legislator*, 85, 95–96.

14 For a discussion of the Buddhist idyll in the *Dīgha Nikâya*, see J. S. Strong, *Aśoka*, 44–45.

15 T. Adorno, and M. Horkheimer, *Dialectic of Enlightenment*, 105.

16 See M. Foucault, *The Use of Pleasure*, 99–108.

17 Shelley is here entering a contemporary debate, conducted in Monboddo and Ritson, among others.

18 See Deleuze and Guattari, '1440: The Smooth and the Striated', *A Thousand Plateaus*, 474–500, an analysis of how the space of the desert, the nomadic space, may be contrasted with the space of the state, of striated cultivation.

19 It also alludes to the first glimpse of Eden in Milton, *Paradise Lost*, IV.325–52.

20 See *V, J* VI.5–7.

21 J. Turner, *Reckoning with the Beast*, 7.

22 Ibid. 8.

23 William Cowper, *Poetic Works*, ed. H. S. Milford.

24 *J* I.159; c.f. VI.7.

25 Cf. *Prometheus Unbound*, III.iv.77: 'All things had put their evil nature off.'

26 Shelley is echoing not Monboddo, but Pufendorf, a source for Defoe's *Mere Nature Delineated* (1726); see M. E. Novak, *Defoe and the Nature of Man*, 26–27.

27 See *J* I.158; c.f. VI.6.

28 *V, J* VI.7; c.f. Ritson, *Animal Food*, 56.

29 M. Mack, *Pope*, 769. Cheyne and Hartley both wrote on the natural diet.

30 Alexander Pope, 'Cruelty to Put a Living Creature to Death', *The Guardian* lxi (21 May 1713); see Mack, *Pope*, 73.

31 Mack, *Pope*, 491.

32 Ibid. 590.

33 Ibid. 757, 621.
34 Ibid. 800.
35 Especially 'But just disease to luxury succeeds' (165), which rewrites *Paradise Lost*, XI.466–95.
36 Shelley, note 17 to *Queen Mab*, *J* 1.163, footnote 1, and *V*, *J* VI.15, footnote 1.
37 See Byron, *The Complete Poetical Works*, 1.239.
38 Lord George Gordon Byron, *Byron's Letters and Journals*, 1.163, II.76, 80, 132, II.89, show a dislike of Pratt for his patronization of this poet.
39 *The Edinburgh Review*, 1 (1802–3), 108–11.
40 James Montgomery's *Poems on the Abolition of the Slave Trade* suggests other parallels with Shelley in its language of 'NATURE FREE' (7), *Prometheus Delivered*, and the use of Trotter (95).
41 Aristotle, *Politics*, 16–17 (1.ii.4, 1253b).
42 Pratt, *Humanity*, 38–39.
43 Plutarch, *Moralia* XII.541. There are many other examples in Plutarch's two extant essays on vegetariansim.
44 Pratt, *Humanity*, 40.
45 Ibid. 41.
46 Ibid. 41.
47 Ibid. 85–86.
48 See *Queen Mab* 1.33–34, III.197, IV.3, VII.20.
49 Cf. Thalaba's discovery of the language of nature written on the forehead of a locust (*Thalaba* III.181).
50 Cf. John Stewart, *The Revelation of Nature*, viii (a similar revision of Pope).
51 W. Keach, *Shelley's Style*, 80–81 (*Queen Mab*), 81–87 (*Alastor*).
52 Ibid. 98; also Clark, *Embodying Revolution*, chapter 4.
53 *L* 1.352.
54 Shelley, *Alastor; or, the Spirit of Solitude: and Other Poems* (London: printed for Baldwin, Cradock and Joy, and Carpenter and Son, 1816).
55 Cameron, ed., *Shelley and his Circle*, IV.487–568.
56 Shelley, *Complete Poetical Works*, ed. N. Rogers, 1.333.
57 See R. A. Lanham, *Rhetorical Terms*, 113.
58 Bodleian MS Shelley Adds. c.4., 28v.
59 William Lambe is also cited in 'Vegetable System', *J* VI.342.
60 Ibid. VI.336.
61 Cf. Southey, *Thalaba*, IX.280: 'The Sledge goes rapidly'; 288, the boat 'Without an oar, without a sail'; 290–93, 'The little boat moved on'; 'The little boat falls rapidly.'
62 M. Crucefix, 'Wordsworth, Superstition, and Shelley's *Alastor*', *Essays in Criticism* XXXIII:2 (April, 1983), 126–47; 145. Crucefix claims that this would tie *Alastor* with the poem *Superstition* which was included in the same volume (130).
63 Ibid. 137.
64 Ibid. 140.

65 *J* 1.159.
66 G. K. Blank, *Wordsworth's Influence on Shelley*, 42.
67 Crucefix, 'Wordsworth, Superstition, and Shelley's *Alastor*', 132–42.
68 Wordsworth, *Poetical Works*, v.95.
69 Shelley, *Peter Bell the Third, J* iii.280; the passage is from *The Excursion*, viii.568–71.
70 The wood-dwelling hermit feeding squirrels appeared in the excised Wordsworth passage (*Poetical Works*, v.95); compare the *Alastor* narrator's sympathy for the 'kindred' 'bird, insect, or gentle beast' (13–15).
71 Cf. Wordsworth, *The Excursion*, iii.148–52.
72 Samuel Taylor Coleridge, *The Rime of the Ancient Mariner* 238–39, 272–91. All references to Coleridge are from *Coleridge*, ed. H. J. Jackson. For a discussion of the politics of the 'populous', see the chapter, 'Malthus, Godwin, Wordsworth, and the Spirit of Solitude', in Ferguson, *Solitude and the Sublime*, 114–28.
73 Clark, *Embodying Revolution*, 55.
74 Shelley would have known about this passage of Cowper through Ritson, *Animal Food*, 90–92.
75 See S. Curran, *Poetic Form and British Romanticism*, 116–19.
76 For a concise and witty explanation of bad infinity, see S. Zizek, *The Sublime Object of Ideology*, 64–66.
77 Hogle, *Shelley's Process*, 48. Freud only conceived of *thanatos* while generating the notion of the Oedipus complex, having reversed his initial theory that anxiety is caused by sexual repression.
78 See Deleuze and Guattari, 'The Desiring Machines', *Anti-Oedipus*, 1–50, especially 16–18.
79 Shortly after writing of adolescent love, St Augustine discusses the Manichean belief that if a 'sanctified' person ate a fig then 'particles of the true and supreme God' which 'were supposed to be imprisoned in the fruit', according to its dualist theory, would be 'released'; Saint Augustine, *Confessions*, 67 (iii.10). It is possible to speculate that since the beneficent God is immaterial light in Zoroastrianism, then Shelley's interest in representing glowing fruit (lit as from within), for example in *Marenghi* or *Laon and Cythna*, may derive somewhat from his reading of Augustine.
80 See Deleuze and Guattari, 'November 28, 1947: How Do You Make Yourself a Body Without Organs?', *A Thousand Plateaus*, 149–66.
81 I am using Marilyn Butler's portmanteau word for Wordsworth, Coleridge, and Southey as poetic collaborators. Shelley is addressing all three poets in the narrative and figurative structures of the poem.
82 Hogle, *Shelley's Process*, 54.
83 Ibid. 56.
84 Shelley, *Laon and Cythna; or, the Revolution of the Golden City: a Vision of the Nineteenth Century. In the Stanza of Spenser* (London: printed for Sherwood, Neely and Jones, and C. and J. Ollier, 1818).

85 R. Girard, *Violence and the Sacred*, 4.
86 *The Quarterly Review*, XXI:xlii (April, 1819).
87 Ibid. xlii.463.
88 Ibid. xlii.463.
89 Ibid. xlii. 463–64.
90 Ibid. xlii.467.
91 Ibid. xlii.461.
92 Numbers in round brackets denote canto line numbers in *J*.
93 Camporesi, *Bread of Dreams*, 28–29, 40–41.
94 See chapter 5 for a developed discussion of this theme.
95 M. Butler's *Romantics, Rebels and Reactionaries* discusses the 'Cult of the South' well.
96 *The Wanderer and the Nightingale* (1818) describes an inhumane man destroying the nightingale whose song creates an Orphic space; cf. *The Witch of Atlas*, 92–95. For a theoretical exposition of the Utopian force of Orphic imagery, see H. Marcuse, *Eros and Civilization*, chapter 8 ('The Images of Orpheus and Narcissus').
97 Bodleian MS Shelley Adds. e.4, 46v.
98 Shelley, *Poetical Works*, ed. T. Hutchinson, 570.
99 *L* II.43. See J. Drew, *India*, 259.
100 Shelley, *Prometheus Unbound: a Lyrical Drama in Four Acts with Other Poems* (London: C. and J. Ollier, 1820).
101 Cf. the cannibalistic snakes which are 'Inseparable parts' of the self-tortured Zohak in Southey, *Thalaba* v.302.
102 Shelley, *Shelley's Poetry and Prose* , ed. D. H. Reiman and S. B. Powers, 184.
103 *V, J* VI.6–7.
104 Baker, C., 90–92.
105 Shelley was interested in describing possible relationships between Brahminism and other cultures in *Prometheus Unbound*: 'and the Celt knew the Indian' (II.iv.94).
106 See chapter 4 for a discussion of *A Refutation of Deism* and *Epipsychidion*.
107 Later (IX.164–65), Khawla makes a wax model of Thalaba from a mixture which includes the stomach contents of the ounce (mandrake); cf. the benign version in *The Witch of Atlas* (especially in the context of the 'Samian sage' and Shelley's renewed interest in Mrs Boinville in 1820).
108 Adorno and Horkheimer, *Dialectic of Enlightenment*, 17–18, 31, 180–81.
109 For further discussion, see Deleuze and Guattari, *Anti-Oedipus* and *A Thousand Plateaus*, both rather eclectic and surrealist accounts of the differences outlined here.

4 APOLLO IN THE JUNGLE: HEALTHY MORALS AND THE BODY
BEAUTIFUL

1 The phrase is used in a critique of Thomas Tryon: John Field, *The
Absurdity and Falseness of Thomas Trion's* [sic] *Doctrine Manifested*, 14.
'Mute eloquence' is used by Young.
2 Hogle, *Shelley's Process*, 92–93.
3 To a certain extent even Foucault falls into this error, despite his
collaboration with Deleuze and Guattari (Ibid. 109).
4 Shelley, *Queen Mab*, *J* 1.164–65.
5 Plutarch, *Plutarch's Moralia*, XII.537.
6 Ibid. XII.547. The passage is *Moralia*, 994B.
7 Ibid. XII.551–53; *Moralia*, 994F–995B.
8 Ibid. XII.541; *Moralia*, 993B.
9 Ibid. XII.553; *Moralia*, 995C.
10 Ibid. XII.553–55; *Moralia*, 995C.
11 *V*, *J* VI.14.
12 Plutarch, *Plutarch's Moralia*, XII.573; *Moralia*, 998B–C.
13 Shelley was admired for this in J. H. Williams, *The Ethics of Diet*, 3.
14 *V*, *J* VI.5.
15 Ibid. VI.5.
16 Ibid. VI.5.
17 Ibid. VI.5.
18 Milton, *Paradise Lost*, XI.477ff.
19 *V*, *J* VI.5.
20 A translation of the epigraph on the title page of *V*: '"You rejoice, O
crafty son of Iapetus, that you have stolen fire and deceived Jupiter; but
great will thence be the evil both to yourself and to your posterity. To
them this gift of fire shall be the gift of woe; in which, while they delight
and pride themselves, they shall cherish their own wickedness"' (*J*
VI.347).
21 *V*, *J* VI.5.
22 Ibid. VI.6; see Horace, *Odes*, 15 (*Odes* 1.3.27).
23 Ibid. VI.6.
24 Ibid. VI.6.
25 Ibid. VI.6.
26 Ibid. VI.6.
27 Ibid. VI.6.
28 Ibid. VI.6–7; see John Frank Newton, *The Return to Nature*, 6–9. The
quotation from Pliny on page 6 is incorrect. The correct sentence reads
'Animal occidit primus Hyperbius Martis filius, Prometheus bovem',
from *Natural History* VII.lvi.209 (not section 57, as Shelley claims); see
Pliny, *Natural History*, II.646.
29 Ibid. VI.7.
30 C.f. Lévi-Strauss, *The Raw and the Cooked*, 140–41, 336, 337–38.
31 *V*, *J* VI.7.

32 Ritson, *Animal Food*, 45–47.
33 *V, J* vi.7. This passage is adapted from Owenson's novel, *The Missionary*: see Drew, *India*, 260. For a discussion of the characteristic rhetoric of 'penury, disease, and crime' (the 'miasmatic tricolon'), see the final chapter.
34 For a discussion of Shelley's use of 'recall' in *Prometheus Unbound* as a kind of Hegelian *Aufhebung*, see C. Jacobs, *Uncontainable Romanticism*, 25–27; on figuration in particular in this context, see C. Chase, *Decomposing Forms*, 23.
35 *V, J* vi.7.
36 See Clark, *Embodying Revolution*, chapters 1 and 2.
37 *Queen Mab* note 17, *J* 1.159.
38 James Henry Lawrence, *The Empire of the Nairs*, 1.iii, 13, 27.
39 *V, J* vi.7–8. See Shelley, *The Poems of Shelley*, ed. K. Everest and G. Matthews, 1.412, for an account of Shelley's reading of Cuvier in Lambe.
40 Ibid. vi.8.
41 Ibid. vi.8.
42 Ibid. vi.8.
43 Abraham Rees, *Cyclopaedia*, xxiii.Hh-Hhv (there is no numbered pagination).
44 *V, J* vi.8.
45 Ibid. vi.9.
46 Ibid. vi.9. See Shelley, *Poems*, ed. Everest and Matthews, 1.413 (on Rousseau).
47 *V, J* vi.9.
48 Ibid. vi.9.
49 Ibid. vi.8.
50 Ibid. vi.9–10.
51 Ibid. vi.10.
52 'VSys', *J* vi.340: 'See Queen Mab, p.223.' Page 223 of the 1813 edition of *Queen Mab* is the main body of this paragraph (expounding the need for a sociopathology).
53 *V, J* vi.10.
54 Shelley would have found precedents for this, with an emphasis on diet, in Trotter's *Nervous Temperament*.
55 *V, J* vi.7.
56 Ibid. vi.6.
57 Ibid. vi.10.
58 Ibid. vi.10.
59 Ibid. vi.10; cf. 'It strikes at the root of the evil', and *Queen Mab* iv.80–85.
60 Ibid. vi.10.
61 Ibid. vi.10.
62 Ibid. vi.10.
63 Ibid. vi.11–12.
64 Ibid. vi.12.

65 Ibid. VI.12.
66 Ibid. VI.13.
67 See Plato, *Phaedrus*, 57.
68 *V, J* VI.13–14.
69 Ibid. VI.15.
70 Ibid. VI.14–15; 15 footnote 1.
71 Ibid. VI.16.
72 Ibid. VI.17.
73 Ibid. VI.6.
74 (*J* i.152, 420).
75 See T. Weiskel, *The Romantic Sublime*, 190.
76 *V, J* VI.6
77 Ibid. VI.6.
78 Ibid. VI.7.
79 Ibid. VI.13.
80 Ibid. VI.14.
81 Ibid. VI.14.
82 'VSys', *J* VI.335.
83 Ibid. VI.340.
84 *J* I.145.
85 Shelley, *Adonais: an Elegy on the Death of John Keats, Author of Endymion, Hyperion etc.* (Pisa: printed by the author, 1821).
86 See 'The Rhetoric of Temporality', in P. De Man, *Blindness and Insight*, 187–228.
87 Compare the 'self-destroying poisons' which the Maniac desires to drink in *Julian and Maddalo* (1818–19), 436.
88 See Trotter, *Nervous Temperament*, 72.
89 N. Goslee, 'Dis-Personing: Drafting as Plot in *Epipsychidion*', paper given at the international conference, *Shelley: Poet and Legislator of the World* (New York: 20–23 May, 1992). B. C. Gelpi's work on *Epipsychidion* at the MLA (1992) showed links between recall and progress (without raising Shelley's anxieties about the implicit violence of this procedure, either in political reform or in the act of love): the poem appears to oppose to the violence of figuration the endless transference of repression (Colonus = ivy = buried Oedipus; a rather Kristevan, 'pre-Oedipal' reading; see B. C. Gelpi, *Shelley's Goddess*, 204.
90 *V, J* VI.17.
91 'VSys', *J* VI.335.
92 Shelley, *Shelley's Prose*, ed. D. L. Clark, 91.
93 Ibid. VI.339.
94 Ibid. VI.337; the passage is from *The Curse of Kehama* IX.86–87. Southey had his own opinions about diet and poetry: see Robert Southey, *Southey's Common-Place Book*, 20.
95 Ibid. VI.340.
96 Ibid. VI.340–41.
97 Ibid. VI.341.

98 Bodleian MS Shelley Adds. c.4, 268v.
99 I am indebted to E. B. Murray for his help in dating 'Vegetable System'.
100 Bodleian MS Shelley Adds. c.4, 269v.
101 Euripides, *Ion, Hippolytus, Medea, Alcestis*, 237.
102 Mary Shelley, *Journal*, II.646.
103 'VSys', *J* VI.336; c.f. *J* VI.44; see Cicero, *De natura deorum*, vol. XIX of the Loeb edition of Cicero, 55 (i.54); iii.88 describes Pythagoras' objections to the sacrifice of blood.
104 *V*, *J* VI.16.
105 Shelley, *A Refutation of Deism*, *J* VI.44.
106 'VSys', *J* VI.335.
107 Ibid. VI.335.
108 Ibid. VI.335.
109 Ibid. VI.337.
110 Ibid. VI.339.
111 C.f. *V*, *J* VI.5.
112 'VSys', *J* VI.335.
113 Shelley, 'On the Punishment of Death', *J* VI.190; 'A Philosophical View of Reform', *J* VII.8.
114 'VSys', *J* VI.344, footnote 1.
115 Bodleian MS Shelley Adds. c.4, 267r.
116 Ibid. 267v; Ingpen and Peck misread this as 'politicians' dreams' (*J* VI.336).
117 Ibid. 267v; a slash denotes a new line; angled brackets denote a cancellation mark.
118 Ibid. 267v.
119 William (and Alexander) Smellie, *The Philosophy of Natural History*, I.60–61.
120 Bodleian MS Shelley Adds. c.4, 272v.
121 Ibid. 268v.
122 Ibid. 271r.
123 Ibid. 271r.
124 Ibid. 271r. Shelley uses James Easton, *Human Longevity*.
125 See John Abernethy, *Hunter's Theory of Life*, 14; the increased secular tone of 'Vegetable System' compared with the Fall narratives of *V* is reminiscent not of the vitalist Abernethy but of his radical pupil, William Lawrence.
126 Bodleian MS Shelley Adds. c.4, 271v.
127 Ibid. 271v.
128 'VSys', *J* VI.340, footnote 1; probably referring to John Abernethy, *Local Diseases*, 17–18. Also, see John Abernethy, *Surgical Observations*, 144–47 (on the relationship between digestive disorders and the brain).
129 Bodleian MS Shelley Adds. c.4, 271v.
130 *J* VI.339; surely Shelley is trying to demonstrate how wild boars are mutated into domestic pigs (how many domesticated bears are there?).
131 Bodleian MS Shelley Adds. c.4, 271v.

132 Lambe, *Constitutional Diseases*, 10.
133 Bodleian MS Shelley Adds, c.4, 269r.
134 Ibid. 270r.
135 See M. Butler, *Burke, Paine, Godwin, and the Revolution Controversy*, 161.
136 Bodleian MS Shelley Adds. c.4, 268r.
137 Ibid. 270v.
138 Shelley, *A Refutation of Deism: in a Dialogue* (London: printed by Schulze and Dean, 1814).
139 Shelley, *A Refutation of Deism*, J VI.35.
140 Ibid. VI.35.
141 Ibid. VI.36, my emphasis.
142 Ibid. VI.36.
143 Ibid. VI.43–46.
144 Ibid. VI.46.
145 Ibid. VI.50–53.
146 Hogg, *Life*, II.485.
147 Shelley, *A Refutation of Deism*, J VI.49.
148 Ibid. VI.52.
149 Ibid. VI.50.
150 Ibid. VI.51, footnote 1; Shelley also quotes part of Plutarch's second essay on vegetarianism; Jones is misleading about exactly which passage is quoted here (*L* 1.381); Shelley also quotes the second passage of Plutarch quoted at the end of *Queen Mab* note 17 (*Moralia* XII.994F–995B).
151 I am grateful to Nicolas Rasmussen for helping me to research this information.
152 Shelley, *A Refutation of Deism*, J VI.51.
153 Ibid. VI.52.
154 Ibid. VI.35.
155 Ibid. VI.52.
156 *V, J* VI.10.
157 William Blake, *Songs of Experience* ('The Human Abstract', 1).
158 J. F. MacCannell, *The Regime of the Brother*, 40. Rousseau is analysed as a primal figure in the construction of fraternity, 'insisting on the primacy of egoism and narcissism [rather than the sexual relationship] in the construction of human society' (43).
159 Shelley, *A Refutation of Deism*, J VI.45.
160 Ibid. VI. 50. Cf.*Queen Mab* VIII.107:

> All things are recreated, and the flame
> Of consentaneous love inspires all life:
> The fertile bosom of the earth gives suck
> To myriads, who still grow beneath her care.

161 Ibid. VI.42–43.
162 Shelley, 'On the Game Laws', *Shelley's Prose*, ed. D. L Clark, 342.
163 Ibid. 342.

164 Ibid. 342.
165 Ibid. 342.
166 Ibid. 342; angled brackets denote a cancellation in the manuscript.
167 Ibid. 342.
168 Ibid. 342.
169 Ibid. 342.
170 Ibid. 342.
171 Ibid. 342–43; there are a number of syntactical hiatuses in the passage. Deletions in the manuscript are given here between ⟨ ⟩ marks.
172 Thomas, *Man and the Natural World*, 296.
173 Ritson, *Animal Food*, 199–200.
174 See B. H. Bronson, *Ritson*, II.545–46.
175 Adams, *The Sexual Politics of Meat*, 99–104.
176 Ritson, *Animal Food*, 1–11.
177 A translation of the Greek epigraph (from Archimedes) to *Queen Mab* (*J* i.63).
178 Ritson, *Animal Food*, 51, 71–78, 148–56, and chapter ix *passim*.
179 A. O. Lovejoy, 235.
180 Ritson, *Animal Food*, 15.
181 Ibid. 16.
182 Ibid. 20.
183 Ibid. 33.
184 *The Edinburgh Review*, II (1803–4), 129.
185 Ibid. II.129.
186 *L* I.344.
187 M. Crucefix, thesis, *The Development of Shelley's Conception of Language*, part ii.
188 James Burnet (Lord Monboddo), *Language*, I.198–202.
189 Ibid. I.203–5.
190 Ibid. I.205.
191 Ibid. I.206–7.
192 Ibid. I.206.
193 Ibid. I.207.
194 Ibid. I.207.
195 Ibid. I.209.
196 Ibid. I.212.
197 Ibid. I.219.
198 Ibid. I.318–19.
199 Ibid. I.210.
200 Ibid. I.216. For a current refutation of these ideas, see M. Midgley, *Beast and Man*, 27–29, on the sociability of aggressive, and therefore protective, carnivores, and the cruelty of some herbivores.
201 Compare the position outlined in volume v of James Burnet (Lord Monboddo), *Antient Metaphysics*.
202 Ritson, *Animal Food*, 31–39.
203 See D. King-Hele, *Erasmus Darwin*, 93, 173.

204 *L* 1.129.
205 Ritson, *Animal Food*, 39. C.f. *V, J* vi.5.
206 Ibid. 51.
207 Trotter, *Nervous Temperament*, title page; the quotation is from Shakespeare, *Macbeth*, iv.iii.67.
208 *V, J* vi.11.
209 Trotter, *Nervous Temperament*, 23.
210 Ibid. 25.
211 Ibid. 44.
212 Ibid. 26.
213 Ibid. 233.
214 Ibid. 29.
215 Ibid. 33.
216 Ibid. 41.
217 Trotter's monarchism can be understood from a reading of his collected poems, *Sea Weeds*.
218 *V, J* vi.10.
219 Ibid. vi.11; Shelley refers to Lambe's *Constitutional Diseases* in 'VSys', *J* vi.342, although Ingpen and Peck misplace the footnote, which should really refer to the sentence on 'Constitutional diseases' on the same page (Bodleian MS Shelley Adds. c.4, 269v).
220 Ibid. vi.11.
221 Crook and Guiton, *Shelley's Venomed Melody*, 77.
222 *The Monthly Gazette of Health; or, Popular Medical, Dietetic, and General Philosophical Journal*, iii (1818), 787–91 (including an article on vegetable diet).
223 William Lambe, *Reports*, 33–34.
224 Ibid. 34.
225 Ibid. 37–38.
226 Ibid. 33.
227 William Lambe, *Additional Reports*, 201–2.
228 Ibid. 242.
229 Ibid. 243.
230 Ibid. 243.
231 Ibid. 238.
232 See *J* vi.13–15. Plato, *Laws*, 1.493 (bloodless sacrifices in early times, vegetarian food), 1.377 (agriculturalism, anti-commercialism, especially the attitude towards trading and usury, cf. ii.171). Compare Plato, *The Republic*, 1.76–77 (war is caused among other things by the luxury of meat creating a squeeze on agricultural territory).
233 Lambe, *Additional Reports*, 245.
234 Ibid. 246–47.
235 Marquis de Condorcet, *Outlines*, 365.
236 Ibid. 73–74.
237 P. Magli, 'The Face and the Soul', in M. Feher, R. Nadaff, and N. Tazi, eds., *Fragments*, ii.86–127.

238 Ibid. ii.122.
239 Lambe, *Additional Reports*, 226–27.
240 Ibid. 519.
241 Magli, 'Face', 93–94.
242 Ritson, *Animal Food*, 76, 137.
243 Lambe, *Additional Reports*, 203.
244 Ibid. 204.
245 Ibid. 207.
246 Ibid. 216–17.
247 Ibid. 225–26.
248 Ibid. 229.
249 Ibid. 220.
250 The Medici Venus dates from the time of Augustus. The Apollo Belvedere could be found in the Belvedere gallery in the Vatican, and was discovered at Antium in 1485.
251 Lambe, *Additional Reports*, 230.
252 Ibid. 208–9; Lambe is quoting Forster.
253 Ibid. 211.
254 Cf. *V, J* vi.12: 'when the benefits of vegetable diet are mathematically proved'.
255 J. F. Blumenbach, *Natural History*, 1 ('In some cases *natural bodies* have such a close resemblance to the products of art, that it is difficult to distinguish one from the other class'), 16 (on climate and food).
256 J. Derrida, *Of Grammatology*, 144–45.
257 See Leask, *British Romantic Writers and the East*, 30.
258 Newton, *The Return to Nature*, 15, 4–5.
259 Ibid. 2.
260 Ibid. 70, 75.
261 Ibid. 35–36.
262 Ibid. 31.
263 Ibid. 74.
264 Ibid. 66.
265 Ibid. 36.
266 Ibid. 36, footnote.
267 Ibid. 40.

5 INTEMPERATE FIGURES: RE-FINING CULTURE

1 F. S. Ellis, *Concordance*, 'blood', 'gore', 'flesh'.
2 *V, J* vi.14.
3 *OED*, 'disfigure', v.3.
4 Shelley, *St Irvyne; or, the Rosicrucian: a Romance. By a Gentleman of the University of Oxford* (London: printed for J. J. Stockdale, 1811), *J* v.128.
5 Ibid. v.199.
6 P. De Man, 'Shelley Disfigured', *The Rhetoric of Romanticism*, 93–123.
7 *L* i.267.

8 Ibid. I.268.
9 Ibid. I.269.
10 Shelley, *The Assassins*, *J* VI.157.
11 The Assassins may be modelled partly on the Essenes. I am grateful to Paul Dawson for pointing this out to me.
12 Shelley, *The Assassins*, *J* VI. 157–58.
13 Ibid. VI.159–60.
14 The close of Mary Shelley's *The Last Man* is similar to this story.
15 Shelley, *The Assassins*, *J* VI.158.
16 Ibid. VI.160.
17 Ibid. VI.162.
18 Ibid. VI.156–57.
19 Ibid. VI.164.
20 Ibid. VI.164.
21 Ibid. VI.163. Cf. Southey, *Thalaba* IX.148: '"When to thy tent the venemous [sic] serpent creeps / Dost thou not crush the reptile?"' This view is opposed by Thalaba, and it is possible, considering Shelley's by-heart knowledge of Southey's poem, and his love for it, that *The Assassins* is intended to counteract the force of such opinions.
22 Ibid. VI.165.
23 Ibid. VI.164.
24 Ibid. VI.164.
25 Ibid. VI.165.
26 Edmund Burke, *Philosophical Enquiry*, 102.
27 Mary Shelley, *Frankenstein*, 167.
28 Shelley, *The Assassins*, *J* VI.169–70.
29 Ibid. VI.170–71.
30 See Leask, *British Romantic Writers and the East*, 78–79.
31 Neville Rogers' version (from Shelley, *Complete Poetical Works*) will be printed here.
32 *V*, *J* VI.6.
33 The Upas tree is also the tree of knowledge of good and evil here. 'A tree alleged to have existed in Java...with properties so poisonous as to destroy all animal and vegetable life to a distance of fifteen or sixteen miles around it' (*OED*, 'upas', 1). It was mentioned in *The London Magazine* of 1783, used by Erasmus Darwin, and then in Blake, Southey (*Thalaba*) and Shelley. See Southey, *Thalaba* IX.200: 'The Upas Tree of Death'.
34 Cf. Euripides, *Bacchanals*, *Madness of Helen*, *Children of Hercules*, *Phoenician Maidens*, *Suppliants*, 61 (699–700). Shelley's lines substitute milk (always positively valorized in his texts) for wine; however, the reference to Cadmus may be an indirect attack on Godwin's censure of revolutionary violence.
35 See *Laon and Cythna*, II.i.1–9; on suckling and humanity, see *Rosalind and Helen*, 396–404. For the dietary importance of mother's milk, see *V*, *J*

VI. 17 and B. C. Gelpi, 'The Nursery Cave: Shelley and the Maternal' in G. K. Blank, ed., *The New Shelley*, 42–63, especially 52 ('when Harriet refused to breast-fed [sic] Ianthe and insisted on hiring a wet-nurse, Shelley's horror, allegedly so strong that he attempted to suckle the child himself, stemmed from the fact that "The nurse's soul would enter the child"'). Faciality is also involved in the discourse of the breast and of milk, something that the commencement of *Laon and Cythna* II demonstrates in its juxtaposition of 'The starlight smile of children', 'the sweet looks / Of women' and 'the fair breast from which I fed' (1–2).

36 *V*, *J* VI. 18.

37 Thomas Trotter, *An Essay; Medical, Philosophical, and Chemical, on Drunkenness*, chapter iii. See Leask, *British Romantic Writers and the East*, 173–75.

38 Ibid. 15. This is further evidence for the role of vegetarianism and temperance as a limit-case humanism, distinguishing man from animals in terms of what is natural.

39 Ibid. 41.

40 Ibid. 42.

41 Ibid. 43.

42 Ibid. 57.

43 Ibid. 199.

44 Ibid. 160–62.

45 Ibid. 162–63.

46 Ibid. 4, 8.

47 Ibid. 5–6.

48 Ibid. 55–56.

49 Ibid. 52.

50 *The Republican* I (1819), 3, 6, 49.

51 Ibid. 1.12.

52 Shelley, *An Address, to the Irish People* (Dublin: 1812), *J* v.226.

53 See the discussion of Shelley, *Proposals for an Association of those Philanthropists, who Convinced of the Inadequacy of the Moral and Political State of Ireland to Produce Benefits which are Nevertheless Attainable are Willing to Unite to Accomplish its Regeneration* (Dublin: printed by I. Eton, 1812), in chapter 6, for an understanding of the difference in address towards the upper-class reformers.

54 Shelley, *An Address*, *J* v.229; see 230.

55 Ibid. v.232.

56 Cf. *Epipsychidion*, 259–66. Shelley, *Epipsychidion: Verses Addressed to the Noble and Unfortunate Lady Emilia V – Now Imprisoned in the Convent of –* (London: C. and J. Ollier, 1821).

57 For a study of the relationship between Dionysus and diet, see M. Detienne, *Dionysos*.

58 Shelley, *Rosalind and Helen: a Modern Eclogue; with Other Poems* (London: printed for C. and J. Ollier, 1819) (written 1817–18).

59 For the identification of Lionel with Shelley, see Clark, *Embodying Revolution*, 159–60.

60 Cf. the taming of the 'sanguine' beasts at the witch's fountain in *The Witch of Atlas* (92–95) and *Orpheus*, 98–124 (another version of Isaiah).

61 See Euripides, *Euripides: Cyclops*, 174.

62 Ibid. 98.

63 Ritson, *Animal Food*, 124.

64 Ibid. 127; the Cyclopes are a Homeric paradigm for the European encounter with a barbarian culture; cf. the racism of describing Africans as '*anthropophagi*' (137).

65 Euripides, *Cyclops*, 118.

66 Scrivener, *Radical Shelley*, 18.

67 R. Wells, *Wretched Faces*, Ibid. 13, 14–15.

68 Ibid. 20.

69 Ibid. 31.

70 See *J* 1.425; 'not a part of the Shelley-Rolls MS'. The poem appears without the stanza in Shelley, *The Poetical Works of Percy Bysshe Shelley*, ed. W. M. Rossetti.

71 Shelley, *The Cenci. A Tragedy, in Five Acts* (London: printed for C. and J. Ollier, 1819).

72 See Adams, *The Sexual Politics of Meat*, 63–82.

73 Thomas Hobbes, *Leviathan*, 15.

74 See A. McWhir, 'The Light and the Knife: Ab/Using Language in *The Cenci*', *Keats-Shelley Journal* xxxviii (1989), 145–61.

75 M. Worton, 'Speech and Silence in *The Cenci*', in M. Allott, ed., *Essays on Shelley*, 105–24.

76 See Keach, *Shelley's Style*, 26–27.

77 G. Hough, *A Preface to the 'Faerie Queene'*, 106–11; Hough acknowledges his debt to Northrop Frye's schematization of figurative language in this passage.

78 *J* vi.16, 340.

79 Dawson, *The Unacknowledged Legislator*, 216.

80 Shelley, *Oedipus Tyrannus; or, Swellfoot the Tyrant. A Tragedy. In Two Acts. Translated from the Original Doric* (London: published for the Author by J. Johnston, 1820).

81 For a more contextual discussion, see N. I. White, 'Shelley's Swell-Foot the Tyrant in Relation to Contemporary Political Satires', *PMLA* xxxvi (1921), 332–46.

82 Printed as a broadside in Dublin, this poem coincides with Shelley's declared adoption of the natural diet.

83 See R. Woodman, 'Nietzsche, Blake, Keats and Shelley: the Making of a Metaphorical Body', *Studies in Romanticism* xxix:1 (Spring 1990), 115–49.

84 See R. Bartel, 'Shelley and Burke's Swinish Multitude', *Keats-Shelley Journal* xviii (1969), 4–9.

85 K. Marx, *Selected Writings*, 482–83.
86 Mary Shelley's note to *Swellfoot*, *J* II.350.
87 See M. Foucault, *Discipline and Punish*, 60–61.
88 G. Bateson, 'Men are Grass: Metaphor and the World of Mental Process', in Thompson, ed., *Gaia*, 44–45.
89 Ibid. 45–46.
90 Compare the comic 'Order! order! be not rash!' (II.i.117).
91 See Jehan de Grise, *The Romance of Alexander*, Bodleian MS 264, 81v.
92 See M. M. Bakhtin, *The Dialogic Imagination*, 72, 79, for a discussion of the socially sustaining role of medieval license; see E. R. Curtius, *European Literature and the Latin Middle Ages*, 94–98, for a discussion of the inherent conservatism of the *adynaton/impossibilia* topos.
93 Shelley, 'On the Devil, and Devils', *J* VII.98–99.
94 See Ritson, *Animal Food*, 98.
95 Shelley, 'On the Devil', *J* VII.95.
96 See P. Stallybrass and A. White, chapter 1, 'The Fair, the Pig, Authorship', in *The Politics and Poetics of Transgression*.
97 Medwin, *Life*, II.164–65.
98 *DNB*, 'Leighton, Alexander'.
99 Cf. *V*, *J* VI.13–15.
100 W. Benjamin, *One-Way Street*, 359.
101 *V*, *J* VI.14.
102 William Wordsworth, *Prose Works*, III.81.
103 Ibid. I.141 (the preface to the 1850 edition of *Lyrical Ballads*).
104 Shelley, 'A Defence of Poetry', *J* VII.134.
105 Ibid. VII.132.
106 In *Epipsychidion*, Shelley's 'constant recollections' of the thing (the Lacanian and Kantian *das Ding*) are the 'paradoxical' promise of the future which can never be attained; hence the idea of the endless 'business' of Utopianism (in which case, the act of remembering is part of the technohumanistic sublime).

6 SUSTAINING NATURES: SHELLEY AND ECOCRITICISM

1 *V*, *J* VI.13, 15.
2 *L* II.303.
3 Thomas Malthus, *Population*, 37.
4 Ibid. 39–48.
5 Ibid. 47; see Milton, *Paradise Lost*, XII.646.
6 Here Malthus is unlike his brother, whose work on 'nature' was a translation of Girardin on the picturesque.
7 Malthus, *Population*, 73.
8 Ibid. 75.
9 Ibid. 76.
10 Ibid. 77, 79.

11 Ibid. 90.
12 Ibid. 113.
13 Ibid. 139–40.
14 Condorcet, *Outlines*, 4.
15 Malthus, *Population*, 144–45, my italics.
16 Ibid. 152–53.
17 Ibid. 155.
18 Ibid. 164.
19 Ibid. 165.
20 Ibid. 179.
21 Ibid. 181–83.
22 Ibid. 182–83.
23 Ibid. 183–209.
24 Ibid. 187.
25 C. Gallagher, 'The Body Versus the Social Body in the Works of Thomas Malthus and Henry Mayhew', *Representations* xiv (Spring, 1986), 83–106.
26 Shelley, *Proposals*, *J* v.265–66.
27 Ibid. v.266, my emphasis.
28 Ibid. v.266.
29 See the subtitle of Ross, *Strange Weather*: '*Culture, Science, and Technology in the Age of Limits*'.
30 Shelley, *Proposals*, *J* v.254.
31 Ibid. v.255; c.f. v.258.
32 Ibid. v.253–54, v.255.
33 Ibid. v.255.
34 Ibid. v.264.
35 Ibid. v.253.
36 Shelley, *Declaration of Rights*, *J* v.274.
37 Shelley, *Proposals*, *J* v.266–67.
38 Ibid. v.267.
39 Shelley, *An Address*, *J* v.239.
40 Ibid. v.239.
41 Shelley, 'A Philosophical View of Reform', *J* vii.29.
42 Ibid. vii.30.
43 Ibid. vii.30–31.
44 Ibid. vii.32.
45 *The Republican* vi (May 24–December 27 1822), 315.
46 Ibid. vi.316. *The Republican* was shortly to announce the death of Percy Shelley: 'The celebrated author of "Queen Mab" is no more!' (vi.380).
47 Shelley, 'A Philosophical View of Reform', *J* vii.33.
48 Reiman and Powers' edition (Shelley, *Poetry and Prose*) is used in quoting this poem.
49 'VSys', *J* vi.340.
50 See Zizek, *The Sublime Object of Ideology*, 21–23 ('The Social Symptom'), for further discussion.

51 For example, the radicalism of another reference to the Upas tree, echoed in *V*: 'Let the axe / Strike at the root, the poison-tree will fall' (IV.82, on the causes of violence and war); c.f. *J* VI.10, 15.
52 *J* VI.14.
53 Jonathan Bate, *Romantic Ecology*, 85–115.
54 Ibid. 33, 53–54.
55 'VSys', *J* VI.341.
56 For example, *V*, *J* VI.13–15.
57 Wells, *Wretched Faces*, 3–11.
58 Ibid. 134.
59 Ibid. 134.
60 Ibid. 135.
61 *The Black Dwarf* I (1817), 271.
62 Samuel Jackson Pratt, *Bread*, 34.
63 Ibid. 85.
64 Ibid. 36.
65 Ibid. 40.
66 Ibid. 40.
67 Ibid. 41.
68 Ibid. 41.
69 Ibid. 43; c.f. *J* VI.17.
70 Ibid. 74.
71 Ibid. 75.
72 Ibid. 76.
73 Ibid. D IV.
74 Anon, *An Address*, 6.
75 Ibid. 6.
76 I am indebted to Terry Eagleton for his valuable comments on this matter.
77 Shelley, *Hellas: a Lyrical Drama* (London: C. and J. Ollier, 1822).
78 See the discussion of *Queen Mab* VIII in chapter 3.
79 See the discussion of Pope in chapter 3.
80 See C. Trungpa, *Crazy Wisdom*, 79–81.
81 *J* III.57.
82 See Godwin, *Of Population*, 446–47, 450–51.
83 Ibid. 309, 340.
84 M. Bookchin, *Remaking Society*, 30.
85 Ibid. 21–25.
86 Ibid. 30–39. See Scrivener, who cites Bookchin in *Radical Shelley* (35–36, 319n, 326n).
87 Ibid. 154. See 'A New Vision of Community', section 2 in Clark, ed., *Renewing the Earth*.
88 *V*, *J* VI.15, footnote 1. The reference is to *Bread*, note K (page 77), a discussion of a certain Joseph Smith of Wolvercot.
89 Holmes, *Pursuit*, 165.
90 *L* 1.351, footnote 2.

91 *J* vii.327.
92 *V, J* vi.14.
93 Ibid. vi.15.
94 See D. Harvey, *Postmodernity*, 127.
95 C. Bartolovich, 'Boundary Disputes: Textuality and the Flows of Transnational Capital', *Mediations* xvii:1 (December 1992), 22–23.
96 Salaman, *Potato*, 501.
97 *V, J* vi.14.
98 Ibid. vi.13.
99 Holmes, *Pursuit*, 592.
100 *L* 1.213.
101 Ibid. ii.182.
102 Bodleian MS Shelley Adds. e.6, 172–55 (rev).
103 Ibid. 171.
104 Ibid. 160.
105 T. Tokoo, 'The Contents of Shelley's Notebooks in the Bodleian Library', *Humanities: Bulletin of the Faculty of Letters, Kyoto Prefectural University*, 36 (December 1984).
106 Bodleian MS Shelley Adds. e.6, 2–3.
107 Ibid. 6.
108 Ibid. 6–7.
109 P. Dawson, 'Shelley and Ecology', originally given as a paper at the international Shelley conference (New York, 20–23 May, 1992), soon to be published in B. Bennett and S. Curran, eds., *Shelley: Poet and Legislator of the World* (Baltimore: Johns Hopkins University Press, forthcoming).
110 Appadurai, ed., *The Social Life of Things*, 38.
111 Haraway, *Simians, Cyborgs, and Women*, 151.
112 Ibid. 208–209: 'Late twentieth-century bodies do not grow from internal harmonic principles theorized within Romanticism.'
113 Ibid. 67.
114 Ibid. 67.
115 M. Taussig, 'History as Commodity in Some Recent American (Anthropological) Literature', *Food and Foodways* ii:2 (1987), 151–69; 159–60 quoted here. This is a trenchant review of S. Mintz, *Sweetness and Power*.
116 Ross, *Strange Weather*, 53–54.

Bibliography

MANUSCRIPTS

de Grise, Jehan, *The Romance of Alexander*, Bodleian MS 264.
Bodleian MS Shelley Adds. c.4
Bodleian MS Shelley Adds. e.4.
Bodleian MS Shelley Adds. e.6.
Bodleian MS Shelley Adds. e.12.

THE WORKS OF SHELLEY

UNLESS OTHERWISE INDICATED, ALL REFERENCES TO SHELLEY'S
POETRY AND PROSE ARE FROM THE 'JULIAN' EDITION:

Shelley, Percy Bysshe, *The Complete Works*, ed. Ingpen, R. and Peck, W. E.,
10 vols. (London and New York: Ernest Benn, 1926–30).

OTHER COLLECTIONS CITED:

The Poetical Works of Percy Bysshe Shelley, ed. Rossetti, W. M., 2 vols.
(London: Moxon, 1870).
Poetical Works, ed. Hutchinson, T. (Oxford and New York: Oxford
University Press, 1970).
Complete Poetical Works, ed. Rogers, N., 4 vols. (only two published)
(Oxford: the Clarendon Press, 1972, 1975).
Shelley's Poetry and Prose, ed. Reiman, D. H. and Powers, S. B. (New York
and London: W. W. Norton, 1977).
The Poems of Shelley, ed. Everest, K. and Matthews, G. (London and New
York: Longman, 1989).
Shelley's Prose: or the Trumpet of a Prophecy, ed. Clark, D. L. (London:
Fourth Estate, 1988).

ALL REFERENCES TO SHELLEY'S LETTERS ARE FROM:

The Letters of Percy Bysshe Shelley, ed. Jones, F. L., 2 vols. (Oxford
University Press, 1964).

275

The new Clarendon Press edition of Shelley's prose and letters, edited by E. B. Murray and T. Webb, was unavailable at the time of writing.

SECONDARY TEXTS

BIBLIOGRAPHIES

Dunbar, C., *A Bibliography of Shelley Studies: 1823–1950* (Kent: Dawson, 1976).

Erdman, D. V., ed., *The Romantic Movement: a Selective and Critical Bibliography for 1979–86*, 7 vols. (New York and London: Garland, 1980–87).

Houghton, W. E., ed., *The Wellesley Index to Victorian Periodicals 1824–1900: Tables of Contents and Identification of Contributors with Bibliographies of their Articles and Stories*, 5 vols. (Canada: University of Toronto Press and London: Routledge and Kegan Paul, 1966–89).

The Modern Language Association of America, *MLA International Bibliography of Books and Articles on the Modern Languages and Literatures* (New York: MLA, 1969–).

Reiman, D. H., ed., *The Romantics Reviewed: Contemporary Reviews of British Romantic Writers*, 9 vols. (New York and London: Garland, 1972).

DICTIONARIES

The Oxford Companion to Classical Literature, ed. Howaton, M. C., 2nd edn. (Oxford and New York: Oxford University Press, 1989).

The Oxford English Dictionary, ed. Murray, J. A. H, *et al.*, 2nd edn. (Oxford: the Clarendon Press, 1933-).

Lewis and Short, *A Latin Dictionary*.

Dictionary of National Biography.

PERIODICALS (EIGHTEENTH AND NINETEENTH CENTURIES)

The Black Dwarf.

The Edinburgh Review.

The Gentleman's Magazine and Historical Chronicle.

The Guardian.

The Medical Adviser.

The Medusa; or, Penny Politician.

The Monthly Gazette of Health ; *or, Popular Medical, Dietetic, and General Philosophical Journal.*

The Republican.

The Theological Enquirer.

THESES CONSULTED

Crucefix, M., *The Development of Shelley's Conception of Language: an Examination of the Contemporary Study of Language within which Shelley's own*

Thought Developed and its Significance for Some of his Major Poems (Oxford: D.Phil thesis, 1985).

OTHER SECONDARY TEXTS

Abernethy, John, *On the Constitutional Origin and Treatment of Local Diseases* (London: Longman, Hurst, Rees, Orme and Brown, 1809).
An Enquiry into the Probability and Rationality of Mr. Hunter's Theory of Life; being the Subject of Two Anatomical Lectures Delivered before the Royal College of Surgeons, of London (London: Longman, Hurst, Rees, Orme and Brown, 1814).
Surgical Observations on the Constitutional Origin and Treatment of Local Diseases; and on Aneurisms, 5th edn. (London: Longman, Hurst, Rees, Orme and Brown, 1820).
Accum, Frederick, *A Treatise on Adulterations of Food, and Culinary Poisons, Exhibiting the Fraudulent Sophistications of Bread, Beer, Wine, Spiritous Liquors, Tea, Coffee, Cream, Confectionery, Vinegar, Mustard, Pepper, Cheese, Olive Oil, Pickles, and Other Articles Employed in Domestic Economy. And Methods of Detecting Them* (London: Longman, Hurst, Rees, Orme and Brown, 1820).
Adams, C., *The Sexual Politics of Meat: a Feminist-Vegetarian Critical Theory* (Cambridge: Polity Press, 1990).
Adorno, T. and Horkheimer, M., *Dialectic of Enlightenment*, tr. Cumming, J. (London and New York: Verso, 1979).
Allott, M., ed., *Essays on Shelley* (Liverpool University Press, 1982).
Anon, *Adam's Luxury, and Eve's Cookery; or, the Kitchen-Garden Display'd. In Two Parts* (London: printed for R. Dodsley, 1744).
Anon, *An Address, in Verse, to the Author of the Political and Philosophical Essay on the French Revolution* (London: printed for J. Owen, 1793).
Appadurai, A., ed., *The Social Life of Things: Commodities in Cultural Perspective* (Cambridge University Press, 1986).
Arbuthnot, John, *An Essay Concerning the Nature of Aliments, and the Choice of them, According to the Different Constitutions of Human Bodies. In which the Different Effects, Advantages, and Disadvantages of Animal and Vegetable Diet, are Explain'd*, 2nd edn., with *Practical Rules of Diet in the Various Constitutions and Diseases of Human Bodies* (London: printed for J. Johnson, 1732).
Arnold, M., *The Complete Works of Matthew Arnold*, vol. IX (Ann Arbor: University of Michigan Press, 1973).
Aristotle, *The Politics*, tr. Rackham, H. (Cambridge, Mass.: Harvard University Press, 1944).
Augustine, *Confessions*, tr. Pine-Coffin, R. S. (London: Penguin, 1961).
Axon, W. E. A., *Shelley's Vegetarianism* (Manchester: The Vegetarian Society, 1891).

Axon, W. E. A. and E., *Ninety-Two Years of the Vegetarian Society* (Manchester: The Vegetarian Society, 1939).

Baker, C., *Shelley's Major Poetry: the Fabric of a Vision* (Princeton: Princeton University Press, 1948).

Bakhtin, M. M., *The Dialogic Imagination: Four Essays*, ed. Holquist, M., tr. Emerson, C. and Holquist, M. (Austin: University of Texas Press, 1981).

Barkas, J., *The Vegetable Passion: a History of the Vegetarian State of Mind* (London: Routledge and Kegan Paul, 1975).

Barrell, J., *The Infection of Thomas De Quincey: a Psychopathology of Imperialism* (New Haven and London: Yale University Press, 1991).

Bartel, R., 'Shelley and Burke's Swinish Multitude', *Keats-Shelley Journal* XVIII (1969), 4–9.

Bartolovich, C., 'Boundary Disputes: Textuality and the Flows of Transnational Capital', *Mediations* XVII:1 (December 1992), 21–33.

Bataille, G., *The Accursed Share: an Essay on General Economy*, tr. Hurley, R., vol. 1 (New York: Zone Books, 1988).

Bate, J., *Romantic Ecology: Wordsworth and the Environmental Tradition* (London and New York: Routledge, 1991).

Bateman, Thomas, *Reports on the Diseases of London, and of the State of the Weather, from 1804 to 1816; Including Practical Remarks on the Causes and Treatment of the Former; and Preceded by a Historical View of the State of Health and Disease in the Metropolis in Past Times; in which the Progress of the Extraordinary Improvement in Salubrity, which it has Undergone, the Changes in the Character of the Seasons in this Respect, and the Causes of these, are Traced down to the Present Period* (London: printed for Longman, Hurst, Rees, Orme and Brown, 1819).

Baudrillard, J., *The Mirror of Production* (St Louis: Telos Press, 1975).

Beavan, A. H., *James and Horace Smith: Joint Authors of 'Rejected Addresses; a Family Narrative Based upon Hitherto Unpublished Private Diaries, Letters, and Other Documents'* (London: Hurst and Blackett, 1899).

Beddoes, Thomas, *Hygëia: or Essays Moral and Medical on the Causes Affecting the Personal State of our Middling and Affluent Classes*, 3 vols. (Bristol: printed for Richard Phillips, 1802).

Behn, Aphra, *The Works of Aphra Behn*, ed. Summers, M., vol. VI (London: William Heinemann and Stratford-on-Avon: A. H. Bullen, 1915).

Behrendt, S. C., *Shelley and his Audiences* (Lincoln and London: University of Nebraska Press, 1989).

Benjamin, W., *Illuminations*, ed. Arendt, H., tr. Zohn, H. (London: Harcourt, Brace and World, 1973).

One-Way Street and Other Writings, tr. Jephcott, E. and Shorter, K. (London: Verso, 1979; paperback, 1985).

Bennett B. and Curran S., eds., *Shelley: Poet and Legislator of the World* (Baltimore: Johns Hopkins University Press, forthcoming).

Blake, William, *William Blake's Writings*, ed. Bentley, G. E., 2 vols. (Oxford: the Clarendon Press, 1978).

Blank, G. K., *Wordsworth's Influence on Shelley: a Study of Poetic Authority* (Hampshire and London: the Macmillan, 1988).

Blank, G. K., ed., *The New Shelley: Later Twentieth-Century Views* (Hampshire and London: Macmillan, 1991).

Blumenbach, J. F., *A Manual of the Elements of Natural History*, tr. Gore, R. T. (London: Simpkin and Marshall, 1825).

Blunden, E., *Leigh Hunt: a Biography* (London: Cobden-Sanderson, 1930).

Bookchin, M., *Remaking Society: Pathways to a Green Future* (Boston: South End Press, 1990).

Bourdieu, P., *Outline of a Theory of Practice*, tr. Nice, R. (Cambridge University Press, 1977; repr. 1991).

Distinction: a Social Critique of the Judgement of Taste, tr. Nice, R. (London: Routledge, 1989).

Boyle, T. C., *The Road to Wellville* (New York: Viking, 1993).

Braudel, F., *Civilization and Capitalism, 15th–18th Century*, tr. Reynolds, S., vol. 1 (*The Structures of Everyday Life*) (Berkeley and Los Angeles: University of California Press, 1992).

Bronson, B. H., *Joseph Ritson, Scholar-at-Arms*, 2 vols. (Berkeley: University of California Press, 1938).

Brotherton, Joseph, *The First Teetotal Tract. On Abstinence from Intoxicating Liquor. First Published in 1821* (Manchester: 'Onward' Publishing Office and London: S. W. Partidge, 1890).

Burke, Edmund, *Reflections on the Revolution in France and on the Proceedings in Certain Societies in London Relative to that Event. In a Letter Intended to have been Sent to a Gentleman in Paris* (London: J. Dodsley, 1790).

A Letter from the Right Honourable Edmund Burke to a Noble Lord, on the Attacks Made upon him and his Pension, in the House of Lords, by the Duke of Bedford and the Earl of Lauderdale, early in the Present Sessions of Parliament (London: printed for J. Owen and F. and C. Rivington, 1796).

A Philosophical Enquiry into the Origin of our Ideas of the Sublime and the Beautiful, ed. Boulton, J. T. (Oxford: Basil Blackwell, 1987).

Burnet, James (Lord Monboddo), *Of the Origin and Progress of Language*, 6 vols. (Edinburgh: printed for A. Kincaid and London: T. Cadell, 1773–92).

'Lord Monboddo's Account of Peter the Wild Boy, formerly brought from the Woods of Germany', *The Gentleman's Magazine and Historical Chronicle*, LV (1785), 113–14.

Antient Metaphysics. Volume Fifth, Containing the History of Man in the Civilized State (Edinburgh: printed for Bell & Bradfute and London: T. Cadell, 1797).

Butler, M., *Romantics, Rebels and Reactionaries: English Literature and its Background 1760–1830* (Oxford University Press, 1981; repr. 1989).

Burke, Paine, Godwin, and the Revolution Controversy (Cambridge University Press, 1984; repr. 1989).

'The First *Frankenstein* and Radical Science', *The Times Literary Supplement* (9 April, 1993), 12–14.

Byron, Lord George Gordon, *The Complete Poetical Works*, ed. McGann, J., 5 vols. (Oxford: the Clarendon Press, 1980–86).

Byron's Letters and Journals, ed. Marchand, L. A., 12 vols. (London: John Murray, 1973–82).

Cameron, K. N., *The Young Shelley: Genesis of a Radical* (London: Victor Gollancz, 1951).

Cameron, K. N., ed., *Shelley and his Circle 1773–1822*, vols. III–IV (Cambridge, Mass.: Harvard University Press and London: Oxford University Press, 1970).

Camporesi, P., *Bread of Dreams: Food and Fantasy in Early Modern Europe* (Cambridge: Polity Press, 1989).

Chapman, M. and Macbeth, H., eds., *Food for Humanity: Cross-Disciplinary Readings* (Oxford: Centre for the Sciences of Food and Nutrition, 1990).

Chase, C., *Decomposing Forms: Rhetorical Readings in the Romantic Tradition* (Baltimore and London: Johns Hopkins University Press, 1986).

Cheyne, George, *An Essay of Health and Long Life* (Dublin: printed for George Ewing, 1725).

Cicero, *De natura deorum*, vol. XIX of the Loeb edition of Cicero, ed. Page, T. E., Capps, E. and Rouse, W. H. D, tr. Rackham, H. (London: William Heinemann and New York: G. P. Putnam's Sons, 1933).

Clairmont, Claire, *The Journals of Claire Clairmont*, ed. Stocking, M. K. (Cambridge, Mass.: Harvard University Press, 1968).

Clark, D. L., 'The Date and Source of Shelley's "A Vindication of Natural Diet"', *Studies in Philology* XXXVI (1939), 70–76.

Clark, J., ed., *Renewing the Earth: the Promise of Social Ecology; a Celebration of the Work of Murray Bookchin* (London: Green Print, 1990).

Clark, T., *Embodying Revolution: the Figure of the Poet in Shelley* (Oxford: the Clarendon Press, 1989).

Coleridge, Samuel Taylor, *Samuel Taylor Coleridge*, ed. Jackson, H. J. (Oxford and New York: Oxford University Press, 1985).

Condorcet, Marquis de, *Outlines of an Historical View of the Progress of the Human Mind* (London: printed for J. Johnson, 1785).

Conrad, P., *The Everyman History of English Literature* (London and Melbourne: J. M. Dent and Sons, 1985; paperback, 1987).

Cowper, William, *Poetic Works*, ed. Milford, H. S. (London: Oxford University Press, 1905; repr. with revisions, 1967).

Crab, Roger, *The English Hermite, or, Wonder of this Age. Being a Relation of the Life of Roger Crab, Living near Uxbridg [sic], Taken from his own Mouth, Shewing his Strange Reserved and Unparallel'd Kind of Life, who Counteth it a Sin against his Body and Soule to Eate any Sort of Flesh, Fish, or Living Creature, or to Drinke any Wine, Ale, or Beere. He can Live with Three Farthings a Week. His Constant Food is Roots and Hearbs, as Cabbage, Turneps, Carrets, Dock Leaves, and Grasse; also Bread and Bran, without Butter or Cheese: his Cloathing is Sack-Cloath. He left the Army, and Kept a Shop at Chesham, and hath now Left off That, and Sold a Considerable Estate to Give to the Poore,*

Shewing his Reasons from the Scripture, Mark. 10.21 Jer.35. (London, 1655; repr. 1725).

Crary, J., and Kwinter, S., eds., *Incorporations* (New York: Urzone, 1992).

Crook, N., and Guiton, D., *Shelley's Venomed Melody* (Cambridge University Press, 1986).

Crowe, Henry, *Zoophilos: or, Considerations on the Moral Treatment of Inferior Animals* (London: printed for the author, 1819).

Crucefix, Martin, 'Wordsworth, Superstition, and Shelley's *Alastor*', *Essays in Criticism* XXXIII: 2 (April, 1983), 126–47.

Curran, S., *Poetic Form and British Romanticism* (New York and Oxford: Oxford University Press, 1986; paperback, 1989).

Curtius, E. R., *European Literature and the Latin Middle Ages*, tr. Trask, W. R. (New York: Princeton University Press, 1953).

Davy, Humphry, *Elements of Agricultural Chemistry, in a Course of Lectures for the Board of Agriculture* (London: printed for Longman, Hurst, Rees, Orme & Brown and Edinburgh: printed for A. Constable, 1813).

Dawson, P., *The Unacknowledged Legislator: Shelley and Politics* (Oxford: the Clarendon Press, 1980).

De Almeida, H., *Romantic Medicine and John Keats* (New York and Oxford: Oxford University Press, 1991).

De Bolla, P., *The Discourse of the Sublime: Readings in History, Aesthetics and the Subject* (New York and Oxford: Basil Blackwell, 1989).

De Man, Paul, *Blindness and Insight: Essays in the Rhetoric of Contemporary Criticism* (London: Methuen, 1983).

The Rhetoric of Romanticism (New York: Columbia University Press, 1984).

De Quincey, Thomas, *Confessions of an English Opium-Eater* (London: Taylor and Hessey, 1822).

Defoe, Daniel, *Mere Nature Delineated: or, a Body without a Soul. Being Observations upon the Young Forester Lately Brought to Town from Germany. With Suitable Applications. Also, a Brief Dissertation upon the Usefulness and Necessity of Fools, whether Political or Natural* (London: printed for T. Warner, 1726).

Deleuze, G. and Guattari, F., *Anti-Oedipus: Capitalism and Schizophrenia*, tr. Hurley, R., Seem, M. and Lane, H. (Minneapolis: University of Minnesota Press, 1983).

A Thousand Plateaus: Capitalism and Schizophrenia, tr. Massumi, B. (Minneapolis: University of Minnesota Press, 1987).

Derrida, J., *Of Grammatology*, tr. Spivak, G. C. (Baltimore and London: Johns Hopkins University Press, 1987).

Desmond, A. J., *The Politics of Evolution: Morphology, Medicine, and Reform in Radical London* (University of Chicago Press, 1989).

Detienne, M., *Dionysos at Large*, tr. Goldhammer, A. (Cambridge, Mass. and London: Harvard University Press, 1989).

Dombrowski, D. A., 'Vegetarianism and the Argument from Marginal

Cases in Porphyry', *Journal of the History of Ideas* XLV: 1 (January–March 1984), 141–43.

Douglas, M., *Purity and Danger: an Analysis of the Concepts of Purity and Taboo* (London and New York: Ark, 1984).

'Eschewing the Fat: Food Faddism in the Light of Global Famine', *Times Literary Supplement* (30 July 1993), 3–4.

Drew, J., *India and the Romantic Imagination* (Oxford and New York: Oxford University Press, 1987).

Drummond, J. C. and Wilbraham, A., *The Englishman's Food: a History of Five Centuries of English Diet* (London: Jonathan Cape, 1939; repr. Pimlico, 1991).

Dryden, John, *The Poems of John Dryden*, ed. Kinsley, J., vol. IV (Oxford: the Clarendon Press, 1958).

Duffy, E., *Rousseau in England: the Context for Shelley's Critique of the Enlightenment* (Berkeley: University of California Press, 1979).

Eagleton, T., *The Ideology of the Aesthetic* (Oxford: Basil Blackwell, 1990).

Easton, James, *Human Longevity: Recording the Name, Age, Place of Residence, and Years, of the Decease of 1712 Persons, who Attained a Century, & Upwards, from A. D. 66 to 1799, Comprising a Period of 1733 Years. With Anecdotes of the Most Remarkable* (Salisbury: J. Easton, 1799).

Ellis, F. S., *A Lexical Concordance to the Poetical Works of Percy Bysshe Shelley: an Attempt to Classify Every Word Found Therein According to its Signification* (London: Bernard Quaritch, 1892).

Engels, F., *The Condition of the Working Class in England*, ed. Kiernan, V. (London: Penguin, 1987).

Erdman, D. V., *Commerce des Lumières: John Oswald and the British in Paris, 1790–1793* (Columbia: University of Missouri Press, 1986).

Erskine, Thomas, *The Speech of Lord Erskine in the House of Peers on the Second Reading of the Bill for Preventing Malicious and Wanton Cruelty to Animals* (London: Richard Phillips, 1809).

Cruelty to Animals: the Speech of Lord Erskine, in the House of Peers, on the Second Reading of the Bill for Preventing Malicious and Wanton Cruelty to Animals (Edinburgh: printed for Alexander Cawrie, 1809).

Euripides, *Bacchanals, Madness of Helen, Children of Hercules, Phoenician Maidens, Suppliants*, tr. Way, A. S. (London: William Heinemann and New York: Macmillan, 1912).

Euripides: Cyclops; Introduction and Commentary, ed. Ussher, R. G. (Rome and London: Edizioni dell' Ateneo e Bizzari, 1978).

Ion, Hippolytus, Medea, Alcestis, ed. Goold, G. P., tr. Way, A. S. (Cambridge, Mass.: Harvard University Press and London: William Heinemann, 1980).

Featherstone, M., Hepworth, M. and Turner, B., eds., *The Body: Social Process and Cultural Theory* (London, Newbury Park and New Delhi: Sage Publications, 1991).

Feher, M., Nadaff, R. and Tazi, N., eds., *Fragments for a History of the Human Body*, 3 vols. (New York: Urzone, 1989).

Ferguson, F., *Solitude and the Sublime: Romanticism and the Aesthetics of Individuation* (London and New York: Routledge, 1992).

Fiddes, N., *Meat: a Natural Symbol* (London and New York: Routledge, 1991).

Field, John, *The Absurdity and Falseness of Thomas Trion's* [*sic*] *Doctrine Manifested, in Forbidding to Eat Flesh* (London: printed for Thomas Howkins, 1685).

Foucault, M., *The Order of Things* (London: Tavistock Publications, 1970). *Discipline and Punish: the Birth of the Prison*, tr. Sheridan, A. (New York: Pantheon, 1977). *The Use of Pleasure: the History of Sexuality*, vol. II (London: Penguin, 1987).

Gallagher, C., 'The Body Versus the Social Body in the Works of Thomas Malthus and Henry Mayhew', *Representations* xiv (Spring 1986), 83–106.

Geertz, C., *The Interpretation of Cultures: Selected Essays* (New York: Basic Books, 1973).

Gelpi, B. C., *Shelley's Goddess: Maternity, Language, Subjectivity* (Oxford and New York: Oxford University Press, 1992).

Girard, R., *Violence and the Sacred*, tr. Gregory, P. (Baltimore and London: Johns Hopkins University Press, 1977; repr. 1986).

Godwin, William, *An Enquiry Concerning Political Justice, and its Influence on General Virtue and Happiness* (London: printed for G. G. and J. Robinson, 1793). *Of Population: an Enquiry Concerning the Power of Increase in the Numbers of Mankind, Being an Answer to Mr. Malthus's Essay on that Subject* (London: Longman, Hurst, Rees, Orme and Brown, 1820).

Goldsmith, Oliver, *Collected Works of Oliver Goldsmith*, ed. Friedman, A., vols. II and IV (Oxford: the Clarendon Press, 1966).

Goslee, N., 'Dis-Personing: Drafting as Plot in *Epipsychidion*', paper given at the international conference, *Shelley: Poet and Legislator of the World* (New York: 20–23 May, 1992).

Grabo, C., *The Magic Plant: the Growth of Shelley's Thought* (Chapel Hill: University of North Carolina Press, 1936).

Hall, E., *Inventing the Barbarian: Greek Self-Definition through Tragedy* (Oxford: the Clarendon Press, 1989; paperback, 1990).

Haraway, D. J., *Simians, Cyborgs, and Women: the Reinvention of Nature* (London: Verso, 1991).

Hargrove, E. C., ed., *The Animal Rights/Environmental Ethics Debate: the Environmental Perspective* (Albany: State University of New York Press, 1992).

Hartley, David, *Observations on Man, his Frame, his Duty, and his Expectations*, 2 vols. (London: Leake and Frederik, Hitch and Austen, 1749).

Harvey, D., *The Condition of Postmodernity: an Enquiry into the Origins of Cultural Change* (Oxford: Basil Blackwell, 1989).

Hay, D., Linebaugh, P., Rule, J. G., Thompson, E. P., and Winslow, C., eds., *Albion's Fatal Tree: Crime and Society in Eighteenth-Century England* (New York: Pantheon, 1975).

Haydon, Benjamin Robert, *The Diary of Benjamin Robert Haydon*, ed. Pope, W. B., 5 vols. (Cambridge, Mass.: Harvard University Press, 1960–63).

The Autobiography and Memoirs of Benjamin Robert Haydon (1786–1846), ed. Taylor, T., 2 vols. (London: Peter Davies, 1926).

Hazlitt, William, *The Complete Works of William Hazlitt*, ed. Howe, P. P., 21 vols. (London and Toronto: J. M. Dent and Sons, 1930–34).

Hesse, H., *The Glass Bead Game*, tr. Winston, R. and C. (London: Penguin, 1972 (published in German, 1943)).

Hobbes, Thomas, *Leviathan*, ed. Tuck, R. (Cambridge University Press, 1991).

Hogg, Thomas Jefferson, *The Life of Percy Bysshe Shelley*, 2 vols. (London: Edward Moxon, 1858).

The Athenians: Being Correspondence between Thomas Jefferson Hogg and his Friends Thomas Love Peacock, Leigh Hunt, Percy Bysshe Shelley, and Others, ed. Scott, W. S. (London: the Golden Cockerel Press, 1943).

Hogle, J. E., *Shelley's Process: Radical Transference and the Development of his Major Works* (Oxford University Press, 1988).

Holmes, R., *Shelley: the Pursuit* (London: Weidenfeld and Nicolson, 1974; repr. Penguin, 1987).

Holmes, S. W., 'Browning: Semantic Stutterer', *PMLA* lx (1945), 231–55.

Horace, *Horace: the Odes and Epodes*, tr. Bennett, C. E. (Cambridge, Mass.: Harvard University Press and London: William Heinemann, 1978).

Hough, G., *A Preface to the 'Faerie Queene'* (London: Duckworth, 1962).

Huet, M. H., *Monstrous Imagination* (Cambridge, Mass.: Harvard University Press, 1993).

Jacobs, C., *Uncontainable Romanticism: Shelley, Brontë, Kleist* (Baltimore and London: Johns Hopkins University Press, 1989).

Jameson, F., *The Prison House of Language: a Critical Account of Structuralism and Russian Formalism* (Princeton University Press, 1972).

Jeanneret, M., *A Feast of Words: Banquets and Table Talk in the Renaissance* (University of Chicago Press, 1991).

Jerome, N. W., Kandel, R. F., and Pelto, G. H., eds., *Nutritional Anthropology: Contemporary Approaches to Diet and Culture* (New York: Redgrave, 1980).

Keach, W., *Shelley's Style* (New York and London: Methuen, 1984).

Keats, John, *The Letters of John Keats, 1814–1821*, ed. Rollins, H. F., 2 vols. (Cambridge, Mass.: Harvard University Press, 1958).

King-Hele, D., *The Essential Writings of Erasmus Darwin* (London: Mac-Gibbon and Kee, 1968).

Kristeva, J., *Powers of Horror: an Essay on Abjection*, tr. Roudiez, L. S. (New York: Columbia University Press, 1982).

Lambe, William, *A Medical and Experimental Inquiry, into the Origin, Symptoms, and Cure of Constitutional Diseases. Particularly Scrophula, Consumption, Cancer, and Gout* (London: printed for J. Mawman, 1805).

Reports of the Effects of a Peculiar Regimen on Scirrhous Tumours and Cancerous Ulcers (London: printed for J. Mawman, 1809).

Additional Reports of the Effects of a Peculiar Regimen in Cases of Cancer, Scrofula, Consumption, Asthma, and other Chronic Diseases (London: printed for J. Mawman, 1815).

Lanham, R. A., *A Handlist of Rhetorical Terms: a Guide for Students of English Literature* (Berkeley, Los Angeles and London: University of California Press, 1969).

Lawrence, James Henry, *The Empire of the Nairs; or, the Rights of Women. An Utopian Romance, in Twelve Books*, 4 vols. (London: printed for T. and E. T. Hookham, 1811).

Lawrence, John, *A Philosophical Treatise on Horses, and on the Moral Duties of Man towards the Brute Creation* (London: T. N. Longman, 1796–98).

Leahy, M. P. T., *Against Liberation: Putting Animals in Perspective* (London: Routledge, 1991).

Leask, N., *British Romantic Writers and the East: Anxieties of Empire* (Cambridge University Press, 1992).

Lévi-Strauss, C., *The Raw and the Cooked: Introduction to a Science of Mythology: 1*, tr. Weightman, J. and D. (London: Jonathan Cape, 1970; repr. Penguin, 1986).

Liu, A., *Wordsworth: the Sense of History* (Stanford University Press, 1989).

Lovejoy, A. O., *The Great Chain of Being: a Study in the History of an Idea* (Cambridge, Mass.: Harvard University Press, 1936).

Lovett, William, *The Life and Struggles of William Lovett, in his Pursuit of Bread, Knowledge and Freedom; with Some Short Account of the Different Associations he Belonged to, and of the Opinions he Entertained* (London: Trübner and Co., 1876).

MacCannell, J. F., *The Regime of the Brother: After the Patriarchy* (London and New York: Routledge, 1991).

Mack, M., *Alexander Pope: a Life* (New Haven and London: Yale University Press, 1985).

Malthus, Thomas, *An Essay on the Principle of Population, as it Affects the Future Improvement of Society. With Remarks on the Speculations of Mr. Godwin, M. Condorcet, and Other Writers* (London: printed for J. Johnson, 1798).

Marcuse, H., *Eros and Civilization: a Philosophical Inquiry into Freud* (London: Allen Lane, 1969).

Marx, K. *Selected Writings*, ed. McLellan, D. (London and New York: Longman, 1977).

Massumi, B., *A User's Guide to Capitalism and Schizophrenia: Deviations from Deleuze and Guattari* (Cambridge, Mass. and London: MIT Press, 1992).

McCalman, I., *Radical Underworld: Prophets, Revolutionaries and Pornographers in London, 1785–1840* (Cambridge University Press, 1988).

McGann, J., *The Romantic Ideology: a Critical Investigation* (Chicago and London: University of Chicago Press, 1983).

McWhir, A., 'The Light and the Knife: Ab/Using Language in *The Cenci*', *Keats-Shelley Journal* xxxviii (1989), 145–61.

Medwin, Thomas, *Oswald and Edwin: an Oriental Sketch* (Geneva: printed by J. J. Paschoud, 1820).

The Life of Percy Bysshe Shelley, 2 vols. (London: Thomas Cautley Newby, 1847).

The Life of Percy Bysshe Shelley, ed. Buxton Forman, H. (London: Oxford University Press, 1913).

Mellor, A., review of Huet, M. H., *Monstrous Imagination*, in *The New York Times Books Review* (25 April 1993), 7.

Midgley, M., *Beast and Man: the Roots of Human Nature* (Brighton: the Harvester Press, 1979; repr. London: Methuen, 1980).

Miller, D., *Material Culture and Mass Consumption* (Oxford and New York: Basil Blackwell, 1987).

Milton, John, *Paradise Lost*, ed. Fowler, A. (London and New York: Longman, 1968, 1971).

John Milton: Complete Shorter Poems, ed. Carey, J. (London and New York: Longman, 1968, 1971).

Mintz, S. W., *Sweetness and Power: the Place of Sugar in Modern History* (New York: Viking, 1985).

Montgomery, James, *Poems on the Abolition of the Slave Trade; Written by James Montgomery, James Grahame, and E. Benger* (London: printed for R. Bowyer, 1809).

Moore, Thomas, *Memoirs, Journal and Correspondence of Thomas Moore*, ed. Russell, Lord John, 8 vols. (London: Longman, Brown, Green and Longmans, 1853–56).

Newton, John Frank, *The Return to Nature, or, A Defence of the Vegetable Regimen; with Some Account of an Experiment Made During the Last Three Years in the Author's Family* (London: T. Cadell and W. Davies, 1811).

Nicholson, E. B., *The Rights of an Animal: a New Essay in Ethics* (London: Kegan Paul, 1879).

Nicholson, George, *On the Conduct of Man to Inferior Animals* (Manchester: G. Nicholson, 1797).

Nicholson, George, ed., *On Food*, in *The Literary Miscellany: or, Selections and Extracts, Classical and Scientific, in Prose and Verse* (Ludlow: G. Nicholson, 1803).

Nietzsche, F., *The Birth of Tragedy*, in *The Birth of Tragedy and the Genealogy of Morals*, tr. Golffing, F. (New York and London: Doubleday, 1956).

Werke, ed. Schelchta, K., 6 vols. (München-Wien: Carl Hanser Verlag, 1980).

Novak, M. E., *Defoe and the Nature of Man* (London: Oxford University Press, 1963).

Oswald, John, *The Cry of Nature; or, an Appeal to Mercy and to Justice, on Behalf of the Persecuted Animals* (London: printed for J. Johnson, 1791).

The Government of the People; or, a Sketch of a Constitution for the Universal

Common-Wealth (Paris: printed at the English Press, First Year of the French Republic (1793)).

Poems; to which is Added, The Humours of John Bull, an Operatical Farce, in Two Acts. By Silvester Otway (Oswald's pseudonym) (London: printed for J. Murray, 1789).

Outram, D., *The Body and the French Revolution: Sex, Class, and Political Culture* (New Haven and London: Yale University Press, 1989).

Ovid, *Ovid in Six Volumes,* tr. Miller, F. J., 6 vols. (Cambridge, Mass.: Harvard University Press and London: William Heinemann, 1984).

Paine, Thomas, *Rights of Man: Being an Answer to Mr. Burke's Attack on the French Revolution* (London: printed for H. D. Symonds, 1792).

Agrarian Justice, Opposed to Agrarian Law, and to Agrarian Monopoly; Being a Plan for Meliorating the Condition of Man, by Creating in Every Nation a National Fund, to Pay to Every Person, when Arrived at the Age of Twenty-One Years, the Sum of Fifteen Pounds Sterling, to Enable Him, or Her to Begin the World; and also, Ten Pounds Sterling per Annum During Life to Every Person Now Living of the Age of Fifty Years, and to All Others when they shall Arrive at that Age, to Enable them to Live in Old Age without Wretchedness, and Go Decently out of the World (Paris: W. Adlard and London: printed for T. G. Ballard, and Evans and Bone, 1797).

Paley, M. D., 'Mary Shelley's *The Last Man*: Apocalypse without Millenium [sic]', *Keats-Shelley Review* iv (1989), 1–25.

Paley, William, *The Principles of Moral and Political Philosophy* (London: printed for R. Faulder, 1785).

Palmer, R., *A Touch of the Times: Songs of Social Change 1770 to 1914* (London: Penguin, 1974).

Parker, R., *Miasma: Pollution and Purification in Early Greek Religion* (Oxford: the Clarendon Press, 1983; paperback, 1990).

Parry, J. 'Death and Digestion: the Symbolism of Food and Eating in North Indian Mortuary Rites', *Man* xx: 4 (December 1985), 612–30.

Paulson, R., *Representations of Revolution (1789–1820)* (New Haven and London: Yale University Press, 1983).

Peacock, Thomas Love, *The Works of Thomas Love Peacock,* ed. Brett-Smith, H. F. B. and Jones, C. E., 10 vols. (London: Constable & Co. and New York: Gabriel Wells, 1924–34).

Memoirs of Shelley, with Shelley's Letters to Peacock, ed. Brett-Smith, H. F. B. (London: Henry Frowde, 1909).

Phillips, Sir Richard, *Golden Rules of Social Philosophy; or, a New System of Practical Ethics* (London: printed for the author, 1826).

Plato, *Laws,* tr. Bury, R. G., 2 vols. (London: William Heinemann and Cambridge, Mass.: Harvard University Press, 1952).

Phaedrus, ed. Burnett, J. (Oxford: the Clarendon Press, 1901).

Phaedrus and the Seventh and Eighth Letters, tr. Hamilton, W. (London: Penguin, 1973).

The Republic, tr. Shorey, P., 2 vols. (London: William Heinemann and Cambridge, Mass.: Harvard University Press, 1956).

Pliny, *Natural History*, tr. Rackham, H., vol. II (London: William Heinemann and Cambridge, Mass.: Harvard University Press, 1947).

Plotz, J., 'On Guilt Considered as One of the Fine Arts: De Quincey's Criminal Imagination', *The Wordsworth Circle*, XIX:2 (Spring 1988), 83–88.

Plutarch, *Plutarch's Moralia*, tr. Cherniss, H. and Helbold, W. C., vol. XII (London: William Heinemann and Cambridge, Mass.: Harvard University Press, 1957).

Pope, Alexander, *The Poems of Alexander Pope* (The Twickenham Edition, general editor Butt, J.), vol. VIII, *The Iliad of Homer*, ed. Mack, M. et al. (London: Methuen and New Haven: Yale University Press, 1967).

The Poems of Alexander Pope: a One-Volume Edition of the Twickenham Text, with Selected Annotations, ed. Butt, J. (London and New York: Routledge, 1963; repr. 1989).

'Cruelty to Put a Living Creature to Death', *The Guardian* lxi (21 May 1713).

Porter, R., ed., *Consumption and the World of Goods* (London and New York: Routledge, 1993).

Pottle, F. A., *Shelley and Browning: a Myth and Some Facts* (Chicago: the Pembroke Press, 1923).

Pratt, Samuel Jackson, *Humanity, or the Rights of Nature, a Poem; in Two Books* (London: T. Cadell, 1788).

A Poetical and Philosophical Essay on the French Revolution, Addressed to the Right Hon. Edmund Burke (published anon.) (London: printed for J. Ridgway, 1793).

Bread; or, the Poor. A Poem. With Notes and Illustrations (London: printed for Longman, Rees and Becket, 1802).

Rabisha, William, *The Whole Body of Cookery Dissected, Taught and Fully Manifested ... According to the Best Tradition of the English, French, Italian, Dutch, etc., or a Sympathie of all Varieties in Naturall Compounds in that Mysterie* (London: printed for Giles Calvert, 1661).

Rajan, T., *Dark Interpreter: the Discourse of Romanticism* (Ithaca and London: Cornell University Press, 1980).

Rees, Abraham, *The Cyclopaedia; or, Universal Dictionary of Arts, Sciences, and Literature*, 41 vols. (Philadelphia: Samuel Bradford, Murray, Fainman and Co., 1810–24).

Reiman, D. H., ed., *Shelley and his Circle 1773–1822*, vols. V–VI (Cambridge, Mass.: Harvard University Press, 1973).

Ritson, Joseph, *An Essay on Abstinence from Animal Food, as a Moral Duty* (London: Richard Phillips, 1802).

Ronell, A., *The Telephone Book: Technology, Schizophrenia, Electric Speech* (Lincoln and London: the University of Nebraska Press, 1989).

Ross, A., *Strange Weather: Culture, Science, and Technology in the Age of Limits* (London and New York: Verso, 1991).

Rousseau, Jean-Jacques, *Emilius; or, an Essay on Education*, tr. Nugent, 2 vols. (London: printed for J. Nourse and P. Vaillant, 1763).

St Clair, W., *The Godwins and the Shelleys: the Biography of a Family* (London: Faber and Faber, 1989; paperback, 1990).

Salaman, R. N., *The History and Social Influence of the Potato* (Cambridge University Press, 1949; repr. 1986).

Scarry, E., *The Body in Pain: the Making and Unmaking of the World* (Oxford and New York: Oxford University Press, 1985).

Literature and the Body: Essays on Populations and Persons (Baltimore: Johns Hopkins University Press, 1988).

Schecker, P., ed., *An Anthology of Chartist Poetry: Poetry of the British Working Class, 1830s–1850s* (Rutherford, Madison and Teaneck: Fairleigh Dickinson University Press and London and Toronto: Associated University Presses, 1989).

Scrivener, M. H., *Radical Shelley: the Philosophical Anarchism and Utopian Thought of Percy Bysshe Shelley* (Princeton University Press, 1982).

Shakespeare, William, *The Complete Works*, ed. Wells, S. and Taylor, G. (Oxford: the Clarendon Press, 1986).

Shelley, Harriet, *Letters from Harriet Shelley to Catherine Nugent* (London: privately printed, 1889).

Shelley, Mary Wollstonecraft, *The Last Man. By the Author of Frankenstein*, 3 vols. (London: Henry Colburn, 1826).

Frankenstein or the Modern Prometheus: the 1818 Text, ed. Rieger, J. (Chicago and London: University of Chicago Press, 1974, 1982).

The Journals of Mary Shelley 1814–1844, ed. Feldman, P. R. and Scott-Kilvert, D., 2 vols. (Oxford: the Clarendon Press, 1987).

Singer, S. and Ashworth Underwood, E., *A Short History of Medicine* (Oxford: the Clarendon Press, 1962).

Smellie, William (and Alexander), *The Philosophy of Natural History*, 2 vols. (Edinburgh: printed for the Heirs of C. Elliot and London: printed for C. Elliot, T. Kay, T. Cadell and G., G., J. and J. Robinsons, 1790, 1799).

Smith, W. D., *The Hippocratic Tradition* (Ithaca and London: Cornell University Press, 1979).

Smith, William, *A Sure Guide in Sickness and Health, in the Choice of Food, and Use of Medicine* (London: printed for J. Bew and J. Walter, 1776).

Southey, Robert, *Thalaba the Destroyer* (London: printed for Longman and Rees, 1801).

The Curse of Kehama (London: printed for Longman, Hurst, Rees, Orme & Brown and Edinburgh: J. Ballantyne, 1810).

Southey's Common-Place Book. Fourth Series. Original Memoranda, Etc., ed. Warter, J. W. (London: Longman, Brown, Green & Longmans, 1851).

Stafford, B. M, *Body Criticism: Imaging the Unseen in Enlightenment Art and Medicine* (Cambridge, Mass.: MIT Press, 1991).

Stallybrass, P. and White, A., *The Politics and Poetics of Transgression* (Ithaca: Cornell University Press, 1986).

Stewart, John, *The Revelation of Nature, with the Prophesy* [sic] *of Reason* (New York: printed by Mott and Lyon, 'in the fifth year of intellectual existence, or the publication of the apocalypse of nature, 3000 years from the Grecian olympiads, and 4800 from recorded knowledge in Chinese tables of eclipses, beyond which chronology is lost in fable' [1796?]).

Opus Maximum ; *or, the Great Essay to Reduce the Moral World from Contingency to System, in the Following Sciences: Psyconomy; or, the Science of the Moral Powers; in Two Parts: 1st, Containing the Discipline of the Understanding; 2nd, the Discipline of the Will: Mathemanomy; or, the Laws of Knowledge: Logonomy; or, the Science of Language: Anagognomy; or the Science of Education: Ontonomy; or, the Science of Being* (London: printed for J. Ginger, 1803).

Strong, J. S., *The Legend of King Aśoka: a Study and Translation of the Aśokâvadâna* (Princeton University Press, 1983).

Tannahill, R., *Food in History* (London: Penguin, 1973; revised, 1988).

Taussig, M., 'History as Commodity in Some Recent American (Anthropological) Literature', *Food and Foodways* II:2 (1987), 151–69.

Taylor, Thomas, *A Vindication of the Rights of Brutes* (London: printed for Edward Jeffrey, 1792).

Tester, K., *Animals and Society: the Humanity of Animal Rights* (London and New York: Routledge, 1991).

Thomas, K., *Man and the Natural World: Changing Attitudes in England 1500–1800* (London: Allen Lane, 1983; repr. Penguin, 1984).

Thompson, E. P., *The Making of the English Working Class* (London: Victor Gollancz, 1963; repr. with revisions, Penguin, 1988).

Thompson, William, *Appeal of One Half of the Human Race, Women, against the Pretensions of the Other Half, Men, to Retain them in Political, and thence in Civil and Domestic Slavery* (London: Virago, 1983; first published, 1825).

Thompson, W. I., ed., *Gaia: a Way of Knowing; Political Implications of the New Biology* (Great Barrington, Mass.: Lindisfarne Press, 1987).

Thomson, Alexander, *Memoirs of a Pythagorean, in which are Delineated the Manners, Customs, Genius, and Polity of Ancient Nations* (London: printed for G., G., J. and J. Robinson, 1785).

Thomson, James, *Complete Poetical Works of James Thomson*, ed. Robertson, J. L. (Oxford: the Clarendon Press, 1908).

The Seasons and the Castle of Indolence, ed. Sambrook, J. (Oxford: the Clarendon Press, 1972; repr. 1989).

Tokoo, T., 'The Contents of Shelley's Notebooks in the Bodleian Library', *Humanities: Bulletin of the Faculty of Letters, Kyoto Prefectural University*, 36 (December 1984).

Trelawny, Edward John, *Records of Shelley, Byron, and the Author*, 2 vols. (London: Basil Montagu Pickering, 1878).

Trotter, Thomas, *An Essay; Medical, Philosophical, and Chemical, on Drunkenness and its Effects on the Human Body* (London: Longman, Hurst, Rees and Orme, 1804).

A View of the Nervous Temperament; Being a Practical Enquiry into the Increasing Prevalence, Prevention, and Treatment of those Diseases Commonly Called Nervous, Bilious, Stomach and Liver Complaints, Indigestion, Low Spirits, Gout, etc. (Newcastle and London: printed for Longman, Hurst, Rees, and Orme, 1807).

Sea Weeds: Poems, Written on Various Occasions, Chiefly During a Naval Life (London: Longman & Co. and Edinburgh: D. Lizars, 1829).

An Essay, Medical, Philosophical, and Chemical on Drunkenness and its Effects on the Human Body, ed. Porter, R. (London: Routledge, 1988).

Trungpa, C., *Crazy Wisdom*, ed. Chodzin, S. (Boston and London: Shambhala, 1991).

Tryon, Thomas, *Pythagoras His Mystic Philosophy Revived; or, the Mystery of Dreams Unfolded* (London: printed for Thomas Salisbury, 1691).

Turner, J., *Reckoning with the Beast: Animals, Pain, and Humanity in the Victorian Mind* (Baltimore and London: Johns Hopkins University Press, 1980).

Vitale, M., 'The Domesticated Heroine in Byron's *Corsair* and William Hone's Prose Adaption', *Literature and History* x (1984), 76–78.

Weiskel, T., *The Romantic Sublime: Studies in the Structure and Psychology of Transcendence* (Baltimore and London: Johns Hopkins University Press, 1976; repr. paperback, 1986).

Wells, R., *Wretched Faces: Famine in Wartime England, 1793–1801* (Gloucester: Alan Sutton and New York: St Martin's Press, 1988).

Whale, J., and Copley, S., eds., *Beyond Romanticism: New Approaches to Texts and Contexts, 1780–1832* (London and New York: Routledge, 1992).

White, N. I., 'Shelley's Swell-Foot the Tyrant in Relation to Contemporary Political Satires', *PMLA* xxxvi (1921), 332–46.

Williams, J. H., *The Ethics of Diet: a Catena of Authorities Deprecatory of the Practice of Flesh-Eating* (London: F. Pitman, John Heywood and Manchester: J. Heywood, Deansgate and Ridgefield, 1883).

Williams, R., *Culture and Society: Coleridge to Orwell* (London: Chatto and Windus, 1958; repr. The Hogarth Press, 1987).

Wollstonecraft, Mary, *Original Stories from Real Life; with Conversations, Calculated to Regulate the Affections, and Form the Mind to Truth and Goodness* (London: printed for J. Johnson, 1791).

A Vindication of the Rights of Woman (London: J. Johnson, 1792).

Woodman, R., 'Nietzsche, Blake, Keats and Shelley: the Making of a Metaphorical Body', *Studies in Romanticism* xxix: 1 (Spring 1990), 115–49.

Wordsworth, William, *The Poetical Works of William Wordsworth*, ed. de Selincourt, E. and Darbyshire, H., 5 vols. (Oxford: the Clarendon Press, 1940–49; repr. 1952).

The Prose Works of William Wordsworth, ed. Owen, W. J. B. and Smyser, J. W., 3 vols. (Oxford: the Clarendon Press, 1974).

William Wordsworth, ed. Gill, S. (Oxford and New York: Oxford University Press, 1984; repr. 1986, 1987).

Xenophon, *Memorabilia and Œconomicus*, tr. Marchant, E. C., with *Symposium and Apology*, tr. Todd, O. J. (Cambridge, Mass.: Harvard University Press and London: William Heinemann, 1979).

Yorke, Henry Redhead, *Letters from France, in 1802* (London: printed for H. D. Symonds, 1804).

Young, Thomas, *An Essay on Humanity to Animals* (London: T. Cadell, W. Davies and W. H. Lunn and Cambridge: J. Deighton, 1798).

Zizek, S., *The Sublime Object of Ideology* (London and New York: Verso, 1989, 1991).

A LIST OF POSTHUMOUS PUBLICATIONS OF SHELLEY'S PROSE ON THE NATURAL DIET:

Shelley, Percy Bysshe, *A Vindication of Natural Diet* (London: the Shelley Society, 1884, 1886).

A Vindication of Natural Diet (London: F. Pitman and Manchester: J. Heywood and Officers of the Vegetarian Society, 1884).

A Vindication of Natural Diet by Percy Bysshe Shelley and Extracts from the Works of Dr Lambe (London: C. W. Daniel, 1904).

A Vindication of Natural Diet (London: C. W. Daniel, 1922).

On the Vegetable System of Diet: Now First Printed from the Original Manuscript (an offprint of the *Julian* text for private circulation) (Bungay: R. Clay and Sons, 1929).

An Essay on the Vegetable System of Diet (Widdington, Newport: the Linden Press, 1940).

On the Vegetable System of Diet (Essex: printed for the London Vegetarian Society by C. W. Daniel, 1947).

A Vindication of Natural Diet and Extracts from the Works of Wm. Lambe, M. D. (Essex: C. W. Daniel, 1947).

A Vindication of Natural Diet (repr. of Pitman's edition, published by the Shelley Society, London) (Folcroft, PA: Folcroft Library Editions, 1975).

Index

293

Butchers, butchery, 15, 23, 62, 93–96, 110,
147–48, 151, 196–201
Butler, Marilyn, 241 (introduction, note 5),
258 (chapter 3, note 81)
Byron, George Gordon, Lord, 72, 76, 78,
80, 94, 235
works: *The Corsair*, 83; *Darkness*, 106, 173,
220–21; *Don Juan*, 137, 156

Cain and Abel, 110, 113, 115, 183, 215
Cameron, Kenneth Neil, 100, 256 (chapter
3, note 2)
Cannibalism, 13, 25–26, 40–41, 55, 71–72,
76, 84–86, 111–12, 155, 164, 174,
180–81, 185–86, 195, 217
Carlile, Richard (*The Republican*), 19–20, 35,
37, 183, 215
Capitalism, 9, 14, 18, 37, 42–43, 51–52, 56,
85, 137, 168, 187, 197, 199, 205–6, 208,
212–13, 216–17, 218–19, 220, 227–28
Carnivores, carnivorousness, 25–26, 34, 47,
48, 71–72, 106, 134, 135, 138, 147,
155–56, 172, 182, 186, 196–202, 223
Chase, Cynthia, 241 (introduction, note 2),
261 (chapter 4, note 34)
Cheyne, George, 41, 89, 90
Christianity, 28, 62–63, 73, 74, 85, 89, 99,
101, 110, 113, 138, 145–49, 175, 182,
191, 202–4, 235, 239
Jesus, 213
Cicero, Marcus Tullius, 118, 142, 253
(chapter 2, note 102)
City (and urbanization), 13, 14, 15, 65,
104, 116, 133, 159, 160, 165, 167, 187,
207, 210
Clairmont, Claire, 72
Clark, David Lee, 60
Clark, Timothy, 107
Class, 11, 14, 17–18, 21, 27, 35–38, 54, 68,
118, 152, 158–62, 165, 168–69, 171–72,
178, 183–84, 187–91, 196, 209, 212,
215, 231–32, 236, 240
Cobbett, William, 19, 229
Coleridge, J. T., 110–11
Coleridge, Samuel Taylor, 51, 105, 126
Colonialism, 23–26, 55–56, 79
see also 'slavery', 'race'
Commodities, 5, 13, 34, 112, 172, 183, 236,
210
see also 'capitalism'
Condorcet, Marquis de, 51, 162–63, 210–11
Cooking, 16–18, 47, 48, 118, 130, 135, 186,
202
Cowherd, William, 16
Cowper, William, 41, 89, 95, 107, 126

Crab, Roger, 41
Crook, Nora, and Guiton, Derek, 57, 58
Crowe, Henry, 28
Crucefix, Martin, 102
Cultural studies, 8, 234
Culture (concept of), 3, 7, 6–8, 42–43,
87–88, 134–35, 168–69, 170, 172–73,
188, 204, 205–6, 224, 228, 236
Curran, Stuart, 241 (introduction, note 2),
258 (chapter 3, note 75)
Cuvier, Georges, 147

Darwin, Erasmus, 156, 182
Davy, Humphry, 232
Dawson, Paul, 2, 192 (quoted), 233, 268
(chapter 5, note 11)
Death, 23, 80, 106–7, 110, 126, 178–79
De Certeau, Michel, 237
Deconstruction, 5, 12, 109, 129, 148, 166,
172–73, 234–35
see also 'disfiguration', 'Derrida'
Defoe, Daniel, 48
Deleuze, Gilles, and Guattari, Félix, 2, 7,
108, 137
De Quincey, Thomas, 11, 68
Derrida, Jacques, 130, 166, 241
(introduction, note 2)
Descartes, René, 143
Desmond, A. J., 241 (introduction, note 6)
Deterritorialization, 51–52
De Waal, 230
Didacticism, 4, 192
Diet (as a way of life), 10, 18–21, 49, 54,
63–64, 158, 168–69, 175, 188–89, 240
Dionysus, 174, 180
Disfiguration, 12, 42, 52, 127–29, 138–41,
144, 153, 157, 167–69, 172–73, 174–75,
202, 234–35, 240
see also 'deconstruction'
Disgust, aversion, horror, 1, 38–39, 73, 112,
131, 134, 162, 177, 193
Douglas, Mary, 7
Drinking, 1, 3, 15, 47, 49, 50, 61, 62, 63, 67,
70, 72, 74, 78, 96, 100, 101, 116, 117,
120, 131, 134, 152, 177–78, 180,
181–86, 192–93, 198
Drummond, A. C., and Wilbraham, A., 2
Dryden, John, 28, 245 (chapter 1, note 115)

Eagleton, Terry, 247 (chapter 1, note 179),
273 (chapter 6, note 76)
Eating, study of, 1, 13, 52, 110, 112, 114,
121, 164–65, 207–8, 234–35, 237–38
Ecology, ecocriticism, 1, 2, 136–37, 205–6
deep, 227, 229

TITLES PUBLISHED